INTRODUCTIONS TO NIETZSCHE

Friedrich Nietzsche (1844–1900) is one of the most important philosophers of the last two hundred years, whose writings, both published and unpublished, have had a formative influence on virtually all aspects of modern culture. This volume offers introductory essays on all of Nietzsche's completed works and also his unpublished notebooks. The essays address such topics as his criticism of morality and Christianity, his doctrines of the will to power and the eternal recurrence, his perspectivism, his theories of tragedy and nihilism, and his thoughts on ancient and modern culture. Written by internationally recognized scholars, they provide the interested reader with an up-to-date and authoritative overview of the thought of this fascinating figure.

ROBERT B. PIPPIN is the Evelyn Stefansson Nef Distinguished Service Professor of Philosophy, and the Chair of the John U. Nef Committee on Social Thought, at the University of Chicago. His publications include *The Persistence of Subjectivity* (Cambridge, 2005), *Hegel's Practical Philosophy* (Cambridge, 2008), *Nietzsche, Psychology and First Philosophy* (2010), *Hollywood Westerns and American Myth* (2010), and *Hegel on Self-Consciousness: Desire and Death in Hegel's Phenomenology of Spirit* (2010).

INTRODUCTIONS TO NIETZSCHE

EDITED BY
ROBERT B. PIPPIN

CAMBRIDGE
UNIVERSITY PRESS

CAMBRIDGE
UNIVERSITY PRESS

University Printing House, Cambridge CB2 8BS, United Kingdom

One Liberty Plaza, 20th Floor, New York, NY 10006, USA

477 Williamstown Road, Port Melbourne, VIC 3207, Australia

314-321, 3rd Floor, Plot 3, Splendor Forum, Jasola District Centre, New Delhi - 110025, India

79 Anson Road, #06-04/06, Singapore 079906

Cambridge University Press is part of the University of Cambridge.

It furthers the University's mission by disseminating knowledge in the pursuit of education, learning and research at the highest international levels of excellence.

www.cambridge.org
Information on this title: www.cambridge.org/9780521189910

© Cambridge University Press 2012

First published 2012
Reprinted 20122

A catalogue record for this publication is available from the British Library

Library of Congress Cataloging in Publication data
Introductions to Nietzsche / edited by Robert B. Pippin.
pages   cm
Includes bibliographical references and index.
ISBN 978-1-107-00774-1 (hardback) – ISBN 978-0-521-18991-0 (paperback)
1. Nietzsche, Friedrich Wilhelm, 1844–1900.   I. Pippin, Robert B., 1948– editor of compilation.
B3317.I67   2012
193 – dc23   2011050264

ISBN   978-1-107-00774-1   Hardback
ISBN   978-0-521-18991-0   Paperback

Contents

Note to the reader

The essays in this volume originally appeared as introductions to the editions of Nietzsche's works which are published in the series Cambridge Texts in the History of Philosophy. They were brought together in this single volume in order to give the interested reader a rich and wide-ranging overview of Nietzsche's philosophical thought. The Press is grateful to the authors of these essays for permission to reproduce them. The select bibliography, which is conveniently organized by theme, has been created especially for the volume and aims to offer a useful resource to accompany the essays.

Chronology of Nietzsche's life and works

1844	Friedrich Wilhelm Nietzsche born on 15 October in Röcken, in the Prussian province of Saxony
1849	His father dies (at the age of 36)
1858–64	Attends the classics-oriented boarding-school Schulpforta; plays the piano and composes
1864	Enters Bonn University to study classical languages and literatures
1869	Associate professor of classical philology (before even completing his Ph.D.) at the Swiss university at Basel
1870	Full professor at Basel; enlists as a medical orderly in the Franco-Prussian War, contracting serious illnesses
1872	First book *The Birth of Tragedy* appears (and is met with scholarly derision) – his only major classical studies publication
1873–4	Publishes the first three *Untimely Meditations*, including the essays *On the Uses and Disadvantages of History for Life* and *Schopenhauer as Educator*
1876	Writes a fourth *Meditation* in homage to Wagner, but his enthusiasm for Wagner cools
1878	The first volume of *Human, All Too Human* (638 aphorisms) appears; Wagner sends him *Parsifal*, and their estrangement deepens
1879	Resigns (with pension) from his position at Basel, incapacitated by health problems; begins spending his summers in the Swiss Engadine region, and his winters in northern Italy, living in boarding-houses
1879–80	Writes two sequels to *Human, All Too Human*, subsequently published as the two parts of its second volume (another 758 aphorisms)

1881 Publishes *Daybreak* (575 aphorisms); alternative periods of depression and exhilaration; first summer in Sils Maria, where the idea of "eternal recurrence" comes to him

1882 The year of his intense but short-lived relationship with Lou Salomé, which ends badly; publishes the initial four-part version of *The Gay Science* (342 aphorisms and reflections)

1883 The first two parts of *Thus Spoke Zarathustra* are written and published; estrangement from family and friends; depression; resolves against living in Germany; Wagner dies

1884 Completes and publishes the third part of *Zarathustra*; breaks with his sister Elizabeth, unable to endure her anti-Semitic, pro-"Teutonic" fiancee Bernard Förster (she marries him the next year, to Nietzsche's disgust and distress, accompanying him to Paraguay where he sought to found a Teutonic colony)

1885 The fourth part of *Zarathustra* is written, but is only privately printed and circulated; condition worsens

1886 *Beyond Good and Evil* (296 aphorisms and reflections in nine parts, plus a poem "Aftersong") is published; new editions of most pre-*Zarathustra* works are prepared and supplied with prefaces

1886–7 An expanded second edition of *The Gay Science* is prepared and published, with a new preface and fifth part consisting of 41 additional reflections, and an appendix of poetry, "Songs of Prince Vogelfrei"

1887 *On the Genealogy of Morals* appears, consisting of a preface and three "essays" (of 17, 25, and 28 numbered sections, respectively); completes orchestral score for *Hymnus an das Leben*; begins working on magnus opus, to be called *The Will to Power*

1888 *The Case of Wagner* is published; and *Twilight of the Idols, The Antichrist, Nietzsche contra Wagner, Dionysian Dithyrambs* (a collection of poems), and *Ecce Homo* are all written; *The Will to Power* project is dropped, in favour of a projected four-part *Revaluation of All Values*; condition deteriorates

1889 Collapses in early January in Turin, at the age of 44 (never recovers, living his final eleven years in invalid insanity in the care of his mother and sister); *Twilight of the Idols* is published in January

1892 First public edition of the fourth part of *Zarathustra* appears

1893   Sister returns from Paraguay, and – under the name Elizabeth
           Förster-Nietzsche – assists their mother in the management
           of her brother's affairs

1895   *The Antichrist* and *Nietzsche Contra Wagner* are published

1897   Mother dies, leaving complete control of his care – and of his
           literary estate – to Elizabeth, who exploits his growing fame
           and fosters the assimilation of his thought to right-extremist
           political purposes during the next four decades

1900   Nietzsche dies, on 25 August, in Weimar

1901   Sister publishes an arrangement of selections from his note-
           books of 1883–8 under the title *The Will to Power*, and in his
           name

1908   *Ecce Homo* is finally published

1910–11   First edition of Nietzsche's collected works is published under
           the supervision of Elizabeth – including a greatly expanded
           edition of *The Will to Power*

                                                            Richard Schacht

Introduction

Robert Pippin

Anyone who has heard anything about Nietzsche has probably heard him associated with many of the following phrases: God is dead. Everything, all of nature and certainly the human world, is will to power, a constant zero-sum game struggle for dominance and mastery. Judaism and Christianity are slave moralities. The motivation for and the meaning of the Christian religion reside in a feeling of "*ressentiment*" against the stronger, the masters. The Christian moral tradition has culminated in nihilism. Nihilism means "Nothing is true; everything is allowed." Contemporary morality is herd morality. We require now a transvaluation of values, and it must be beyond good and evil. The representative of these new values will be an Overman or Superman (*Übermensch*). Everything recurs eternally. There are no objective values or universal moral principles. All understanding is perspectival. Even "physics" is an "interpretation." "One law for the lion and the lamb" is unacceptable; true human excellence is possible only for an elite few. Our sense of conscious control over what to believe and what to do is an illusion. Consciousness itself is an illusion.

These ideas occur in works that often have hyper-dramatic, apocalyptic titles, as if to suggest some great historical moment was upon us, all written in a "loud," hyperbolic, often figurative style: *The Dawn, The Joyous Science, Beyond Good and Evil, Thus Spoke Zarathustra, The Anti-Christ, The Twilight of the Idols*. There is even a book *The Will to Power*, often referred to and cited by scholars, that is not a book at all, but a collection of his notes, his *Nachlass*, arranged by his nutty sister to suit more her ends than his. Some of these books seem to be little more than collections of aphorisms; some look like sociological or historical essays; others read like religious sermons, or prophecies, or biblical imitations, or political pamphlets. Some seem to be all of the above at once. Moreover, these books are often treated as exemplifying phases in the development of Nietzsche's thought; early, middle, and late, usually. And scholars argue about whether, and if so how much, Nietzsche changed his mind throughout these periods.

Such widespread notoriety for Nietzsche's ideas – that is, the way his ideas have become labeled, overly familiar, T-shirt material even – and the highly unusual and unprecedented literary form of his published works, and the uncertainty about what he believed when and about how to make use of his unpublished notes, have all understandably made it difficult for both friendly and hostile commentators and critics to settle on any common view of Nietzsche's philosophy and his legacy. In many significant cases, there is not even agreement about what the controversies, the opposing sides, are. Some of the terms and catchphrases are so familiar that they have become clichés and we take too much for granted in invoking them. How could God have died, for example? If Nietzsche means that the existence of God has become less credible for people, then for which people, and why not say that instead of that he died (and that we killed him but cannot own up to the fact)? Why is the Overman mentioned so infrequently if he is so important? For that matter why does Zarathustra, who first introduces him, stop mentioning him around the middle of *Thus Spoke Zarathustra*? What could Nietzsche mean by the "will to power" for human beings when he denies that there is any psychological faculty like the will? Why does he say that "truth is a woman" and philosophers are clumsy lovers? And so on.

Not surprisingly, this has all led to wide variations in the reception of Nietzsche's works. He was largely unknown during his brief lifetime, or at least during his life of sanity. (Nietzsche was born in October of 1844, and went mad in Turin in January of 1889 at the age of forty-four. He lived another ten years before dying in August of 1900.) His books sold poorly, and he lived a somewhat isolated and lonely life. But as with the fate of some artists who start to sell only after they have died, after Nietzsche went insane, and during the period between 1890 and 1918, he became world famous, the originator of a kind of avant-garde philosophy, a philosophy in style and substance and atmosphere like avant-garde and modernist movements in art, music, and literature. Those who found official bourgeois culture philistine, materialistic, small-minded, smug, self-satisfied, and conformist found a voice in Nietzsche, as did those who found it sexually repressive, timid, boring, and hostile to change.

This all began to change during and immediately after the First World War, and the legacy of this change in the perception of Nietzsche remained until well after the Second World War. (For some critics it is still a jus-tifiable association.) For Nietzsche was claimed during the war by the nationalist right in Germany as a philosopher who appreciated the glories of "strength," war, militarism, and the need for a revival of the German *Volk*. And he was just as eagerly associated with those traits and views by the English propaganda machine. That common three-quarters profile of the glaring Nietzsche, with the huge moustache, became a staple of such war propaganda against "the Hun." The Germans had started the war because they were by nature war-mongers and power hungry, and you could see all those traits in that typical German philosopher, Nietzsche.[1]

In effect this all led to the fact that Nietzsche would be ultimately claimed not by the traditional right in Germany, the aristocratic, religious (often Catholic), land-owning right, but by the *petit bourgeois* "radical right" and their "intellectuals," the core of what would become the Nazi movement. Their complaint was, they thought, Nietzsche's, that the West had sunk into nihilism, a diffident toleration of morally corrosive groups, a sterile cosmopolitanism, all the dangerous traits typical of democracies, and had adopted a foolishly narrow reliance on reason as a guide to life. And the solution was to create a new mythology and a radical reformation of German society. Such an association of Nietzsche with a "blood and soil" irrationalism would be cemented further by his popularity among the hacks and propagandists who became the official Nazi "philosophers." Nietzsche, who had nothing but contempt for nationalism and was often as brutal a critic of German culture and history as Heine, nevertheless found himself painted with the same anti-Nazi brush, and it would be some time before his thought could be discussed in any way not shadowed by this association.

It is also true that in this same period, Nietzsche had become important for social critics of bureaucratized bourgeois society (like Max Weber), and he would also become important for the "critical theory" brand of neo-Marxism. Nietzsche's genealogical method, applied to morality, was an important example of what they considered to be "ideology critique," and Nietzsche's suspicions about the Enlightenment, especially about the pretension of some social group to authority on the basis of some appeal to a supposedly disinterested, neutral standard of rationality, resonated with such thinkers. His influence was easy to see in later books like Horkheimer and Adorno's *The Dialectic of Enlightenment*.[2] However it would take a full generation after the Second World War before Nietzsche could be again

---

[1] I follow here the very helpful account by Steven E. Aschheim, *The Nietzsche Legacy in Germany* (Berkeley: University of California Press, 1994).

[2] Max Horkheimer and Theodor Adorno, *The Dialectic of Enlightenment*, trans. E. Jephcott (Stanford University Press, 2002). The book first appeared in 1944.

claimed by the left, especially by the "68'ers" dissatisfied with the prudent, rational moderation of traditional liberalism.

For after the Second World War, all things German were under suspicion of some sort of intellectual complicity with Nazism. Many thinkers like Hegel and Nietzsche and Heidegger (who became a party member) were listed as enemies of "the open society," and Germany itself was thought to be haunted by a dark, romantic, irrationalist, counter-Enlightenment specter. In the case of Nietzsche, his rehabilitation or decontamination in Anglophone philosophy in essence began in 1950 with the publication of Walter Kaufmann's *Nietzsche: Philosopher, Psychologist, Anti-Christ*.[3] Kaufmann occupied a position of great academic importance in America (he was a philosophy professor at Princeton) and was a noted translator and critic as well. His book argued in detail against characterizations of Nietzsche as anti-Semitic, as a totalitarian thinker, or as a German nationalist, and he tried to show that Nietzsche was not just an avant-gardist of importance to the literary and artistic worlds, but that he was a challenging, even a great, original philosopher in his own right. Arthur Danto's 1964 book, *Nietzsche as Philosopher*,[4] was also an important if somewhat isolated event, and in the 1970s there finally began to appear high-quality secondary literature such as John Wilcox's 1974 book, *Truth and Value in Nietzsche*,[5] and Tracy Strong's 1975 book on Nietzsche and politics, *Friedrich Nietzsche and the Politics of Transfiguration*.[6] And when the Routledge "Arguments of the Philosophers" series brought out Richard Schacht's lengthy 1983 book *Nietzsche*,[7] the idea that Nietzsche, whatever else he was doing in his books, was making philosophical claims and devising ways to defend them, was becoming more firmly established.

By the mid-1980s, it was also widely known that Nietzsche had become an unavoidable figure in Europe – in France, Germany, and Italy especially. Heidegger's lecture courses on Nietzsche in the 1930s and 1940s had been published in German in the early 1960s and an English translation had appeared in the late 1970s. Books by Sarah Kofman, Giles Deleuze, Jacques Derrida, Jean Granier, Gianni Vatimo, Pierre Klossowski, and Karl Löwith had also claimed Nietzsche as a philosopher, but in a very different way from in Anglophone work. The latter tended to be organized in the traditional sub-disciplines of professional philosophy and so treated Nietzsche's epistemology, metaphysics, aesthetics, value theory, moral psychology, etc. as distinct separable themes, and he was said to have

[3] Princeton University Press, 1975.   [4] repr. New York: Columbia University Press, 2005.
[5] Ann Arbor: University of Michigan Press, 1974.   [6] repr. Urbana: University of Illinois Press, 1999.
[7] repr. New York: Routledge, 1985.

a "perspectivist" epistemology, a relativist moral theory, and so forth. The European approaches tended to treat very sweeping issues in what might loosely be called accounts of possible meaning in language and thought (or even "the meaning of being") and the possibility of meaningfulness in action, and they portrayed Nietzsche as having much more radical positions, not subsumable in the traditional categories of the profession. An important book during this period was Alexander Nehamas's *Nietzsche: Literature as Life*.[8] Nehamas was able to show convincingly that Nietzsche's philosophy was not subject to the "self-refutation" and other paradoxes into which Nietzsche's critique of "truth" or his insistence that "there were no facts, only interpretations," or his anti-dogmatism were taken to have led him. And Nehamas also took up some of the themes of the European commentators, especially the importance of the unusual style of Nietzsche's writings and the omnipresent need for interpretation in any relation to the world and in the self's very relation to itself. Nehamas argued that these all needed to be modeled on the relation of an author to a text.

More recently, many philosophers interested in Nietzsche have focused attention on what appear to be Nietzsche's doubts about the transparency of consciousness to itself, doubts that the way things *seem* to a subject of thoughts and deeds, apparently "in charge" of what it decides to believe and do, can be correct. In some passages, Nietzsche appears to appeal to non-conscious and corporeal factors ("instincts" or "drives") as the proper *explicans* of conscious phenomena like believing or acting, and he appears to claim that these causal determinants of behavior operate, as it were, "behind the back" of what is accessible to consciousness. As the interest in "naturalizing" epistemology, moral theory, and aesthetics grows apace in Anglophone philosophy, interest in Nietzsche as a forerunner and interesting defender of such claims has also grown.[9]

II. THE NIETZSCHE PROBLEM

As already noted, Nietzsche does not state positions and argue for them in the manner traditional in modern philosophy; he does not write extended essays with chains of argument, considerations of counter-arguments and counter-examples, and there is widespread disagreement about how to understand his very different works, works which are different both from the tradition and from each other. But even though most of his work is

---

[8] Cambridge, Mass.: Harvard University Press, 1985.
[9] Richard Schacht and John Richardson have published important interpretations of a "naturalist" Nietzsche but probably the most influential work has been by Brian Leiter.

diagnostic and critical, he does seem almost everywhere concerned with various dimensions of what he would recognize as the chief Socratic question (even though he disagreed vigorously with Socrates's supposedly "dogmatic" answer): how ought one to live? It is true that he denies there is any "one size fits all" answer to this question, but he clearly believes that some sorts of answers – a life of Christian piety, or Kantian moral rectitude, or a devotion to the "ascetic ideal" – cannot be successful answers, at least not *now*, and these arguments alone inevitably imply something about how one ought to live now. And he does explicitly, if often figuratively, sketch out some traits required for anyone to live well.

So even though in the early writings he was worried about many of the implications of an overly historicized perspective on ourselves, there is no question that Nietzsche thinks that something in the shared form of life characteristic of modern European societies – their inheritance of a Christian and so universalist view of morality, and both the Greek and modern enlightenments' "faith" in the value of truth – has gone dead in some way. Various propositions may still evoke assent; we avow belief and commitment, but, he seems to say, these are not deeply held commitments, capable of inspiring great sacrifice. (People may still go to church on Sunday but they do not live genuinely Christian lives, as Kierkegaard might put a similar point.) And so any possible answer we can give to such a Socratic question must take account of our living in the shadow of this event. The two most prominent names for such crisis are, in the published work, the death of God, and, in those works as well but especially in the unpublished notes, "nihilism." (In the Prologue to *Thus Spoke Zarathustra*, Nietzsche also makes in a literary way the paradoxical point that one of the chief features of such a crisis, a feature that seems to drive him to rhetorical desperation, is that it is unnoticed. People are perfectly satisfied and experience no disorienting loss.) Sometimes the problem itself is described as a kind of failure of desire, as if there is nothing worth wanting, at least not badly enough to help organize a life, give it direction. People don't want the sorts of things that could serve this life-orienting function. They certainly want things, perhaps even greatly want them: security, peace, comfort, pleasure. But, Nietzsche seems to think, these are precisely the sorts of essentially unimportant things that must be risked if anything worthwhile is to be achieved.

Typically, almost all these points are made in an imagistic way. So in the Preface to *Beyond Good and Evil*, he notes that our long struggle with and often opposition to and dissatisfaction with our own moral tradition, European Christianity, has created a "magnificent tension (*Spannung*) of spirit in Europe, the likes of which the earth has never known: with such a tension in our bow we can now shoot at the furthest goals." But, he goes on, the "democratic enlightenment" also sought to "unbend" such a bow, "to insure that spirit should not experience itself so readily as 'need.'"[10] This latter formulation coincides with a neatly made point in *The Gay Science*. In discussing "the millions of young Europeans who cannot endure boredom and themselves," he notes that they would even welcome "a yearning to suffer something in order to make their suffering a likely reason for action, for deeds." In sum: "neediness is needed!" (*Not ist nötig.*)[11] Another imagistic formulation of the death of desire occurs in *Ecce Homo* in a passage that has not been much commented on, even though it is a concise expression of the uniqueness of his position. He notes what is happening to us as " . . . one error after another is calmly put on ice; *the ideal is not refuted – it freezes to death –.*"[12]

In §38 of *The Twilight of the Idols*, a section called "Expeditions of an untimely man" in a passage called "My conception of freedom," Nietzsche offers a kind of counter-picture to the psychological complacency of "the last men," the rather bovine, self-satisfied creatures Zarathustra must try to rouse to action and a new way of life. By contrast what one needs is

That one has the will to self-responsibility. That one preserves the distance that divides us. That one has become more indifferent to hardship, toil, privation, even to life. The man who has become free . . . spurns the contemptible sort of well-being dreamed of by shopkeepers, Christians, cows, women, Englishmen and other democrats. The free man is a warrior.[13]

The passage goes on like this, praising danger, risk, and strength, but, as he tries to characterize what he calls "psychologically true" (*psychologisch wahr*) about freedom, Nietzsche adds something that is easy to overlook.

How is freedom measured, individuals as in nations? By the resistance which has to be overcome, by the effort it costs to stay aloft. One would have to seek the highest type of free man where the greatest resistance is constantly being overcome.

But such a constant self-overcoming, if left at this, is an oddly formal criterion. Nietzsche clearly does not think that Christian ascetic practices

[10] *Beyond Good and Evil: Prelude to a Philosophy of the Future*, trans. Judith Norman (Cambridge University Press, 2002), p. 4, translation altered.
[11] *The Gay Science: With a Prelude in German Rhymes and an Appendix of Songs*, trans. Josefine Nauckhoff and Adrian del Caro (New York: Cambridge University Press, 2001), §56, p. 64.
[12] *The Anti-Christ, Ecce Homo, Twilight of the Idols, and Other Writings*, trans. Judith Norman (Cambridge University Press, 2005), p. 116, translation altered.
[13] Ibid., p. 92.

such as fasting and self-flagellation, the constant attempt to overcome the desires and demands of the body, however difficult and even futile, are admirable. The struggle against resistance and the willingness to endure and persevere are obviously markers of a sort for the kind of commitment that Nietzsche is searching for under contemporary conditions, but such a picture is incomplete without some sense of the goal for the sake of which such struggle is undertaken.

And with that question we come to what must be the most frequently asked question, not just by long-time devoted readers but by students encountering Nietzsche for the first time. As anyone who has taught Nietzsche to the young realizes, he was not exaggerating very much when he described himself this way in *Ecce Homo*: "I am no man. I am dynamite." The confidence and rhetorical power with which he attacks the Christian religion and institutions like morality and the culture of commercial republics can be both thrilling and shattering to first-time readers. But almost everyone, when they have caught their breath and started thinking, always asks: "But how *does* he think we ought to live? What is he affirming?"

In one respect of course, such a question, if understood in a certain way, betrays a deep misunderstanding of Nietzsche. He clearly wants to answer, as Zarathustra does at the end of "The Spirit of Gravity" section of *Thus Spoke Zarathustra*, "'This – it turns out – is *my* way – where is yours?' That is how I answered those who asked me 'the way.' *The* way after all – it does not exist!"[14] But it would also be bad faith to pretend that we are left with *no* sort of Nietzschean response to the Socratic question, even if that response will not be a new catechism or rule-book. We have already seen that what he is dissatisfied with inevitably suggests something of what he approves of. And even if such an approval is "just an interpretation" or even "only his interpretation," and even if he is not trying to convince us that his is "true," that it is the only response and suggestion possible, he is clearly trying to change our minds about what is central to any state of living well. What is central is, characteristically, presented in a complexly figurative way.

III. NIETZSCHE'S IDEAL: "*AMOR FATI*"

This is the formulation he introduces in the *The Gay Science* and returns to ever after:

---

[14] *Thus Spoke Zarathustra*, ed. R. Pippin and A. del Caro (Cambridge University Press, 2006), p. 156.

. . . I, too, want to say what I wish from myself today and what thought first crossed my heart this year – what thought shall be the reason, warrant and sweetness of the rest of my life! I want to learn more and more to see what is necessary in things as beautiful – thus I will be one of those who make things beautiful. *Amor fati*: Let that be my love from now on! I do not want to wage war against ugliness. I do not want to accuse; I do not even want to accuse the accusers. Let *looking away* be my only negation! And, all in all and on the whole: some day I want only to be a Yes-sayer![15]

In *Nietzsche Contra Wagner*, the stress is on necessity again, and he insists explicitly that with respect to everything necessary, "one should not only bear it, one should love it. *Amor fati*, that is my innermost nature."[16] The key to all this, and so the key to being able to "love life" again, is, apparently, "only, one loves differently . . . It is the love of a woman who makes us doubt."[17] So this appears to add another condition to "learning to see the necessary as beautiful"; to wit: loving a different way, as in loving someone about whose love for us we are always in doubt. All this is intriguing, perhaps, but certainly not immediately helpful.

The two last published references occur in *Ecce Homo*. In the section on *The Case of Wagner*, he again says that what is "necessary" does not injure him and that *amor fati* is "his innermost nature."[18] In "Why I am so Clever," he concludes by stressing again that what is important to him is being able to love one's fate.[19]

My formula for greatness in a human being is *amor fati*: that one wants nothing to be different, not forward, not backward, not in all eternity. Not merely bear what is necessary, still less conceal it – all idealism is mendaciousness in the face of what is necessary – but love it.[20]

Now Nietzsche himself made up the phrase *amor fati*, obviously trying to allude to Spinoza's intellectual love of God, *amor intellectus dei*, and also clearly trying to suggest an ancient pedigree that might help us understand the key terms of necessity, beauty, and love as the chief requirements now for any sort of – however various – greatness. So we need to introduce elements of Nietzsche's treatment of the Greeks to understand what he was trying to say.

In 1870, in one of the several works and lectures that ultimately form the material of *The Birth of Tragedy*, the essay "The Birth of Tragic Thinking"

---

[15] *The Gay Science*, §276, p. 157.   [16] *Nietzche Contra Wagner*, in *The Anti-Christ*, Epilogue §1.
[17] Ibid.   [18] *The Case of Wagner*, in *The Anti-Christ*, §4.
[19] "Why I am so Clever," in *The Anti-Christ*, §4.
[20] *Twilight of the Idols*, in *The Anti-Christ*, §10.

("Die Geburt des tragischen Gedankens"), Nietzsche praises the Greeks for
what in reality he himself invented as a category – the notion of a tragic view
of life itself, *a way of life* embodied and worked out in the tragic dramas.
He says, as he does in his first publication and several times later, that the
Greeks did not have a religion of duty or ascetic practices or intellectuality
(*Geistigeit*), but a "religion of life (*eine Religion des Lebens*)," one in which all
their aesthetic forms breathed out the "triumph of existence, an abundant
feeling of life."[21] This is something that, in the context of his critique of
asceticism and his characterization of Christianity as "life turning against
life," is high praise. It is in this context that he says the deepest wisdom of
this religion was that "even the gods are subject to necessity" (*Ananke*), a
remark that again seems to suggest resignation or at least something other
than the "triumph of existence." But somehow the absolute inescapability
of *Ananke*, even for the beings imagined to be as great as it was possible to
imagine beings to be, made their enthusiastic and full-hearted embrace of
such an existence *in spite of that* all the more beautiful and, to note again
what we are trying to understand, *thereby* (because beautiful) affirmable,
even lovable.

This notion of affirmation is not just the expression of the so-called
"early Nietzsche." Indeed the role of the god who sums up this affirmation, Dionysus, grows again in importance in the so-called "late period."
(Dionysus is an appropriate divinity to evoke fate and even the Eternal
Return version of Nietzschean fatalism because of his status as a birth-
life-death-rebirth god, a symbol of the indestructibility of life, even in its
necessity.) One passage from (the late period) *Twilight of the Idols* (1888) is
particularly telling:

Saying Yes to life even in its strangest and hardest problems, the will to life rejoicing
over its own inexhaustibility even in the very sacrifice of its highest types – *that* is
what I called Dionysian, *that* is what I guessed to be the bridge to the psychology
of the *tragic* poet. *Not* in order to be liberated from terror and pity, not in order to
purge oneself of a dangerous affect by its vehement discharge . . . but in order to
be *oneself* the eternal joy of becoming, beyond all terror and pity – that joy which
included even joy in destroying.[22]

So when Nietzsche appeals to *amor fati* (relatively early, or early middle,
in *Gay Science* (1882)) and late (in *Ecce Homo* (1888)), we can expect a
continuity of the same enthusiasm for this "religion of life," but we also

---

[21] *Kritische Studienausgabe*, ed. G. Colli and M. Montinari (Berlin: de Gruyter, 1988), Bd. I, "Die
Geburt des tragischen Gedankens," p. 588.
[22] *Twilight of the Idols*, in *The Anti-Christ*, §6.

have something of the same question re-emerging in different but very similar forms in all these contexts. I think Nietzsche ultimately means for us not to be able to pose these questions in this form, to understand that the question's form already betrays a misunderstanding, but still one keeps returning to what seem inevitable questions like: *How* could one come to *love* one's fate? What exactly *is* the fate one is supposed to love? Are we to love the fact that everything one does is fated? That one is fated to suffer no matter what, and suffer arbitrarily and so meaninglessly? That one is so often forced to choose among options one would have never wanted to face in the life one would have chosen for oneself? On what *basis*, *why* would anyone have reason to love one's fate? *How* could the Greek religion find a way to turn away from or ignore this endless "necessary" suffering rather than simply die or want to die in response to its truth? Is the effect of tragedy supposed to be mimetic in some way; that *one just sees* that Greek gods and heroes could, to recall Faulkner, not just endure but prevail, and that inspires us to go and do likewise? If the highest types must always be sacrificed, how could one possibly rejoice in the inexhaustibility of *such* a life? What exactly is wrong with what seem such natural, inevitable questions?

To approach these questions, I think we need to take several steps back and get a wider perspective. Whatever "fatalism" is expressed in the ideal of *amor fati*, there is no evidence that Nietzsche is committed to a full-blown universal fatalism as that is usually understood. He certainly does not believe that the gods will determine our significant outcomes no matter what we do, does not believe that attempts at self-understanding, deliberation, action, and creation are all simply pointless because of natural or scientific necessity. (Whatever his "drive theory" is, it does not appear to be of the sort that renders all decisive action impossible. After all, he keeps *calling for* a decisive response to his diagnosis and so appears to believe that such an informed response is possible.) There is certainly no indication that he believes in divine foreknowledge and thus pre-destination, and, although he worries about the enormous new shaping and forming powers of modern societies creating herd societies, he does not believe that the future of societies and individuals in them is fixed by large social forces like capital, or power, or linguistic structures. But the passages we have seen, and many more familiar ones having to do with doubts about the supremacy and power of consciousness, comments about the instinctual and the hidden motivations of which we are not aware, the near omnipresence of self-deceit, do all indicate that he is out to reduce any optimism about what have come to be central requirements of any theory of agency. As suggested a few times now, we can get all the fatalism we need to make sense of what Nietzsche is alluding to by noting simply that for him we are far *less* accessible to ourselves than previously thought, and far less able to determine a unique, willed future than often supposed, even if it is not completely impossible to play a role in determining such a future.

This means for Nietzsche that our deepest intuitions are largely, even if not completely, self-inflating distortions. He means the intuitions that go back to Aristotle on the voluntary and that were radically intensified by the model of agency necessary for morality: intuitions about "inner directed" action, or our exercising some sort of control over events as they unfold, all on the basis of some view about what ought to happen. (Again the comparative status of what now seems "mere fate" is somewhat relative; it depends a great deal on what had been assumed about the scope of agency.) He believes this because all such intuitions presuppose a model of self-knowledge or self-relation about which Nietzsche is clearly quite suspicious. This is a large topic, but a general summary statement would be that for Nietzsche we have grossly inflated our capacity to "master fate" by individual or collective initiative, and that in the most important or decisive instances, our situation is *much* more like what the heroes of Greek tragedy must face, a rule of (blind, purposeless) necessity with which they must find a way to live.

Such suspicions about the putatively decisive role of self-conscious subjectivity are for most people old news, and Nietzsche has been inscribed as one of these Suspicion Masters, together with Marx and Freud, Heidegger, Foucault, structural anthropologists, systems theorists, and many others for some time now. But what we still do not have is something that, I think, Nietzsche on *amor fati* is beginning to try to work out. I mean some clear picture of what it would actually be to lead a life under the assumption that such a suspicion is well founded. (Freud and Heidegger have gone much further in trying to imagine what it would be to live out the implications of the loss of the credibility of the picture of individual centers of agentive power. But even their accounts do not go all that far. Let us say that what they attempted at least raises the question of what Nietzsche's own picture looks like, what plays the role in Nietzsche of the therapeutic attitude or an account of Heideggerian resoluteness.) Even if Nietzsche were a determinist, an instinct or drive theorist, say, what it would be to be *the subject of* such drives (what that would look like, feel like) rather than *merely subject to them* is quite underdetermined by the "sideways on" view offered by the theory itself. Perhaps one of the reasons the attack on subjectivity is so often repeated is that we understand only how to mount the attack, not how to live with or live out its implications. In the simplest obvious sense, any person, post-Nietzschean enlightenment, trying hard *not* to live as if she, as a self-conscious reflective subject, is simply "running the show," is just thereby attempting reflectively and self-consciously to run *that* show. Even if one were somehow to know at a time today that he will not do A when faced with the possibility of doing A tomorrow, he cannot give himself that fact as a *reason* not to do A. And when faced with doing A or not doing A, he must have some reason for doing one rather than the other; he must decide.

In other words, Descartes was surely right that the relation of the mind to the body is not like that of a pilot to a ship, and we might add that it is not like that of a passenger on a remote-controlled vessel either. We cannot wait around to see what our drives, our instincts, the destiny machine, the body, will do. But Nietzsche's deflationary account of reflective consciousness and practical knowledge, or what we have discovered about "our fate," still makes the response he describes or hopes for, *amor fati*, elusive.

For one thing, the picture of *a way of life* as *amor fati* is, quite appropriately, never presented as a recommendation or injunction. One cannot, however convinced of the wisdom of doing so, follow a recommendation to love something just because one is convinced that the recommendation is sound, and so one cannot be enjoined to see one's fate in a beautiful way. The best-known *amor fati* passage from *The Gay Science* is in the appropriately hortatory, subjunctive mood: "*Amor fati: das sei von nun an meine Liebe*," "let *amor fati* be my love from now on," and "*Wegsehen sei meine einzige Verneinung*," "let looking away be my only negation." Indeed the form is rather that of a prayer, certainly an expression of hope, rather than an injunction or even a recommendation about what one ought to do.

As we have seen then, as late as *Twilight of the Idols*, *Ecce Homo*, and *Nietzsche Contra Wagner*, Nietzsche was still appealing to some sort of formulation that returned to his earliest work on the tragic point of view, an ethical outlook informed by the basic orientation to or assessment of life evinced in the classical tragedies. He had of course long since given up the "romantic" idea that any aesthetic experience in modernity – certainly not Wagner's music – could be the transformative or "conversion" experience spoken of earlier. At various points he seemed to hold out some hope that the destructive but "cleansing" effect of the nihilism crisis could effect this conversion. Sometimes he seemed to believe that he and his work alone, functioning like a new Socrates or Jesus, could effect this conversion. But we find him at the end still linking his deepest aspirations for the possibility of a new "post-moral" form of life to an aesthetic appreciation of the beauty of tragic suffering and heroic transcendence of such suffering. By that he seemed to mean that the greatness, the enormity of the risk incurred, the strength and resolve necessary to act in the deeds of tragic heroes was so great that, contra Aristotle, our experience was "beyond" pity and fear. In his account such deeds inspired an experience of their beauty to such an extent that it carried us into an identification of sorts with "the power of life" itself in both its creative and destructive aspects. Whatever this means, it certainly suggests some faith in a wholly transformative experience. That is, what we saw on stage was so beautiful in the grandeur of the attempt that it overcame whatever tendency we might have had to count such fate-defying or fate-indifferent acts as merely futile or perhaps foolhardy (which they might well seem to a person with the virtue of prudence). Indeed Nietzsche is clearly worried that the dominance of reflective, prudent rationality in our own age will make this experience impossible. We will chide Agamemnon for not realizing the absolute value of his daughter's life, or wonder why Orestes could not have brokered a deal between Apollo and the Furies, convinced as we are that killing his mother was going rather far in avenging his father's murder, or wonder why Ajax could not have gotten some therapy, or why Oedipus had to be so hard on himself when he did what he did unintentionally.

As we have seen, Nietzsche thinks the actions in such tragedies are even more beautiful when more hopeless, when they are undertaken in futile but decisive resistance to what the fates decree, when there simply is no answer to such a question about Silenus. We are moved to love a life in which such strategically futile but aesthetically grand gestures are possible, and we are so moved "without guarantees," in the same sense, as he had noted in *Nietzsche Contra Wagner*, that the "love" in *amor fati* is different: "It is the love of a woman who makes us doubt." There is even a slight suggestion that, given the great difficulty of self-knowledge and the truth about our minimal power to order and shape a life on the basis of reflection and human will alone, Nietzsche affirms such a state or fate precisely *because* this great difficulty provides the occasion for great resistance and refusal, sets us obstacles so formidable that struggling with them can elevate deeds to a heroic if doomed status. We might even be said to love these occasions in that sense.

The problem with the picture Nietzsche paints is evident when one starts thinking through the implications of his late references to the tragic poets and *amor fati*. I think that what is behind Nietzsche's *amor fati* picture is something summed up very well by Bernard Williams at the end of his Nietzsche-inspired book, *Shame and Necessity*. It is important enough to quote at length.

We are in an ethical condition that lies not only beyond Christianity but beyond its Kantian and Hegelian legacies. We have an ambivalent sense of what human beings have achieved, and have hopes for how they might live (in particular, in the form of a still powerful ideal that they should live without lies). We know that the world was not made for us, or we for the world, that our history tells no purposive story, and that there is no position outside the world or outside history from which we might hope to authenticate our activities. We have to acknowledge the hideous costs of many human achievements that we value, including this reflective sense itself, and recognize that there is no redemptive Hegelian history or universal Leibnizean cost-benefit analysis to show that it will all come out well enough in the end. In important ways, we are, in our ethical situation, more like human beings in antiquity than any other Western people have been in the meantime. More particularly, we are like those who, from the fifth century and earlier, have left us traces of a consciousness that had not yet been touched by Plato's and Aristotle's attempts to make our ethical relations to the world fully intelligible.[23]

Everything Williams says here is fully "Nietzschean," but he leaves something out. We may have "come out the other side" of our collective experience with Christianity and circled back to a Greek condition pre-Plato and Aristotle. But our situation is also most definitely touched by something new and foreign to Greek ethical life. Before we ended up "back there" we experienced something no Greek ever did: *Nietzsche*, and this despite his resemblance to Callicles or other Sophists or in other guises to Thucydides. Nietzsche may not have a Christian view of intentional action and agency and responsibility, or a Cartesian view of interiority, or a determinist view of psychic mechanisms, but he has certainly not overcome or dispensed with the problem of practical self-knowledge in its *modern* form. Thanks to him and Freud and others, the possibility of such practical self-knowledge, the simple knowledge of what we are doing and why, is immensely more problematic than it was for any ancient dramatist. Modern characters in dramas must suffer a burden no ancient hero ever had to – doubt that they are in fact doing what they take themselves to be doing (their act descriptions may be self-interestedly distorted) and that they are really motivated by what they ascribe to themselves, even sincerely. (For this we don't even need to travel as far as Nietzsche: Shakespeare's Hamlet, Othello, Lear, Macbeth, are enough.) The most important psychological notion in

---

[23] Berkeley: University of California Press, 2008, p. 166.

Nietzsche's genealogy of morality and religion, in his assessment of scientific self-confidence, of democratic politics, and even of philosophy, is self-deceit, a notion unknown to antiquity. And this makes it very unclear that we can respond to ancient dramatic heroes as Nietzsche expects, and all of such doubt is thanks to some degree to Nietzsche himself.

He leaves us, that is, with quite a complicated situation. If we have absorbed, "made corporeal" or incorporated as he once put it, what he had to say about the extraordinary difficulty of adequate self-knowledge, how could we ever be confident enough of our ability to know our own minds well enough to count as full-blooded heroic agents, much less find beautiful and so be swept away by what such heroes do in ancient plays? He has also left us not confident enough of our ability to direct the future in a modern society to count as *effective* agents (or at least nowhere near as confident as the architects of the modern project), but unable to adopt as any sort of credible practical posture the pose of *being fated*. That too – *adopting* such a posture – will still have to count as something we could do or not do.

But this paradoxical dual emphasis both on fate (a restricted scope of effective agency) and the temptation to a self-deceived invocation of fatalism is perhaps what we should expect. The danger of exaggerating our capacity for self-initiated action and so exaggerating a burden of responsibility is, it turns out, as great as the danger of throwing up our hands and in a self-undermining way bemoaning the all pervasive power of fate and the weakness or epiphenomenal status of consciousness and subjectivity itself. Perhaps the best one can say is that Nietzsche is quite good at conveying to us the sense that *this*, this complicated and near paradoxical situation, is what could more properly be said to be our modern fate.

CHAPTER I

Nietzsche: Writings from the early notebooks

Alexander Nehamas

No modern philosopher has been read in as many different ways or appropriated by as many diverse schools of thought, social and political movements or literary and artistic styles as Nietzsche – perhaps, Plato's towering figure aside, no philosopher ever. Notorious during much of the twentieth century as a 'precursor' of German National Socialism, he was also an inspiration to left-wing and avant-garde radicalism in the century's early years as well as to the European and American academic left toward the century's end. Denounced by some for undermining all traditional faith in truth and goodness, he has been praised by others for confronting honestly and truthfully the harmful and deceptive ideals of a self-serving past.

Nietzsche's almost irresoluble ambiguity and many-sidedness are partly generated by his style of writing – playful, hyperbolic, cantering and full of twists and turns – and by his fundamental philosophical conviction that 'the *more* affects we allow to speak about a thing, the *more* eyes, various eyes we are able to use for the same thing, the more complete will be our "concept" of the thing, our "objectivity"'.[1] Nietzsche was intentionally a philosopher of many masks and many voices. His purported objectivity is also due to the fact that most of his writing (more than two thirds of his total output, not counting his voluminous correspondence) has come to us in the form of short notes, drafts of essays and outlines of ideas and books he never published – fragmentary texts that allow great latitude in interpretation. These unpublished writings – his *Nachlass* – were mostly inaccessible until the recent publication of the standard edition of his works.[2] His readers had to rely on a series of different editors who, beginning with his own sister, selected the texts to be published according to their own preconceptions,

---

[1] Friedrich Nietzsche, *On the Genealogy of Morality*, trans. Carol Diethe (Cambridge University Press, 1994), III. 12, p. 92.
[2] Friedrich Nietzsche, *Sämtliche Werke, Kritische Gesamtausgabe*, ed. G. Colli and M. Montinari (Berlin: de Gruyter, 1967–77) (KGW).

arranged them in idiosyncratic ways, and sometimes attributed to him ideas and even whole books he had never himself contemplated.[3]

Because of their intrinsic interest, their bulk, the role they have played in Nietzsche's reception so far and the role they surely should play in trying to come to terms with his sinuous engagement with the world, Nietzsche's unpublished writings deserve serious study and reward careful attention. But, in order to be read at all, these texts – fragments that range from the casual to the polished, from the telegraphic to the discursive, from the personal to the detached, and address, sometimes in considerable detail, topics and problems that preoccupied him throughout his life – must first be placed within a context.

I. READING STRATEGIES

This volume contains an extensive selection from the notebooks Nietzsche kept between 1868, just before he was appointed Professor of Classical Philology at the University of Basel in Switzerland at the age of twenty-four, and 1879, when he resigned his position because of his health and devoted himself full-time to his writing.[4] During that time, Nietzsche composed and published *The Birth of Tragedy* (1872), his four *Untimely Meditations* (1873, 1874, 1876) and *Human, All Too Human*, volumes I and II (1878). Ten years later, in January 1889, Nietzsche collapsed in a public square in the Italian city of Turin and never regained full control of his faculties until his death in 1900. These notes, then, represent his philosophical reflections over more than half of his creative life. They address questions that were central to Nietzsche's early philosophical views: the relative importance of music, image, and word to art and life; the role of ancient Greece – Greek tragedy in particular – as a model for a renewed German culture; and the nature of genius. But they also raise issues with which he grappled throughout his life – the nature of truth, knowledge and language, the connections between art, science and religion, the ancient Greeks' attitudes toward individual and collective goals, the role of philosophers both then and now, and the nature and function of morality. They also reveal different sides of Nietzsche's lifelong involvement with his two great 'educators', the composer Richard Wagner and the philosopher Arthur Schopenhauer.

[3] The most famous among them is the compilation of notes published by Elizabeth Förster–Nietzsche and her collaborators under the title *The Will to Power: Attempt at a Revaluation of All Values*, first in 1901 and then, in expanded form, in 1906. English translation by Walter Kaufmann and R. J. Hollingdale (New York: Random House, 1968).

[4] With one exception: a set of notes on Schopenhauer from 1867–8 which are crucial to the material that follows.

Before we try to look at this material in more detail, though, we must ask how one should go about reading such a collection of semi-independent texts, which shift abruptly from one subject to another, try different tacks only to abandon them and do not generally aim to establish a clear conclusion. The problem of 'reading Nietzsche', a centrepiece of Martin Heidegger's monumental study (published in Germany in 1961),[5] has given rise to a complex debate over whether each of Nietzsche's many voices speaks on its own, independently of the others, whether one among them is authoritative or whether they all harmonise in expressing a single overarching way of looking at the world. The debate was joined by the French philosopher Jacques Derrida,[6] who focused on a sentence, '"I have forgotten my umbrella"', appearing (within quotation marks) in a notebook from 1881–2. Derrida argued that it is impossible to determine precisely the sense of such a sentence and suggested that not only Nietzsche's fragmentary notes but all his writings present a similarly inscrutable face to their interpreters: 'To whatever lengths one might carry a conscientious interpretation', he wrote, 'the hypothesis that the totality of Nietzsche's text, in some monstrous way, might well be of the type "I have forgotten my umbrella" cannot be denied.'[7] On the basis of that hypothesis, Derrida took issue with every attempt to establish a coherent overall interpretation of Nietzsche's work.

The trouble, though, is that, in order to support his reading of this passage, Derrida himself had to place it along with other passages in which, he claimed, Nietzsche expressed similar ideas (for example, sections 365 and 371 of *The Gay Science*). In so doing, he conceded that it is impossible to read anything without bringing some other text – if only the sentences that precede and follow it – to bear upon it. And that, in turn, means that no sentence or statement stands completely on its own, impervious to the pressures of its context. That is not a matter of choice, particularly in the case of Nietzsche's often haphazard notes. Choice enters only when we ask, as we now must, how to select a context within which to read them so as to be able to say something significant about them – even if that is only that they lack all specific meaning.

It won't do, that is, to take each note as a small work in its own right. Consider, for example, note 7[166]:

Euripides and Socrates signify a new beginning in the development of art: *out of tragic knowledge*. This is the task of the future, which so far only Shakespeare

[5] Martin Heidegger, *Nietzsche*, trans. David Farrell Krell, 4 vols. (San Francisco: Harper & Row, 1979–82).
[6] Jacques Derrida, *Spurs: Nietzsche's Styles*, trans. Barbara Harlow (University of Chicago Press, 1979).
[7] Ibid., p. 133.

and our music have completely appropriated. In this sense Greek tragedy is only a preparation: a yearning serenity. – The Gospel according to St John.

The problem here is that, on a theoretical level, it seems close to impossible even to process the words of this passage (unlike the simpler '"I have forgotten my umbrella"') without thinking of what *The Birth of Tragedy* and various other notes have to say about tragedy, Euripides, Socrates, Shakespeare and German music (that is, primarily, Richard Wagner). Each of these passages, in turn, invites (and requires) a reading in the light of still others. For instance, in note 7[131] we read: 'Euripides on the path of science seeks the tragic idea, in order to attain the effect of dithyramb through words. Shakespeare, the poet of fulfilment, he brings Sophocles to perfection, he is the *Socrates who makes music*.' What, then, are we to make of Walter Kaufmann's view that the 'Socrates who makes music' in section 15 of *The Birth of Tragedy* 'is surely an idealized self-portrait: Nietzsche played the piano and composed songs'?[8] And even if we stop that line of questioning there, the reference to the Gospel of St John continues to resist understanding. Why shouldn't we, then, take into account note 7[13], 'The *Gospel according to St John* born out of Greek atmosphere, out of the soil of the Dionysian: its influence on Christianity in contrast to Judaism', which will necessarily send us in ever-new directions?[9]

On a practical level, taking each note as a tiny essay in its own right makes it impossible to keep it securely in mind once we have moved to the next (or the next after that, and so on). Almost as soon as we have read one note, the previous one will have disappeared from memory (try it). Nor again does it improve matters to take the opposite tack and try to read the notebooks as discursive works, containing a more or less unified presentation of interconnected topics in good expository order. In most cases, it is simply impossible to establish such an order and the net result is that the notes fail to make a lasting impression and fade away soon after we have read them.

That is not just an abstract hermeneutical problem: it has affected directly the way in which Nietzsche's notes have been published. Earlier editors, for example, addressed it in the following manner.[10] In his

---

[8] Friedrich Nietzsche, *The Birth of Tragedy*, trans. Walter Kaufmann (New York: Random House, 1966), p. 98, n. 10.

[9] Here is one of them: the Gospel according to St John is not only a Greek legacy to Christianity, it is also 'the most beautiful fruit of Christianity' (10[1]) – a description that cannot be deciphered without following the tangled webs of Nietzsche's views on Christianity, the Dionysian and beauty.

[10] The method is followed, with some individual differences, by the editors of both *Nietzsches Werke* (Leipzig: Kröner, 1901–13) – known as the *Grossoktavausgabe* – and *Nietzsches Gesammelte Werke* (Munich: Musarion, 1920–9) – the *Musarionausgabe*.

correspondence during the decade 1870–9, Nietzsche often referred to an ambitious project that would combine his university lectures on early Greek philosophy with further material in his notes into a work on the cultural significance of philosophy in ancient Greece compared to its role in contemporary Europe. He never settled either on a title or on a structure: his notes contain many different plans and projected outlines, several of them included in this volume. Accordingly, and based on the method Nietzsche's sister Elizabeth used in compiling *The Will to Power*, some of his editors selected various notes and arranged them in several thematically connected groups, as if they were early or unfinished versions of larger works which might have eventually been incorporated into a *magnum opus* treating these issues. And so, in addition to more polished essays like 'On the Pathos of Truth' and 'On Truth and Lie in an Extra-Moral Sense' (both included here), Nietzsche was credited with the following 'potential' works: *The Philosopher: Reflections on the Struggle between Art and Knowledge*, *The Philosopher as Cultural Physician*, *Philosophy in Hard Times* and *The Struggle between Science and Wisdom*.[11]

That way of providing a context for Nietzsche's notes does not only depend heavily on editorial discretion but is also, in a serious sense, circular: it uses as *evidence* for Nietzsche's views 'works' constructed only on the basis of a previous *interpretation* of those very views – how else could one select and order a series of discrete passages into a coherent whole? There is, however, a further difficulty: although Nietzsche might have planned to use a note in a work he was considering at the time, it is impossible to know whether he would have kept it, revised it or even rejected it for the work's final version.

In place of such an 'internal' or 'vertical' approach to the notes, linking them to others that precede or follow them, it might be better to provide them with an 'external' or 'horizontal' context. Without overlooking the notes' internal connections, we should read them alongside the works he published during the 1870s, using both to cast light on one another, add complications to his views or generate uncertainty where only confidence was visible before. The unpublished material can provide us with 'more eyes with which to see the same thing' and thus increase the 'objectivity' with which we can address his intricate, manifold views.[12]

---

[11] That material, along with some of Nietzsche's plans and outlines, appeared (before the relevant volumes of KGW had been published) in an excellent English version, *Philosophy and Truth: Selections from Nietzsche's Notebooks of the Early 1870's*, translated and edited with an introduction and notes by Daniel Breazeale (New Jersey: Humanities Press, 1979).

[12] That should also not exclude other published works, which some of the notes may anticipate, reinforce or, sometimes, contradict.

II. INTELLECTUAL BACKGROUND

Let's begin by considering three topics that preoccupied Nietzsche during the years when he was thinking about, and writing, *The Birth of Tragedy* and, in one way or another, during most of the rest of the 1870s: the philosophy of Schopenhauer, the music of Richard Wagner, and the importance of ancient Greek art and civilisation for a renaissance of German culture.

I Schopenhauer

By far the most important source of philosophical inspiration for the young Nietzsche was the thought of Arthur Schopenhauer (1788–1860), whose major work, *The World as Will and Representation*,[13] Nietzsche read while studying Classics at the University of Leipzig in 1865. 'Here', he wrote in a later autobiographical sketch, 'every line cried Renunciation, Negation, Resignation, here I saw a mirror in which I caught a glimpse of World, Life and my own Mind in frightful splendour,'[14] while in 'Schopenhauer as an Educator', the third of his *Untimely Meditations*, he confessed that, 'though this is a foolish and immodest way of putting it, I understand him as though it was for me he had written'.[15] Nietzsche admired Schopenhauer intensely as an exemplar of what a philosopher should be, and was particularly influenced by his metaphysics, his views on art and his all-encompassing pessimism.

Schopenhauer saw himself as the true heir of Immanuel Kant (1724–1804), who had argued that the objects of our experience are necessarily located in space and time, subject to the law of causality. But space, time and causality apply to things not as they are in themselves but only as they appear to beings like us: they are, so to speak, the filters through which the human mind necessarily perceives and understands the world.[16] The objects of experience, therefore, are not things as they are in themselves, independent of any experiencing subject, the world as it really is, but only things as they appear (to us) – mere 'phenomena' or 'representations'. But

---

[13] WWR; originally published in 1819 and twice revised by Schopenhauer. English translation by E. J. Payne, 2 vols. (Indian Hills, Colo: The Falcon Wing Press, 1958).

[14] 'Rückblick auf meine zwei Leipziger Jahre', in Karl Schlechta, ed., *Werke in Drei Bänden*, vol. III (Munich: Carl Hanser Verlag, 1960), p. 133.

[15] Friedrich Nietzsche, 'Schopenhauer as Educator', in *Untimely Meditations*, trans. R. J. Hollingdale (Cambridge University Press, 1983), p. 133.

[16] A place in space and time makes each thing distinct from every other and causality allows it to interact with every other. The world of experience is subject to the principles of 'individuation' and 'sufficient reason'.

while Kant had concluded that 'how things in themselves may be (without regard to representations through which they affect us) is entirely beyond our cognitive sphere',[17] Schopenhauer was convinced that the real, 'inner' or 'intelligible' nature of the world remains unknown only as long as we limit ourselves to an 'objective' (scientific) standpoint and look at things, *even at ourselves*, from the outside. But in addition to that standpoint, we can also adopt a 'subjective' point of view, and, when we do, when we look at ourselves so to speak from the inside, we find something else: *Will*. It is the will, he argues, that accounts for what from the outside looks like mere bodily movement, an inexplicable succession of stimuli and reactions, and makes it intelligible as a series of actions aimed at satisfying our needs and desires. What *appears* as body and movement when seen from without is an 'objectification' of the will which constitutes our inner reality. In our awareness of ourselves as will, then, we have at least one instance of a direct, unmediated interaction with a thing-in-itself

For various reasons (some better, some worse), Schopenhauer generalised that conclusion to everything in the world – not only human beings but also animals and plants and even, most surprisingly, to inanimate objects. He thought of objects as spaces filled with force and of will as the ultimate metaphysical nature of the world as a whole. Will was for him beyond 'individuation' and 'sufficient reason' – without distinct position in space and time and not subject to the laws of causality. And, most important, it was 'blind': without rhyme or reason, as experience testifies, it is always destroying some of its own parts in order to satisfy the others; the world is finite and if anything is to come into being something else must provide its raw materials.

The will, whether we think of it as nature itself or as it is manifested within each one of us, is eternally dissatisfied, in pain as long as it lacks what it pursues and bored as soon as it obtains it, swinging inexorably between these two sources of suffering – and to no purpose. Schopenhauer's pessimistic conclusion is that nothing in life has a point: all effort is a failure as soon as it succeeds, nothing can affect the world's monstrously indifferent chaos.

Art and beauty, however, can offer a temporary liberation from the will's 'fetters'. Taking the commonplace idea of aesthetic absorption in the most literal terms, Schopenhauer writes that, confronted with a beautiful object, 'we lose ourselves entirely in [it]; in other words, we forget our individuality,

---

[17] Immanuel Kant, *Critique of Pure Reason*, trans. and ed. Paul Guyer and Allen W. Wood (Cambridge University Press, 1998), A190/B234, pp. 305–6.

our will, and continue to exist only as pure subject, as clear mirror of the object, so that it is as though the object alone existed without anyone to perceive it'.[18] At that point, 'all at once the peace, always sought but always escaping us on the former path of the desires, comes to us of its own accord, and it is well with us. It is the painless state Epicurus prized as the highest good and as the state of the gods.'[19] On a more permanent level, what Schopenhauer called 'salvation' is a cessation or denial of willing, accomplished, if at all, only through an ascetic life, a constant effort to overcome the very temptation of striving, a realisation that all goals are completely insignificant and that striving itself is never more than a source of new, continuous suffering.

II Richard Wagner

Nietzsche's love of Schopenhauer's philosophy was matched only by his devotion to the controversial music of Richard Wagner (1813–83), whose equally controversial cultural politics became a source of inspiration for the young scholar. The two met in Leipzig in 1868, where Wagner, himself under the thrall of Schopenhauer, invited Nietzsche to visit him at his house in Tribschen, Switzerland – an invitation that marked Nietzsche's life for ever, since Tribschen was close to Basel, where Nietzsche moved in 1869, and his frequent visits led him into a fateful personal and intellectual friendship with the fiery composer.

In large part, Wagner admired Schopenhauer on account of his view of music. Unlike the other arts, which represent the knowable elements of the everyday world (the Ideas), music – which is non-verbal but nevertheless a vehicle of communication, a 'language' in its own right – is an 'immediate...copy' of reality, that is, the will or the thing-in-itself.[20] Schopenhauer's belief that music (not language) came closest to capturing what the world is really like was a perfect fit with Wagner's contempt for traditional opera, which he accused of subordinating music to language and using it, often deforming it in the process, primarily to illustrate or emphasise the action on the stage. By contrast, Wagner's own music drama (to which denial of the will became a central theme – think of *Tristan and Isolde* or *The Ring of the Nibelung*) made music – the representation of the structure of the will – pre-eminent and used language only to provide its audience with illustrations of the possible objects and activities on which the pure feelings expressed in the music might become focused.

[18] WWR, vol. 1, p. 178.   [19] Ibid., vol. 1, p. 196.   [20] Ibid., vol. 1, p. 257.

Wagner was convinced that his music drama – artistically genuine, philosophically correct and true to the German 'spirit' – would give its audience a direct experience of the nature of the world, their place within it and the bonds of will which, transcending their individual identity, tied them together into a single, unified people (*Volk*). His monumental faith in himself aside, though, was it reasonable to imagine that music, or any art, was capable of such a grandiose metaphysical, cultural and social role? Nietzsche, who, having taken on Wagner's aspirations for a rebirth of German culture, asked that question, believed its answer lay in 'the tragic age' of ancient Greece. What the Greeks had accomplished, especially as it was manifested in the great works of Attic tragedy, established that Wagner's dream was possible and provided a model for the regeneration of the decadent culture of modernity.

III The Greeks

In contrast to most of his contemporaries, Nietzsche wanted philology to shed its scholarly carapace and return to its eighteenth-century origins, when, animated by a sense of kinship between modern Germany and ancient Greece, it studied the Greeks in order to show the emerging German nation how to understand its authentic character and forge a new, unified culture. But, in contrast to its great eighteenth-century admirers, Nietzsche refused to find the heart of Greek culture in what Johann Joachim Winckelmann (1717–68) had famously characterised as 'noble simplicity and quiet grandeur' (*edle Einfalt und stille Größe*). His view of the Greeks was immensely more complex.

In the high points of Greek culture Nietzsche found not a seamless harmony but a host of deeply conflicting tendencies – among them, love of freedom going hand-in-hand with an acknowledgement of the necessity of slavery and devotion to the social unit counterpoised by overweening individual ambition – joined and held together in a dynamic unity. Greek culture was for Nietzsche 'artistic' because it incorporated such oppositions into the balanced structure that is characteristic of great works of art and because the creation and appreciation of art was, as he saw it, its most valued endeavour: 'The Greek artist addresses his work not to the individual but to the state; and the education of the state, in its turn, was nothing but the education of all to enjoy the work of art' (7[121]). The pinnacle of Greek art, in turn, was Attic tragedy, in which the two deepest and most radically opposed tendencies of the 'Hellenic soul' – a deeply pessimistic insight into the real nature of life and the world and a joyful desire to live life to the fullest – found their clearest expression and their final reconciliation. In his interpretation of Greek tragedy Nietzsche combined his interest in Schopenhauer's philosophy, his admiration for Wagner's art and politics, and his devotion to the study of Greece into a radical, extraordinarily ambitious programme for the revival of German culture and, more generally, of the culture of modernity as a whole.

III. THE NOTES

It is impossible to give a comprehensive survey of the material in this volume here. Instead, I will discuss a few specific issues relevant both to Nietzsche's notes and to his published works in order to indicate the various ways in which each kind of writing can cast light on the other. The notes are divided into three sub-periods, corresponding, roughly, with his writing *The Birth of Tragedy*, the *Untimely Meditations* and *Human, All Too Human*.

I 1867–1872

In his 1886 Preface to a second edition of *The Birth of Tragedy*,[21] Nietzsche insisted his early work had already moved well beyond Schopenhauer's thought despite the fact that it still relied on his terminology. In some respects, he was quite right. He was right, for example, that, while Schopenhauer believed that morality – which depends on identifying with others and sharing their suffering – is one of the highest expressions of what it is to be human, his own 'instinct turned *against* morality at the time [he] wrote this questionable book':[22] morality plays no role either in explaining or in justifying life in *The Birth of Tragedy*. He was also right that Schopenhauer could never have imagined such a thing as 'the metaphysical solace which . . . we derive from every true tragedy, the solace that in the ground of things, and despite all changing appearances, life is indestructibly mighty and pleasurable'.[23] Schopenhauer's pervasive pessimism was much more closely aligned with what in *The Birth of Tragedy* Nietzsche calls 'the wisdom of Silenus', whose advice to human beings was that 'the very best thing is . . . not to have been born, not to *be*, to be *nothing*. However, the second best thing for you is: to die soon'.[24] Nietzsche, who was unwilling

---

[21] 'An Attempt at Self-Criticism', in *The Birth of Tragedy*, trans. Ronald Speirs (Cambridge University Press, 1999), pp. 3–12.
[22] Ibid., sec. 5, p. 9.   [23] *The Birth of Tragedy*, sec. 7, p. 39.   [24] Ibid., sec. 3, p. 23.

to accept such a nihilistic view, found much to celebrate in the fact that, even if only 'by means of an illusion spread over things, the greedy Will always finds some way of detaining its creatures in life and forcing them to carry on living'.

That illusion is most forcefully illustrated in tragedy. By combining the Greeks' 'Apollonian' love of the ordered world of individual objects with their 'Dionysian' exaltation in a loss of identity through which (as in communal singing or dance) one is merely part of a larger whole, tragedy offered its audience 'the metaphysical solace that eternal life flows on indestructibly beneath the turmoil of appearances'.[25] Contrary to Schopenhauer's claim that art allows us momentary respite from the torture of willing, Nietzsche sees in it a rekindling of the will: it is precisely at the 'moment of supreme danger for the will [that] *art* approaches as a saving sorceress with the power to heal'.[26]

Why does art spread an 'illusion' over that insight? The reason is that, although Nietzsche rejects Schopenhauer's pessimism, the metaphysical picture that underlies his effort to show that 'only as an *aesthetic phenomenon* [are] existence and the world eternally *justified*'[27] is Schopenhauer's through and through. *In reality*, there is only blind will, working without rhyme or reason, manifesting itself in the individuals and cultures that it will itself eventually destroy. Only through the illusion that the will's creatures provide it with a beautiful spectacle can we come to think of ourselves as *both* creatures (represented by the Apollonian hero on the tragic stage) and creator (represented by the Dionysian chorus in the orchestra whose vision the hero is). And only through that illusion can we be seduced into believing that effort, any effort, is worth making in so far as it provides – for us and for 'that original artist of the world' – yet another beautiful spectacle.

At this point, we can see why it is important to take Nietzsche's notes into account. For there is among them a discussion of Schopenhauer, composed in 1867–8, before he had even met Wagner, in which he makes a set of devastating criticisms of Schopenhauer's metaphysics and, in particular, of the notion of the will (pp. 1–8 below). Nietzsche's criticisms begin with an objection to the legitimacy of the concept of the 'thing-in-itself' that Schopenhauer had adopted from Kant. He goes on to argue, however, that, even if we were to grant that concept to Schopenhauer, we would still have to ask why he believes he can identify the thing-in-itself with the will. 'The will', Nietzsche writes, 'is created only with the help of a poetic intuition,

---

[25] Ibid., sec. 18, p. 85.   [26] Ibid., sec. 7, p. 40.   [27] Ibid., sec. 5, p. 33.

while his attempted logical proofs can satisfy neither Schopenhauer nor us' (p. 3).[28] Further, even if we allow that the thing-in-itself is the will, it is not at all clear how the will, which is beyond experience and therefore altogether unthinkable (since thinking necessarily presupposes the categories of time, space and causality), can be one, eternal (timeless) and free (not bound by reason).[29] Schopenhauer, Nietzsche argues, attributes these features to the world as will only because the world as representation is multifarious, temporal and subject to causality. But, he continues, the realm of the in-itself is not contrary to but incommensurable with appearance: no opposition is possible between them, and none of these features can apply to it.

Nietzsche finds Schopenhauer's system 'riddled [with] a species of extremely important and hardly avoidable contradictions'. He discusses these contradictions in some detail and concludes that Schopenhauer sometimes, when it suits him, thinks of the will as a transcendent thing-in-itself and sometimes, again, as one object among others. Nietzsche, of course, retained his admiration for Schopenhauer himself and for many of his philosophical ideas. This passage shows, though, that from a very early time Schopenhauer's metaphysical picture was not among them. There are, in fact, indications that *The Birth of Tragedy*, without explicitly announcing it, presents an original development of Schopenhauer's view and not a straightforward application of it. And it is possible to argue that, taking advantage of the ambiguity he had himself noted, Nietzsche interprets the will not as the ultimate reality of the world but as the primary manifestation of that reality, itself lying still further and, in itself, completely unknowable.[30] At the same time, though, it is impossible not to wonder why Nietzsche avoids all criticism of Schopenhauer on this issue and why the work seems almost designed to give the overwhelming impression that it follows faithfully in his footsteps. We might, in fact, begin to suspect that Nietzsche may have made a strategic decision to proceed in a way that would not alienate the work's first and ideal reader – Wagner, to whom the work is dedicated and whose friendship with Nietzsche was cemented on their mutual admiration for the philosopher of metaphysical pessimism.

---

[28] For a sympathetic exposition, and measured criticism, of Schopenhauer's arguments on this and many other issues, see Julian Young, *Schopenhauer* (London: Routledge, 2005), pp. 53–88.

[29] I believe 'reason' here refers to the principle of sufficient reason, i.e., causality, which Schopenhauer believed to be incompatible with freedom.

[30] See the excellent discussion in Henry Staten, *Nietzsche's Voices* (Ithaca, N.Y.: Cornell University Press, 1990), pp. 187–216 and James Porter, *The Invention of Dionysus: An Essay on 'The Birth of Tragedy'* (Stanford University Press, 2000), pp. 57–73.

That Nietzsche's decision was in fact strategic is made more likely by another difference between his notes and the published version of *The Birth of Tragedy*. In a notebook dating from the beginning of 1871, there is a long continuous passage which, although originally intended as part of the book, was not included in the final version.[31] The passage contains several views about Greek culture and culture in general that became progressively more prominent in Nietzsche's writings, but not until well after his break with Wagner – most notably the idea that a genuine culture is impossible without a large labouring class, if not a class of actual slaves. This, however, would have seemed intolerable to Wagner, whose vision of a future German culture excluded every vestige of the *de facto* slavery to which capitalism condemns the largest, wage-earning segment of society – and that could certainly be a reason for Nietzsche's tactfully avoiding the issue in a book dedicated to the realisation of the composer's vision.

Whatever the final answer to these questions, it is clear that we cannot avoid asking them once we take, as I believe we should, Nietzsche's notes into account along with *The Birth of Tragedy*. Taken in conjunction with the published works to which they are related, the notes are indispensable to the interpretation of his philosophy.

II 1872–1876

Nietzsche had hoped *The Birth of Tragedy* would have a direct and profound effect on public discourse regarding the culture of the new German *Reich* but, in the event, the book's reception proved a bitter disappointment. It is true that Wagner and his circle were delighted with it, but their numbers were much too small to satisfy Nietzsche and, in any case, their admiration did not remain a source of unequivocal pleasure for long. Wagner himself moved his family to Bayreuth in April 1872 and devoted himself to building a theatre exclusively dedicated – as it still is – to the performance of his works. Nietzsche, to be sure, remained close to him and visited Bayreuth several times, but relations between two men gradually became cooler. In 1876, when Nietzsche arrived for the inauguration of the theatre with the first full performance of *The Ring of the Nibelung*, what he saw, far from a modern equivalent of the ancient dramatic competitions, was just yet another occasion for the display of German bourgeois philistinism – *fast*

---

[31] A different version of that passage, with the title 'The Greek State', was (along with 'On the Pathos of Truth', included in this volume) part of Nietzsche's 'Five Prefaces to Five Unwritten Books', a Christmas gift for Cosima, Wagner's wife, in 1872.

habe ich's bereut ('I have almost regretted it'), he wrote to his sister, with a characteristic pun on the town's name.[32]

Personally and intellectually, these were difficult years for Nietzsche. By the standards of the next decade (the last of his productive career), which saw the publication of at least fourteen books and various other pieces, this period of his life is relatively barren, although his notes indicate that he contemplated several different works. One was a series of thirteen essays, collectively entitled *Untimely Meditations,* only four of which – his total literary output for these years – appeared. The first was an attack on David Strauss, who had combined a demythologised portrait of Jesus with continued faith in the precepts of Christianity, and on the philistinism Nietzsche took him to represent. The second addressed the contributions of the study of history, positive and negative, to the life and flourishing of society, and the third and fourth were accounts of his views on Schopenhauer and Wagner respectively.

Nietzsche's notes of the time reveal his increasing interest in philosophical problems of metaphysics and epistemology as well as in the history of Greek philosophy. He is concerned with the role of philosophy, both in the ancient world and in his own day, within culture – prompted, perhaps, by his own failure to intervene directly in the cultural politics of Germany. He worries about the connections between philosophy, art, science and religion, and speculates on the origins of the desire for knowledge and truth and its effects on life in general. And while he does not abandon the main themes of his earlier years – Schopenhauer, Wagner and the Greeks – he begins to look at them with new and different eyes. Above all, his notes testify to a preoccupation with his writing style and his determination to acquire a voice of his own and, although his language does not yet achieve its later brilliance, it becomes progressively simpler and more straightforward. His 1886 confession that *The Birth of Tragedy* was marred by being framed in the language of Kant and Schopenhauer[33] is clearly anticipated in a note from just this period: 'Everything must be said as precisely as possible and any technical term, including "will", must be left to one side' (19[46]).

Although morality, which was to become one of Nietzsche's main preoccupations, plays no explicit role either in *The Birth of Tragedy* or in the *Untimely Meditations,* his notes show that it was already on his mind well

---

[32] Nietzsche improved on his joke in later years: 'Typical telegram from Bayreuth: *bereits bereut* [already rued]'; see *The Case of Wagner* (1888), included in *Basic Writings of Nietzsche,* ed. and trans. Walter Kaufmann (New York: Random House, 1968), p. 641.

[33] 'An Attempt at Self-Criticism', sec. 6, p. 10.

before it burst forth in *Human, All Too Human* and the works that follow it. Nietzsche is sometimes positive about it – when, for example, he associates it with Schopenhauer's idea of identifying with the suffering of others or with the Christian ideal of love of the neighbour, which he contrasts to the prudential origins of justice (19[93]; see also 19[63]). Sometimes he thinks of it in terms that anticipate 'the morality of custom', which emerges most clearly in *Daybreak* (1881): 'If we could create custom, a powerful custom! We would then also have morality' (19[39]). More often, though, his interest in morality emerges indirectly, particularly in his many discussions of the practical source of those most theoretical of human desires: the 'drive' for knowledge and the 'pathos' of truth.

Along with the problem of the role of philosophy in antiquity and today, with which it is closely connected, the question of the origins of these drives is probably the most important theme in these notes. It is a theme to which Nietzsche returned again and again. He was convinced that 'our natural science, with its goal of knowledge, drives towards *downfall*' (19[198]) and he contrasted 'σοφία' [wisdom], which 'contains within it that which selects, that which has taste', with science, which, 'lacking such a refined taste, pounces on everything worth knowing' (19[86]).[34] Not quite certain that wisdom gives him the right contrast to knowledge, he tries out various candidates, usually art – 'Absolute knowledge leads to *pessimism*; art is the remedy against it' (19[52]) – or philosophy: 'It is not a question of destroying science, but of *controlling* it. For science in all its goals and methods depends entirely on philosophical views, *although it easily forgets this. But the controlling philosophy must also remember the problem of the degree to which science should be allowed to grow: it has to determine **value**!*' (19[24]). His fundamental idea, however, remains unchanged: the unfettered pursuit of knowledge for its own sake, as if everything worth knowing is equally and supremely valuable, leads inevitably to the realisation that knowledge is finally unattainable. The drive to knowledge thus undermines itself and its result is a pessimistic resignation from the pointlessness of life.

Before asking why Nietzsche was tempted by that position, we should note his view that the intellect, the faculty directed at knowledge, is, like all human faculties, primarily

a means of preserving the individual, [and] unfolds its main powers in dissimulation; for dissimulation is the means by which the weaker, less robust individuals survive, having been denied the ability to fight for their existence with horns or

---

[34] 'Science' and 'knowledge' are almost completely interchangeable in such contexts: the German word *Wissenschaft* applies to everything from physics to classics.

sharp predator teeth. In man this art of dissimulation reaches its peak [so] that there is hardly anything more incomprehensible than how an honest and pure drive from truth could have arisen among them. ('On Truth and Lie in an Extra-Moral Sense', p. 254)

This is one of the earliest expressions of an idea that pervades the thought of Nietzsche's later years. Beginning with *Thus Spoke Zarathustra* and throughout the works that followed it, he launched a vehement attack against the assumption that knowledge of the truth has an unconditional and overriding value. He argued that such a belief could not have been based on experience 'if both truth *and* untruth had constantly made it clear that they were both useful, as they are': 'rather it must have originated *in spite of* the fact that the disutility and dangerousness of "the will to truth" or "truth at any price" is proved . . . constantly'.[35] At that time, Nietzsche traced the will to truth to a moral conviction: the principle that deception (even of oneself) is absolutely wrong. That conviction in turn is based on thinking that human beings are radically different from the rest of nature, which depends essentially on deception to accomplish its purposes. Although the essays of the 1870s explicitly reject such a metaphysical picture and insist that we are simply one animal among many, 'On Truth and Lie in an Extra-Moral Sense' locates the origin of the drive for truth and knowledge in our need for social organisation.

The contrast between truth and lie arises because lying, which misuses the valid designations of things, can be harmful to society. That only shows, though, that what we really want to avoid is not the lie, the deception itself, 'but the bad, hostile consequences of certain kinds of deception. Only in a similarly restricted sense does man want the truth. He desires the pleasant, life-preserving consequences of truth; he is indifferent to pure knowledge without consequences, and even hostile to harmful and destructive truths' (p. 255). The origin of the 'pathos' (passion) for truth is therefore profoundly practical: 'Man demands truth and achieves it in moral contacts with others; all social existence is based on this. One anticipates the bad consequences of reciprocal lies. This is the origin of *the duty of truth*' (19[97]).[36] At the same time, though, Nietzsche recognises that telling the truth is not always

---

[35] Friedrich Nietzsche, *The Gay Science*, trans. Josefine Nauckoff (Cambridge University Press, 1981), sec. 344, p. 201. Nietzsche expands this discussion in sections 24–7 of the Third Essay of *On the Genealogy of Morality*.

[36] Nietzsche uses the term *moralisch*, 'moral', in a broad sense and applies it indifferently to both moral and prudential interests. He eventually thinks of morality as a much more specific set of rules, values and practices and distinguishes it not only from prudential but also from other ethical institutions. See, for example, the contrast between 'noble' and 'slave' values in the First Essay of *On the Genealogy of Morality*.

benign and quotes approvingly Benjamin Constant's statement that: 'The moral principle that it is one's duty to speak the truth, if it were taken singly and unconditionally, would make all society impossible' (29[6]). He seems, that is, to be aware that the obligations society imposes upon us can be no more than partial: both truth and untruth are useful. From where, then, does the pathos of truth derive its claim to absolute authority? Nietzsche answers that question through an examination of the general features of language and representation.

In fact, even those 'valid designations' the rules of language specify as true are in reality radically and completely false – they are all, in the appropriate sense, 'lies'. In reality, we are told in 'On Truth and Lie in an Extra-Moral Sense', it is impossible for any human perception, word or sentence to be faithful to the structure of the world.

First of all, Nietzsche claims, we are never aware of things-in-themselves but only of various stimulations of our nerve-endings, and no inference from the properties of a nerve stimulus, which is internal to us, to the properties of a cause outside us is ever legitimate: the in-itself is not subject to the principle of causality or sufficient reason. Second, he argues, on the basis of a version of Schopenhauer's epistemology, that none of the links in the chain that connects a nerve stimulus to an image (perception) and an image to a sound (word) can be an accurate representation of what gives rise to it. Each imposes 'a complete overleaping of the sphere' to which the previous element belongs: it is nothing but a metaphor, and metaphors 'do not correspond in the slightest to the original entities' they attempt to describe (p. 256).

Things get even worse when we introduce the conceptual aspects of language into the picture: while in reality every experience is 'unique' and 'entirely individualised', a concept, which is meant to apply to whole families of such experiences, 'comes into being through the equation of non-equal things. As certainly as no leaf is ever completely identical to another, so certainly the concept of leaf is formed by arbitrarily shelving these individual differences or forgetting the distinguishing feature' (pp. 256–7). Strictly speaking, then, there is no truth at all – all our representations of the world, sensory, perceptual and conceptual, are in principle inadequate to the reality to which they are supposed to correspond. Why, then, do we value truth as we do? Whence the pathos of truth? Nietzsche answers that it lies in *forgetting*. Above and beyond

the obligation that society, in order to exist, imposes on us – the obligation to be truthful, i.e. to use customary metaphors . . . to lie in accordance with a firm convention . . . man forgets that this is his predicament and therefore he lies, in the manner described, unconsciously and according to the habit of hundreds of years – and arrives at a sense of truth precisely *by means of this unconsciousness*, this oblivion. The sense of being obliged to call one thing red, another cold, a third mute, awakens a moral impulse related to truth. (pp. 257–8)

That is, finally, why the unbridled pursuit of knowledge leads to its own 'downfall' (p. 31 above): we *have forgotten* that the obligations of society are conditional. We have forgotten that both truth (lying according to fixed conventions) and untruth (lying in unusual ways) are useful and, more important, that they are both *lies*, since language is necessarily inadequate to the world. Our overvaluation of truth thus leads us into an indiscriminate pursuit of knowledge and, the more we learn, the closer we come to realising the *actual* truth that the truth is completely inaccessible to us.

Nietzsche's view is deeply flawed, but we can address only two of the difficulties it faces here.[37] The first is with the very idea of forgetting. For if, as Nietzsche acknowledges, society constantly requires both truth-telling and lying, how could we ever have forgotten the usefulness of the lie and attributed all value to truth?[38] The second problem is that his epistemology faces serious difficulties of its own. Very briefly, it is impossible to see how Nietzsche can claim both that 'we believe that we know something about the things themselves . . . and yet we possess nothing but metaphors for things which do not correspond in the slightest to the original entities' on the one hand and that 'no leaf is ever completely identical to another' on the other (p. 256). If nothing we say corresponds to the way things are, it is impossible to assert correctly that in reality every leaf (supposing reality contains leaves in the first place) is different from every other. Either language succeeds in describing reality, in which case we can say some true things about it, or it does not, in which case the best we can do is to remain silent. It is not even clear that we can say that our representations can't correspond to the world, because if we knew that we would know *something* about the world – enough, at any rate, to know that we can't possibly represent it: how else could we tell that we can't?

Nietzsche's notes show that he was ambivalent here (e.g., 9[154–63], 29[8]). And that ambivalence, I believe, is why Nietzsche did not publish

---

[37] For a detailed examination of the theoretical claims of 'On Truth and Lie in an Extra-Moral Sense', several of their difficulties and Nietzsche's leaving both behind, see Maudemarie Clark, *Nietzsche on Truth and Philosophy* (Cambridge University Press, 1990), chapters 3 and 4.

[38] Ironically, in *On the Genealogy of Morality* Nietzsche dismisses the 'unhistorical' thinking of 'the English psychologists' who argue that the original sense of the concept 'good' – 'unegoistic' – was gradually forgotten with the question: 'How was such forgetting possible? Did the usefulness of such behaviour suddenly cease at some point?' (I. 2–3, pp. 12–13).

any of his views on metaphysics and epistemology between 1872 and 1876: he seems to have realised that his extreme epistemic pessimism – the idea that all of our beliefs, from the most abstruse to the most common and banal, are necessarily false – was not a sustainable position; but he also seems to have been unable to see his way to formulating a reasonable alternative to it.

What he published, instead, were four essays that he hoped would give him the public voice he had failed to develop through *The Birth of Tragedy* – three, as we have seen, on specific individuals and one on the way in which the study of history can be put to the service of 'life'. By 'life', Nietzsche mainly meant the cultural life of Germany, whose self-satisfaction with its victory in the Franco-Prussian war he considered 'capable of turning our victory into a defeat: *into the defeat, if not the extirpation, of the German spirit for the benefit of the "German Reich"*'.[39] In 'On the Uses and Disadvantages of History for Life' he addresses one of the dangers he saw threatening the 'German spirit': an excessive concern with the past, which, under the delusion that history can be studied scientifically and 'without restraint, . . . uproots the future because it destroys illusions and robs the things that exist of the atmosphere in which alone they can live'.[40] That idea, in turn, bears a complex and illuminating relationship to the notes of this period.

The essay distinguishes three ways of approaching history. *Monumental* history inspires us to 'act and strive' by showing that since greatness was possible in the past it may also be possible in the present; *antiquarian* history shows the worth of the present by tracing it to a past that is perceived with love and loyalty; *critical* history allows us to move beyond our past by 'condemning' various of its parts and loosening their claim to persist: some things – privileges, castes, dynasties – really do deserve to perish. Each makes its own contribution to life but all depend, once again, on a crucial forgetting. A past event appears exemplary and worthy of imitation only by means of forgetting that no effect can be separated from its causes and by wrenching a particular occurrence from a web of relations apart from which it is really unthinkable.[41] One's past appears

[39] This comes from section 1 of 'David Strauss, the Confessor and the Writer,' the first of the *Untimely Meditations*, p. 3. Nietzsche has clearly moderated his early hopes for the future of the *Reich*.

[40] 'On the Uses and Disadvantages of History for Life', *Untimely Meditations*, sec. 7, p. 95.

[41] Nietzsche insists that 'that which was once possible could present itself as a possibility for a second time only if the Pythagoreans were right in believing that when the constellation of the heavenly bodies is repeated, the same things, down to the smallest event, must also be repeated on earth . . . but that will no doubt happen only when the astronomers have again become astrologers . . . [whereas] the truly historical connexus of cause and effect . . . fully understood, would only demonstrate that

unique and pre-eminently valuable only as a result of forgetting anything that did not directly contribute to it, by an extreme narrowing of vision that relates the past to nothing else, gives every one of its parts equal value and finally identifies value with antiquity and rejects anything new and evolving. The passions, errors and crimes of the past, such as they are, can be condemned only by forgetting that we too are ourselves their outcome and that all the condemning in the world cannot alter the fact that we originate in them and that they are part of what makes us what we are.

History served life in the past only because of such forgetting. But the present is different: the 'constellation of life and history' has been disturbed by 'a mighty, hostile . . . gleaming and glorious star' – '*by science, by the demand that history should be a science*' (p. 77). By 'science', Nietzsche understands a particular attitude toward our knowledge of the world, not a particular method of investigation for whose indiscriminateness he feels contempt – 'The drive for knowledge *without choice* is on a par with the indiscriminate sex drive – a sign of *coarseness!*' (19[11]) – and about whose outcome he is deeply pessimistic:

Historical verification always brings to light so much that is false, crude, inhuman, absurd, violent that the mood of pious illusion in which alone anything that wants to live can live necessarily crumbles away: for it is only in love, only when shaded by the illusion produced by love, that man is creative. (p. 95)

Love, which makes one's own deeds seem more beautiful and greater than they are, is contrasted with justice, which accords each thing the attention it deserves: 'he who acts loves his deed infinitely more than it deserves to be loved' (p. 64).[42] Love, too, requires precisely the narrowing of horizon that allows history to serve life, 'an enveloping illusion' that gives its object pride of place in the world and makes it worth pursuing. That illusion is what science refuses to respect and, in its relentless pursuit of the truth, will reveal for what it is.

Knowledge, so to speak, levels the field. Since it reveals nothing that inspires love and attracts our energy and attention to the exclusion of other things, it leaves us listless, unable to make the choices necessary for forging a path to a new future. It forbids us to forget the injustice of love (one

the dice-game of chance and the future could never again produce anything exactly similar to what it produced in the past' (ibid., p. 70). That is bound to cast doubt on the popular interpretation of the idea of the 'eternal recurrence', which appears in sec. 341 of *The Gay Science* and in several of Nietzsche's late works, as a theory that declares precisely the sort of repetition that is said to be impossible here to be a necessary natural phenomenon.

[42] For a contrast between love and justice along a different axis, see 19[93].

illusion) and disowns both art and religion, which 'bestow upon existence the character of the eternal and the stable' (another). Action, though, is impossible without such illusions; to maintain them we must 'restrain' the pathological growth of the historical sense a scientific approach to history brings in its wake (p. 120).

How can the historical sense be restrained? The essay itself offers no unequivocal answer, but Nietzsche's notebooks are clear on the direction of his thought:

If we are ever to achieve a culture, tremendous artistic forces are needed in order to break the boundless drive for knowledge and once more to create a unity. *The supreme dignity of the philosopher manifests itself here, where he concentrates the boundless drive for knowledge and restrains it into a unity.* This is how the ancient Greek philosophers [who lived in the most artistic of cultures] must be understood: they restrain the drive for knowledge. (19[27]; see also 19[24])

Nietzsche sets philosophy 'against the dogmatism of the sciences . . . but only in the service of a culture' (23[7]). Culture is the unified and therefore mutually balanced and restrained expression of the drives of a people (19[42]) and it is perhaps the highest task of philosophy to bring such a unity about.

Philosophy is connected both with science, since both depend on a conceptual representation of the world, and with art, because the purpose of both is to articulate what 'greatness' is and to promote it at the expense of everything else. A sense that what matters is not only truth but 'greatness' as well '*restrains* the drive for knowledge' (19[83]) because it forces us to omit, overlook and ignore: 'it has not the same interest in everything perceived' and directs the drive to truth toward what matters (19[67]; cf. 19[33]). Nietzsche is aware of difficulties here. He confesses to a '[g]reat uncertainty as to whether philosophy is an art or a science' (19[62]) and doubts whether, like art, philosophy can create a culture on its own: '[The philosopher] *cannot create a culture,* but he can prepare it, remove impediments, or moderate and thereby preserve it, or destroy it. (Always exclusively by negation)' (28[2]; cf. 23[14]). Not today, he seems to think: 'For us it is no longer possible to produce a succession of philosophers such as Greece did in the age of tragedy. Their task is now performed *by art alone*' (19[36]). Can philosophy, then, reclaim its ancient status and, if so, how can it find a place next to art and religion?[43]

---

[43] Nietzsche's notes are important in showing that his attitude toward religion during this period was much more positive than one would expect from a reading of his later work.

That he had no answer to that question may be why 'On the Uses and Disadvantages of History for Life' leaves the mechanism that turns history into art relatively obscure. The problem would have been even more pressing when Nietzsche began to work on 'Schopenhauer as Educator' since it might cast doubt on Schopenhauer's own accomplishment and on the claim of the philosopher to join saint and artist in Schopenhauer's pantheon.

Nietzsche resolved that difficulty through a brilliant application of a theme he had introduced both in his notes and in the essay on history. He now located the aim and justification of a genuine culture in the creation of great individuals: 'the *goal of humanity* cannot lie in its end but only *in its highest exemplars*'.[44] Philosophers are among such exemplars because their creative work is not exhausted by their ideas: it includes, crucially, the application of their ideas to life, the demonstration that one can forge a new way of living on the basis of those ideas. But Nietzsche realised that to follow such exemplars could not possibly be to become their disciple: each constellation of views answers to the circumstances, the needs and aspirations of the person who produced it. What exemplary 'educators' can offer to others is a life and accomplishments that, idiosyncratic and unrepeatable as they may be, can be understood as an instance of 'the universal life' which it is everyone's fate – whatever the differences between our specific situations – to live. In his late works, of course, Nietzsche repudiated all claims to universality, which he came to consider pathological,[45] but the present view is not without advantages. It gives philosophy a place next to art because it construes the philosophers' lives and examples as their creative works (see 29[205]). It explains why philosophers can disagree so radically with one another and yet function as exemplars, since each philosophical vision is tied to its creator's own 'want', 'misery' and 'limitedness'.[46] And it allows Nietzsche to proclaim his indebtedness to Schopenhauer at the same time that, on account of such differences, he can also declare himself independent from him. No wonder that, many years later, he claimed that the essay 'registers my innermost history, my becoming'.[47]

---

[44] 'On the Use and Disadvantages of History for Life', p. 111; cf. 19[38].

[45] Compare this passage, along with the earlier and more absolutist 'The single outstanding moral man exercises a magic that causes others to imitate him. The philosopher must spread this magic. What is law for the highest specimen must gradually become the law as such: if only as a barrier for the others' (19[113]), with section 43 of *Beyond Good and Evil*: the pride and the taste of the 'philosophers of the future' would be offended 'if their truth were a truth for everyone (which has been the secret wish and hidden meaning of all dogmatic aspirations so far)' – Nietzsche's own included. Friedrich Nietzsche, *Beyond Good and Evil*, trans. Judith Norman (Cambridge University Press, 2002).

[46] 'Schopenhauer as Educator', p. 142.

[47] *Ecce Homo*, trans. Judith Norman in *Friedrich Nietzsche: The Anti-Christ, Ecce Homo, Twilight of the Idols and Other Writings* (Cambridge University Press, 2005), 'The Untimely Ones', sec. 3, p. 115.

This discussion has not touched either on Nietzsche's extensive comments on Socrates, which are much more ambivalent than his attack in *The Birth of Tragedy*, or on his treatment of early Greek philosophy, which he admired intensely. We merely mentioned his growing disillusion with Wagner, which made him doubt for a while whether he should publish his essay on the composer's significance and accomplishment. And we ignored a host of other important themes and questions. It is time, though, to take a quick look at the material that dates from the years when Nietzsche was writing *Human, All Too Human*, a work in which he truly found his own voice and articulated a radically new and original set of philosophical ideas.

III 1876–1879

Nietzsche's life was in upheaval. His academic career was in a shambles. His health, which had been precarious to begin with, had been further weakened while he served as a medical orderly in the Franco-Prussian war, making everyday life – not to mention writing and meeting his professional obligations – almost impossibly painful. The world around him was brimming with optimism – about the *Reich*, the scientific revolution, technological progress, the successes of capitalism and, variously, both liberalism and imperialism. By contrast, he was convinced that Europe was blissfully unaware of the disastrous collapse, with the erosion of religion during the Enlightenment, of the only authority on which its faith (illusory as it may have been) in the absolute validity of the values that sustained it could be based. But, disillusioned with Wagner and emancipated from Schopenhauer, he was left without a model (illusory as *that* might have been) for an alternative cultural and philosophical project of his own, while his rather vague appeals to 'German youth' in the *Untimely Meditations* had gone, once again, completely unheeded.

It was time to change tack: 'To readers of my writings I want to declare unequivocally that I have abandoned the metaphysico-artistic views that essentially dominate those writings: they are pleasant but untenable. If one takes the liberty of speaking in public early one is usually obliged to contradict oneself in public soon after' (23b[159]).[48] *Human, All Too Human*, which appeared in 1878, was the record of his first effort to think through his problems without Wagner, Schopenhauer or, to a considerable extent, the Greeks. It represents a radical turn away from looking for

---

[48] I use the letter 'b' to distinguish the notebook in question, included in vol. 8 of KSA, from a notebook that bears the same number in vol. 7.

comfort in art and metaphysics and a new respect for science and 'the little unpretentious truths which have been discovered by means of rigorous method... [rather] than the errors handed down by metaphysical and artistic ages and men, which bind us and make us happy'.[49] It proposes to show that both the origins and the consequences of our most hallowed and spiritual aspirations and accomplishments are firmly anchored in the natural world of physics and biology and that instead of having an other-worldly significance they are simply human, all too human.

At the same time, Nietzsche's writing style undergoes an utterly drastic change. The continuous prose of his earlier works gives way to a series of aphoristic passages, ranging from a single line to a few paragraphs, each relatively self-contained, as economical in expression as they are lavish in implication. This style, on which Nietzsche was to depend in most of what he wrote from now on, allows him to look at everything he approaches from many different points of view and gives his thought, despite the confidence of each individual statement, a diverse, multifarious quality that has often been mistaken for inconsistency.

The change in both style and substance is immediately evident in the first notebook from this period, compiled almost immediately following the completion of *Wagner in Bayreuth*. In 1871, Nietzsche had credited the greatest accomplishment of art to 'individuals' who 'are driven ahead... into that devouring brightness – to return with a transfigured look in their eyes, as a triumph of the Dionysian will which, through a wonderful delusion, bends back and breaks even the existence-denying last barb of its knowledge, the strongest spear directed against existence itself' (7[123]). Now he writes, 'The artist needs the infidelity of memory in order not to copy but to transform nature' (17[32]). The sharp distinction between appearance and reality, the essential conflict between art and science, the necessity of a metaphysical illusion – all that is gone. In their place, forgetting, itself shorn of metaphysical garb, provides a natural mechanism for art's transfiguration of the only world we all inhabit. Forgetting has already become for Nietzsche 'not just a *vis inertiae*, as superficial people suppose, but... rather an active ability to suppress, positive in the strongest sense of the word', to which, he will later claim, we owe not only art but even happiness, cheerfulness, hope and pride.[50]

Metaphysics, the belief in a world behind every *possible* appearance, a stable domain of the in-itself in which human beings alone, among all

---

[49] Friedrich Nietzsche, *Human, All Too Human: A Book for Free Spirits*, trans. R. J. Hollingdale (Cambridge University Press, 1996), sec. 3, p. 13.

[50] *On the Genealogy of Morality*, II. 1, p. 38.

natural creatures, have an uneasy share, is now interpreted simply as a response to the human need 'to prefer *any explanation* to none' (19b[107]). But need, Nietzsche writes, 'proves nothing about any reality corresponding to that need'; however necessary it has become, a belief may still be false. But – we find here perhaps for the first time an idea that became central to his thought – to refute a belief created by a need is not to abolish the need: 'By overthrowing a *belief* one does not overthrow the *consequences* that have grown out of it' (19b[97]). To show that there is no metaphysical world (or that, even if there is, it is irrelevant to us)[51] it is not enough to dislodge our faith that the authority of our deepest views and values is absolute, as if it did in fact derive from a world beyond the continual change that deprives the world of phenomena of anything universal or absolute.

Life is partial and limited; it lacks objectivity: 'Love and hate are cataractic and one-eyed, likewise the "will"' (21[40]). But objectivity, the ideal of impartial knowledge, cannot sustain life. It is incapable of providing it with the preferences and values without which it is unthinkable: 'No *ethics* [a way to live] can be based on pure knowledge of things: for that purpose one must be like nature, neither good nor evil' (17[100]). But although we cannot possibly be like nature, we are still natural beings.[52] What has allowed us to separate ourselves from the rest of nature so far is religion and metaphysics: 'How would men look without all these sublime errors – I believe, *like animals*.' But what of it? Depending, of course, on the kind of animal involved, 'the *truth* and *animals* get on well together' (23b[21]).

Metaphysics, then, is essentially a collection of errors, but error – everyday, literal error, not the grand illusions with which Nietzsche had been occupied so far – can have the most beneficial results: 'If men had not built houses for gods architecture would still be in its infancy. The tasks man set himself on the basis of false assumptions (e.g. the soul separable from the body) have given rise to the highest forms of culture. "Truths" [he continues, problematically] are unable to supply such motives' (23b[167]). The question, for whose answer Nietzsche was to search for the rest of his life, is how to eliminate the need that gave rise to particular errors yet preserve the useful consequences many of them may have had.

---

[51] *Human, All Too Human*, sec. 9.
[52] It is clear that Nietzsche is trying out various paths here: 23[9], for example, proposes a reductionist view – often wrongly identified with 'naturalism' – to the effect that all that happens biologically 'is determined by chemical laws just as a waterfall is determined by mechanical laws', while the notion of 'drive' applies only when psychological phenomena 'have not yet been traced to their chemical and mechanical laws'. But see *Beyond Good and Evil*, sec. 9, for an indication of his attitude toward that proposal, as well as the opening section of *Human, All Too Human*, which shows how broadly he understands the idea of 'chemistry'.

Perhaps we should think of *The Birth of Tragedy* itself as a great work that is based on the most erroneous views. Nietzsche, however, was not so charitable and he focused on its errors more than its greatness. One such error, he makes it very clear, was his overvaluation of tragedy and drama in general: 'Dramatists are *constructive* geniuses, not original finders like epic poets. *Drama* is *lower* than the epic – coarser audience – democratic' (27[19])]). And along with his rejection of drama comes his final renunciation of Wagner, whom he now demotes – rather cruelly, perhaps – from 'musician' (or, in Wagner's own terms, 'dramatist of reality' – a dramatist whose raw material is music and whose subject is the world beyond appearance) to 'dramatist' (someone who, in the end, is only capable of representing everyday reality without discerning the fissures through which different alternatives to it appear possible): 'His soul does not *sing*, it *speaks*, but it speaks as the supreme passion does. What is *natural* to him is the tone, the rhythm, the gestures of the spoken language; the music, on the other hand, is never quite natural, but a kind *of learnt* language with a modest stock of words and a *different* syntax' (27[47]).[53]

He describes *Human, All Too Human* as an 'atonement' for *The Birth of Tragedy*, which he suspects, to the extent that it had an influence on Wagner, of having caused him 'some harm'! 'I regret this very much,' he concludes (30[56]). He criticises *The Birth of Tragedy* for the view that the world has an 'author' (30[51]) or an 'artist-creator' (30[68]) who provides it with an aesthetic justification, and he even expresses considerable scepticism regarding his understanding of Greek philosophy: was it perhaps due simply to 'the ears of a man in great need of art' (30[52])? His self-criticism is relentless and sweeping, clearing the ground for the immense project he is beginning to set for himself and which he will pursue until the end of his life: how to find a way to live and thrive in a world that provides no absolute foundation for value, imposes no requirements and offers no pre-established paths for anyone to follow.

Nietzsche was engaged in this radical revaluation of his own values while, having resigned his professorship, he was also preparing himself for a solitary, nomadic life with minimal resources, and his notes testify to that as well:

I conclude: *Restricting* our *needs*. With regard to these (e.g. our food, clothing, shelter, heating, climate etc.) we must *all* make sure that we become *experts*. *Building our lives on as many or as few foundations as we can adequately judge* –

---

[53] It is important to contrast this note with Nietzsche's earlier views in 12[1]; see also 29b[15], where he claims that both tragedy and comedy supply a 'caricature, not an image, of life'.

that is how we promote general morality, i.e. we force every craftsman to treat us *honestly* because we are *experts*. If we do not want to become experts in any one need we must *deny* that need to ourselves: this is the new morality. (40[3])

This is all very serious business, as Nietzsche was always ready to remind his readers. But he also expected more from them than just earnest agreement since nothing, including seriousness, is ever good or bad in itself (23b[152]). As we follow him through his notes' labyrinthine paths and leave him just as they have led him to the threshold of his greatest accomplishments, we can do no better than keep with us, as our own version of Ariadne's thread, the world of the very last note included in this volume:

Shame on this lofty semi-idiotic seriousness! Are there no little lines around your eyes? Can't you lift a thought on your fingertips and flick it up in the air? Does your mouth have only this one pinched, morose expression? Do your shoulders never shake with laughter? I wish you would once in a while whistle and behave as if you were in bad company, instead of sitting together with your author in such a respectable and unbearably demure way. (47[7])[54]

---

[54] I gratefully acknowledge Raymond Geuss' comments and suggestions on an earlier version of this Introduction.

CHAPTER 2

Nietzsche: The Birth of Tragedy

Raymond Geuss

Cosima Wagner's thirty-third birthday, her first since she and Wagner had married, fell on 25 December 1870. Wagner's present to her was the newly composed 'Siegfried Idyll'. He secretly arranged for a small group of musicians to assemble in the morning on the stairs outside her bedroom and they began to play as she awoke. One of the guests present at this performance was the newly appointed 26-year-old Professor of Classical Philology at the University of Basel, Friedrich Nietzsche. Nietzsche was an ardent admirer of Wagner's music, and he and Wagner shared an enthusiasm for the philosophical pessimism of Arthur Schopenhauer. The world as we know it, Schopenhauer thought, the world of objects in space and time held together by relations of cause and effect, was nothing but a representation, an illusion generated by the unending play of a metaphysical entity which he called 'the Will'. This Will, the underlying reality of the world, expressed itself in a variety of ways in the human world, most keenly in the form of sexual desire; it had each human individual in its grip and drove each of us on to forms of action that inevitably ended either in disgusting satiation or in frustration. The very nature of the universe precluded the possibility of any continuing human happiness. The best we could hope for, Schopenhauer argued, was momentary respite from the continual flux of willing and frustration through the contemplation of art. Aesthetic experience could have this effect because it is radically disinterested and thus extracts us from the world of willing. Music, in particular, is inherently non-representational, and Schopenhauer draws from this fact the stunning conclusion that music both gives us virtually direct access to ultimate reality, and is also one of the best ways available to us of distancing ourselves from the relentless throb of the Will.

This heady combination of extreme pessimism, sexual fantasy presented as metaphysics and the deification of music was irresistible to Wagner, the unemployed kapellmeister who had spent a decade of his life in exile following his participation in the failed revolution of 1849 and who had experienced some difficulty in controlling the attractions the wives of various of his patrons and associates held for him. He was delighted to find a young academic who shared so many of his own passionate interests and Nietzsche became a frequent visitor at Wagner's house in Tribschen, near Lucerne, and an intimate friend of the family. On that Christmas morning he, too, had a present for Cosima, the manuscript of a study entitled 'Die Entstehung des tragischen Gedankens'. In turn he received a copy of Wagner's recent essay 'Beethoven' and a piano reduction of the first act of *Siegfried*. In the evening there were two further performances of the 'Siegfried Idyll', and Wagner read aloud from the text of *Die Meistersinger*. The next day Nietzsche's manuscript was read aloud and discussed. On 1 January 1871 Nietzsche returned to Basel and began work on his first book, *The Birth of Tragedy out of the Spirit of Music*, using some of the material he had originally elaborated in Cosima's birthday present. He dedicated the book to Wagner.

By 1886, when he was preparing a second edition of the work, Nietzsche claimed to have long since changed his mind about Wagner (and about Schopenhauer). As he would later put it, he had eventually overcome these two youthful enthusiasms, exchanging Schopenhauerian pessimism for a fully affirmative attitude towards life and coming to see Wagner as a *décadent* and the embodiment of everything that was to be rejected in modern culture. So the view has sometimes been expressed that the 'mature' Nietzsche became just as committed an anti-Wagnerian as his younger self had been pro-Wagner. This in turn has been taken to mean that one should read the main text of *The Birth of Tragedy* through the eyes of the 1886 Preface in which the mature anti-Wagnerian corrects the errors of his youth. Although the later Nietzsche did doubtless occasionally write things that could be interpreted as putting the matter in these simple terms – that he outgrew a deluded, early admiration for Wagner and his music and moved to a position of clear-sighted, unconditional rejection – it would be a mistake to take passages in which Nietzsche makes claims like this simply at face value. After all, Nietzsche prided himself on his ability to see things from a variety of different perspectives, even (and especially) when that resulted in holding views that to lesser minds would have seemed inconsistent, and he also prided himself on his ability to adopt a variety of different disguises or masks for his own deeper and more considered views. The later anti-Wagnerian pose is one such mask, a particular form of self-dramatization adopted at a certain time for particular reasons, and it must be treated with the same suspicion Nietzsche uses in analysing the self-interpretations of others.

Matters must from the very start have been slightly complicated at least on a personal level for the youthful Wagnerite in Tribschen, if only because Wagner in his own way was just as much an egocentric megalomaniac as Nietzsche was. At the time Cosima noted in her diary that for all his professed admiration of and devotion to Wagner the man and his music, Nietzsche seemed to be making a concerted effort to 'defend himself' against the overwhelming direct impact of Wagner's personality, and she suspected that he was preparing in some way to take revenge (*sich rächen*) for having been thus assaulted.[1] In addition, Nietzsche was in love with Cosima, and if the ageing Wagner had been able to detach her from her husband (the conductor Hans von Bülow), why could not the mustachioed young Professor of Philology and former artillerist, in turn, play Tristan to Wagner's Marke? Finally, Nietzsche fancied himself a composer, going so far as to make presents of various of his compositions to Cosima and to play some of them in the presence of 'the Master' (as he called Wagner, following Cosima's usage). These compositions caused Wagner much amusement, and while Cosima seems to have been well bred enough to confine her slighting comments about them to her diaries, Wagner let no opportunity pass to remind Nietzsche that he was a dilettante, whose 'music' deserved no serious attention. Correspondingly, throughout his life, even when he is writing in his most explicitly anti-Wagnerian mode, there is ample evidence of Nietzsche's continuing love of Wagner's music which clearly had a very powerful hold over him to the very end. Thomas Mann seems to me to get the matter right when he says that even Nietzsche's criticism of Wagner is 'inverted panegyric... another form of glorification' ('Panegyrikus mit umgekehrtem Vorzeichen... eine andere Form der Verherrlichung'), an expression of one of the major experiences of Nietzsche's life, his deep love–hate of Wagner and his music.[2] The love was there virtually from the beginning, as was the hate; both lasted to the very end.

Still, between 1871 and 1886 Nietzsche had clearly changed some of his views very significantly. In the new introduction to the second edition, Nietzsche does criticize some aspects of his youthful work quite severely, especially its breathless, hyperbolic style. He does not, however, completely repudiate it, but rather does his best to integrate some of its central claims into the course his thinking was later to take, to find in it the germs of ideas that he was later to develop more fully. This means that we are invited to read the text from a double perspective: that of the youthful follower of

[1] Cf. *Wagner-Handbuch*, ed. U. Müller and P. Wapnewski (Stuttgart, Kröner Verlag, 1986), pp. 114f.
[2] Thomas Mann, *Leiden und Größe Richard Wagners*, in *Gesammelte Werke in dreizehn Bänden* (Frankfurt-on-Main, Fischer, 1960), vol. IX, p. 373.

the Master – who, whatever his private reservations might have been, in the 1870s seriously proposed changing his profession to that of travelling lecturer on Wagnerism and propagandist for 'the idea of Bayreuth' – and that of the highly, if ambiguously, critical Nietzsche of the late 1880s.

The Birth of Tragedy is directed at two slightly different issues: on the one hand it is an attempt to answer a number of questions about culture and society: what is a human culture? Why is it important for us to participate in one? Are all human cultures fundamentally of the same type or do they differ in important ways? Under what circumstances will a human culture flourish, and under what circumstances will it become 'decadent' and decay or even 'die'? The highest form of culture we know, Nietzsche thinks, is that of ancient Greece, and the most perfect expression of that culture is fifth-century Attic tragedy, but the depredations of time make our knowledge of that culture at best fragmentary and indirect. Attic tragedy was a public spectacle in which poetry, music, and dance were essential constituents, but the tradition of ancient music and dance has been completely lost, so we cannot know (Attic) tragedy as the ancients would have known it. The most vital contemporary form of culture is Wagnerian music-drama, which is also something to which we have full and immediate access,[3] so it makes sense to study the general questions about the nature of culture by looking at the origin, the flourishing, and the decline of Attic tragedy in the light of our experience of Wagner's music-drama. In this sense *The Birth of Tragedy* is a specific intervention in a debate that was conducted during the nineteenth century about what form modern society and modern culture should take. Roughly speaking, *The Birth of Tragedy* asks: how can we remedy the ills of 'modern' society? Nietzsche's answer is: by constructing a new 'tragic culture' centred on an idealized version of Wagnerism.

The second set of issues with which *The Birth of Tragedy* is concerned derives from the tradition of Western philosophical theology. The second basic question is: 'Is life worth living?' Nietzsche's answer is (roughly): 'No (*but* in a tragic culture one can learn to tolerate the knowledge that it is not).' Obviously the two questions are intimately connected.

The argument in the text falls into roughly three parts. The first part (§§ 1–10) describes the origin of tragedy in ancient Greece as the outcome of a struggle between two forces, principles, or drives. Nietzsche names each of these principles after an ancient Greek deity (Apollo, Dionysos) who can be thought of as imaginatively representing the drive in question in an

---

[3] Although when *The Birth of Tragedy* was written most of Wagner's music-dramas had never been staged and Nietzsche will have known them through piano reductions of the scores.

especially intense and pure way. 'Apollo' embodies the drive toward distinction, discreteness and individuality, toward the drawing and respecting of boundaries and limits; he teaches an ethic of moderation and self-control. The Apolline artist glorifies individuality by presenting attractive images of individual persons, things, and events. In literature the purest and most intense expression of the Apolline is Greek epic poetry (especially Homer). The other contestant in the struggle for the soul of ancient Greece was Dionysos. The Dionysiac is the drive towards the transgression of limits, the dissolution of boundaries, the destruction of individuality, and excess. The purest artistic expression of the Dionysiac was quasi-orgiastic forms of music, especially of choral singing and dancing.

Although these two impulses are in some sense opposed to each other, they generally coexist in any given human soul, institution, work of art, etc. (although one will usually also be dominant). It is precisely the tension between the two of them that is particularly creative. The task is to get them into a productive relation to each other. This happens, for instance, when the Dionysiac singing and dancing of a chorus is joined with the more restrained and ordered speech and action of individual players on a stage, as in Attic tragedy. The synthesis of Apollo and Dionysos in tragedy (in which the musical, Dionysiac element, Nietzsche claims, has a certain dominance) is part of a complex defence against the pessimism and despair which is the natural existential lot of humans.

Tragedy consoles us and seduces us to continue to live, but the synthesis it represents is a fragile one, and the second part of Nietzsche's text (§§ 11–15) describes how the balance is upset by the arrival of a new force, principle, or drive, which Nietzsche associated with Socrates. Socrates does not try to attain metaphysical consolation through the dissolution of boundaries (Dionysos) or glory in the loving cultivation of individual appearance (Apollo); rather, his life is devoted to the creation of abstract generalizations and the attainment of theoretical knowledge, and he firmly believes that the use of reason will lead to human happiness. Socratic rationalism upsets the delicate balance on which tragedy depends, by encouraging people not to strive for wisdom in the face of the necessary unsatisfactoriness of human life, but to attempt to use knowledge to get control of their fate. 'Modern culture' arises in direct continuity out of such Socratism.

The third and final part of the text (§§ 16–25) describes the modern (i.e. late nineteenth century) state of crisis in which we are being forced to realize the limits of our Socratic culture and the high price we have had to pay for it. History, Nietzsche believes, is about to reverse direction and move us backward from the Socratic state to one in which tragedy will once again be possible (§ 19). The main evidence for this is recent (as of 1870) developments in philosophy and music. Schopenhauer and Kant show the limits of rationalism, and music, especially the music of Beethoven, has rediscovered the Dionysiac. Wagner's music-dramas are a first attempt to marry the Dionysiac power of the modern symphony orchestra to Apolline epic speech and action (in the interests of a pessimistic philosophy derived from Schopenhauer). At the end of his life Socrates realized that he had missed out completely on something and tried to 'write music';[4] he failed, but we can and should adopt the ideal of the *musiktreibender Sokrates*, of a figure who can integrate art and knowledge into cultural forms that will make our lives tolerable again.

As mentioned above, *The Birth of Tragedy* was one of the last and most distinguished contributions to a Central European debate about the ills of modern society. This was a debate in which many of the participants, oddly enough, were broadly in agreement on a complex diagnosis of the problem, although, of course, they disagreed on the treatment. The diagnosis was that life in the modern world lacks a kind of unity, coherence, and meaningfulness that life in previous societies possessed. Modern individuals have developed their talents and powers in an overspecialized, one-sided way; their lives and personalities are fragmented, not integrated, and they lack the ability to identify with their society in a natural way and play the role assigned to them in the world wholeheartedly. They cannot see the lives they lead as meaningful and good. Schiller, Hölderlin, Hegel, Marx, Wagner, Nietzsche (and many other lesser-known figures) all accept versions of this general diagnosis. Theoretical and practical reactions to this perceived problematic state differ enormously. Some (like the later Schiller) thought that what was needed was a new elitist classicism; others (such as Marx) thought that only radical political action directed at changing the basic economic structure of society could deal effectively with the situation. The strand of response to this perceived problem that is most important for the genesis of Nietzsche's views is Romanticism. As Nietzsche himself points out in the introduction to the second edition, *The Birth of Tragedy* is a work of Romanticism. It is concerned with the description of a highly idealized past which is analysed so as to highlight its contrast with and superiority to the 'modern' world, and it ends with a peroration which calls for the utopian construction of a form of society and culture which will break radically with the present and re-embody some of the positively valued features of this past. Earlier Romantics had been obsessed with one or the

---

[4] Plato, *Phaedo* 60e 5ff.

other of two such idealized past societies. Some gave their allegiance to an idealized antiquity, presenting some version of the the ancient city-state (especially the Athens of the fifth and fourth centuries BC) as the model for a harmonious and satisfying human life; others, and this came to be thought the more characteristically Romantic option, followed the lead of the poet Novalis in praising the purported all-encompassing unity of the Catholic Middle Ages.[5] There are strong elements of both of these views in Wagner, whose ideas about the work of art are strongly informed by his reading of Attic tragedy (especially the *Oresteia*), but who tends to derive the plot and setting of his music-dramas from the Middle Ages (and who, of course, ends his productive life with the *catholisant Parsifal*). Nietzsche belongs firmly in the first of the two camps.

His version of the story begins by distinguishing his view from what he takes to be the assumptions of prevailing humanist accounts of antiquity. The 'ancient world' was not itself a single unitary phenomenon which deserves unqualified and indiscriminate admiration. Rather there is a robust, creative, and admirable part, 'archaic Greece', the period from Homer to some time in the middle of the fifth century, and then a period of decadence and decline. It is 'archaic Greece' that we should study if we wish to see a model of the best kind of society humans can aspire to.

Archaic Greek society, Nietzsche claims, is different from and superior to the modern world because archaic Greece was an *artistic* culture, whereas modern culture is centred on cognition ('science') and 'morality'. The culture of archaic Greece, Nietzsche claims, was not just 'artistic' in that it produced a lot of excellent art, but it was in some sense fundamentally based on and oriented to art, not theoretical science or a formally codified morality. Art was pervasively integrated into all aspects of life and was perceived to be of fundamental significance. Art told the archaic Greeks who they were and how it was best for them to act. Children were taught not biology, geography, mathematics, and a catechism of rules for behaviour (based either on Revelation or on rational argumentation), but athletics, music, dancing, and poetry. The final standards of evaluation and approbation in more or less any area of life were aesthetic. As adults the basic way people argued about what to do was by citing not statistics or scientific theories, but chunks of Homer, Simonides, or Pindar. Homer, in particular, it was thought, must be the universal expert and authority on everything *because* he was the best poet, i.e. was aesthetically superior to all other

---

[5] Cf. Novalis, 'Christianity or Europe', in *The Early Political Writings of the German Romantics*, ed. F. Beiser (Cambridge University Press, 1996), pp. 59ff.

poets. Plato's Socrates has an uphill battle in many of the dialogues trying to wean his contemporaries from this habit. As Wagner had emphasized, Attic 'tragedy', the most characteristic form of this ancient artistic culture, was not originally a mere 'aesthetic phenomenon' confined to one rather marginal sphere of life, but was rather a highly public event at the very centre of the political, religious, and social life of Athens. The production of tragedies was publicly funded and attendance at the theatre was such an important part of what it was to be an Athenian citizen, in fact, that indigent citizens eventually would have their tickets paid for them, just as they would eventually be paid to attend the Assembly or to serve on juries. The period of greatest dramatic creativity in Athens was also the period during which Athens held hegemony over the so-called 'Delian League'. The League was a military alliance originally directed against the Persian empire, which, however, eventually became in effect an Athenian empire. Most of the 'allied' members of the League were forced to pay assessed contributions which were used for the upkeep of the Athenian fleet and for public works (such as building the Parthenon) in Athens. The poet Sophocles, we know, in addition to writing tragedies, also served on the board of generals and was one of the overseers entrusted with collecting the contributions from the allies. On the day on which the main dramatic festival began, then, all the citizens (ideally) and representatives of the 'allies' assembled in the theatre in front of the altar to Dionysos which stood in the centre of the theatre and observed the sacrifices which were offered to the god, including a sacrifice by the generals. Then the 'tribute' from the 'allies' was carried across the stage to be stored in the Athenian temples that served as treasuries. Finally the dramatic competition proper could begin.

To the contemporary reader it seems odd that Nietzsche, who, following Wagner, emphasizes so strongly the role tragedy played in unifying Athenian culture, has nothing to say about any possible connection between artistic achievement and that archetypically Athenian institution, democracy. Apoliticism was not a necessary part of Romanticism. Indeed some of the early Romantics (the two Schlegels) had been keen republicans – Nietzsche criticizes them on just this account in *The Birth of Tragedy*. The Wagnerian *Gesamtkunstwerk*, modelled on Wagner's ideas about Attic tragedy, was to be an institution of spiritual *and* political regeneration. It was, of course, not uncommon in the humanistic tradition at the end of which Nietzsche stands to admire Athens *despite* its 'democratic' institutions (and in earlier and more pervasively Christian periods, also *despite* its paganism). Nietzsche's utter contempt for 'democracy' seems to be one of the most basic features of his intellectual and psychological make-up. It certainly antedated the development of any of his characteristic philosophic views. He is said to have resigned from a student fraternity because he disapproved of its excessively democratic admissions policies. It is true that virtually no one in the nineteenth century would have thought of 'democracy' in the way that has become customary here in Western Europe at the end of the twentieth century, as self-evidently the only justifiable form of political organization,[6] but even by the standards of his period Nietzsche's political views were not enlightened. Wagner's political reputation has been tarnished by his anti-Semitism, by his later accommodation to the political powers-that-be in Germany – he would do almost anything, even kowtow to Bismarck (not to mention King Ludwig of Bavaria), to get his Festspielhaus built – and by the attractiveness of his aesthetics to the National Socialists. He was also first and foremost a creative artist who, although intellectually extremely active and sometimes insightful, was not always terribly clear or consistent in the general ideas he held. Left Hegelian, anarchist, republican, pacifist, 'communist', nationalist, and various other kinds of political ideas jostled one another in his mind without apparently disturbing him too much. Still, he remained committed until the end of his life to the idea of a total revolution (i.e. a cultural *and* political revolution) which would abolish the state and introduce a form of radical social egalitarianism. The Festspielhaus itself in Bayreuth embodies Wagner's egalitarian ideal architecturally in the complete absence of separate boxes or special loges where members of an elite could segregate themselves from the other members of the audience: as in an ancient theatre, there are just plain rows of identical benches with each member of the audience the equal of each other, just as (ideally) among the citizens of the ancient democracies. This is the direct architectural denial of one of Nietzsche's central ideas, that of *Rangordnung*, of 'rank-ordering'.

Although politics is absent from the text as we now have it (apart from the odd *obiter dictum*), a sustained discussion of politics was an integral part of the original series of overlapping projects that eventually became *The Birth of Tragedy*. Thus the essay that has come to be known as *The Greek State* was originally part of an early draft of *The Birth of Tragedy*,[7] and Nietzsche must have made a conscious decision to exclude it from the

---

[6] Cf. John Dunn, 'Conclusion', to *Democracy: The Unfinished Journey*, ed. John Dunn (Oxford University Press, 1992).

[7] Reprinted in Nietzsche, *On the Genealogy of Morality*, ed. by K. Ansell-Pearson (Cambridge University Press, 1994), pp. 176ff.

published version. In this essay Nietzsche expresses his early political views with great clarity and force. In contrast to Wagner's view (as expressed in his *Das Kunstwerk der Zukunft*) that the artistic culture of ancient Greece could not be revived because it *deserved* to perish – founded as it was on slavery – and that a fully satisfactory work of art '*of the future*' could belong only to a society that had abolished not only chattel-slavery but its modern equivalent, the wage-slavery characteristic of capitalist societies, Nietzsche asserts that slavery is an essential feature of any society that aspires to high cultural attainments. He does seem to think it is rather a shame that this is the case, but he never suggests that the price is not worth paying.

'Modern culture', in the sense of that term Nietzsche insists on using, starts in mid-fifth-century Athens with Socrates. It is essentially theoretical or scientific in that it assumes that *knowledge* (not custom or the most aesthetically pleasing words of the best poets) should be our guide in life. The good man (and, on Socrates' reading of it, this means the man who was leading a good life) was the man who had a certain kind of knowledge. To be sure, the 'knowledge' the real historical Socrates sought (as far as we can tell, which is not very far, since the historical Socrates notoriously wrote nothing) is not exactly scientific knowledge, certainly not in the sense that term had come to have by the end of the nineteenth century; it is a kind of 'moral knowledge', but Nietzsche assumes that there is a distinct, important, historically continuous line of development from the Socratic quest to the nineteenth-century ideal of the pursuit of objective, scientific knowledge for its own sake. This part of his view is not worked out in any great detail, but Nietzsche clearly holds that it is appropriate to call 'modern' nineteenth-century culture 'Socratic' in the wider sense of being essentially devoted to the pursuit and application of propositionally articulated 'theoretical knowledge' and incapable of conceiving that anything else could be an appropriate guide for how to live. Such Socratism, Nietzsche argues, is a fundamentally optimistic view, and that brings us to the second of the two sets of issues *The Birth of Tragedy* addresses, the question whether life is worth living (and if so for what reasons).

Plato's Socrates explicitly holds that no ill can befall a good man, a man with the appropriate kind of knowledge, and that this knowledge is accessible to humans (through 'dialectic', the give-and-take of argument in the attempt to discover formal definitions of human 'excellence'), and the nineteenth century is unreflectively convinced that the accumulation of scientific knowledge will lead to increased human happiness. Christianity too can be seen as contributing a separate strand to the genesis of the

characteristically modern form of optimism:[8] the world is finally created
by an omnipotent and all-benevolent God who will take care that in the
larger scheme of things all is for the best. It is one of Nietzsche's major
claims in *The Birth of Tragedy* that archaic Greece did not share this
optimism about knowledge, the Christian metaphysical optimism about
the final nature of the universe, or indeed optimism in any form. The
archaic equivalent of the biblical claim that God looked on the world and
saw that it was good (or the Socratic claim that no harm can ever befall
the good man) is the wisdom of Silenus that never to have been is the
best state of all for humans. This 'wisdom' was *not* necessarily expressed
in propositional form – it was a kind of non-theoretical, non-discursive
knowledge, as Aeschylus puts it in *Agamemnon* (line 177) a 'pathei mathos',
a knowing in and through experiencing/suffering, a knowing embodied
perhaps tacitly in one's attitudes and behaviour even if one never formulated
it clearly (although, as we have seen, various archaic thinkers *did* formulate
it explicitly). The very fact that the Athenians organized so much of their
political, social, and religious life around a ritualized representation of
catastrophic destruction (i.e. tragedy) shows that they must in some sense
have been metaphysical pessimists. How else, Nietzsche argues, could one
explain the keen, addictive pleasure the Athenians and, following them,
many others through the ages have taken in watching a basically admirable,
heroic individual destroy himself in the pursuit of truth and knowledge, as
Oedipus does?

One possibility, of course, is to attribute to the Athenians (and to us)
some kind of deep-seated sadism – we just, in fact, take such pleasure in
making other people suffer that we even enjoy artistic representations of
other people's sufferings. The later Nietzsche does propose versions of this
view,[9] but in *The Birth of Tragedy* he gives a rather more complex account.
People enjoy watching tragedy because they in some sense understand that
in watching this ritual self-destruction they are gaining insight into the
fundamental human condition (perhaps into the very nature of reality),

---

[8] In the Preface to the second edition of *The Birth of Tragedy* Nietzsche claims that the absence of any
extended discussion of Christianity in the first edition is a sign that even then he was a committed
anti-Christian. This is pretty clearly another instance of Nietzsche's attempt to project views he later
developed back on to his early work. To the extent to which there is any reference at all to Christianity
in *The Birth of Tragedy* it takes the form of a discussion of the *Dionysiac* standing of at least one
strand of Christianity (§ 23, cf. § 17 very end, § 12). In later writings Nietzsche goes out of his way to
emphasize that Christianity is a historically composite phenomenon comprising a number of different
strands. So there may be a Dionysiac Christian religiosity (speaking in tongues in the early church),
and also a more rationalist version of Christianity (Leibniz). In the following discussion 'Christianity'
means the kind of Christianity of the roughly 'rationalist' theological tradition (including Aquinas).
[9] Cf. *Beyond Good and Evil* § 229f; *Genealogy of Morality*, II. § 7.

i.e. because they recognize that Oedipus' fate is *the human fate*, and in particular in some sense *their own fate*. People in some sense take pleasure in knowing this truth. Since, however, this kind of knowledge of the truth is useless in helping them avoid their inevitable fate (death and dissolution), this is a masochistic form of knowledge. The situation, however, is even more complex, because while dissolution of our identity and individuality is in one sense what we fear most, it is *also* potentially the highest and most intense kind of pleasure (Isolde's 'unbewußt / höchste Lust'). Presumably the pleasure results from the fact that in losing our individuality we are (if Schopenhauer is right) returning to our original state, a state which is metaphysically speaking what we always *really* were. Getting back to that fundamentally natural state, after the brief sojourn in the illusory world of 'individuality', is experienced as pleasurable. We take pleasure in watching Oedipus' demise because deep down we know we would experience our *own* dissolution as deeply pleasurable (and also horrible). The pleasure we experience in various mundane orgiastic experiences when the sense of separate, differentiated self is lost is a vague analogue of the real pleasure (and horror) of genuine self-dissolution. Finally, just as dissolution of identity is both horrible and pleasurable, so equally knowledge that our identity is an illusion doomed imminently to be dissolved is both attractive – which explains partly the appeal of tragedy – and repulsive. In fact, Nietzsche claims, full, undiluted knowledge of the metaphysical truth about the world would be strictly intolerable to humans; it would produce in us a nausea in the face of existence that would literally kill us. The paradoxical duality in tragedy (pain and pleasure: 'unbewußt / höchste Lust') mirrors an underlying metaphysical paradox: what we take to be most real about ourselves, our very individuation as separate beings, is nothing but an illusory appearance generated by a non-individuated metaphysical entity (the Will). This is what makes tragedy the highest form of art, and, as such, 'the true *metaphysical* activity' ('An Attempt at Self-criticism' § 5; cf. also 'Foreword to Richard Wagner').

Oedipus' fate, then, is a paradigm instance of what it is to be human and a good artistic representation of a basic metaphysical feature of the universe. First of all, the social identity which Oedipus believes is his and which he takes to be robust and firmly founded – that he is the all-knowing, omnicompetent saviour of Thebes – shows itself in the course of the drama to have been an illusion which gradually is dissolved. This is an artistic expression of the basic metaphysical truth that our prized individuality, even our very spatio-temporal distinctness itself, is only a momentary illusion. Second, Oedipus is shown to be untiring in his attempts to discover the truth, but discovery of that truth does him (and Thebes) ultimately no good at all. By answering the riddle of the Sphinx, he frees the city from her depredations, but the end result of this is the plague with which the tragedy opens. Application of human intelligence has merely replaced one evil with another. The truth about himself, which Oedipus pursues so keenly throughout most of the play, is utterly intolerable to him when he attains it – that is why he blinds himself. That knowledge itself is, as Nietzsche puts it, an 'enormous offence against nature' (§ 9) which nature itself will avenge is the basic mythic truth which tragedy transmits and Oedipus instantiates. This is what makes tragedy literally incomprehensible to the optimistic Socrates with his faith in 'knowledge'.

Even if, however, this cognitive account of tragedy explains why the Athenians were addicted to it, it does not answer the further question. If the knowledge of reality *is* really so terrible that no one can tolerate it, how can the audience in a tragedy survive a performance? The answer is that tragedy transmits the basic pessimistic truth about the world and human life while at the same time enveloping it with an illusory appearance which makes it (just barely) tolerable.

Tragedy originally arises, Nietzsche claims, from the dancing and music-making of a frenzied chorus in the grip of a Dionysiac 'intoxication' (*Rausch*). Collective music-making is the form of art that brings us as close as it is possible for us to come to the experience of the basic truth that our individual identity is an illusion. Pure, unadulterated Dionysiac music, however, is so close to the basic reality of the world that it is dangerous. No one, Nietzsche suggests (falsely, no doubt, but that is another matter), could really survive a simple *listening* to (the Dionysiac truth embodied in) the music to the third act of *Tristan* without the words and staging.

Fully formed tragedy has come into existence when words and stage-action are added to the collective, orgiastic music-making of the chorus. The words and the stage-action as it were deflect and dilute the impact of that reality, making it tolerable to humans. They do this by constructing a realm of what Nietzsche calls *Schein*, i.e. of appearance or semblance.

Tragedy is a constructed realm of *Schein* in two senses. First, the actor on stage is not really the mythic king of Thebes, Oedipus (although he in some sense 'seems' to be), but some Athenian citizen in a mask. One has failed to experience the tragedy if one sees only one's friend and fellow actor up there on the stage parading around in an odd mask. One has also failed if one thinks that it *really is* Oedipus up there, that the blood dripping down from his eyes is real blood, etc.

In a second sense, the words and action in tragedy generate a *Schein* in that they seem to individuate what is happening and give the audience distance from it. What is actually happening in the performance of a tragedy is that each member of the audience is being confronted with a general, but existentially pertinent, truth about what human life is and must be (namely one form of catastrophe or another), but the appearance is created that what is happening on stage is happening to some particular *other* individual, to Oedipus, or Tristan (not to you, the individual member of the audience).

When Pentheus in Euripides' *Bacchae* is torn limb from limb by his mother and her friends, presumably this is already a version *ad usum delphini* of Dionysiac experiences that were even more savage and pleasurable, but which few of the participants survived. This is not yet the deepest form of Dionysiac experience because it is 'already' corrupted and distorted by the principle of individuation, i.e. the pleasure and pain are represented as distributed to *different* individuals at *different* times: physical pain to Pentheus, physical pleasure at one point in time to his mother, but then at a later time distress. The genuine aboriginal Dionysiac experience would be most intense pleasure and most intense pain at the same time and in the same person (or rather in the same collectivity with no distinction of person). So again the best example would be if Isolde at the end of *Tristan* were to sing her part without words, as a kind of *vocalise*, in a performance without a separate audience, apart from the musicians, and the collectivity composed of Isolde and the members of the orchestra expired at the end in a paroxysm of self-inflicted intolerable pleasure-and-pain.

The production of individuated *Schein* is the work of 'Apollo' and it is this work that allows the spectators to survive. Tragedy requires the cooperation of Dionysos with Apollo, of music *and* words. Pure or absolute Dionysiac music (which would have to be purely instrumental music with no accompanying words) would be too direct an expression of this truth; we survive a Wagnerian music-drama (as the ancient Athenians had survived an Aeschylean tragedy) only because of the illusions Apollo creates. Success in tragedy consists in combining appropriately the most deeply Dionysiac music with the most highly articulated and pleasing Apolline illusions. Great tragedy can be a central part of a culture only if the members of that culture are psychically vital and robust enough to tolerate engagement with the truth which tragedy transmits.

Socrates correctly diagnoses tragedy as a purveyor of *Schein*, but fails utterly to see the point of this *Schein*. Part of the reason for this, Nietzsche thinks, is that Socrates is a deeply abnormal, unhealthy man, a man of stunted and perverted instincts and a diseased intellect that has run wild. His abnormality take the form of a kind of hyperintellectualized simple-mindedness. When he looks at tragedy, he fails to see it as an instance of a kind of self-sufficient *Schein* which confronts us with a deep truth about life, and thinks it is *just* a simple lie/illusion. That is not to say that Socratism is not itself a tissue of illusions. 'On Truth and Lying in a Non-Moral Sense' is precisely an extended analysis of the various 'illusions' Nietzsche thinks inherently constitutive of the Socratic way of life. Socrates, Nietzsche thinks, is committed not just to the self-evidently false beliefs that no harm can befall the good man, and that no one does 'wrong' willingly, but also to the equally false view that concepts can tell us something about the essence of the world, that the world is composed of identical cases that can be correctly subsumed under general concepts, and so on.

The human situation, then, is dire indeed if tragedy is an illusion, and the only alternatives to it – Socratism or Christianity – are equally illusions. In fact, according to Nietzsche, the only choice we have is (one or another kind of) illusion *or* death. That is one way of expressing what it means to say that Nietzsche's view is pessimistic. If this is the case, though, what reason can we have to prefer the illusions of a tragic culture to the illusions of Socratism? Why should we bother actively to seek tragedies out? Why should *we* (late-nineteenth-century Central Europeans) try to build theatres to expose ourselves to these illusions? Why should we try to construct a new 'tragic' culture?

There are several interconnected reasons for preferring tragic to Socratic illusions. First, Socratic illusions and the form of life associated with them are not finally stable. In the end even Socrates himself felt the need for 'music',[10] and this will be the fate of every Socratic culture. The history of philosophy also shows a natural development from Socrates to the insight attained in Kant (according to Nietzsche) and Schopenhauer that the everyday world investigated by the scientific optimist is a mere illusion and that one must look beyond it (to Kantian 'faith' or Schopenhauer's pessimism) for any final human meaning. Second, although both tragedy and Socratism are 'illusions', *Schein* (in *one* sense of that highly equivocal term), Nietzsche believes that some kinds of *Schein* can be closer to the truth than others. This is one of Nietzsche's more interesting ideas and it is a shame that he never develops it in any detail. Tragedy, in any case, Nietzsche clearly thinks, is closer to the truth than Socratic 'illusions' are.

[10] Cf. above, footnote 4.

Finally, Socratic illusions just are not as inherently satisfying as the illusions of a full tragic culture.

That brings us to the second of the two main topics of *The Birth of Tragedy*. Clearly the book is intended as a contribution to philosophical theodicy. The text states several times that 'only as an aesthetic phenomenon can the world be justified'.[11] The task of giving a theodicy in the Western theological tradition was that of trying to show argumentatively that the world, despite appearances to the contrary, really was in essence good, and not just 'good' in some very abstract sense, but good *for us*. By showing this, philosophers thought they could vindicate the claim that human life was potentially worthwhile for those living it, and thus that it was rational for us to adopt a fundamentally optimistic attitude toward our respective lives and toward the world as a whole. The history of philosophical theodicies in the West is long and convoluted, and I will mention only two of the various approaches that have been taken. One historically important strand of argument depends on the claim that the existence of evil is a logically necessary concomitant of the existence of free human choice, and the existence of such free choice is an overriding good. Since whatever evil exists in the world is there for the sake of the realization of the overwhelming good of human freedom, it makes sense to see the world as a whole as good. Another approach claims that the world as a whole was created by a rational god attempting to maximize the number and variety of created beings in the most parsimonious way. This project, it is claimed, is inherently rational and good, and what we call 'evil' can be shown to be a necessary, but subordinate, or merely local aspect of it.

Most of these traditional arguments presuppose the existence of an omnipotent god who created the world as a whole according to a rational plan and who cares for the good of each individual person, and they argue from that to the view that the existence of evil in the world is *compatible with* having an optimistic attitude toward the world as a whole and human life. So 'theodicy' can be a useful exercise for people who *already* have the appropriate religious belief in the existence of an omnipotent, benevolent creator of the world, but Nietzsche in *The Birth of Tragedy* is adopting a post-Christian view which does not assume such a religious belief.

The claim that the world can be justified only as an aesthetic phenomenon is to be read in two ways, negatively and positively. First of all it asserts that none of the traditional ways of justifying existence by reference to formal rationality, the exigencies of freedom of the will, or principles

[11] § 5, cf. 3, 'An Attempt at Self-criticism' § 5.

such as parsimony, efficiency, plenitude of being etc. works. Second, it asserts positively that one way of justifying the world (or 'life' or whatever) *does* work, namely contemplation of the world as an aesthetic phenomenon. This presumably means that each feature of the world is justified because *that* feature is one the world must have if it is to present an aesthetically pleasing spectacle (or perhaps, *the* most aesthetically pleasing spectacle) to an appropriately sophisticated observer. The first thing to notice is that the very term 'justification' (*Rechtfertigung*) might be thought to belong to the Socratic sphere which it is purportedly the whole intention of *The Birth of Tragedy* to undercut, because the most normal way (at least now) to take it is as a request for some kind of general theoretically based discursive structure. One could, of course, use 'justify' in a more general sense to mean simply 'to cause to seem to be worthwhile or good'. One must be careful not to go too far down this road, because getting drunk or taking various drugs can be a very effective way for me to be caused to come to see the world as good or various activities as 'worthwhile', but it is not clear that this is a model for 'justification' in any interesting sense. The question is whether there is something between sheer *Rausch* on the one hand, and Socratic argumentation on the other. Nietzsche claims that art is located precisely there and that may well be right, but it is not clear how we can get clarity about where this 'there' is. To give too discursive an account would be self-defeating. Perhaps that is part of the reason for the dithyrambic style of *The Birth of Tragedy*, and Nietzsche's comment in the Preface to the second edition ('An Attempt at Self-criticism' § 3) that he ought to have expressed himself by singing rather than by speaking in prose is perhaps more than just a joke (although, given what we know about Nietzsche's abilities as a composer, we should probably be very pleased we have the text we do).

In addition, if *The Birth of Tragedy* is to be a satisfactory aesthetic theodicy we need to know who is making the basic aesthetic judgment on which the theodicy rests. The answer to this question is not as obvious as it might seem, because in the main text Nietzsche uses as his example of an aesthetic theodicy the 'Homeric' view that the world is justified *because* it presents an engaging aesthetic spectacle *to* the Olympian gods (§ 5). When Nietzsche later refers to *The Birth of Tragedy* as containing an 'artiste's metaphysics' ('Attempt at Self-criticism' § 2) I think he has in mind a metaphysics which is a secularized descendant of this 'Homeric' view. The non-individuated reality behind all appearances, what Nietzsche calls *das Ur-Eine* ('the primordially One') (*passim*), is itself a kind of artist. In an image taken over from Heraclitus (fragment 52 [Diels–Kranz]; *The*

Birth of Tragedy § 24; *GM* II. 16) Nietzsche writes that this primordial unity is like a child playing in the sand on the beach, wantonly and haphazardly creating individuated shapes and forms and then destroying them, taking equal pleasure in *both* parts of the process, in both creation (Apollo) and destruction (Dionysos). Our world is nothing but a momentary configuration of shapes in the sand. The child's play does not in any significant sense follow 'rational' principles and has no purpose beyond itself. It is 'innocent' and 'beyond good and evil' (to use Nietzsche's own later expression). The only sense that can be made of the whole activity is whatever aesthetic sense it makes for the child to create or erase one form rather than another. From the fact, though, that the world presents a pleasing aesthetic spectacle to certain gods (especially to the wanton Heraclitean child), and is in *this* sense 'justified', it does not obviously follow that *I* will find *my* life worth living, especially if my role in the spectacle is that of victim, and even more so if there are cogent philosophical arguments, such as one finds in the work of Schopenhauer, to the effect that the *only* kind of role available for a human is that of one or another kind of victimization or frustration. The world and life may come to *seem* 'justified' for us to the extent to which we, through various aesthetic experiences, can come close to identifying ourselves in the primordial child and seeing the beauty of the play. Successful (great) tragedy may allow us that momentary identification and vision, but that identification is nonetheless in one important sense an illusion. In *one* sense the child who in metaphysical play creates and destroys the world is our underlying reality (because it is the underlying reality of everything), but in the usual sense of 'identical' we are not 'identical' with that child, 'we' are one of the insubstantial shapes with which it plays.

The important difference between Nietzsche's 'theodicy' and previous Christian ones is that *he* will come increasingly to distinguish three separate things which views like traditional Christianity connect: theodicy ('the world is justified'), optimism ('our life can be worth living') and affirmation. Affirmation is not exactly the same thing as optimism (at least as traditionally understood), if only because it is usually assumed that an 'optimistic' position is one that claims that we can see our lives as they really are, *without* illusions, and still find them worthwhile. Nietzsche, however, thinks that this is not possible for us. However beautiful the play from the point of view of *das Ur-Eine*, *we* are momentary illusory shapes doomed to the ineluctable frustration of the desires we necessarily have, and we cannot even tolerate the knowledge that this is our situation. Metaphysically, then, pessimism is true; what Nietzsche wishes to investigate is whether affirmation in any sense is possible under these circumstances, and he seems to find that possibility embodied in tragedy.

Paradoxically, if Dionysos and Apollo are successfully brought into alliance in a given tragedy, the result will be a transformation of 'pessimism' – not into optimism, to be sure, but into a kind of affirmation; that is, the *Schein* that arises will not sap the audience's strength, paralyse its will or lead to demoralization, but rather will energize the members of the audience to go on living. To be more exact, it requires great strength to produce and appreciate tragedy because it takes us so close to the basic horror of things, but if one can tolerate this, the result is an increase rather than a decrease in one's ability to live vividly (and create further great art – Nietzsche seems sometimes rather to confuse these two).

That tragedy can have this life-enhancing effect is one of the things that permits Nietzsche later (in the 1880s when he writes the Preface to the second edition) to claim that in *The Birth of Tragedy* he had *already* moved beyond Schopenhauer and away from pessimism in the strict sense. It is not hard to see how Nietzsche could have thought this. To admit the existence of a life-enhancing form of pessimism (if such a form did exist) would seem to mean at least that 'pessimism' must be a much more highly ambiguous phenomenon than had previously been thought.

Nietzsche's views on pessimism and its modalities shifted significantly from the early 1870s to the mid-1880s. In the earlier period he is still attempting to assimilate archaic Greece more or less straightforwardly to Schopenhauer, and is satisfied to point out that *both* Schopenhauer and Aeschylus (purportedly) are 'pessimistic' (compared with the optimism of Christianity and the modern belief in science, progress etc.). Later (for instance, in *Human, All Too Human*) he comes to claim that the whole discussion of optimism or pessimism as basic attitudes towards the world makes sense only if one assumes an outmoded theological view of the world. So presumably we should try to adopt a form of life that was 'beyond optimism and pessimism', one which we did not find it necessary to interpret in terms of either of these two concepts. Still later (in the Preface to the second edition of *The Birth of Tragedy* and other writings) he seems to find his way back again to a more complex understanding of the problems associated with 'pessimism'. He claims to find the unitary notion of 'pessimism' (which he had used in the main text of *The Birth of Tragedy*) over-simple, and he distinguishes between different types of pessimism – a pessimism of weakness (Schopenhauer), and a pessimism of strength (archaic Greece). The archaic Greeks are 'pessimists', but 'pessimists of strength', *not*, as Nietzsche claims in the main body of *The Birth of Tragedy*, pessimists in the sense in which Schopenhauer is a pessimist (and what Nietzsche now calls 'pessimism of weakness'). That is, he seems to think that what is finally significant in a philosophy is whether or not it contributes to an affirmation of this world, and that one can in some sense distinguish issues of pessimism/optimism from issues concerning affirmation or negation of *this* world, our world of everyday life. Since both Schopenhauer and Christianity agree that *this* world is not to be affirmed, they are really instances of the same kind of weakness, and the difference in their metaphysical views (that the Christian thinks the underlying *reality* of the world, God, is to be affirmed while Schopenhauer thinks this underlying reality, the Will, is to be negated) is irrelevant.

How exactly are we to construct a new tragic culture? Obviously part of the project will be to get rid of the various forms of optimism that cloud our vision, primarily Christianity and the nineteenth-century 'scientific world view'. The image of the *musiktreibender Sokrates* that dominates the latter parts of *The Birth of Tragedy* might be taken as suggesting that the new tragic world view will not just turn its back completely on the existing 'theoretical culture', but will pass through it, assimilate it completely, and emerge, as it were, beyond on the other side of it. How exactly Wagner and Ranke can be brought together, though, is not completely clear.[12] Perhaps in the new tragic culture people will *know* theoretically, in the way Schopenhauer claims to 'know', that our situation in the world is ultimately hopeless. We will *know* in a grounded way that our choice is illusion or death and will still choose life-invigorating illusions. In this we will differ from the ancients. Apolline art in the ancient world was not a reasoned and theoretically grounded response to the inherent worthlessness of our lives, but an instinctive reaction of exceptionally vital people. We will be able to choose *Schein* knowing in the fullest sense that it is *Schein*.

The relation of a work of philosophical speculation, like *The Birth of Tragedy*, to empirical scholarship is complex. Greece is important in the work primarily because of the tacit assumption that it is the paradigmatic artistic culture, and thus that it will exhibit in an especially transparent way the articulations one will need to grasp in order to understand just what a successful artistic culture would be like. So the *The Birth of Tragedy* could in principle contain a certain number of factual errors, idiosyncratic interpretations, empirically unsupported hypotheses, and wilful conflation

---

[12] In one of the fragmentary notes Nietzsche wrote while working on the preliminary sketches of *The Birth of Tragedy* he claims that Shakespeare is the 'musiktreibender Sokrates' (*Sämtliche Werke: Kritische Gesamtausgabe*, ed. G. Colli and M. Montinari (Berlin, de Gruyter, 1967ff., 7(131))), but, apart from half a dozen other fragments, he never develops this line of thought any further.

of things that do not perhaps really belong together – as, in fact, it does – without losing its value completely. At a certain point, of course, if the number of errors or of unsupported speculative claims became too great, the whole project would collapse, although even then it would not be completely clear that the problem lay in Nietzsche's theory of the three factors in every culture (the Dionysiac, the Apolline, and the Socratic); it might just be that Greece was not as good an instance of a (tragic) culture as we had thought.

Nietzsche's hopes for *The Birth of Tragedy* seem to have been both very exaggerated and very naive. He expected the work to be received with enthusiasm by all young Germans eager for cultural renewal, especially Wagnerians, but he also expected that the more open-minded members of the academic community of philologists would recognize the work as a pathbreaking new way of studying the ancient world. The second of these hopes was very quickly and thoroughly dashed. An initial review by Ulrich von Wilamowitz-Möllendorff was harshly critical, indeed dismissive of Nietzsche's whole project. Apart from various points of detail, Wilamowitz correctly diagnosed and categorically rejected Nietzsche's attempt to do 'philology' in a way that would make it more like philosophy or art than like a strict 'wissenschaft';[13] the proper mode of access to the ancient world, Wilamowitz asserted, was through the painstaking study of history 'in der askese selbstverläugnender arbeit', not through the mystic insights used in *The Birth of Tragedy*. It is of course perfectly true that, given the choice, Nietzsche would prefer *Weisheit* to *Wissenschaft*, so there was no real response he could make to that basic charge. Nietzsche also hoped for at least understanding, and perhaps some more tangible support, from his former teacher and patron Ritschl. Ritschl, after all, had been the person who had obtained for him his unprecedented university appointment in Basel, and, as editor of an influential journal, had been responsible for the publication of Nietzsche's early philological papers, but Ritschl agreed with Wilamowitz in his judgment of *The Birth of Tragedy*, and privately expressed regret that Nietzsche had wandered off the track from his very promising historical research into a fantastic world of religiously inspired enthusiasms. The review of *The Birth of Tragedy* was Wilamowitz's first publication, but he went on to become by far the most significant German classical philologist of the turn of the century, so his condemnation continued to be extremely influential, and Nietzsche's work was not an object

---

[13] When Wilamowitz wrote his criticism of *The Birth of Tragedy* he was a supporter of one of the movements for reform of German orthography, so, contrary to current practice, he used lower-case for the initial letter of nouns.

of serious consideration in academic philological circles in Germany for 40 years or so. *The Birth of Tragedy* did not succeed in reforming German philology, in changing the way it was done.

With Wagnerians Nietzsche had better luck. Wagner himself was thrilled – not surprisingly, since many of the most central thoughts in *The Birth of Tragedy* are culled from Wagner's own earlier writings or from Wagner's idol Schopenhauer and the book as a whole could easily have carried as its motto: 'Only as a Wagnerian is life worth living (to the extent to which it can be said to be worth living at all).' With the wider public, too, Nietzsche's work slowly established itself, starting in the 1890s, and eventually became so pervasively influential that the history of its reception in twentieth-century culture is too rich and complex to recount here even in outline.

It might seem odd that one of the most influential modern books on Greek tragedy was written by a person who had little real, continuing interest in drama, if the same thing were not also true of the ancient world: Aristotle, to judge by the existing evidence, turned a much keener eye to the reproductive organs of sea-creatures than to the fate of tragedy. If one looks at Nietzsche's life as a whole there are topics to which he returns again and again obsessively. These include the psychology of religion – his friend Lou Andreas-Salomé was right to emphasize this as a central concern – the nature of philosophy (especially as embodied in the person of Socrates), music and musicians (especially Wagner as the archetypical musician), and some general issues about how to understand the 'vitality' of cultures; they do not include drama or tragedy. Ancient tragedy became of special importance to him for a very brief moment under the spell of Wagner. As he wrote in the letter to Wagner to accompany the presentation copy of *The Birth of Tragedy* (2 January 1872), the object of the book was to show that Wagner's art was 'eternally in the right' ('daß *Sie* mit *Ihrer Kunst* in Ewigkeit recht haben müssen'). To put it bluntly, Nietzsche found tragedy especially interesting for as long as he thought it a form of the self-evidently most important and inherently significant cultural phenomenon there was – *music* – and he thought tragedy was essentially music to a large extent because Wagner said so. Wagner, in turn, said so because this was his way of asserting the superiority of his own music-drama *as music* over the purely instrumental music of Beethoven and others. To make the construction work, Nietzsche needed the highly implausible thesis that the highest form of music *must* transform itself into sung words if it is to remain humanly tolerable. Once this claim was dropped there was no reason to give pride of place to drama. Nietzsche's fascination with music (and with the psychology of religion) could take more direct and appropriate forms, and tragedy could leave centre-stage and return to the dusty corners of his consciousness. The subtitle added to the second edition (*Hellenism and Pessimism*) connects Nietzsche's first published book more perspicuously with his continuing philosophical concerns than the original title does.

The idea specifically derived from *The Birth of Tragedy* which has become perhaps most influential in the twentieth century is the conception of the 'Dionysiac' and its role in human life, i.e. the view that destructive, primitively anarchic forces are a part of us (not to be projected into some diabolical Other), and that the pleasure we take in them is real and not to be denied. These impulses cannot simply be ignored, eliminated, repressed, or fully controlled. As Euripides' *Bacchae* shows, they will have their due one way or another and failure to recognize them is just a way of, eventually, giving them free rein to express themselves with special force, destructiveness, and irrationality. In some sense higher culture rests on coming to terms with them, but that does not mean simply letting them play themselves out in a direct and unmodified way. The primitive Dionysiac orgy is *not* an Attic tragedy, and not a form of 'higher culture' at all in this sense, although tragedy is in some sense a development of the orgy. The construction of a higher culture requires *both* a sympathetic recognition of the existence of the Dionysiac *and* an integration of it into an alliance with what Nietzsche calls 'Apollo' and what he calls 'the *daimonion* of Socrates'. Different cultures are different ways of negotiating and renegotiating the terms of this 'alliance', probably a never-ending process.

Reading the later Nietzsche has caused us to be very justifiably suspicious about uncritical use of the concept of progress, but the attempt in the modern world to assimilate or at least to face up to Nietzsche's early views about the Dionysiac seems to me to be not just another instance of the random motion of history, but an undeniably progressive development, difficult as it is to specify exactly what is meant by that. If philosophy, as Nietzsche himself thought, is essentially a matter of asking important questions that no one else had thought to ask, then to have begun to ask the questions he did in *The Birth of Tragedy* is a mark of Nietzsche's significance as a philosopher.

CHAPTER 3

Nietzsche: Untimely Meditations

Daniel Breazeale

Individually and collectively, the four 'untimely meditations' are unquestionably among Nietzsche's most widely neglected works. Published between 1873 and 1876, they seem to lack both the dramatic originality of the work that preceded them (*The Birth of Tragedy*) and the epigrammatic brilliance of the book that followed (*Human, All Too Human*). Their ostensible subjects are so diverse – David Strauss, the study of history, Arthur Schopenhauer and Richard Wagner – that they seem to be connected by little beyond their collective title and common form: namely, that of the traditional polemical essay divided into numbered, untitled sections.

Upon closer examination, however, they reveal a thematic unity that is not always obvious at first. The *Untimely Meditations* contain important, early discussions of such essential 'Nietzschean' subjects as the relationship between life, art and philosophy; the character and cultivation of the 'true self'; education (and its vital erotic dimension), and the difference between genuine wisdom and mere knowledge (or 'science'). Moreover, these four short works – especially the last two – always retained a special, deeply personal significance for their author, who considered them to be key documents for understanding his development as a philosopher. They are not, admittedly, as immediately accessible as many of Nietzsche's other writings, largely because of the way in which the *Untimely Meditations* are related to specific events, authors, and intellectual and cultural movements of his own era. The following remarks do not give even a preliminary analysis of the philosophical *substance* or *content* of these works; instead, they aim to provide readers with some understanding of the specific *context* within which Nietzsche conceived the project of the *Untimely Meditations* and with an appreciation of its significance within the larger context of his thought and development.

At the age of just 24 Nietzsche accepted an appointment as an Associate Professor of Classical Philology at the University of Basel, where his duties also included teaching Greek in the *Pädagogium* (the senior class of the high school). He arrived in Basel 19 April 1869, six weeks prior to the beginning of the summer semester. One of the chief attractions of Basel for Nietzsche was that Richard Wagner and Cosima von Bülow (who were not actually married until 1870) were then living in nearby Tribschen. Nietzsche had become personally acquainted with Wagner at a private party in Leipzig the previous fall, where he and the 54-year-old composer were immediately attracted to each other, at least in part on the basis of their shared enthusiasm for Schopenhauer's philosophy. Though Nietzsche already had some acquaintance with Wagner's music, he could hardly have been prepared for the tremendous personal impact made upon him by Wagner. He immediately plunged into an intense study of the voluminous writings of the composer whom he began describing in his letters of this period as 'my mystagogue' and 'the living exemplar of what Schopenhauer calls a genius'.[1] Nietzsche called on the Wagners for the first time on 17 May and visited Tribschen twenty-three times over the next four years. Indeed, he became almost a part of the family and was present for many holidays and special occasions. He was such a frequent visitor that a special 'thinking room' was reserved for the use of 'the professor'.

The young classicist proved to be a diligent and popular professor; he began to publish the expected philological articles in professional journals and seemed well launched upon a brilliant, albeit conventional academic career. He also began to receive offers from other universities and was quickly promoted (in 1870) to Full Professor. Nietzsche, however, had more ambitious and unconventional plans for himself, plans closely related to his enthusiasm for Schopenhauer and Wagner and to his rapidly growing concern with questions of cultural, educational and social reform. As his inaugural lecture on 'Homer and Classical Philology' demonstrated, he never subscribed to the professional ideal of 'pure, disinterested science' or 'knowledge for its own sake'; instead, he believed scholars in general and classical philologists in particular had a special role to play in the increasingly urgent task of cultural renewal – a conception of the academic calling which he believed he shared with his distinguished colleague at Basel, Jacob Burckhardt, author of *The Civilization of the Renaissance in Italy* (1860).

[1] See Nietzsche's letters to Richard Wagner, 21 May 1870 and to Erwin Rohde, 9 December 1868. Nietzsche's letters are here cited by recipient and date. Translations from his correspondence are my own and are based upon the critical edition edited by Giorgio Colli and Mazzino Montinari, *Nietzsche Briefwechsel. Kritische Gesamtausgabe* (Berlin and New York, Walter de Gruyter, 1975ff.). For a recent study of Nietzsche's complex relationship to Wagner during the Basel period, see Carl Pletsch, *Young Nietzsche: Becoming a Genius* (New York, Free Press, 1991).

Even during his student days at Leipzig, Nietzsche had toyed with the idea of switching from classical philology to philosophy,[2] and the idea seems to have reoccurred to him at Basel, for during his fourth semester there he unsuccessfully petitioned to be appointed to a recently vacated chair of philosophy and to have his own chair filled by his friend Erwin Rohde. Even if his burning interest in cultural and philosophical issues could not be adequately reflected in his classes and lectures (with the exception, perhaps, of his lectures on pre-Platonic philosophy), he was determined that these interests should receive prominent expression in his first book. Encouraged by the Wagners at every step of the way, he transformed his manuscripts on 'The Dionysian Worldview' and 'The Origin of Tragic Thought' into the stunning *Birth of Tragedy from the Spirit of Music*, the second half of which was devoted largely to Wagner's 'art of the future' and to the prospects for a *rebirth* of tragic culture in late-nineteenth-century Germany.

After being rejected by one publisher, *The Birth of Tragedy* was finally published at the beginning of 1872 by Wagner's publisher, E. W. Fritsch.[3] At this time, Nietzsche was at the height of his popularity as a professor in Basel and was just beginning a series of five, well-attended public lectures 'On the Future of Our Educational Institutions', in which he sharpened and amplified his critique of the 'disinterested pursuit of pure science' and called for nothing less than a complete reform of higher education and a total cultural revolution. As if in response to this call, Wagner's ambitious plans for establishing a permanent 'festival theatre' at Bayreuth were gathering momentum, and Nietzsche was intimately and enthusiastically involved in this planning process from the start, at one point even offering to resign his professorship so that he could become a full-time lecturer and fund-raiser on behalf of the festival theatre project. Only a few months later, in April 1872, the Wagners relocated to Bayreuth, thus bringing to a rather abrupt end what were unquestionably the happiest three years of Nietzsche's life.

Barely a month later, another event occurred that had equally fateful consequence for Nietzsche's future: the publication of a pamphlet by the then-young classicist Ulrich von Wilamowitz-Möllendorf savagely attacking *The Birth of Tragedy* and directly challenging the professional competence of

---

[2] Nietzsche's intention to switch from philology to philosophy during his later years at Leipzig is documented in his letters to Paul Deussen, end of April/beginning of May 1868 and to Rohde, 3 April and 3 or 4 May 1868. He even went so far as to make extensive notes for a projected dissertation on the topic 'Teleology since Kant' (see Nietzsche, *Frühe Schriften*, Band 3, ed. Hans Joachim Mette and Karl Schlechta [München, Beck, 1994], pp. 371–95; trans. Claudia Crawford in *The Beginnings of Nietzsche's Theory of Language* [Berlin and New York, Walter de Guyter, 1988], pp. 238–53).

[3] See William H. Schaberg, *The Nietzsche Canon: A Publication History and Bibliography* (Chicago and London, University of Chicago Press, 1995), pp. 19–26.

its author.[4] Wagner's and Rohde's public efforts to defend Nietzsche were to no avail; indeed, they only served to reinforce the growing doubts about his professional soundness. The impact of Wilamowitz's pamphlet upon Nietzsche's career was swift and dramatic. Whereas twenty-one students (out of a total student population at the University of Basel of 156) had enrolled in his lectures during the summer semester of 1872, only two enrolled for the winter semester of 1872–3 – and neither was a student of classical philology.[5]

During this period, Nietzsche himself was more preoccupied than ever with such 'non-philological' subjects as philosophy, science and the theory of knowledge, though he usually tended to focus his own reflections on these topics through the lens provided by his ongoing and intensive study of the pre-Platonic philosophers. It was during this period that he began such well-known works as the 'On Truth and Lies in a Nonmoral Sense' and 'Philosophy in the Tragic Age of the Greeks', neither of which was published until many years after his death. As his letters and notebooks make clear, he expected that his next book would be explicitly devoted to philosophy and philosophers, though he seems never to have made up his mind about the precise form that his projected '*Philosophenbuch*' would take – whether it would be limited to the early Greeks, or would also include more general reflections on philosophy and epistemology.[6]

It was also during this period that Nietzsche's health began to deteriorate progressively and rapidly, a process that may have begun in Fall 1870 when he contracted dysentery and diphtheria while serving briefly in the Prussian medical corps during the Franco-Prussian War. In any event, he took the first of several sick leaves from his university during Spring 1871, though his health continued to decline. He was granted a sabbatical leave for the entire academic year of 1876–7, though once again any improvement in his physical condition was only temporary (in part, no doubt, because he

[4] Ulrich Wilamowitz-Möllendorf, *Zukunftphilologie! eine Erwiderung auf Friedrich Nietzsches Geburt der Tragödie*, conveniently available in *Der Streit um Nietzsches 'Geburt der Tragödie'. Die Schriften von E. Rohde, R. Wagner, U. v. Wilamowitz-Möllendorf*, ed. Karlfried Gründer (Hildesheim, Olms, 1969), pp. 27–55. For a succinct but detailed summary of Wilamowitz-Möllendorf's case against *Die Geburt der Tragödie*, see J. H. Groth, 'Wilamowitz-Möllendorf on Nietzsche', *Journal of the History of Ideas*, 11 (1950), 179–90.

[5] See Richard Frank Krummel, *Nietzsche und der deutsche Geist. Ausbreitung und Wirkung des Nietzschean Werkes im deutschen Sprachraum bis zum Todesjahr des philosophen* (Berlin and New York, Walter de Gruyter, 1974), p. 14.

[6] Regarding this project and the manuscripts associated with it, see Nietzsche's letters to Rohde, 21 November 1872, 7 December 1872, and 22 March 1873, as well as the editor's introduction to *Philosophy and Truth: Selections from Nietzsche's Notebooks of the Early 1870's*, ed. and trans. Daniel Breazeale (Atlantic Highlands, NJ, Humanities Press, 1979).

never ceased to devote himself to his studies and his writings). Finally, in Spring 1879, he was forced by the parlous state of his health to resign his position at the University of Basel, from which he received thereafter a modest pension.

Returning to the years immediately following the publication of *The Birth of Tragedy*: Nietzsche visited Bayreuth for the second time in April 1873, more than three years prior to the completion of the theatre and the inauguration of the festival. As was his custom, he brought along a work-in-progress to read to the Wagners, in this case, the manuscript of 'Philosophy in the Tragic Age of the Greeks'. Wagner, who was totally preoccupied by the urgent demands of the Bayreuth project, proved to be less than enthusiastic about Nietzsche's expenditure of his talent and energy upon a subject as 'remote' (and as unrelated to Wagner's own interests) as pre-Platonic philosophy. This cool reception may help explain why Nietzsche never actually published his profoundly original study of early Greek philosophy, even though he prepared a fair copy for the printer.

No doubt chastened by his visit to Bayreuth, and certainly sharing some of Wagner's frustration and despair over the many obstacles and setbacks encountered by the festival theatre project, Nietzsche returned to Basel and immediately threw himself into an entirely new literary project, one that would be of unmistakable relevance to the concerns he shared with Wagner. The ironically titled *Untimely Meditations* are the fruits of this reorientation of Nietzsche's efforts. The first contribution to the series, *David Strauss, the Confessor and the Writer*, was completed in only a few months in the Spring and Summer 1873. Thanks in part to the timely personal intervention of Wagner with Fritsch, the book was published that August, by which time Nietzsche was already at work on the next contribution to the series.

The original plan was to write and to publish two *Untimely Meditations* per year until the series was complete. Like many authors, Nietzsche was inordinately fond of drawing up plans and outlines, and his notebooks of this period are filled with drafts for the projected series of *Untimely Meditations*. Most, though not all, of these outlines project a total of thirteen separate titles. The following list, from early 1874, is representative:

> Strauss
> History
> Reading and Writing
> The One Year Volunteer
> Wagner
> Secondary Schools and Universities

Christian Disposition
The Absolute Teacher
The Philosopher
People and Culture
Classical Philology
The Scholar
Newspaper Slavery[7]

Other outlines include such additional topics and titles as: 'Literary Musicians (How the Followers of a Genius Cancel His Effects)', 'Military Culture', 'Natural Science', 'Commerce', 'Language', 'The City', 'The Path to
Freedom', 'Woman and Child', and 'Those Who Are Frivolous'.[8]

That the first *Untimely Meditation* was devoted to Strauss was, in fact,
something of an accident and directly reflects several conversations and
letters exchanged between Nietzsche and the Wagners in the immediately
preceding months, in which Wagner had expressed to Nietzsche his deep-
seated personal animus against the aging Strauss (with whom Wagner had
previously engaged in several vitriolic public disputes). David Friedrich
Strauss was a theologian and philosopher closely identified with the so-
called 'Young Hegelian' movement and best known – then and now – for
his *The Life of Jesus* (1835/6), a pioneering effort to present a 'demytholo-
gized' portrait of Jesus as a historical person and moral teacher. It quickly
became a *cause célèbre*, and the resulting controversy destroyed Strauss's
academic career. Nietzsche himself had been profoundly affected by the
liberal humanism of Strauss's work, which he first read while he was a high
school student at Pforta. Indeed, some interpreters believe Strauss's book
was an important contributing factor in Nietzsche's own abandonment of
Christianity only a year later, during his first year in college (1865). Strauss

---

[7] 16[10], 1876, IV/2: 385. Unless otherwise indicated, all quotations from Nietzsche's published and
unpublished writings are cited from *Nietzsches Werke. Kritische Gesamtausgabe*, ed. Giorgio Colli and
Mazzino Montinari (Berlin and New York, Walter de Gruyter, 1967ff.) Passages from his unpublished
notes (*Nachlass*) are identified by 'fragment' number (e.g., '16[10]', date, and volume and page number
(e.g., 'IV/2: 385'). Unless otherwise identified, all translations are my own.

[8] See 19[330], Summer 1872–beginning of 1873, III/4: 106; 29[163–4], Summer–Fall 1873, III/4: 307–8;
30[38], Fall 1873–Winter 1873/4, III/4: 354–5; 32[4], beginning of 1874–Spring 1874, III/4: 368–9;
and 16[11], 1876, IV/2: 385. Regarding Nietzsche's various (and ever-changing) plans for a series of
'Untimely Meditations', see his letter to Malwida von Meysenbug, 25 October 1874, in which he
states that the series will consist of thirteen 'Meditations' and that he hopes to finish the series in the
next five years, and his letter to Hans von Bülow, 2 January 1875, 'I have put aside the next five years
for working out the remaining ten "Untimely Meditations".' Many different lists of the projected
series of *Unzeitgemässe Betrachtungen* are to be found in Nietzsche's *Nachlass* from this period. In
English, see Breazeale, *Philosophy and Truth*, pp. 162–3 and Nietzsche, *Unmodern Observations*, trans.
William Arrowsmith (New Haven and London, Yale University Press, 1990), pp. 321–2.

later abandoned the radical Hegelianism of his youth and championed instead an eclectic and more socially conservative materialist philosophy, though he remained a staunch critic of Christianity. This is the position expounded by Strauss in his work of 1882, to which the title of Nietzsche's first *Meditation* directly alludes, *The Old Faith and the New: A Confession*, a rather innocuous and prolix work of Strauss's final years.

The real subject of the first *Untimely Meditation* is not David Strauss at all, but the smug and false complacency of the 'cultivated' German bourgeoisie in the aftermath of Prussia's victory over France in the Franco-Prussian War and the subsequent establishment of the second German *Reich*. Nietzsche's *David Strauss* was meant as a direct rebuke and challenge to the hoard of uncultivated chauvinists who interpreted Prussia's military victory as a clear sign of the superiority of their own popular culture and received ideas. Upon these self-satisfied newspaper readers and consumers of culture Nietzsche bestowed the fitting name *Bildungsphilister* or 'cultivated philistines' (a term he later – albeit mistakenly – claimed to have coined).[9]

The enormous difference between a *genuine* and a merely *popular* culture was a theme very close to Nietzsche's heart during the early Basel period and is explored, for example, in his lectures 'On the Future of Our Educational Institutions'. That he should have selected precisely Strauss as the illustration and embodiment of the kind of 'cultural philistine' he wished to unmask seems to have been little more than a concession to Wagner, without whose urging Nietzsche would certainly never have concerned himself with *The Old Faith and the New*. In fact, Nietzsche soon came to regret the strident and personal tone of his polemic. When Strauss died shortly after its publication, Nietzsche confessed, in a letter of 11 February 1874 to his friend Gersdorff, that 'I very much hope that I did not make his last days more difficult and that he died without knowing anything of me.' (In fact, the aged Strauss was familiar with Nietzsche's book and professed to be puzzled by the motives for such a vitriolic personal attack.)

It is, however, a relatively simple matter to appreciate the first *Meditation* while ignoring Nietzsche's graceless defamation of Strauss and his heavy-handed criticism of Strauss's literary style. What gives the essay enduring value is precisely the way it calls into question the relationship between 'genuine' and 'popular' culture, a question that has, of course, lost none of

---

[9] See Nietzsche's claim in *Ecce Homo*, 'Why I Write Such Good Books', 'The 'Untimely Ones', 2. In fact, as Walter Kaufmann points out in his translation of *Ecce Homo*, this term had been used earlier by Gustav Teichmüller. See Nietzsche, *Ecce Homo* (with *On the Genealogy of Morals*), trans. Walter Kaufmann (New York, Random House, 1967), p. 277.

its urgency over the past century and a quarter. Though Nietzsche's attempt to provide a positive description of genuine culture ('unity of artistic style in all the expressions of the life of a people', p. 5) may strike the reader as unduly abstract and in need of further elaboration, what he has to say about the deficiencies of an 'entertainment culture' ruled by public opinion is certainly not without contemporary relevance. Nor is there anything obsolete about his harsh indictment of intellectuals and academics for their participation in the debasement of the idea of culture, for their failure to assume any responsibility for the abject state of contemporary culture and society and, above all, for their fundamental hypocrisy.

Though the first *Meditation* is today the most neglected of the four, it was the one that attracted the greatest attention and public comment from Nietzsche's contemporaries. It sold more copies than any of the other *Untimely Meditations*, though it still fell short of the optimistic expectations of both the author and publisher. It also received more than a dozen (generally hostile) reviews.[10] Nietzsche professed to be pleased by the stir and was delighted that his book had, in his words, 'found a public'.

Maintaining the rigorous production schedule he had imposed upon himself, Nietzsche devoted the last half of 1873 to composing the second *Untimely Meditation, On the Uses and Disadvantages of History for Life*, which was published in February 1874. Though he had already published two books, it is significant that this was the first that was not written under the direct influence of Wagner (who greeted its publication without enthusiasm and described it as 'very abstract' and 'somewhat arbitrary'[11]). This might suggest that it more accurately reflects Nietzsche's own concerns during this period, though once again he employs other authors as foils for his own systematic discussion of 'the uses and disadvantages of history for life': one positive foil, the Austrian dramatist Franz Grillparzer, and a negative one, the German philosopher Eduard von Hartmann.

Hartmann's *Philosophy of the Unconscious* (1869), an uneasy blend of Schopenhauerian and Hegelian elements, was a work that Nietzsche had studied closely and that influenced his views concerning the origin of language. In the second *Meditation*, however, Nietzsche is primarily concerned only with Hartmann's complacent 'historicism', which, on Nietzsche's reading at least, is simply a means for deifying success and idolizing whatever

---

[10] See Schaberg, *Nietzsche Canon*, pp. 32–5, and Krummel, *Nietzsche und der deutsche Geist*, pp. 17–23.
[11] For Wagner's private reaction to the second *Meditation*, see Cosima Wagner, *Diaries*, ed. Martin Gregor-Dillon and Dietrich Mack, trans. Geoffrey Skelton (New York, Harcourt Brace Jovanovich, 1976), vol. 1, p. 735.

happens to be the case: a philosophy of history ideally suited for the cultural philistines portrayed in the first *Meditation*.

What Nietzsche seems to have admired about Grillparzer, whose *Political and Aesthetic Writings* (1871) he was reading at the same time he was composing the second *Meditation*, is his direct and eloquent appeal to 'correct' (immediate) *feeling* as the highest criterion of moral and aesthetic judgment, as well as his conception of the 'plastic' or creative power of human beings and societies to overcome and to transform themselves. As in his earlier use of Strauss as a rhetorical means for introducing his own thoughts on the differences between genuine and spurious culture, however, Nietzsche's highly original discussion of the relationship between history (and the study of history) and human life is not really dependent upon his choice of this particular pair of contemporary thinkers to illustrate certain points in his discussion.

Though the second *Untimely Meditation* is sometimes read as a blanket rejection of 'historicism', this is far from the truth. What Nietzsche rejects in neo-Hegelian philosophies of history (such as Hartmann's) is not the basic thesis that every aspect and expression of human life is unavoidably conditioned by history, but rather, the progressive or whiggish consequences that are typically – albeit, in Nietzsche's view, quite illicitly – drawn from this thesis. It is not historicism per se to which he objects in this *Meditation*, but rather the unexamined teleology that usually accompanies it.

'History', of course, can mean either the past itself or the study or knowledge of the past, and the second *Meditation* is concerned with the 'use and disadvantages for life' of history in both senses of the term, though, admittedly, Nietzsche does not always bother to make this distinction clear to his readers. Despite the fact that the attention of commentators has generally been focused upon his discussion of various approaches to the *study* of the past (and, more narrowly, upon his influential distinction between 'monumental', 'antiquarian' and 'critical' approaches to 'history'), a perhaps more important feature of the second *Meditation* is precisely the way in which its author seeks simultaneously to concede the inescapable historicity of human existence and to affirm the creative capacity of human beings to overcome themselves and their past. One of the things that Nietzsche attempts to do in this brief text is thus to begin constructing a new account of our relationship to time in general and to the past in particular – a project that, by the time of *Thus Spoke Zarathustra* (1883–5), will come to occupy the very centre of his attention. In the language of *On the Uses and Disadvantages of History for Life*, the project is to show how human life requires us to adopt *both* a 'historical' and an 'ahistorical' perspective upon ourselves.

This recognition of our complex relationship to history and to time clearly has direct and important implications for Nietzsche's conception of the self; and one of the central questions explored by the *Untimely Meditations* as a whole is: What constitutes one's 'true self'? This question, which is merely touched upon in the second essay, where it is discussed in conjunction with Nietzsche's rejection of the claim that the 'true self' is something purely 'inward' and private, is explored in much greater detail in the third.

Despite the fact that *On the Uses and Disadvantages of History for Life* has attracted more attention from twentieth-century commentators than the other three *Meditations* combined, it was the least successful with Nietzsche's contemporaries, receiving only one review and selling fewer copies than the others.[12] By Fall 1874, at a time when Nietzsche was negotiating with a new publisher, Ernst Schmeitzner (and thus trying to put the best possible public face on his literary prospects), his private letters reveal how deeply disappointed and depressed he was by the public reception of the first two *Untimely Meditations*. Reflecting upon his literary prospects, in a letter to Rohde of 15 November 1874, he can only quip, 'What a future!'

Schopenhauer as Educator was written during Summer 1874 and published (by his new publisher, Schmeitzner) on Nietzsche's 30th birthday, 15 October. Many of the notes incorporated into this third *Untimely Meditation* were originally written during the preceding summer and fall and were intended for use in two separate *Meditations*, one to be devoted to 'the philosopher', and the other to 'the scholar'. Traces of this dual origin can still be discerned in the published text of *Schopenhauer*, which devotes as much space to a polemic against mere 'scholars' or 'academic philosophers' as it does to characterizing the 'genuine philosopher'.

As virtually everyone who has written on the third *Meditation* has observed, what is conspicuous by its absence in *Schopenhauer as Educator* is any serious discussion of Schopenhauer's actual philosophy. Though there are numerous citations from him, almost all of these are from the 'popular' writings contained in his collected *Parerga und Paralipomena* (1857) or in his posthumously published papers. There is, however, an excellent reason for Nietzsche's relative silence concerning Schopenhauer's principal work, *The World as Will and Representation* (1818), and for his complete disregard of Schopenhauer's most characteristic philosophical doctrines. The simple truth is, as Nietzsche revealed in his 1886 preface to volume 2 of

---

[12] See Krummel, *Nietzsche und der deutsche Geist*, pp. 24–5 and Schaberg, *Nietzsche Canon*, pp. 37–40.

the second edition of *Human, All Too Human*, that by the time he wrote *Schopenhauer* he himself 'no longer believed in Schopenhauer'. And there is plenty of documentary evidence from Nietzsche's own correspondence and unpublished papers, as well as from the testimony of friends such as Paul Deussen, to show that he began to have serious reservations about the most central doctrines of Schopenhauer's philosophy only a few short years after his dramatic 'conversion' to Schopenhauerianism as a student in Leipzig during Fall 1865.[13] By 1871 at the latest, he had privately rejected not only Schopenhauer's 'world-negating' pessimism, but also his fundamental dualism of 'appearance' ('representations') and 'reality' (the 'will' qua 'thing in itself'). Even if one remains suspicious of Nietzsche's later claim that 'I distrusted Schopenhauer's system from the start',[14] there still can be no doubt that by the time he wrote the third *Meditation* he had long since jettisoned any allegiance he may once have had to the two most distinctive features of Schopenhauer's philosophical system.

[13] Paul Deussen, *Errinerungen an Friedrich Nietzsche* (Leipzig, Brockhaus, 1901), p. 38. For evidence from Nietzsche's own hand, see the manuscript 'Zu Schopenhauer', written in early Spring 1868, that is, just a few years after his first encounter with Schopenhauer's writings. In this early, unpublished text Nietzsche severely criticizes Schopenhauer's separation of the (unitary) will from its manifold appearances (representations) and challenges his interpretation of the latter as the transcendent ground of the former (see *Frühe Schriften*, Band 3, pp. 352–61; trans. in Crawford, *Beginnings of Nietzsche's Theory of Language*, pp. 226–38). This same criticism recurs in later notebook entries from the Basel period, including: 7[161–72], end of 1870–April 1871, III/3: 209–14; 5[77–81], September 1870–January 1871, III/3: 114–19; and 12[1], Spring 1871, III/3: 380–1. See too Nietzsche's letter to Deussen, October/November 1867, in which he declines to spell out his objections to Schopenhauer's philosophy on the grounds that '*Weltanschauungen* are neither created nor destroyed by means of logic.' For a detailed discussion of Nietzsche's early criticism of Schopenhauer, see Sandro Barbera, 'Ein Sinn und unzählige Hieroglyphen: Einige Motive von Nietzsches Auseinandersetzung mit Schopenhauer in der Basler Zeit', in '*Centauren-Geburten': Wissenschaft, Kunst und Philosophie beim jungen Nietzsche*, ed. Tilman Borsche, Federico Gerratana, and Aldo Venturelli (Berlin and New York, Walter de Gruyter, 1994), pp. 217–33.

[14] 30[9], Summer 1878, IV/3: 382. See too the comment from the 1886 preface to the new edition of *Human, All Too Human*, vol. 2:

My writings speak *only* of my own overcomings. 'I' am in them, together with everything that is inimical to me... To this extent, all my writings... are to be *dated back* – they always speak of something 'behind me.' – some, e.g., the first three *Untimely Meditations*, even to a period prior to that in which I experienced and produced a book published before them... When, in the third *Untimely Meditation*, I went on to give expression to my reverence for my first and only educator, the *great* Arthur Schopenhauer – I would now express it much more strongly, also more personally – I was already deep in the midst of moral skepticism and destructive analysis, *that is to say in the critique and likewise the intensification of pessimism as understood hitherto*, and already 'believed in nothing any more', as the people put it, not even in Schopenhauer: just at that time I produced an essay I have refrained from publishing, 'On Truth and Lie in an Extra-Moral Sense' (trans. R. J. Hollingdale, [Cambridge], 1996), p. 29).

See too 6[4], Summer 1886–Spring 1887, VIII/1: 238–9 and 10[B31], Spring 1880–Spring 1881, V/1: 748–9.

Why then does Nietzsche, writing in 1874, still consider Schopenhauer to be the very exemplar of a philosophical educator? The answer to this question lies in the radically new conceptions of both 'education' and 'philosophy' that are propounded in this text – though neither will seem all that new to readers acquainted with Nietzsche's unpublished notes from the immediately preceding years, for much of the content of *Schopenhauer* is directly anticipated in 'The Philosopher as Cultural Physician' and other posthumously published notes and manuscripts originally intended for use in the 'philosophers' book' project.

As described in the third *Meditation*, the philosophers' task is 'to be lawgivers as to the measure, stamp and weight of things' (p. 144) and to provide their contemporaries with a new 'picture of life' (p. 141); and it is precisely by establishing these new values and by erecting this 'new image of man' (p. 150) that a philosopher 'educates' others. He does not, however, accomplish these things primarily by what he writes in his books or by the doctrines he propounds in his system, but rather by *the example of his own life*. This is precisely how Nietzsche had interpreted the task and accomplishment of the pre-Platonic philosophers in 'Philosophy in the Tragic Age of the Greeks', and it is also how he interprets Schopenhauer's accomplishment as a philosophical educator in this essay. Nietzsche thus feels free to ignore Schopenhauer's philosophical doctrines in a book entitled *Schopenhauer as Educator* because he contends that the real achievement of any philosopher – Schopenhauer included – lies precisely in the *example* he provides to others of 'the courageous visibility of the philosophical life' (p. 137).

To be 'educated' by a philosopher, therefore, has nothing to do with sub-scribing to his favourite theories or philosophical doctrines: one is educated by Schopenhauer if one's own manner of living has been decisively affected by his 'example'. The word 'example' is here placed within quotation marks for the simple reason that the 'example' provided to Nietzsche by Schopen-hauer was not really that of his actual life, though Nietzsche certainly did admire him for his rejection of all academic and institutional ties in favour of a more independent mode of living. Though a few anecdotes are sprinkled throughout the third *Meditation*, Nietzsche is clearly not inter-ested in relating Schopenhauer's biography. What he holds up to his readers instead is something altogether different, a mere 'image' of human life: not an idealized version of the actual person, Arthur Schopenhauer; still less, an ideal embodiment of the world-denying philosophy expounded in *The World as Will and Representation*; but rather, 'the Schopenhauerian image of man' (pp. 152–5).

What directly inspired – and thus educated – the young Nietzsche was a certain notion of human possibility, an image of a particular way of living and of a particular kind of person, an image that he apparently constructed for himself as he continued to read and to reflect upon Schopenhauer throughout the late 1860s and early 1870s. Nietzsche's image of the 'Schopenhauerian man', whom he describes as 'voluntarily taking upon himself the suffering involved in being truthful' (p. 152) and as a 'destroying genius',[15] resembles neither Arthur Schopenhauer himself nor Schopenhauer's ideal of the world-denying 'saint', but is instead a product of Nietzsche's own philosophical imagination. He associated this image with Schopenhauer primarily out of simple gratitude for the fact that he had arrived at this 'image of human life' through years of sustained, critical reflection upon Schopenhauer's arguments and assumptions – as well, no doubt, as through reflection upon the well-documented contradiction between Schopenhauer's life and his philosophy.[16]

That Nietzsche drew from his personal encounter with Schopenhauer's philosophy conclusions radically at odds with those drawn by Schopenhauer himself does not imply that there is anything disingenuous about his description, in 1874, of Schopenhauer as his most important 'educator'. On the contrary, he was grateful for precisely this reason, as is apparent from the following note, written four years later: 'The Schopenhauerian man drove me to skepticism against everything I had previously defended and held worthy of high esteem – including the Greeks, Schopenhauer, and Wagner – against the genius, the saint – the pessimism of knowledge. By means of this *detour* I arrived at the *heights* with the fresh wind'.[17] The thesis of the third *Meditation* is that true education involves the *liberation* of the self from everything foreign to it, including those elements of oneself that one judges to be incompatible with one's true (future) self. Schopenhauer 'educated' Nietzsche by provoking and inspiring him to 'become himself', even if this should involve – as it certainly did – a decisive rejection of Schopenhauer's philosophy.

---

[15] 'I achieved the greatest pathos when I sketched the Schopenhauerian person: the *destroying* genius, against all becoming' (27[34], Spring–Summer 1878, IV/3: 351).

[16] 'Even as I was celebrating Schopenhauer as my educator, I had forgotten that for a long time before that none of his dogmas could withstand my mistrust. I paid no attention, however, to how often I had scribbled "poorly demonstrated" or "indemonstrable" or "exaggerated" beneath his sentences, because I reveled with gratitude in the powerful impact that Schopenhauer – freely and bravely standing before things and against them – had on me a decade earlier' (10[B31], Spring 1880–Spring 1881, V/1: 748–9).

[17] 27[80], Spring–Summer 1878, IV/3: 358.

Schopenhauer as Educator remains one of Nietzsche's most personal and stimulating books, valuable not merely as an essential document for understanding his own spiritual development, but also as an early and eloquent exploration of some of his most characteristic themes and ideas. Particularly noteworthy is the discussion, which begins on the very first page, of the deeply problematic conception of the 'true self'. Here one finds Nietzsche already striving to defend a novel conception of genuine selfhood as a never-to-be-completed process of self-development and self-overcoming, a philosophical project that recognizes the elements of truth contained in both essentialist and existentialist theories of the self, while committing itself fully to neither. The 'true' self, according to the author of *Schopenhauer as Educator*, is neither an externally given and unchangeable 'essence' (such as Schopenhauer's 'intelligible character') nor an arbitrary and freely-willed 'construct'. My true self is something I have to 'become', but it is also what I already 'am'. The implications of this new conception of the self are by no means fully apparent in the third *Meditation*, nor are the difficulties it raises fully explored. For this, one will have to wait another decade or more. But the basic idea of the 'Nietzschean self' – as well as the fundamental problems raised by such an idea – is already present in *Schopenhauer as Educator*.

The substantial riches of the third *Untimely Meditation* were largely lost on Nietzsche's contemporaries and have been only rarely recognized by subsequent generations of readers and interpreters. Despite the vigorous promotional efforts of Nietzsche's new publisher, the third *Meditation* sold almost as few copies as the second and received only a few uncomprehending reviews.[18]

Even before the publication of the third essay, Nietzsche was already at work on the next instalment. Over the course of the following year (1875), however, he seems to have gradually lost interest in and enthusiasm for the entire project. This surely had something to do with the poor sales of the first three *Meditations* and with their apparent failure to achieve what Nietzsche himself described as their primary goal: namely, to attract the kind of readers and followers who might be interested in the further development of his ideas.

As the many notes accumulated by Nietzsche for the project indicate, the fourth *Meditation* was originally intended to be an explicit coming to terms on his part with an issue that he had at least touched upon in all

---

[18] See Schaberg, *Nietzsche Canon*, pp. 41–5 and Krummel, *Nietzsche und der deutsche Geist*, pp. 26–8.

of the first three: the origin, status and value of 'disinterested scholarship', particularly as embodied in his own discipline of classical philology. The working title for the new book was, accordingly, 'We Philologists'. Some time during Summer 1875, however, Nietzsche abandoned further work on this nearly completed project and began instead to make notes for a completely different topic, with the title *Richard Wagner in Bayreuth*.

The period 1874–5 was a particularly difficult one for everyone concerned with the Bayreuth project, which was beset by such serious financial and technical difficulties that Wagner himself considered abandoning it. It was also during this time that the first overt signs of tension began to appear between Wagner and Nietzsche, whose private notebooks begin to contain unflattering and critical remarks about Wagner. Outwardly, however, Nietzsche was still very much the faithful Wagnerian, having dutifully travelled to Bayreuth for the ceremonial laying of the corner-stone of the festival theatre in May 1872 (an event rather lugubriously described in the opening passage of *Wagner in Bayreuth*) and also having – at no small personal expense – become an official 'patron' of the festival.[19] He was also still prepared to spring to Wagner's public defence and to subordinate his own projects to the requirements of 'the movement' – as he did, for example, when he agreed, in October 1873, to write an 'Exhortation to the Germans' to raise funds for the Bayreuth project, a document that was subsequently (and prudently) rejected by the officers of the Wagnerian Society as poorly suited for its intended purpose.

A new coolness nevertheless seems detectable in Nietzsche's relationship with the Wagners, beginning perhaps during his visit to Bayreuth in August 1874, when he and Wagner quarrelled openly over Nietzsche's admiration for Wagner's great rival, Brahms, and over other musical matters. Nietzsche subsequently turned down repeated invitations from the Wagners to spend the Christmas holidays 1874 with them and to attend the rehearsals scheduled for Summer 1875. (Wagner's plan called for a summer of rehearsals a year prior to the actual first performance of the *Ring* cycle.) It was under these circumstances that he began to write *Richard Wagner in Bayreuth*. Though he had mentioned a *Meditation* with this title more than a year earlier (in a letter to Gersdorff of 11 February 1874), it is difficult not to see his decision to revive this project as an effort to demonstrate his fealty to the maestro who was irritated by his absence from Bayreuth that summer.

---

[19] The cost of becoming an official patron of the Bayreuth project was 900 marks, which, as Schaberg points out (*Nietzsche Canon*, p. 36), amounted to more than a quarter of Nietzsche's entire salary for 1872 (3,200 marks).

Whatever Nietzsche's actual reasons for beginning this new essay may have been, he soon began to have serious reservations about continuing the series of *Untimely Meditations*, and, in a letter of 7 October 1875, he confided to Rohde that he was abandoning the *Meditation* on Wagner on the grounds that 'it is of value only for me, as a way of orienting myself with respect to the most difficult points of our recent experience'. It was around this same time that a young musician named Heinrich Köselitz, who, at Nietzsche's suggestion, adopted the stage name 'Peter Gast', entered his orbit and began to serve as his assistant; and it is largely due to Gast's intervention that the fourth *Untimely Meditation* was ever published at all. Gast read the unfinished manuscript of *Wagner in Bayreuth* in Spring 1876 and insisted that it should be completed and published. Once again Nietzsche maintained that the piece was too 'personal' for publication, though he agreed to allow Gast to make a fair copy for presentation to Wagner on his birthday (22 May). Eventually, however, he decided instead to add some additional material to this manuscript and, as he had intended, have it published as the fourth *Untimely Meditation*. Printing was completed over the summer, and Nietzsche was able to present Wagner with a copy in August, during the first Bayreuth festival.

Richard Wagner in Bayreuth remains to this day one of Nietzsche's least popular and least read works, and it is not difficult to see why. It wholly lacks the stylistic unity of the other three *Untimely Meditations*, in part, perhaps, because it contains so many (usually unidentified) quotations from and paraphrases of Wagner's overwrought prose. Even for the specialist, it is a difficult and sometimes painful work to read, and one suspects that it must have been an equally difficult and painful book for Nietzsche to write. There is certainly something forced and deeply ambivalent about the overall tone of this essay, and again one suspects that this is an all-too-accurate reflection of the author's own profound ambivalence about his subject.

Just as *Schopenhauer as Educator* was written some years after Nietzsche had ceased to be an adherent of Schopenhauer's philosophy, so was *Wagner in Bayreuth* written at a point in his life when he had already formulated (albeit only privately) the basic elements of the devastating critique of Wagner as a 'histrionic romantic' that he would make public only many years later. Schopenhauer, however, was dead, whereas Wagner was not only very much alive, but was also extremely sensitive to any appearance of criticism or disloyalty on the part of his friends and allies. Hence Nietzsche's dilemma: he *did* admire Wagner and was certainly grateful to him (as to Schopenhauer) for the inspiration of his example and for his assistance in helping Nietzsche 'become himself'; on the other hand, he harboured increasingly serious reservations about Wagner's art and personality, not to mention his even stronger reservations about Bayreuth and the 'Wagnerians'. The problem was how to write a book, intended for the public, in which he could express his admiration without violating his intellectual integrity. Though it cannot be said that Nietzsche succeeded fully in resolving this problem, his strategy seems clear: to use Wagner's own words against Wagner himself. By quoting copiously from his writings, Nietzsche would erect a certain (Wagnerian) *ideal* of art and of culture, an ideal to which he himself once subscribed whole-heartedly and to which he could still subscribe at least in part. It would then be left up to the readers to determine for themselves – assisted, perhaps, by a few discreet suggestions from the author – how far short Wagner's actual achievement was from this ideal.

Despite the difficulties of 'reading' the fourth *Meditation* – or perhaps because of them – *Wagner in Bayreuth* remains a key document for anyone interested in Nietzsche's biography and intellectual development. Its interest, however, is not merely psycho-biographical; it too contains its share of stimulating and original ideas concerning such topics as the relationship between art and science, the origin of language and (returning to the theme of the first *Meditation*) the origin and task of culture.

The completion of *Wagner in Bayreuth* coincided with yet another crisis in Nietzsche's health, one which forced him to cancel his classes several weeks prior to the end of the summer semester of 1876 and to apply (successfully) for a sabbatical leave for the following academic year. First, however, he had to attend the Bayreuth festival, which he dutifully did. Though he managed to attend the first performances of the *Ring*, the festival proved to be such a torment to him and the sight of the assembled Wagnerians was so repugnant that he soon sought refuge in the nearby village of Klingenbrunn. Just a few months later he was a thousand miles away, living in Sorrento with Paul Rée and working on an entirely new literary project.

The project in question, to which Nietzsche had given the tentative title 'The Free Spirit', had originally been intended as the next instalment in the series of *Untimely Meditations*. Some time during the year in Italy, however, Nietzsche underwent what he later described in a letter of 19 February 1888 to Georg Brandes as 'a crisis and shedding of the skin' and reconceived the structure and form of his next literary work accordingly. The title too was altered: it now became *Human, All Too Human* – a book as different in tone and in content from *Richard Wagner in Bayreuth* as the landscape and climate of Sorrento is from that of Bayreuth, and the first book by Nietzsche to be published with no indication of the author's academic degree and institutional affiliation.[20]

Coinciding as it did with the first Bayreuth festival, *Wagner in Bayreuth* naturally received a bit more partisan attention from the public and the press than the previous two instalments in the series, though it too fell far short of the publisher's and author's expectations.[21] In reply to an inquiry from Schmeitzner about the possibility of continuing the series, Nietzsche replied on 2 February 1878, 'shouldn't we consider the *Untimely Meditations* finished?' Seven years later he briefly considered reviving them and adding one to three new 'Untimely Ones'.[22] Nothing came of this, however, though a distant echo of it may still be detected in the name that Nietzsche gave to the longest section of one of his last works (*Twilight of the Idols*): 'Streifzüge eines Unzeitgemässen' or 'Skirmishes of an Untimely Person'.

In 1886, after he had at last obtained the publication rights to all of his earlier writings, Nietzsche immediately began preparing new, expanded editions and adding new prefaces and other new material. The only exceptions were the *Untimely Meditations* and Parts I–III of *Thus Spoke Zarathustra*, which were reissued in their original forms (though *Zarathustra* I–III were bound in a single volume.) The 'new editions' of the four *Untimely Meditations* that were issued in late 1886 are therefore identical to the first editions.

Though some commentators have interpreted Nietzsche's failure to provide the *Meditations* with new prefaces as a sign of his relatively low regard for them, the opposite would seem to be the case. These four short works were (along with *Zarathustra* I–III) alone given the honour of being judged to stand in no need of additional introduction, defence or explanation. This is why Nietzsche could instruct his publisher, in a letter of 29 August 1886, that 'the four *Untimely Meditations* are the only ones that I wish to leave as they are'.

Given the relative neglect of these four texts by commentators and interpreters, one might be surprised not only at the number of references to them one finds in Nietzsche's later correspondence and notebooks, but also at the profound personal significance he evidently attached to his '*Unzeitgemässen*' or 'Untimely Ones' (which is how he customarily referred to them). Not only did he repeatedly recommend them as essential

---

[20] On the title page of the first edition of *The Birth of Tragedy* the author is identified as 'Friedrich Nietzsche, Professor of Classical Philology at the University of Basel'. The title pages of all four of the *Untimely Meditations* identify him as 'Dr. Friedrich Nietzsche, Professor of Classical Philology at the University of Basel'.

[21] See Schaberg, *Nietzsche Canon*, pp. 49–51.   [22] See 35[48], May–June 1885, VII/3: 256–7.

documents for understanding the *development* of his thought, but he also
described them as – and, indeed, claimed that he had explicitly intended
them to serve as – 'lures' or 'fish hooks' for attracting and capturing the
attention of the readers he was so desperately trying to reach.[23] Admittedly,
Nietzsche viewed virtually *all* of his writings as, in this sense, 'bait'; but
some bait is better than others, and of all of his writings none, in his view,
was better-suited for this important function than the *Untimely Meditations*, especially the third one. As he declared to Brandes, in a letter of 10
April 1888: 'This short work serves as my sign of recognition: the person
who does not find himself addressed *personally* by this work will probably
have nothing more to do with me.'

As mentioned, Nietzsche believed that the *Untimely Meditations* were
also especially useful for providing his readers (once 'hooked', like Brandes)
with essential insight into the development of his philosophy and with an
understanding of what he was trying to accomplish in his later writings.
His letter to Brandes thus continues: 'The *Untimely Meditations*, youthful
writings in a certain sense, merit the closest attention for [understanding]
my development.'

In addition, they always retained a profound and essentially *private*
meaning for their author. The deeply personal significance of these texts
is alluded to, albeit elliptically, in a fragment from Spring or Summer
1877: 'Heart first poured out in *Untimely Meditations*'.[24] Five years later,
in mid-December 1882, Nietzsche seemed to reaffirm this sentiment
when he presented Lou Salomé with a copy of *Schopenhauer as Educator*,
accompanied by the comment, 'this book contains my deepest and most
fundamental feelings'.

Among the 'fundamental feelings' that 'pour from Nietzsche's heart' in
the *Untimely Meditations*, perhaps the most obvious is his angry and sometimes bitter *rejection* of so many of the most distinctive features of the
cultural, political and intellectual landscape of late nineteenth-century
European (and especially German) civilization, with a special animus
reserved for the profession to which he himself devoted more than a
decade of his life. Rejection, however, is by no means the only 'deep'
feeling expressed in these works, which also bear convincing witness to
their author's candid and enthusiastic *veneration* for certain powerful ideals and for particular individuals (above all, Schopenhauer and Wagner)
whom he treats as personal embodiments of them. Still more importantly,

---

[23] See, for example, Nietzsche's letter to Elisabeth Förster-Nietzsche, 15 August 1885.
[24] 22[48], Spring–Summer 1877, IV/2: 483.

the *Meditations* testify poignantly to their author's *growing awareness of his own unique task and individual vocation as a thinker*. Let us consider each of these 'basic sentiments' in turn.

The *negative pathos* that pervades all four of the *Meditations* is impossible to miss and was uppermost in Nietzsche's mind when, in a letter to Hans von Bülow of 2 January 1875, he reported his decision to set aside the next five years 'for working out the remaining ten *Untimely Meditations* and thus for clearing my soul as much as possible of this polemical-passionate garbage'. The *Untimely Meditations* provided the young Nietzsche with an effective and badly needed vehicle for 'externalizing' and 'getting rid of' what he characterized as 'everything negative and rebellious that is hidden within me'.[25]

It was in the *Untimely Meditations* that Nietzsche first found the courage to 'say No' to his age and to his fellow scholars, and hence to significant parts of his own self; and this alone would have been a sufficient reason for him to accord these texts a special place in his heart. Saying No to oneself, however, is not without its costs, as few have appreciated better than Nietzsche, the future exponent of *amor fati*. And indeed, the *Meditations* sometimes threaten to become unbalanced by their author's polemical zeal and to be overwhelmed by a seething spirit of resentment. Thus it is perhaps fortunate that the original series was never completed. This, at any rate, seems to have been Nietzsche's later opinion, when, in the previously cited letter to Brandes, he notes that there were originally supposed to be thirteen essays and then adds: 'fortunately, my health said No!'

The *Untimely Meditations* are, however, just as important for what they *praise* as for what they *reject*, even though, as we have now had several occasions to note, much of this same praise was also a means for distancing – and thereby separating – the author of these paeans from certain powerful influences and stimuli. This is especially true of the last two, which, for all their overt praise of 'Schopenhauer' and 'Wagner', are demonstrably products of a mind that has already largely freed itself from the direct influence of either of these two heavily idealized figures.

The personal significance for Nietzsche of these works thus had nothing to do with the alleged accuracy of his portraits of the subjects. What mattered to him instead were the *new ideals* of culture and of humanity that he was able to project *under the inspiration* – or, to use a term he himself employed in this context in *Ecce Homo*, under the 'signs' – of

[25] Letter to Malwinda von Meysenbug, 25 October 1874.

'Schopenhauer' and 'Wagner'.[26] Even if there is a certain amount of wishful thinking contained in Nietzsche's later claim that his earlier praise of them was *nothing* but a device for freeing himself of their influence, and even if the praise and veneration expressed for them in the *Untimely Meditations* was to a certain degree sincere and heartfelt: even this is something toward which Nietzsche later expressed his personal gratitude, as, for instance, in the following passage from an unpublished draft, written in August or September 1885, for a preface to a collected edition of the *Meditations*:

What I, in my 'younger years', once wrote about Schopenhauer and Richard Wagner – or rather, what I *painted* about them, and perhaps in an all too audacious, overly-confident and overly-youthful 'fresco' style – is something I certainly have no desire to examine in detail today as 'true' or 'false'. But suppose that I was wrong in what I wrote: at least my error dishonored neither them nor me. It *is* something to err in *such a way*! It *is* also something for precisely *me* to be led astray by such errors. At that time, moreover, when I had resolved to paint portraits of 'the philosopher' and 'the artist' – to render, as it were, my own 'categorical imperative': at such a time it was also an inestimable benefit for me not to have to apply my own colors to an empty canvas containing nothing real, but rather to be able to paint, so to speak, upon shapes that were already sketched out in advance. Without realizing it, I was speaking only for myself – indeed, at bottom, only of myself.[27]

This passage points directly to what was unquestionably for Nietzsche himself the most poignant and significant feature of the *Untimely Meditations*: namely, the many specific ways in which these texts so clearly *anticipate* and *foreshadow* the future direction of his thinking. In the view of their author, these youthful works constituted a series of *public pledges* and *solemn promises* concerning his own future *tasks* and *projects*. The note just cited, for example, concludes with the observation that, 'Anyone who reads these texts with a young and fiery soul will perhaps guess the solemn vow with which I then bound myself to my life – with which I resolved to live *my own* life.'

Nowhere is the extraordinary *personal* significance of the *Untimely Meditations* for Nietzsche himself more clearly expressed than in the draft of a

---

[26] 'Basically, what I was trying to do in these works was something altogether different from psychology: an incomparable problem of education, a new concept of *self-discipline, self-defence* to the point of hardness, a way toward greatness and world-historical tasks was seeking to find its first expression. Broadly speaking, I made use of two famous and even now altogether unspecified types, as one takes advantage of an opportunity, in order to communicate something, in order to avail oneself of a few more formulas, signs, and linguistic devices' (*Ecce Homo*, 'Why I Write Such Good Books', 'The Untimely Ones', 3).

[27] 41[2], August–September 1885, VII/3: 404–5.

letter from this same period (August 1885) to an unidentified correspondent, to whom Nietzsche confides, 'For me, my "Untimely Ones" signify
promises. What they are for others, I do not know. Believe me, I would have
ceased living a long time ago if I had turned aside even a single step from
these promises! Perhaps someone will yet discover that from *Human, All
Too Human* on I have done nothing but fulfill my promises.' This claim,
which is publicly repeated in Nietzsche's discussion of the *Meditations* in
Ecce Homo, occurs over and over again in the correspondence of his final
years, where he reiterates his description of the *Untimely Meditations* as
'personal confessions', 'public pledges' and 'solemn promises to myself'.[28]

What exactly was it that Nietzsche believed he had 'promised' himself
and his readers in these early works? What did he think he had 'publicly
pledged' to do? A partial answer to this question may be inferred from a
remark contained in a letter he sent to Peter Gast at the very moment when
he believed he had finally fulfilled his earlier promise, that is, immediately
after the completion of Part I of *Zarathustra*: 'It is curious: I wrote the
commentary prior to the *text*! Everything was already *promised* in *Schopenhauer as educator*. But there was still a long way to go from "Human, All
Too Human" to the "Superhuman".'[29] This and many other similar passages strongly suggest that Nietzsche believed that in *Schopenhauer* and the
other 'Untimely Ones' he had not only pledged himself publicly to pursue
a certain *set of questions* ('my task'), but had also provided unmistakable
public hints about *how* these same questions were to be *answered* and *how*
he intended to *accomplish* his task.

In fact, it is not difficult for a reader familiar with Nietzsche's later works
to find in the *Untimely Meditations* clear anticipations of many characteristically Nietzschean themes and theses, including, but by no means limited
to: a global critique of various forms of dualism (including that of the
'outer' and 'inner' selves, as well as the metaphysical dualism of the 'real'
and 'apparent' worlds); a definition of the 'genuine philosopher' (in con-
tradistinction to the mere 'scholar' or 'academic labourer') as a creator of
values and critic of both science and art; the presupposition of a hyperbolic
Kantian scepticism with respect to the limits of knowledge, coupled with
an endorsement of an instrumental 'perspectivism' with respect to actual
knowledge claims; an insistence that neither science nor morality is self-
grounding and an appeal to 'life' itself as the highest standard or criterion of

---

[28] See Nietzsche's letters to Georg Brandes, 19 February and 10 April 1888.
[29] Letter to Peter Gast, 21 April 1883.

judgment; a recognition of the need for various sorts of 'illusion' (uneasily coupled with an insistence that intellectual integrity requires us to identify these illusions as such); and a definition of 'culture' as 'unity of style'.

Some distinctively 'Zarathustrian' doctrines are also anticipated in the *Untimely Meditations*, including: a critique of complacent 'omnisatisfaction' (whether of the 'cultural philistine' or of the 'last man'); an insistence that 'being oneself' requires 'overcoming oneself'; an emphasis upon the personal and cultural importance of positing an ideal of a 'higher' form of humanity; a recognition of the creative and productive power of negation and destruction; a clear awareness of the inescapably temporal and 'this-worldly' character of the human condition; and even (especially in the second *Meditation*) some oblique play with the idea of 'eternal recurrence'.

It is also in the *Untimely Meditations* that Nietzsche first begins to perfect what is perhaps the most original feature of his own philosophical practice: namely, the method of 'genealogical' analysis, which is employed in these early texts to illuminate the origin of such problematic phenomena as 'the pure will to truth', 'the selfless man of science' and conventional morality. One even finds in the *Meditations* unmistakable anticipations of what is arguably the most important achievement of Nietzsche's final years: his analysis of the inevitability of nihilism, a topic that is distantly foreshadowed in his critique of the failure of secular humanists such as Strauss to recognize the intimate connection between their own progressive liberalism and those religious standards they reject, as well as their failure to anticipate the dire and inexorable consequences of their withdrawal of faith in the latter.

In addition to any purely doctrinal continuity between the *Untimely Meditations* and Nietzsche's later writings, there is also another sense in which he believed that his distinctive 'task' and 'promise' were first made public in them – a sense that has less to do with his later writings than with his radically altered *mode of life* in the years following their publication. One of the central theses of the *Meditations* is that every genuine and original thinker requires a degree of *radical personal independence* that is simply incompatible with any sort of institutional affiliation or sponsorship. It is the very independence of the true philosopher's mode of living that confirms his or her right to be taken seriously as a philosophical educator.

There is a familiar and frequently reproduced photograph of Nietzsche, taken at Basel around 1874, which bears the inscription, 'Friedrich the Untimely One'. Nothing testifies more poignantly to his rapidly growing awareness of his own, distinctive 'task' than this presumptuous inscription;

for when he wrote these books and signed this photograph Nietzsche was still an 'academic labourer', a Professor of Classical Philology. One of the implicit promises made by the man who signed himself so is, therefore, that he will not put himself forward as a philosopher in his own right until he has first *established his right* to do so – not through any process of academic certification, but by successfully establishing his own independent mode of living, that is, through the 'courageous visibility' of his own 'philosophical life'. All reasons of health aside, this is why Nietzsche simply had to leave Basel and the academy for an independent career as a free-lance author of books 'for everyone and no one'.[30]

Nietzsche's pride in having actually followed the path he laid out for himself in the third *Meditation* is evident in a letter written just after he reread the *Untimely Meditations* in 1884: 'I have *lived in the very manner* that I sketched out for myself in advance,' he reports with transparent delight, and then adds: 'In case you should find the time to look at *Zarathustra*, take *Schopenhauer as educator* along with you as well, simply for the sake of comparison. (The *error* of the latter is that it is *not* really about Schopenhauer, but almost solely about me – but I myself did not realize this as I was writing it.)'[31]

This last point was elaborated publicly four years later, in *Ecce Homo*, where Nietzsche insisted that the *real* subject of the third and fourth *Meditations* was Nietzsche himself: '*Richard Wagner in Bayreuth* is a vision of my future, and, in contrast, *Schopenhauer as Educator* records my innermost history, my *becoming* – and, above all, my *promise!*'[32] A controversial claim, to be sure, and one which every reader of the *Untimely Meditations* must decide for himself or herself.

---

[30] On the title page of *Thus Spoke Zarathustra*, the title is followed by the words 'a book for everyone and no one'.
[31] Letter to Franz Overbeck, August 1884.
[32] *Ecce Homo*, 'Why I Write Such Good Books', 'The Untimely Ones', 3.

CHAPTER 4

Nietzsche: Human, All Too Human

Richard Schacht

'*Human, All Too Human* is the monument of a crisis.' With these apt words Nietzsche began his own reflection, in his autobiographical *Ecce Homo* (1888),[1] on this remarkable collection of almost 1,400 aphorisms published in three instalments, the first of which had appeared in 1878, ten years earlier. The crisis to which he refers was first and foremost a crisis of multiple dimensions in his own life. *Human, All Too Human* was the extended product of a period of devastating health problems that necessitated Nietzsche's resignation in 1879 from his professorship in classical philology at Basel University. These problems were to plague him for the remaining decade of his brief productive life (which ended with his complete physical and mental collapse in January 1889, at the age of 44, from which he never recovered in the eleven years of marginal existence that remained to him before his death in 1900). *Human, All Too Human* also marked Nietzsche's transition from the philologist and cultural critic he had been into the kind of philosopher and writer he came to be.

But the crisis was above all a crisis in Nietzsche's intellectual development; and although it was very much his own, it presaged the larger crisis toward which he came to see our entire culture and civilization moving, and subsequently came to call 'the death of God'.[2] In his own case, this crisis was precipitated not only by his deepening appreciation of the profound and extensive consequences of the collapse of traditional ways of thinking, but also – and more immediately – by his growing recognition of the insufficiency of the resources of both the Enlightenment and the Romanticism to which he had been so strongly attracted to fill the void. The three instalments of *Human, All Too Human* are no less important for the insight they yield into the kind of struggle in which Nietzsche was

---

[1] *On the Genealogy of Morals/Ecce Homo*, trans. Walter Kaufmann (New York, 1967), p. 283 ('Why I Write Such Good Books': *Human, All Too Human*, §71).
[2] See, e.g., *The Gay Science*, trans. Walter Kaufmann (New York, 1974), §§108, 125 and 343.

engaged than they are for the many sparks that fly in the course of his efforts to find new ways to go on.

The world around Nietzsche did not appear to be a world headed for crisis. The ordeals, horrors and dramatic changes of the century to come were largely unimagined, and indeed unimaginable, even to Nietzsche, who was far more prescient than most – even to the point of deeming the advent of air travel to be inevitable (1:267). In 1876, when he began working on the material that was published two years later in what is now the first volume of *Human, All Too Human*, Europe was again at (relative) peace. It had been ten years since the Austro-Prussian War that had left Prussia dominant in Central Europe; and it had been five years since the brief Franco-Prussian War (in which Nietzsche had briefly served as a volunteer medical orderly, with disastrous consequences for his health), which further enhanced and extended Prussia's sway, this time at France's expense. German unification under Prussian leadership had been achieved in 1871, and the new *Reich* appeared to be thriving, with Wilhelm on the throne and (more importantly) Otto von Bismarck at the helm.

Everything seemed to be coming along very nicely for Western civilization in general, Europe in particular and Germany more specifically. It was the heyday of European imperialism, with India recently incorporated into the British Empire, and much of the rest of the non-Western world coming under European sway. The industrial revolution was sweeping all before it, and capitalism was triumphant. New technologies and modes of transportation and communication were transforming Western societies. (Nietzsche himself must have been one of the very first philosophers to own one of the newly invented typewriters, although it proved to be of little use to him.) Despite the success of conservative elements of European societies in retaining their social position and political power, forces preparing the way for their eventual replacement by more popular forms of social, cultural, economic and political organization – for better or for worse – were gathering.

The physical sciences were advancing spectacularly; and while the influence of Karl Marx and Sigmund Freud had yet to be felt, the social and historical disciplines were maturing, and the biological sciences were coming on strong. Charles Darwin already loomed large. His *Origin of Species* had been published in 1859, and his *Descent of Man* in 1871. Germany, making up for lost time, was emerging as an economic, political and technological powerhouse, as well as the world's new leader in many of the sciences. It also continued its century-long dominance in philosophy, with ever-mutating forms of idealism, neo-Kantianism, naturalism and materialism competing in the aftermath of Hegel. Religion, enjoying official state status in many countries and the unquestioning allegiance of the vast majority of their populations, seemed immune from serious challenge. The arts, literature and music were flourishing as well, in Germany as elsewhere in Europe; and in 1876 the frenzy surrounding Richard Wagner – to which Nietzsche was no stranger – rose to new heights, with the opening of Bayreuth, and the performance of the first complete four-opera cycles of Wagner's monumental *Ring of the Nibulungs*.

Yet Nietzsche was convinced that all was far from well. He was repelled by the popular culture and brave new social, economic and political world burgeoning around him, and could no longer take seriously the intellectual and religious tradition associated with it. By 1876 he also found himself increasingly estranged from the newly fashionable alternatives to the tradition that its critics and rivals had been touting, including his erstwhile idols and mentors Arthur Schopenhauer and Wagner. Everywhere he looked, even at those things and thinkers supposedly representing the pride of our culture and the zenith of humanity, what he saw was not only far from divine but all-too-human.

Nietzsche had long yearned – and continued to yearn throughout his productive life – for a higher humanity with a worth great enough to warrant the affirmation of life even in the absence of any transcendently supplied meaning. He now had come to the hard realization that the only possible way to that higher humanity required an uncompromising examination of everything human and all-too-human that at once stands in our way and is our point of departure, and a sober stocktaking of what there is to work with in undertaking what he was later to call the enhancement of human life. The idea and ideal he seized upon at this juncture to guide and accompany him was that of the 'free spirit', older and wiser heir of the Enlightenment. Nietzsche paid explicit tribute to the ethos of this newly adopted lineage in his dedication of the first edition of *Human, All Too Human* to Voltaire, Enlightenment thinker *par excellence*, who had died exactly a century earlier, and whose spirit he now embraced.

Human, All Too Human was Nietzsche's second book; and it was as far removed from the kind of book professors of classical languages and literatures were supposed to write as anything could be. His first book, *The Birth of Tragedy* (1872), had been a scandal in the eyes of his scholarly colleagues owing to its disregard of prevailing norms of scholarship and its blatant advocacy of Wagner as the reincarnation of the spirit of the tragic culture of the Greeks – but it at least had a recognizably classical literary topic. *Human, All Too Human*, as initially published, was a volume of 638 aphorisms – that is, short observations and reflections ranging from one or two sentences to a long paragraph, of a relatively self-contained nature. This style was a radically new one for Nietzsche, reminiscent of the writings of such observers of the human scene as Montaigne and La Rochefoucauld. Nietzsche had long greatly admired their manner of thought and expression, and found himself drawn to emulate them in his search for a voice that lent itself both to his own changing temperament and circumstances and to the decidedly unphilological tasks towards which he was turning.

The publication of *Human, All Too Human* completed Nietzsche's estrangement from his erstwhile scholarly profession, from which he officially retired shortly thereafter. It also completed his much more painful estrangement from Wagner, whose devoted admirer, champion and intimate younger friend Nietzsche had been. Nietzsche himself claimed to have begun writing the book in reaction to the first Bayreuth production of Wagner's *Ring* cycle, the entire social spectacle of which appalled him; and although he in fact would appear to have begun work on it some months earlier, in the spring of 1876, it certainly was written during a period in which his formerly close relationship to Wagner had become severely strained. Nietzsche knew that Wagner would loathe the book; and its dedication to Voltaire was undoubtedly a very deliberate gesture of defiance and independence in Wagner's direction. Eight years after its first publication, when Nietzsche republished it, he dropped the dedication – perhaps because he no longer wanted Voltaire to be taken as paradigmatic of his evolving conception of the 'free spirit', but perhaps also because Wagner by then had died, and such gestures were no longer either needed or fitting.

In his discussion in *Ecce Homo* of the 'crisis' of which *Human, All Too Human* was the 'monument', Nietzsche goes on to say of it: 'Here I liberated myself from what in my nature did not belong to me.' He had given *Human, All Too Human* the subtitle 'A Book for Free Spirits'; and he went on to characterize the 'free spirit' in similar language, as 'a spirit that has *become free*, that has again taken possession of itself'.[3] Among the things he clearly had in mind were his attachments to Schopenhauer and Wagner, who had been at the centre of his intellectual life for the previous decade. They had been the subjects of his last two major publications prior to *Human, All Too Human*, in which he had lavished praise upon them even

---

[3] *Ecce Homo*, p. 283.

while privately beginning to distance himself from them: *Schopenhauer as Educator* (1874) and *Richard Wagner in Bayreuth* (1876), the final two essays of his four-part *Untimely Meditations*.

A student of classical languages and literatures rather than of philosophy, it had been Nietzsche's accidental discovery of Schopenhauer's magnum opus *The World as Will and Representation* in 1865 that had introduced – and seduced – him to philosophy. His spiritual seduction by Wagner three years later (in 1868) influenced him even more profoundly. The spell cast upon him by the two of them together is very apparent both in his thinking and enthusiasms in *The Birth of Tragedy* and in the fact that he ventured to write and publish such a book. Nietzsche's father had died when he was a young child; and he in effect adopted Schopenhauer as his intellectual godfather and Wagner as his emotional and spiritual father figure. It was for good reason that it occurred to him to write in aphorism 381 of the first volume of *Human, All Too Human*: 'Correcting nature. – If one does not have a good father one should furnish oneself with one.' Yet by the time he wrote these words he was well beyond this point, attempting to liberate himself from the fathers with whom he had furnished himself.

It is well worth bearing in mind who the Nietzsche was who published this book of aphorisms in 1878. Neither he nor anyone else had the slightest idea of what he would go on to do and become. He was a 33-year-old philology professor whose health and academic career were both failing badly. His youthful vigour and promise were now but sadly faded memories to his professional colleagues. His only book, published six years earlier, was the scandalous *Birth of Tragedy*; and his only subsequent publications of any significance were the two essays just mentioned and two previous 'untimely meditations', *David Strauss, the Confessor and the Writer* (1873) and *On the Uses and Disadvantages of History for Life* (1874). His enthusiasm for and association with Wagner had earned him a certain notoriety, but it had done him no good academically; and he otherwise had little reputation at all, except perhaps as a gamble that had appeared not to be working out. He was not thought of as a philosopher, having had no philosophical training and having published nothing resembling a conventional philosophical treatise. He had written a short, ambitious but sketchy essay, 'On Truth and Lies in a Nonmoral Sense', several years earlier; but it remained unfinished, and he never did publish it. His thoughts had indeed begun to turn toward philosophy, and he had even gone so far as to apply for the Chair in Philosophy at Basel when it became vacant; but he was unsuccessful in this attempt to switch professions, for reasons that are easy enough to understand.

Even if *Human, All Too Human* had been published by a professional philosopher, it very probably would not have been regarded as a contribution to the philosophical literature by academic philosophers either in Nietzsche's own time or subsequently. Nor is it clear that it should be; for there is much in it that does not seem to have much to do with philosophical matters. Even the ideas on philosophical topics it addresses are seldom presented in recognizably philosophical ways. More of it can be seen as having philosophical relevance in retrospect, particularly if one looks back upon it with Nietzsche's later writings in mind, and if one's idea of philosophical relevance has been influenced by the impact of his thinking with respect to the philosophical enterprise. Even so, however, all three instalments of the work are very much the product of a mind in transition, moving in many different directions and in many different ways, heedless of disciplinary boundaries and norms, with only Nietzsche's interests and intellectual conscience as his map and compass.

The aphoristic form Nietzsche adopted (and adapted to his purposes) in *Human, All Too Human* had long been a favoured literary form of observers of the human scene who preferred to comment incisively on many things, rather than writing essays about a selected few. But this form may also have been virtually necessitated by Nietzsche's increasingly severe and disabling health problems, which frequently rendered him incapable of writing or even thinking for extended periods of time. He had to make maximum use of the short periods of respite that came to him between frequent and extended bouts of misery. He struggled to surmount his wretched condition, and did so to much greater effect than most people in his situation could; but it was a hard and tortured struggle, giving poignant significance to his subsequent emphasis upon 'hardness', self-mastery, self-discipline, and to his refusal to become preoccupied and deterred by suffering. The flair he discovered in himself for aphoristic writing at this time thus accorded well with necessity. It would be unwarranted, however, to assume that Nietzsche's recourse to it is indicative of the absence of any underlying unity and coherence of thought and intention here and subsequently. So he himself observes in aphorism 128 of the second instalment, very much to this point: '*Against the shortsighted.* – Do you think this work must be fragmentary because I give it to you (and have to give it to you) in fragments?'

Nietzsche had long been plagued by poor eyesight and eye pain that would afflict him when he either read or wrote extensively, by migraine headaches and by indigestion and other gastric problems that made him pay a high price for departures from the blandest of diets. His problems were compounded by a variety of ailments – dysentery and diphtheria among them – he contracted while serving as an orderly during the Franco-Prussian War, the effects of which continued to plague him. And the syphilis he seems somehow to have acquired (despite leading a virtually celibate life), that was the likely cause of his final collapse a dozen years later, may well have begun to contribute to the deterioration of his health during the gestation period of *Human, All Too Human*.

So Nietzsche went from one health crisis to another, finding the rigours and burdens of his academic position increasingly difficult to bear, despite the fact that he rarely had as many as a dozen students attending his lectures. He often was unable to read or write, and frequently was obliged to take medical leaves from his teaching. His collapses were all too common, and at times he was virtually an invalid. He visited clinics, spas and specialists, whose diagnoses and prescriptions may often have only made things worse. Alternating bouts of blinding headaches and wracking vomiting would last for days; and his lecturing became ever more sporadic and difficult. Finally, in the spring of 1879, he submitted his resignation, receiving a small pension that was his sole income thereafter. He then left Basel and began the nomadic life – moving from boarding-house to boarding-house in search of the right climate and conditions – that he would lead for the decade of active life remaining to him prior to his collapse.

It is miraculous that anyone with such severe problems and living such a life could have written anything at all, let alone the series of brilliant books that Nietzsche managed to complete in this period, beginning with the first volume of *Human, All Too Human*. And to all of this must be added the publication history of these books, which compounds the miracle. This history was troubled by Nietzsche's often strained relations with his publishers and printers, and plagued by such other all-too-human difficulties as his eye problems, requiring him to resort to dictation much of the time, and to reliance on the assistance of others to put his manuscripts together, as well as making proof-reading a torment. But worst of all, Nietzsche's publication history is a veritable chronicle of failure. A recent study by William Schaberg makes all of this painfully clear, setting out the whole long and sorry story in depressing detail.[4] *The Birth of Tragedy* sold modestly well, and attracted a good deal of attention – even if much of it was hostile. But the same cannot be said of any of Nietzsche's subsequent books, during his sentient lifetime. Prior to his collapse, none of them sold more than a few hundred copies, and few of them attracted any attention whatsoever.

---

[4] *The Nietzsche Canon: A Publication History and Bibliography* (Chicago, 1995).

Human, All Too Human is a vivid case in point. Of the 1,000 copies in the first printing of the original version, only 120 were sold in 1878; and more than half remained unsold in 1886, when Nietzsche reacquired them and repackaged them with a new introduction as the first volume of the two-volume second edition. The supplement he published in 1879 under the subtitle 'Assorted Opinions and Maxims' sold even more poorly: of the 1,000 copies printed, only a third had been sold by 1886. The second supplement *The Wanderer and His Shadow*, published a year later, fared even worse: fewer than 200 of its initial 1,000 copies had been sold by 1886, when Nietzsche acquired the rights to both supplements and republished them with a new introduction, as the second volume of the second edition of *Human, All Too Human*. There was no true reprinting of additional copies until 1893, when another printing of 1,000 copies of the combined work was run; and its sales remained slow even after his later works began to receive more attention.

Human, All Too Human attained greater circulation and availability as part of the editions of his collected works that began to appear after Nietzsche's death; but it was long eclipsed by *The Birth of Tragedy* before it and by *Thus Spoke Zarathustra* and its sequels after it, both in Europe and in the English-speaking world. The same is true of the other two works in Nietzsche's 'free spirit' series, *Daybreak* and *The Gay Science*. The neglect of *Human, All Too Human* in the English-speaking world is at least partly owing to Walter Kaufmann's lack of interest in it. It was through his translations and his widely read study *Nietzsche: Philosopher, Psychologist, Antichrist*, first published in 1950, that many English-speaking readers after World War II became interested in and acquainted with Nietzsche. Kaufmann translated Nietzsche's first book, *The Birth of Tragedy*, and virtually everything Nietzsche published from *The Gay Science* onward; but he never got around to translating any of the things Nietzsche published in the interval, during the crucial period in which he published not only the three instalments of *Human, All Too Human* but also the four *Untimely Meditations* and *Daybreak*, except for brief excerpts which he inserted in other volumes. Indeed, even Kaufmann's translation of *The Gay Science* was something of an afterthought, appearing long after most of his other translations.[5]

Kaufmann can hardly be blamed for having the interests he did, and for the things he did not choose to do; but they had consequences, since there were no other readily available complete translations of *Human, All*

[5] In 1974 (see note 2).

Too Human or *Daybreak* in English until the early 1980s, when Marion Faber translated the first volume of *Human, All Too Human* (published by the University of Nebraska Press) and Hollingdale's Cambridge University Press translations appeared. Their long inaccessibility ensured that these works, and Nietzsche's thinking during the period in which he wrote them, would remain virtually unknown to English-speaking readers during the preceding three decades. (They likewise had been virtually invisible previously, when Nietzsche was known mainly second-hand in the English-speaking world, and was commonly assumed to be the proto-Nazi he had been made out to be by Nazi propaganda.)

The problem was compounded by Kaufmann's treatment of *Human, All Too Human* (and *Daybreak* and *The Gay Science* as well) in his popular intellectual-biographical study, which had little competition for nearly two decades. This entire period, for Kaufmann, was a gestation period in Nietzsche's thought, of little interest in its own right. He appears to have deemed it deserving of comment at all chiefly for the anticipations to be found in some aphorisms of ideas that became prominent in his later thinking, and for the ammunition other aphorisms afford that were useful in combating Nietzsche's Nazi misinterpretation. So *Human, All Too Human* is relegated to a few pages, in a chapter entitled 'Discovery of the Will to Power'. 'There would be little sense', Kaufmann wrote (without explanation), 'in trying here to sample the gems of *Human, all-too-Human* or [*Daybreak*].' He restricted himself to asserting, with a few illustrations, that, 'Proceeding quite unsystematically and considering each problem on its own merits, without a theory to prove or an axe to grind, Nietzsche reverts now and then to explanations in terms of what he was later to call a will to power.'[6] The works of this period, for Kaufmann, were of significance primarily as the record of Nietzsche's development from the author of *The Birth of Tragedy* into a psychological thinker on a par with Freud, with his further transformation into a philosopher coming somewhat later.

There certainly is some truth in this. *Human, All Too Human* undeniably does show us Nietzsche as psychologist both under development and at work, inventing a kind of psychologizing for which he found a wealth of applications all around him – socially, culturally, behaviourally, intellectually, even philosophically – and simultaneously inventing himself as a new kind of thinker capable of employing this sort of analysis to

---

[6] Walter Kaufmann, *Nietzsche: Philosopher, Psychologist, Antichrist*, 4th edn. (Princeton, 1974), pp. 157, 158.

fascinating and important effect. He was not operating in a void. He had some brilliant aphoristic predecessors, the inspiration of such Enlightenment exemplars as Voltaire, and the benefit of reading his 'educator' and philosophical-psychological mentor Schopenhauer. He also had the more immediate example and encouragement of his newfound friend Paul Rée, who had just written a book in a somewhat similar spirit entitled *Psychological Observations*. Rée's influence was readily and profusely acknowledged by Nietzsche, who went so far as to say that his own position at this time could be called 'Réealism'; and it was evident to all who knew him – including the Wagners, who bitterly lamented it (all the more because Rée was Jewish).

But the results were much more than the sum of their influences even here. And they also added up to something that was much more than psychology as well. It is true enough that Nietzsche's thinking continued to develop, even from one book to the next in this period, as well as over the course of the next decade; and that, as Kaufmann maintained, Nietzsche's philosophical maturity was yet some time off. Yet his accomplishment in the three instalments of *Human, All Too Human* is remarkable in its own right, and can stand on its own feet. If he had died without publishing another thing (as might very well have happened), it would have been sufficient to earn him an important place in the intellectual history of the past several centuries – even if a somewhat different one than he has come to have.

The gulf that separates this work from Nietzsche's previous published writings is wide. The enthusiasms, aspirations and assumptions that so strikingly pervade and animate his earlier work are no longer in evidence. It is a much more sober and analytical, colder and wiser thinker who is at work here. Its author is still hopeful of finding both a diagnosis and a cure to what ails our culture and threatens its future, and resists Schopenhauer's pessimism; but he is as disillusioned now with Wagner, the new *Reich* and other pied pipers of modern times as he earlier had been with traditional religious consolations and their philosophical cousins. He has become convinced that only something like a continuation and radicalization of Enlightenment thinking, getting to the bottom of things and ruthlessly exposing all false hopes and dangerous palliatives, can afford us at least the possibility of a future worth having and a life worth living. Nietzsche's dedication to Voltaire was more than a slap at Wagner (although that it surely was). It also was the announcement of a major intellectual reorientation, placing him squarely in the often calumnied but courageous tradition of Enlightenment thought and effort.

For the Nietzsche of *Human, All Too Human* nothing is beyond criticism – and there is a strong suspicion that (as he would later put it) all 'idols' of our reverence will turn out to be hollow and all-too-human when subjected to critical scrutiny. His new 'psychological' tools are brought to bear upon them, with results that amply support this suspicion. But there is more to the outlook and way of thinking that he is devising and putting into practice here than this. In 'On Truth and Lies in a Nonmoral Sense', some five years earlier, Nietzsche had begun sketching a fundamentally and severely naturalistic picture of our general human condition, in a world over which no benevolent deity reigns and in which no beneficent rationality is at work. We are depicted as alone and adrift in a godless universe, a mere cosmic accident, ill-equipped either to comprehend what is going on or to do much about it; and we are kidding ourselves if we think otherwise – although we seem almost irresistibly drawn to do so. Can we live without such illusions? Nietzsche was at first inclined to doubt it – as one sees in *The Birth of Tragedy*, written at about the same time.

By the time of *Human, All Too Human*, he seems to have resolved to try. The power of myths and illusions to sustain anyone possessed of an uncompromising intellectual conscience is undermined when one sees through them; and so one may have little other choice, if – as for Nietzsche – Kierkegaardian leaps of faith are out of the question, and a Schopenhauerian negation of life is repellent. *Human, All Too Human* is a work of cold passion, in which nothing more is assumed about our humanity than the picture sketched in the 'Truth and Lies' essay, and in which everything in human life that might seem to be of loftier origins is called before the tribunal of scrutiny, with humbling results. Yet the spirit of the investigation is profoundly and pervasively affirmative; for the passion that drives it is not only that of an honesty that will tolerate no nonsense or groundless wishful thinking, but also of a desperate search for enough to work with and ways of doing so to sustain ourselves despite all. To call this 'secular humanism' would be to sell it short; for while Nietzsche's outlook is radically secular, he is far from taking humanity either in general or as embodied in each and every one of us to be the locus of meaning and value. But it is a kind of tough-minded and yet doggedly affirmative naturalism, the upshot of which is that our all-too-human humanity leaves a good deal to be desired, and yet gives us something to work with that is not to be despised.

But if we are to make something worthwhile of ourselves, we have to take a good hard look at ourselves. And this, for Nietzsche, means many things. It means looking at ourselves in the light of everything we can learn about the world and ourselves from the natural sciences – most emphatically including evolutionary biology, physiology and even medical science. It also means looking at ourselves in the light of everything we can learn about human life from history, from the social sciences, from the study of arts, religions, languages, literatures, mores and other features of various cultures. It further means attending closely to human conduct on different levels of human interaction, to the relation between what people say and seem to think about themselves and what they do, to their reactions in different sorts of situations, and to everything else about them that affords clues to what makes them tick. All of this, and more, is what Nietzsche is up to in *Human, All Too Human*. He is at once developing and employing the various perspectival techniques that seem to him to be relevant to the understanding of what we have come to be and what we have it in us to become. This involves gathering materials for a reinterpretation and reassessment of human life, making tentative efforts along those lines and then trying them out on other human phenomena both to put them to the test and to see what further light can be shed by doing so.

This multi-perspectival and multi-directional method, which Nietzsche employed with increasing dexterity and ingenuity throughout the remainder of his productive life, finds its first extended trials and applications in *Human, All Too Human*. The results are uneven, as one might expect – and indeed as is always the case in Nietzsche's writings (or, for that matter, in the case of anyone who engages in such a complex, uncertain and adventuresome sort of interpretive enterprise). Distinguishing between genuine insights and personal preferences, prejudices, over-generalizations, irresistible puns and other such inspirations is not easy. It often can be done better by others than by oneself – even if one's intellectual conscience is as alert and vigorous as Nietzsche's, to whom the all-too-human was no stranger. But by precept and example he invites us to subject him to the same sort of scrutiny to which he subjects others; and that is something many will want to do. He only asks that one be prepared to have one's very objections subjected in turn to the same searching critical assessment – for they too may be questionable.

Nietzsche himself looked back on *Human, All Too Human* twice in print. The final time was in his rather creatively and grandiosely self-interpretive *Ecce Homo*, in 1888, in the course of a review of all of his main publications under the characteristically immodest heading 'Why I Write Such Good Books'. The occasion of his first subsequent retrospective – the reissuing of all three instalments together in 1886 – may itself have had its all-too-human motivations (not the least of which was Nietzsche's hope that by repackaging them with new prefaces he might be able to sell more of them and attract more attention to them). Nonetheless, the two new prefaces he wrote on this occasion are of no little interest; and it is important for readers to bear in mind that they were written long after the material they precede – eight years after the first volume, and six and seven years after the two parts of the second volume. Indeed, the prefaces themselves were written at different times and places – the former in Nice, on the French Mediterranean coast in Spring 1886, and the latter in Sils Maria, in the mountainous Swiss Engadine region, in September of that year. They both deserve close reading, both before and after one has made one's way through the maze of the 1,400 aphorisms.

In the first preface Nietzsche sees himself at the time of the first volume as already burdened with the large and heavy questions that compelled him toward philosophy, and also as struggling to achieve the intellectual and spiritual freedom and resources needed to deal with them, which he feels he had lacked in sufficient measure previously. He also sees himself as having been in a precarious state of health both physically and intellectually, slowly convalescing from the maladies of both sorts that had threatened to engulf him. The same theme is sounded again in the second preface; and there he makes it even clearer what the chief dangers were to which he had to develop resistance and learn to overcome. He refers to these writings as 'a continuation and redoubling of a spiritual cure, namely of the *anti-romantic* self-treatment that my still healthy instinct had itself discovered and prescribed for me against a temporary attack of the most dangerous form of romanticism', and as the expressions of a 'courageous pessimism' that is the 'antithesis of all romantic mendacity' (II:P:2, 4).

As Nietzsche observes in the first preface, his determination to resist and reject all such temptations (which for him could be summed up in a single name: Wagner) was still immature here, and was not yet 'that *mature* freedom of spirit which is equally self-mastery and discipline of the heart and permits access to many and contradictory modes of thought', and which he evidently feels he subsequently had come to attain (I:P:4). But he sees himself in *Human, All Too Human* as having been on the way to it. And it is of no little importance to the understanding of Nietzsche both to observe that he not only places this interpretation upon the direction and outcome of his own intellectual development, and to recognize what is fundamental to it: the repudiation of 'all romantic mendacity', and its replacement by the cultivation of the intellectual conscience and analytical, critical and interpretive abilities of the 'free spirit' he was attempting to become and conjure among his readers by his own example.

Nietzsche thus saw himself here as having turned away from the Wagnerian–Schopenhauerian Romanticism of *The Birth of Tragedy* (of which he was explicitly critical along these very lines in a new preface to that work also written in 1886, entitled 'An Attempt at Self-Criticism'). In doing so, and partly as a way of doing so, he had turned with all the self-discipline and intellect he could muster in an analytical direction, replacing art with science as his new paradigm of high spirituality. Thus, in the preface to the second volume, he refers to the various instalments of *Human, All Too Human* as '*precepts of health* that may be recommended to the more spiritual natures of the generation just coming up as a *disciplina voluntatis* [discipline of the will]' (II:P:2). It is a discipline as much needed today as it was needed by Nietzsche himself and by 'the generation just coming up' in his own time.

This in part answers the question of the intended audience of these volumes. Nietzsche did not think of himself, either at this time or later, as writing primarily for professional philosophers, or even for students in philosophy courses. He clearly was moving in what he conceived to be a philosophical direction; but he was writing first and foremost for inquiring and adventuresome minds of sufficient sophistication to keep pace with him, whoever and wherever they may be – not only in academia but also among the intelligent reading public. He hoped in particular to be able to reach the better minds of the younger generation, who might be more receptive than their elders to challenges to preconceived ideas and assumed values. Yet he also had hopes of having the sort of wider impact Voltaire and other firebrands of the Enlightenment had had a century earlier.

At the same time Nietzsche worried about what the likes of the Wagners and the few colleagues who had not given up on him would think of it. For a time he even considered publishing the first volume anonymously or under a pseudonym. *Human, All Too Human* may not seem to us today to be scandalously radical, however provocative it may be on some topics; but at the time Nietzsche rightly feared that it would be deeply offensive to many of its readers – not in the ways *The Birth of Tragedy* had been to his fellow philologists, but in an almost opposite way. Now it was those who had been enamoured of Nietzsche the romantic who were offended, by his abandonment of Romanticism in favour of a coldly and severely analytical Naturalism – for which he sought the widest possible audience. Beyond the circle of those who already knew of him, however, Nietzsche need not have worried about the scandalousness of his new venture – for, to his dismay, no one else paid the slightest attention. Even today, few recognize it as the gold mine it is, not only as an excellent way of becoming acquainted with his thinking, but also for its wealth of ideas worth thinking about.

It does not do full justice to these ideas to characterize them as 'psychological', let alone as revolving around the 'discovery of the will to power' (as Kaufmann suggests). Nietzsche himself, in his 1886 preface to the first volume, observes that although he may not have realized it at the time, it eventually dawned upon him that 'it is *the problem of order of rank*' – that is, the problem of values and their revaluation and ordering – 'of which we may say it is *our* problem'; and that, to position themselves to address this problem adequately, 'we free spirits' first have to become 'adventurers and circumnavigators of that inner world called "man", as surveyors and [measurers] of that "higher" and "one [above] the other" that is likewise called "man" – penetrating everywhere, almost [!] without fear, disdaining nothing, losing nothing, asking everything, cleansing everything of what is chance and accident in it and as it were thoroughly sifting it . . . ' (1:P:7).

That is a fair characterization of what Nietzsche does in *Human, All Too Human*; and it is in that sense that the term 'psychological' applies to his task and way of going about it. 'Psychology' in his time, after all, was not a discipline in its own right, separate and distinct from philosophy, but rather was conceived both loosely and strictly as a part of it; and in Nietzsche's hands it retained this intimate connection with philosophy as he came to understand and practice it. Philosophy for him revolves around the exploration of things human, and is first and foremost the attempt to comprehend them – even if that comprehension is not an end in itself. It prepares the way for the further comprehension of the whole complex matter of value, as it relates to issues of quality and worth in and about human life, in the service of its enhancement. In *Human, All Too Human* Nietzsche took (and in his prefaces saw himself as taking) major steps in that direction. He had yet to learn to temper his new enthusiasm for the natural sciences, to figure out how to revisit the perspectives relating to the arts and culture he had known so well without becoming captive once again to them, to supplement both with yet others and to develop the ability to make larger interpretive sense of our humanity in the light of this multiplicity of perspectives upon it. But he was on his way.

This assessment of the place of *Human, All Too Human* in the context of Nietzsche's larger intellectual development has the virtues of acknowledging the great differences between it (and its companion volumes in the 'free spirit' series) and his earlier writings, and also of coherently relating his later writings to both. Many readers – and interpreters – make the mistake of regarding these 'free spirit' works as a kind of interlude between *The*

Birth of Tragedy and *Thus Spoke Zarathustra*, and of reading them – if at all – from the perspective of his later writings, in relation to which they are generally found to pale by comparison, both rhetorically and philosophic- ally. It would make a good deal more sense to view his later writings in the perspective of his 'free spirit' works, taking *Human, All Too Human* as one's point of departure, and regarding *Zarathustra* as an interlude between the last of them (the first four-part version of *The Gay Science*) and the continuation of Nietzsche's aphoristic works, beginning with *Beyond Good and Evil* and the expanded version of *The Gay Science* he published a year later. For the continuities between them are strong, even if Nietzsche's arsenal of perspectives grows, his philosophical sophistication increases, his rhetoric sharpens and heats up, and his intellectual pendulum swings back from its scientifically-oriented extreme point in the direction of his artistic and cultural concerns and sensibility (moving subsequently in considerably shorter arcs in the general vicinity of the centre of the spectrum they mark out).

This even applies to the organization of *Human, All Too Human* and the two later works that are not devoted to specific topics or figures, *Beyond Good and Evil* and *Twilight of the Idols*. Like both of them, the first version of *Human, All Too Human* does have an organization, in the form of the division of the volume into parts with headings. Interestingly enough, all three have the same number of major parts – nine – plus an epilogue. And there is a striking similarity among the headings as well. Each starts out with sections on topics relating to philosophers and philosophy; each has a section relating to morality, and another to religious and metaphysical matters; each has a section on social and political matters, and another on cultural and intellectual topics; and each, at some point, contains a collection of one-liners on a variety of sensitive topics guaranteed to offend almost everyone. To be sure, the parallels are not exact; but they are close enough to warrant the suggestion of a continuity of form – and in content there are not only significant differences but also remarkable similarities. One might well ask oneself in what ways Nietzsche's thinking changed on these matters from his initial discussions of them in *Human, All Too Human* to *Beyond Good and Evil* to *Twilight*, what his reasons may have been (if he does not make them explicit) – and whether the changes were invariably for the better.

The two parts of the second volume of *Human, All Too Human* were not supplied with the same sorts of headings, or indeed with any subheadings at all. Most of the aphorisms in them can easily be assigned to one or another of those Nietzsche uses in the first volume, however; for they chiefly range over and fall into the same general topics. An examination of the list of these topics makes it clear both that *Human, All Too Human* is far from being as formless as it is often taken to be, and also that Nietzsche's interests include but are not restricted to issues that are normally deemed 'philosophical'. The first (appropriately enough), 'Of First and Last Things', deals with metaphysical thinking – but in a curiously detached sort of way, more as a phenomenon to be understood than a set of arguments to be engaged head on. The same sort of approach is taken to morality in the second ('On the History of Moral Sensations' – Nietzsche's first go at what he came to call the 'genealogy of morals'); to religion in the third ('The Religious Life'); and to art in the fourth ('From the Souls of Artists and Writers'). In each case Nietzsche is proposing that we make the experiment of looking at these seemingly sublime things as *human* phenomena – experiences and activities of human beings – asking what is going on when such things occur in human life, and shifting the presumption from their sublimity to the suspicion that their appearance of sublimity may well be deceiving.

In the next four sections Nietzsche turns his attention to the domain of cultural, social and interpersonal relationships and types. There is more to culture than art and literature; and he attempts to bring it into focus in the fifth section ('Tokens of Higher and Lower Culture'). Social institutions and relationships are the logical next stop, in the sixth section ('Man in Society'), with family matters coming next ('Woman and Child'), followed by political life ('A Glance at the State'). If in the first four sections he surveys things that claim some sort of transcendent significance, of the sort Hegel sought to express in his characterization of their domain as that of 'absolute spirituality', here Nietzsche surveys those things that flesh out what Hegel had called 'the life of a people' on the level of its 'objective spirituality'. These too are among the chief sorts of things in terms of which our humanity and human meaning and worth are commonly conceived. If one asks what it is that sets us apart from and above other creatures whose existence is merely animal, and is not permitted to give a quick religious or metaphysical answer appealing to transcendent principles and powers, this is a fair inventory of possible answers. That is the larger (and genuinely if unconventionally philosophical) point of these collections of reflections, many of which might not appear to have any philosophical significance whatsoever.

In the final section Nietzsche turns to what he considers to be left after one has considered all of these other dimensions of human life: what we are or can be on our own, as individuals, within or by ourselves ('Man Alone with Himself'). Later he would add another item to the first four on the list, belonging with them, but not yet as problematical in his eyes as he subsequently recognized it to be: scientific thinking, of the very sort he had become so enamoured of and reliant upon here. Like the glasses with which one may be provided to deal with vision problems, and to which one may become so accustomed that one ceases to be aware of them, this sort of thinking can come to be taken for granted beyond the point to which reliance upon it is warranted. To his great credit, Nietzsche was far quicker than most to become sensitive to the limitations of ways of thinking to which he was attracted – and then, having done so, to get past his disappointment with them and ascertain the best uses that might be made of them, their limitations notwithstanding. In *Human, All Too Human*, however, his romance with the sciences was still young, and this process had yet to run its course.

The expression Nietzsche adopted to characterize the kind of thinker and human being he conceived himself to have become – or at any rate to have been on the way to becoming – at the time of *Human, All Too Human* is that which he features in its subtitle: 'free spirit', *Freigeist. Human, All Too Human* is proclaimed in its subtitle to be 'A Book for Free Spirits'. Three years after the publication of its first instalment, when Nietzsche published the first version of *The Gay Science*, he had the following printed on the back cover: 'This book marks the conclusion of a series of writings by FRIEDRICH NIETZSCHE whose common goal it is to erect *a new image and ideal of the free spirit.*' He then went on to list *Human, All Too Human* and its supplements and sequels up to and including *The Gay Science*.[7]

But this did not mark the end of Nietzsche's attachment to the idea of the 'free spirit'. It reappears very significantly in *Beyond Good and Evil*, as the heading of the second part of the book in which, following his largely critical first part 'On the Prejudices of Philosophers', he proceeds to set forth a variety of his own ideas on a broad range of philosophical issues. And it reappears again not only in his retrospective *Ecce Homo*, as one would expect, but also in *Twilight of the Idols*, in a section bearing the heading *'My conception of freedom'*.[8] From first to last it is invoked to convey the double meaning of both liberation from things that have tended to hinder and hobble one, and of determination to undertake tasks requiring independence, strength, courage and imagination. Nietzschean free spirits are not necessarily philosophers; but Nietzschean philosophers

---

[7] *The Gay Science*, trans. Kaufmann, p. 30.
[8] *Twilight of the Idols*, in *The Portable Nietzsche*, ed. and trans. Walter Kaufmann (New York, 1954), 'Skirmishes of an Untimely Man', §39.

are necessarily free spirits. Voltaire, for Nietzsche, was an exemplary free spirit, as the original dedication of *Human, All Too Human* indicated: 'To Voltaire's memory, in commemoration of the day of his death, 30 May 1788.' His example would appear to have taught Nietzsche the erstwhile devoted disciple of Wagner something he came to realize he badly needed to learn.

The 'free spirit' is 'a spirit that has *become free*', as Nietzsche emphasizes in his remarks on *Human, All Too Human* in *Ecce Homo*. In the things that matter most, Rousseau was both right and wrong – right in observing that people are 'everywhere in chains', but wrong in supposing them to be 'born free'. True freedom of the spirit is something that is acquired – if at all – with difficulty, and only by a few. Indeed, in Nietzsche's 1886 preface to the first volume he even goes so far as to allow that he was obliged to *invent* the 'free spirits' to whom the book is addressed, since '"free spirits" of this kind do not exist, did not exist' – although he says 'I had need of them', all the more so because he lacked the kind of actual companionship and comradeship that people of this sort could provide. 'That free spirits of this kind *could* one day exist', on the other hand, and indeed that they *will* one day exist, he does not doubt. 'I see them already *coming*', he optimistically asserts (1:P:2); and in any event the statement on the back cover of *The Gay Science* makes it clear enough that he hoped and intended *Human, All Too Human* to speed the day, by both precept and example.

But the same could be said for all of Nietzsche's aphoristic works, after as well as before *Thus Spoke Zarathustra*. It is perhaps less true of *Zarathustra* itself, despite Zarathustra's repeated proclamations that he wants no disciples and wants his companions to think for themselves; for it is hard (though not impossible) to read and experience *Zarathustra* as a non-tendentious work. And it likewise is perhaps less true of Nietzsche's polemical later works – against Wagner, against Christianity and even (in *On the Genealogy of Morals*) against the kind of morality he considered to have come to prevail in the Western world. Polemics may have their place in the liberation of fettered spirits from the shackles that bind them, and so in making it possible for some people who might not otherwise do so to become free spirits; but they are far from sufficient to complete the process, and can easily subvert it – as the responses of many people to what they find in some of Nietzsche illustrate well enough.

Unfortunately for Nietzsche's reception, his free-spirited side has all too often been overshadowed and even eclipsed by the appearance of a much more impassioned and seemingly dogmatic side, frightening some and exciting others – for equally dubious reasons in either case. Neither the fact that this appearance has been seen in markedly different (and incompatible) ways, nor the objection that it is only an appearance rather than the dark side of the reality of his thought, has sufficed to keep it from long impeding his interpretation and assessment. The best remedy for this predicament is to direct attention to those works in which Nietzsche is engaged in his free-spirited labours, from *Human, All Too Human* to *The Gay Science* and *Beyond Good and Evil* to *Twilight of the Idols*. This is not to expurgate him; for there is plenty in each of these books to worry about and argue with, and much that is all-too-human in him no less than in his targets. But in these volumes he for the most part carries on in the manner of the kind of 'free spirit' he seeks to evoke and encourage. If one would understand the sort of thing he has in mind in speaking of philosophers and philosophy of the future as he would have them be, one would do well to begin – as he did – with this idea in mind, as the presupposition of anything further that a Nietzschean kind of philosophy might involve.

There is no better commentary in Nietzsche on what free-spiritedness meant to him, as the idea took shape in and beyond *Human, All Too Human*, than the paragraph with which he concludes the part of *Beyond Good and Evil* entitled 'The Free Spirit'. It deserves to be read together with the prefaces to the two volumes of *Human, All Too Human* he shortly went on to write. With them in mind one can turn to *Human, All Too Human* itself and see why Nietzsche was not content to allow it to go unnoticed even after he had gone on to publish a good many other things – and why there may be no better introduction to his thought and thinking.

At home, or at least having been guests, in many countries of the spirit; having escaped again and again from the musty agreeable nooks into which preference and prejudice, youth, origin, the accidents of people and books or even exhaustion from wandering seemed to have banished us; full of malice against the lures of dependence that lie hidden in honors, or money, or offices, or enthusiasms of the senses; grateful even to need and vacillating sickness because they always rid us from some rule and its 'prejudice,' grateful to god, devil, sheep, and worm in us; curious to a vice, investigators to the point of cruelty, with uninhibited fingers for the unfathomable, with teeth and stomachs for the most indigestible, ready for every feat that requires a sense of acuteness and acute senses, ready for every venture, thanks to an excess of 'free will,' with fore- and back-souls into whose ultimate intentions nobody can look so easily, with fore- and backgrounds which no foot is likely to explore to the end; concealed under cloaks of light, conquerors even if we look like heirs and prodigals, arrangers and collectors from morning till late, misers of our riches and our crammed drawers, economical in learning and forgetting, inventive in schemas, occasionally proud of tables of categories, occasionally pedants, occasionally night owls of work even in broad daylight; yes, when it is necessary even scarecrows – and today it is necessary; namely, insofar as we are born, sworn, jealous friends of *solitude*, of our own most profound, most midnightly, most middaily solitude; that is the type of man we are, we free spirits! And perhaps *you* have something of this, too, you that are coming? you *new* philosophers? –[9]

[9] Trans. Walter Kaufmann (New York, 1966), §44.

CHAPTER 5

Nietzsche: Daybreak

Maudemarie Clark and Brian Leiter

THE PLACE OF *DAYBREAK* IN THE NIETZSCHEAN CORPUS

Nietzsche began compiling the notes that would comprise *Daybreak* in January of 1880, finishing the book by May of the following year. Like all of Nietzsche's books, it sold poorly (fewer than 250 copies in the first five years, according to William Schaberg). Unlike most of his other works, however, it has been sadly neglected during the Nietzsche renaissance of the past three decades. *Daybreak* post-dates his famous, polemical study of classical literature, *The Birth of Tragedy* (1872) – the book that, at the time, destroyed Nietzsche's professional reputation in classical philology (the subject he taught at the University of Basel, until ill health forced his retirement in 1879). *Daybreak* also post-dates a somewhat less-neglected prior volume, *Human, All Too Human: A Book for Free Spirits* (1878–80), the book often said to constitute the highwater mark of Nietzsche's "positivist" phase (in which he accepted, somewhat uncritically, that science was the paradigm of all genuine knowledge).

Daybreak's relative obscurity, however, is due more to his subsequent writings, which have overshadowed it in both the classroom and the secondary literature: *The Gay Science* (1882), the four books of *Thus Spoke Zarathustra* (1883–84), *Beyond Good and Evil* (1886), *On the Genealogy of Morality* (1887), and, to a lesser extent, the works of his last sane year (1888): *Twilight of the Idols*, *The Antichrist*, and *Ecce Homo*. Even the compilation made (against Nietzsche's wishes) from his notebooks after his mental collapse (in January 1889) and subsequently published as *The Will to Power* (first German edition, 1901) has received more scholarly scrutiny than *Daybreak* – a book Nietzsche intended to publish, and one that he pronounced (in late 1888) the "book [in which] my campaign against morality begins" (*Ecce Homo*, "Why I Write Such Good Books," sub-section 1 of section on *Daybreak*).[1]

---

[1] We will generally refer to Nietzsche's texts by their standard English-language acronyms: D = *Daybreak*; HA = *Human, All Too Human*; BGE = *Beyond Good and Evil*; GM = *On the Genealogy of*

This last observation is of crucial importance: for as he goes on to tell us in the same passage, *Daybreak* "seeks [a] new morning . . . [i]n a *revaluation of all values*, in a liberation from all moral values." The book, in short, marks the beginning of Nietzsche's central philosophical project: a revaluation of all values, a thorough-going critique of morality itself. It is the book that broaches "[t]he question concerning the origin of moral values" (*ibid.*), the question he returns to in *Beyond Good and Evil* (esp. Section 260) and, most famously, in the *Genealogy*. More importantly, it is the book that first develops in a substantial way themes that mark the "mature" Nietzsche: for example, his critique of the conventional view of human agency, as well as his development of a "naturalistic" conception of persons.

That it is a serious mistake to neglect *Daybreak*, and that this new edition presents a splendid opportunity for students and scholars to reconsider its central place in the corpus, we hope will become apparent in the following pages. We also hope to demonstrate how wrong-headed is the following common view of *Daybreak*, most recently expressed by the editors of *The Cambridge Companion to Nietzsche*: "Nietzsche seems bent [in *Daybreak*] on conveying a particular type of experience in thinking to his readers, much more than he is concerned to persuade his readers to adopt any particular point of view." Nietzsche's ambitions are, we will show, far more philosophically substantial, as would befit the book in which Nietzsche's "campaign against morality" begins. First, however, we must set the intellectual stage on which *Daybreak* enters.

NIETZSCHE AND NIETZSCHE'S GERMANY

The widespread pedagogic practice of treating Nietzsche as a figure of "nineteenth-century philosophy," along with Hegel and Marx, actually does considerable violence to the real intellectual history of Germany. While Hegel did dominate German philosophical life in the first quarter of the century, by 1830 his influence was waning seriously. By the 1840s and 1850s, Hegel's critics – Karl Marx, Arthur Schopenhauer, and Ludwig Feuerbach, among others – were both better known and more widely read than Hegel. By the time Nietzsche (born 1844) was being educated at the post-secondary level, it was not Hegel's Idealism that dominated the intellectual landscape, but rather Schopenhauer's own more Kantian metaphysical system, as well as the broad-based intellectual movement known as "German

Morality; EH = *Ecce Homo*. Roman numerals refer to major parts or chapters; Arabic numerals refer to sections, not pages.

Materialism," of which Feuerbach was an early figure. (There is no evidence, however, that Nietzsche ever read Marx, who was not himself part of the "Materialist" movement at issue here.) For purposes of understanding Nietzsche, the key German figures are really Kant, Schopenhauer, and the Materialists.

Nietzsche, of course, was trained not in philosophy *per se*, but in classical philology, the exacting study of the texts and cultures of the ancient world. Unlike contemporary literary theorists, nineteenth-century German classicists viewed the interpretation of texts as a *science*, whose aim was to discover what texts *really mean* through an exhaustive study of language, culture and context. Nietzsche proved a brilliant student, and was awarded a professorship in 1869, even before earning his doctorate. Yet Nietzsche was always ill-at-ease with the narrow academic horizons of professional philology. He sought to do more than solve mere scholarly "puzzles"; he wanted to connect the study of classical civilization to his far more pressing concern with the state of contemporary German culture. It was this project he undertook in *The Birth of Tragedy*, a book that was, not surprisingly, poorly received by his academic peers.

Evidence of Nietzsche's classical training and his admiration of classical civilization abounds throughout *Daybreak*. Two themes, in particular, recur. First, Nietzsche embraced the "realism" of the Sophists and Presocratics, philosophers who had the courage, in Nietzsche's view, to look reality in the eye, and report things as they really are, without euphemism or sentimentality. Nietzsche saw, with good reason, the great Greek historian Thucydides as the embodiment of this perspective on human nature and human affairs, noting that in Thucydides, "that *culture of the most impartial knowledge of the world* finds its last glorious flower: that culture which had in Sophocles its poet, in Pericles its statesman, in Hippocrates its physician, in Democritus its natural philosopher; which deserves to be baptized with the name of its teachers, the Sophists..." (168). Nietzsche himself strives to imitate Thucydides' realistic appraisal of human motivations, for example, when he observes that "egoistic" actions "have hitherto been by far the most frequent actions, and will continue to be so for all future time" (148).

Second, Nietzsche defends the "empiricism" of the Presocratics against the "idealism" of Plato; indeed he sees as fundamental to the whole history of philosophy the dispute between those who accept as the only reality what the "senses" reveal about the world and those who claim that the "real" world exists beyond the sensible world. It is clear where Nietzsche stands on this question. He rejects the "dialectic" method as a way of getting behind "the veil of appearance" – a project he attributes to Plato and Schopenhauer – noting that "For that to which they want to show us the way does not *exist*" (474). Elsewhere in *Daybreak*, he observes: "Thus did Plato flee from reality and desire to see things only in pallid mental pictures; he was full of sensibility and knew how easily the waves of his sensibility could close over his reason" (448; cf. 43). Here we see a characteristic Nietzschean move (to which we will return shortly): to explain a particular philosophical position (e.g. Plato's view that the "real" world is the world of "Forms" or "Ideas," that are inaccessible to the senses) in terms of facts about the person who advances the position (e.g. Plato's excessive sensitivity).

These critical remarks about Plato must be balanced with Nietzsche's admiration for Plato's "genius" (497). Thus, in a remark that remains apt today, Nietzsche contrasts the "Platonic dialogue" in which "souls were filled with drunkenness at the rigorous and sober game of concept, generalization, refutation, limitation" with "how philosophy is done today" in which philosophers "want to be 'artistic natures'" and to enjoy "the divine privilege of being incomprehensible" (544).

Nietzsche's engagement with the classical world marks just one of the three important intellectual influences on his philosophical writing. The other two were the philosophy of Schopenhauer and the German Materialist movement of the 1850s and 1860s. We shall discuss Schopenhauer's impact on Nietzsche in detail below in the context of *Daybreak*'s central theme, the critique of morality. Here we introduce some of the main themes of German Materialism.

German Materialism had its origins in Feuerbach's work of the late 1830s and early 1840s, but it really exploded on to the cultural scene in the 1850s, under the impetus of the startling new discoveries about human beings made by the burgeoning science of physiology. The medical doctor Ludwig Büchner summed up the Materialist point of view well in his 1855 best-seller *Force and Matter*, the book that became the "Bible" of Materialism. "The researches and discoveries of modern times," he wrote in the preface to the eighth edition, "can no longer allow us to doubt that man, with all he has and possesses, be it mental or corporeal, is a *natural product* like all other organic beings." Our evidence of Nietzsche's familiarity with the Materialists is extensive. For one thing, it is impossible that a literate young person in Germany at the time could have been *unfamiliar* with the Materialists. As one critic wrote in 1856: "A new world view is settling into the minds of men. It goes about like a virus. Every young mind of the generation now living is affected by it" (quoted in Gregory, *Scientific*

Materialism, p. 10). More concretely, we do know that Nietzsche read (with great enthusiasm) Friedrich Lange's *History of Materialism* (published 1866), a book which mounted an extensive (but sympathetic) NeoKantian critique of the Materialists. In fact, in a letter of February 1868 (quoted in Stack, *Lange and Nietzsche*, p. 13), Nietzsche called Lange's book "a real treasure-house," mentioning, among other things, Lange's discussion of the "materialist movement of our times," including the work of Feuerbach, Büchner, and the physiologists Jacob Moleschott and Herman von Helmholtz. From Lange, Nietzsche would have learned of the Materialist view that "The nature of man is ... only a special case of universal physiology, as thought is only a special case in the chain of the physical processes of life." Indeed, that he took the lesson to heart is suggested in his autobiography, *Ecce Homo*, where he tells us (in his discussion of *Human, All Too Human*) that in the late 1870s, "A truly burning thirst took hold of me: henceforth I really pursued nothing *more* than physiology, medicine and natural science." A bit earlier in the same work (11:2), he complains of the "blunder" that he "became a philologist – why not at least a physician or something else that opens one's eyes?"

Yet the most compelling evidence of the Materialist impact on Nietzsche is the extent to which Materialist themes appear in Nietzsche's work, including *Daybreak*. The Materialists embraced the idea that human beings were essentially *bodily* organisms, whose attitudes, beliefs, and values were explicable by reference to *physiological* facts about them. Spiritual, religious, and moral explanations of human beings were to be supplanted by purely physical or physiological explanations.

Thus, Moleschott's 1850 work *The Physiology of Food* contained 500 pages of detailed information about the physical and chemical properties of food and human digestion, while his popular companion volume, *The Theory of Food: For the People*, spelled out the implications of this research in terms of the different diets that different types of people need to flourish. In reviewing Moleschott's book, Feuerbach expressed the core idea as follows: "If you want to improve the people then give them better food instead of declamations against sin. Man is what he eats" (quoted in Gregory, *Scientific Materialism*, p. 92). Büchner's *Force and Matter* took a related tack, seeking to explain human character and belief systems in physiological terms. So, for example, he suggested that "A copious secretion of bile has, as is well known, a powerful influence on the mental disposition" and arguing elsewhere in the same work that it was, "Newton's atrophied brain [that] caused him in old age to become interested in studying the ... Bible."

With figures like Moleschott and Büchner ascendant on the intellectual scene, it is hardly surprising to find Nietzsche writing as follows in
Daybreak:

Whatever proceeds from the stomach, the intestines, the beating of the heart, the
nerves, the bile, the semen – all those distempers, debilitations, excitations, the
whole chance operation of the machine of which we still know so little! – had to
be seen by a Christian such as Pascal as a moral and religious phenomenon, and
he had to ask whether God or Devil, good or evil, salvation or damnation was to
be discovered in them! Oh what an unhappy interpreter. (86; cf. 83)

Like the Materialists, Nietzsche replaces "moral" or "religious" explanations
for phenomena with *naturalistic* explanations, particularly explanations
couched in physiological or quasi-physiological language. Thus, he suggests
that "Three-quarters of all the evil done in the world happens out of
timidity: and this [is] above all a physiological phenomenon" (538), and
that "our moral judgments and evaluations . . . are only images and fantasies
based on a physiological process unknown to us" (119). Indeed, he endorses,
as a general explanatory scruple, the view that "all the products of [a
person's] thinking are bound to reflect the condition he is in" (42), noting,
accordingly, that any particular philosophy "translate[s] as it were into
reason" what amounts to a "personal diet" (553).

THE CRITIQUE OF MORALITY

The central theme of *Daybreak* is its attack on morality. The attack proceeds
essentially along two fronts. First, Nietzsche takes traditional morality to
involve *false* presuppositions: for example, a *false* picture of human agency
(roughly, the view that human beings act autonomously or freely, and thus
are morally responsible for what they do). He attacks this picture of agency
from the perspective of a *naturalistic* view of persons as *determined* in their
actions by the fundamental physiological and psychological facts about
them. Second, he takes traditional morality to be inhospitable to certain
types of human flourishing. This second theme, which is less prominent
than the first, is voiced at various points in *Daybreak*: for example, when
Nietzsche complains that morality entails "a fundamental remoulding,
indeed weakening and abolition of the individual" (132), a result of the fact
that "morality is nothing other . . . than obedience to customs" (9), and
thus is incompatible with a "free human being . . . [who] is *determined* to
depend upon himself and not upon a tradition" (9). A variation on this
criticism is also apparent when he observes (*contra* Rousseau) that "Our

weak unmanly, social concepts of good and evil and their tremendous ascendancy over body and soul have finally weakened all bodies and souls and snapped the self-reliant, independent, unprejudiced men, the pillars of a *strong* civilization . . ." (164). The view that morality poses a special threat to human *excellence* or *greatness* is one that will become more prominent in Nietzsche's later works, though it remains visible in this early book as well.

Yet the crux of the argument in *Daybreak* is directed at the problematic presuppositions of morality. As he writes in an important passage on two different ways of "denying" morality:

"To deny morality" – this can mean, *first*: to deny that the moral motives which men *claim* have inspired their actions really have done so – it is thus the assertion that morality consists of words and is among the coarser or more subtle deceptions (especially self-deceptions) which men practise . . . *Then* it can mean: to deny that moral judgments are based on truths. Here it is admitted that they really are motives of action, but that in this way it is *errors* which, as the basis of all moral judgment, impel men to their moral actions. This is *my* point of view: though I should be the last to deny that *in very many cases* there is some ground for suspicion that the other point of view – that is to say, the point of view of La Rochefoucauld and others who think like him – may also be justified and in any event of great general application.

Thus I deny morality as I deny alchemy, that is, I deny their presuppositions [*die Voraussetzungen*, which might also be translated "premises"]: *not* that countless people *feel* themselves to be immoral, but there is any *true* reason so to feel. It goes without saying that I do not deny – unless I am a fool – that many actions called . . . moral ought to be done and encouraged – but I think the one should be encouraged and the other avoided *for other reasons than hitherto*. We have to *learn to think differently* – in order at last, perhaps very late on, to attain even more: *to feel differently*. (D 103)

This important passage is of great value in understanding the argument of *Daybreak*, and we shall have more to say about it, below. Note now, however, the crucial analogy Nietzsche draws between his attack on "morality" and a comparable attack on alchemy. When we deny *alchemy* we don't deny that "countless people" believed themselves to be alchemists, that is, believed themselves to be engaged in the process of transforming the base metals into gold. Rather, we deny a presupposition of their undertaking: namely (to put it in modern terms) the presupposition that the application of forces to the macro-properties of substances can effect a transformation in their micro-properties (i.e. their molecular constitution). So to "deny" morality in a similar fashion is not to deny that people act for *moral* reasons or that they take *morality* seriously, but to "deny" that the reasons for which they do so are sound: the *presuppositions* of morality are as wrong-headed as the presuppositions of alchemy.

We return, below, to the crucial question of what are the "presuppositions" of morality in Nietzsche's sense. Before we do so, however, we will sketch those features of the moral philosophies of Kant and Schopenhauer against the background of which Nietzsche came to understand morality as having false presuppositions.

KANT AND SCHOPENHAUER ON MORALITY

According to Kant and Schopenhauer, actions are praiseworthy from the viewpoint of morality only when done from a moral motive. But these philosophers disagree about the character of moral motivation and therefore about which actions have the special kind of value they both call "moral worth" (or "ethical significance," as Schopenhauer sometimes says).

Kant and Schopenhauer agree that an action is devoid of moral worth if it is motivated purely by a desire for the agent's own happiness. But Kant goes further, claiming that desiring the happiness of others "stands on the same footing as other inclinations" and cannot therefore give moral worth to actions (G 398/66).[2] His reasoning seems to be that the desire for the happiness of another cannot give an action moral worth if the desire for one's own happiness clearly does not. Inclinations and desires may deserve praise and encouragement, but never esteem, the mark of the moral.

Kant considers duty to be the only reasonable alternative to desire or inclination as the source of moral worth. To have moral worth an action must be done from the motive of duty. This means that it is done because one recognizes that one ought to perform the action and that the action is "objectively necessary in itself" regardless of one's own desires or ends (G 414/82). The action is thus motivated by the recognition of a categorical imperative.

If one recognizes an ought statement as a hypothetical imperative, in contrast, one recognizes only a conditioned necessity, the necessity of an action for the achievement of some further end. The shopkeeper recognizes that he ought not cheat his customers because they will buy from his competitors if he does. The necessity he recognizes is thus conditioned by

---

[2] Kant's *Grundlegung zur Metaphysic der Sitten* is cited as "G" followed by the page number in the Academy edition and the page number in H. J. Paton's translation: *The Moral Law: Kant's Groundwork of the Metaphysic of Morals* (London: Hutchinson and Co., 1958).

his own end or desire: to run a successful business. In this case, the necessity of the commanded action can be escaped if he abandons the end or purpose, whereas this is not so in the case of a categorical imperative – the necessity it formulates is not dependent on any of the agent's purposes. There is one purpose Kant thinks we cannot abandon, for "we can assume with certainty that all *do* have [it] by natural necessity": our own happiness. Yet imperatives that affirm the practical necessity of an action as a means to the furtherance of happiness – imperatives of prudence – still count as hypothetical rather than categorical: "an action is commended not absolutely, but only as a means to a further purpose" (G 416/83). To act from the motive of duty, according to Kant, is to act out of reverence for the law: to be motivated sufficiently to perform an action by the recognition of its objective or unconditioned necessity.

Schopenhauer denies that Kant's idea of "objective necessity" adds to our understanding of morality, calling it "nothing but a cleverly concealed and very forced paraphrase of the word *ought*" (BM 67).[3] Arguing that "every *ought* derives all sense and meaning simply and solely in reference to threatened punishment or promised reward" (BM 55), he further denies that the recognition of an ought ever involves "unconditioned necessity." The Kantian notions of absolute obligation, law, and duty are derived from theology, he claims, and have no sense or content at all apart from the assumption of a God who gives the law (BM 68). For we simply can make no sense of the idea of law, and thus of how a law could confer on us duties or obligations, unless we regard obedience as promising reward and disobedience as threatening punishment. Even if we assume that God has laid down a law, Schopenhauer would refuse it moral status. Because even a divine command would acquire the status of law only by being able to promise reward and threaten punishment, it could only be a hypothetical imperative. "Obedience to it is, of course, wise or foolish according to circumstances; yet it will always be selfish, and consequently without moral value" (BM 55).

According to Schopenhauer, then, an ought statement never counts as a categorical imperative or moral judgment, but can only be what Kant would have called a "judgment of prudence." An action performed for the sake of duty, simply because one recognizes that one ought to do it, is selfish rather

---

[3] Schopenhauer's *Die beiden Grundprobleme der Ethik* is cited as "BM," followed by the page number in the translation by E. F. J. Payne: *On the Basis of Morality* (Indianapolis: Bobbs-Merrill, 1965). Schopenhauer's *Die Welt als Wille und Vorstellung* is cited as "WW," followed by the volume and page number in the translation by E. F. J. Payne: *The World as Will and Representation* (New York: Dover, 1966).

than morally motivated. Schopenhauer thus argues against Kant within the latter's own terms. If Kant accepted Schopenhauer's motivational claim – which he in fact explicitly rejects – that "nothing can induce us to obey except *fear* of the evil consequences of *disobedience*" (BM 142), he would have to admit either that there are no morally motivated actions, or that he had characterized them incorrectly.

The latter choice seemed obvious to Schopenhauer, who believed that few "are not convinced from their own experience that a man often acts justly, simply and solely that no wrong or injustice may be done to another," and that many of us help others with no intention in our hearts other than helping those whose distress we see (BM 138–39). It is to such actions, he claims, that we attribute "real *moral worth*," and they are motivated not by what Kant called "duty," but by compassion, "the immediate *participation*, independent of all ulterior considerations, primarily in the *suffering* of another, and thus in the prevention or elimination of it" (BM 144).

The "ulterior considerations" Schopenhauer regards as incompatible with compassion, and thus with moral worth, are egoistic concerns, concerns for one's own well-being. Schopenhauer agrees with Kant that if an action "has as its motive an egoistic aim, it cannot have any moral worth" (BM 141). Unlike Kant, he does not infer from this that concern for another's happiness cannot give actions moral worth. From the premise that "*egoism* and the *moral* worth of an action absolutely exclude each other," he infers instead that "the moral significance of an action can only lie in its reference to others" (BM 142). He draws this conclusion by way of the claim that the will is moved only by considerations of well-being or suffering. If moral worth does not belong to actions motivated by a concern for one's own well-being or suffering, it must belong to actions motivated by a concern for the well-being and suffering of others.

How then would Schopenhauer answer Kant's implied question as to how concern for others' well-being can give an action moral worth when concern for one's own well-being does not? He could not claim that the sphere of other-regarding behavior simply is the sphere of morality, and thus that only other-regarding behavior is properly called "moral." Neither Schopenhauer nor Kant can regard the issue about moral worth that separates them to be simply a matter of what something is called. Both philosophers assume that moral worth is a higher kind of worth – than, say, intellectual worth, aesthetic worth, or prudential value – and Kant describes moral worth as "that pre-eminent good which we call moral" (G 401/69). Schopenhauer claims not simply that we *call* acting for another's sake "moral," but that so acting has a higher value than acting for one's own sake.

To answer Kant's question he must therefore show that there is a difference between these two kinds of motives that justifies the claim that one is of a higher value than the other. Though Schopenhauer never explicitly tries to answer this question, the kind of answer provided by his theory seems clear: it would be given in terms of his conception of the thing-in-itself.

The distinction between appearances (the "phenomenal" or "sensible" world) and the thing-in-itself (the "noumenal" world) – that is, the distinction between the world as it appears to us and the world as it really is "in-itself" – plays an important role in the moral theories of both Kant and Schopenhauer. In each case, the motive claimed to give moral worth to actions is also claimed to have its source in the noumenal world.

For Kant, all inclinations and desires belong to the phenomenal world – they are the "appearances" in terms of which human actions, insofar as we encounter them in the "sensible world," the world accessible to sense observation, are explained and made intelligible. If human beings belonged solely to the world of appearances, all of their actions "would have to be taken as in complete conformity with the laws of nature governing desires and inclinations" (G 453/121).

Kant's claim that concern for the happiness of others "stands on the same footing as other inclinations" therefore means that it belongs to the world of appearances, that actions motivated by it are merely natural, that they are fully explicable in terms of our status as natural creatures, members of the phenomenal world. That this seems sufficient for Kant to dismiss it as a moral motive suggests that Schopenhauer was right to attribute to him the view he attributed to most philosophers:

It is undeniably recognized by all nations, ages, and creeds, and even by all philosophers (with the exception of the materialists proper), that the ethical significance of human conduct is metaphysical, in other words, that it reaches beyond this phenomenal existence and touches eternity. (BM 54)

This is why Schopenhauer rejects Kant's view of moral worth: if recognizing that one ought to perform an action is always conditioned by fear of punishment or the desire for reward, acting from duty has no metaphysical significance, and therefore no moral worth. Kant would have to agree if he agreed about the role of reward and punishment in the recognition of duty – for he accepts the same principle: whatever belongs only to the phenomenal world cannot be the source of moral worth. That is why he rejects moral theories like Schopenhauer's that locate the source of moral worth in sympathetic concern for others: he regards such concern as rooted in natural inclination, and therefore as devoid of metaphysical significance.

Acting out of reverence for the law, in contrast, does have metaphysical significance for Kant – for it involves recognizing as law the commands of the noumenal self. Although Kant denies that we can have knowledge of the thing-in-itself, he argues that we can make sense of morality only if we take human beings as they are "in-themselves" as autonomous, as legislators of universal law. To act morally is to act out of reverence for the law legislated by the noumenal self – the "true self," one is tempted to say. For Kant the noumenal source of the motive of duty bestows on actions an incomparably higher worth than could come from mere inclination (or anything else that belongs only to the phenomenal or natural world).

Schopenhauer had his own ideas regarding the thing-in-itself with which to counter Kant's suggestion that concern for others is of no more value than other inclinations. He believed that Kant had already shown that time and space do not belong to the thing-in-itself, and therefore that individuality and plurality are foreign to the "true essence of the world" (BM 207). Individuality is only the appearance in time and space of the thing-in-itself, which, in complete opposition to Kant, Schopenhauer took to be blindly striving will (the forerunner, perhaps, of Freud's id). To the extent that we fail to recognize our individuality as mere appearance, we are moved to action only by egoistic concerns. We see the world completely in terms of how it affects our own well-being. If we care about the welfare of others, this is due not to our natural inclinations, but only to the recognition in others of something that lies beyond nature, of our "own self," our "own true inner nature" (BM 209). Schopenhauer again stays within Kant's own terms: compassion, immediate concern for the welfare of another, possesses a higher worth than egoistic inclinations because, rather than being part of our natural equipment, it is a sign of our connection to a reality that goes beyond the phenomenal or natural world. This is basically the same claim Kant makes about the motive of duty. To have moral worth, Schopenhauer and Kant thus agree, actions must be motivated by something of higher value than egoistic concern, something that is rooted in a realm beyond the natural world. They disagree about moral worth because they hold very different views about which human motive is rooted in the noumenal world.

FROM *HUMAN, ALL TOO HUMAN* TO *DAYBREAK*

In *Human, All Too Human*, the work preceding *Daybreak*, Nietzsche began a long effort to free morality from the metaphysical world to which Kant and Schopenhauer had connected it. He set out to show that one need not posit the existence of such a world to explain the so-called "higher" activities – art, religion, and morality – which are often taken as signs of human participation in a higher or metaphysical realm (HA 10). He wanted to explain these "higher" things in terms of the "lower," the merely human. The book's title, he writes in *Ecce Homo*, meant: "'where you see ideal things, I see what is – human, alas, all-too-human!' – I know man better." In this book, Nietzsche continues,

you discover a merciless spirit that knows all the hideouts where the ideal is at home... One error after another is coolly placed on ice; the ideal is not refuted – it *freezes* to death. – Here, for example, "the genius" freezes to death; at the next corner, "the saint"; under a huge icicle, "the hero"; in the end, "faith," so-called "conviction"; "pity" also cools down considerably – and almost everywhere "the thing in itself" freezes to death. (EH III: HA 1)

The ideals Nietzsche places on ice are idealizations, beliefs that certain kinds of persons, activities, or states of mind exceed the standard of the merely human. "The saint" counts as an ideal because saints have been thought to represent "something that exceeded the human standard of goodness and wisdom" (HA 143). Nietzsche places this ideal on ice by showing it to involve an error. He isolates the characteristics regarded as elevating saints above the human standard and explains them as expressions of egoistic drives to which no one would attribute an ideal character. For instance, he explains their self-denial and asceticism in such terms as the lust for power and the desire to excite an exhausted nervous system (HA 135–42).

Applying the same method of "psychological observation" or "reflection on the human, all-too-human" (HA 35) throughout the book, Nietzsche explains many other idealized activities or types in terms of psychological needs that he considers egoistic and merely human. The ultimate effect of this procedure, he says, may be to lay an axe "to the root of the human 'metaphysical need'" (HA 37). Even though "there might be a metaphysical world" (HA 9), if we can explain the so-called higher aspects of human life without positing anything beyond the natural world, "the strongest interest in the purely theoretical problem of the 'thing in itself' and the 'appearance' will cease" (HA 10). If the human world can be explained without the assumption of a metaphysical world, the latter will be of no cognitive interest to us. We can say of it only that it is other than our world – an inaccessible, incomprehensible "being-other,... a thing with negative qualities" (HA 9).

In view of the importance of the noumenal world to the moral theories of Kant and Schopenhauer, we should expect Nietzsche's attack on ideals in

Human, All Too Human to involve a rejection of both. Kant does not play much of a role, however, for, as the following passage suggests, Nietzsche had accepted his "great teacher" (GM: P5) Schopenhauer's criticism of Kant's theory.

For there is no longer any *ought*; for morality, insofar as it was an *ought*, has been just as much annihilated by our mode of thinking as has religion. Knowledge can allow as motives only pleasure and pain, utility and injury. (HA 34)

Nietzsche presumably bases this denial of moral *oughts* on Schopenhauer's argument against Kant's categorical imperative – that a command or rule receives its force as an ought only from an egoistic concern with one's own pleasure or pain, advantage or injury. Schopenhauer's view entails that a belief in *moral* oughts depends on misunderstanding the way in which rules and commands affect behavior. If we realized that people feel obliged to obey them only because of egoistic concerns, we would not think of them as having a kind of *moral* force and thereby misinterpret them as *moral* oughts or categorical imperatives. Following out this line of argument and reflecting on the self-serving origins of just actions, Nietzsche writes (HA 92): "How little moral would the world appear without forgetfulness!" Because *Human, All Too Human* attempts to exhibit the egoistic concerns lying behind our feelings of being obliged to do something, Nietzsche could expect it to undermine our sense that oughts have *moral* force and lead us to agree with Schopenhauer, that obedience to them can only be judged as either "wise or foolish," according to the circumstances.

Schopenhauer had used this argument to support his own view of moral motivation and worth – that compassion, the one non-egoistic motive, rather than Kant's motive of duty, gives moral worth to actions. Nietzsche turns the same kind of argument against Schopenhauer in *Human, All Too Human*. Compassion[4] too can be explained in terms of what is egoistic, or human, all too human:

For it conceals within itself at least two (perhaps many more) elements of personal pleasure, and is to that extent self-enjoyment: first as the pleasure of emotion, which is the kind represented by pity in tragedy, and then, when it eventuates in action, as the pleasure of gratification in the exercise of power. If, in addition to this, a suffering person is very close to us, we rid ourselves of our own suffering by performing an act of pity [or: through compassionate actions]. Apart from a

---

[4] In the following passage, the German word *Mitleid* has been translated as "pity," following the normal practice among translators of Nietzsche, but this is the same word translators of Schopenhauer render as "compassion."

few philosophers, human beings have always placed pity very low on the scale of moral feelings – and rightly so. (HA 103)

The opposition Nietzsche accepts between the moral and the egoistic should actually lead him to a more radical conclusion: that there are no moral actions. For he claims:

No one has ever done anything that was solely for the sake of another and without a personal motive. How indeed *could* he do anything that was not related to himself, thus without an inner necessity (which simply must have its basis in a personal need)? How could the *ego* act without *ego*? (HA 133)

Nietzsche's rhetorical question combined with his claim in the same passage that the whole idea of an "unegoistic action" vanishes upon "close examination," suggests that he considers the whole idea of an unegoistic action unintelligible. That Nietzsche's position is in any case a form of psychological egoism becomes even more obvious when he goes on to quote with approval Lichtenberg and La Rochefoucauld to the effect that we do not really love others – "neither father, nor mother, nor wife, nor child" – but only "the pleasant feelings they cause us" (HA 133). We do not even love others, much less act solely for their sake. As we love only the satisfaction of our own interests, we always act for our own sake. If so, and if, as Nietzsche and Schopenhauer agree, actions cannot be both moral and egoistic, there are no moral actions.

Recall that Schopenhauer views the moral significance of conduct as "metaphysical" in the sense that it "reaches beyond this phenomenal existence" and "directly touch[es] the thing-in-itself" (WW I:422). Because egoistic motives are fully comprehensible in terms of the phenomenal world, they have no moral worth. Unegoistic motives, in contrast, spring from "the immediate knowledge of the numerical identity of the inner nature of all living things" (WW II:609) – an identity which is completely inaccessible to empirical knowledge and is therefore not to be found in the phenomenal world. Moral worth attaches to such motives precisely because they point beyond the phenomenal world to the thing-in-itself.

Schopenhauer's assumption of the "numerical identity" of all living things is among the metaphysical assumptions Nietzsche wanted to show we could dispense with in *Human, All Too Human*. This book began his task of "translat[ing] human beings back into nature" (BG 230), and his first problem was to show that so-called "unegoistic" actions could be so translated. But Schopenhauer's world-view (unlike Kant's) had no room for a natural unegoistic action: actions done for the sake of another have moral significance, which they could not have if they were comprehensible in terms of a natural relation between individuals, which would belong only to the phenomenal world. Schopenhauer recognizes only two kinds of motivation – the egoistic motivation human beings have insofar as they act as individuals, hence as members of the phenomenal or natural world, and the motivation they acquire by seeing through the natural or phenomenal world to the metaphysical unity underlying it. Under Schopenhauer's influence, Nietzsche assumed that explaining human behavior naturalistically (i.e., non-metaphysically) meant explaining it egoistically. Accepting Schopenhauer's account of the natural or phenomenal world, he simply denied that it had any connection to a metaphysical world. *Human, All Too Human*'s psychological egoism amounts to a claim that we can explain human behavior without appeal to a reality lying beyond the natural or phenomenal world, combined with Schopenhauer's assumption that all motivation in the latter world is egoistic.

Looking back on *Human, All Too Human*, Nietzsche claimed to find in it a more important issue than the existence of unegoistic actions. This issue "was the *value* of morality."

> In particular the issue was the *value* of the unegoistic, of the instincts of compassion, self-denial, self-sacrifice, which Schopenhauer had gilded, deified, and made otherworldly until finally they alone were left for him as "values in themselves," on the basis of which he *said No* to life, also to himself. (GM: P5)

Nietzsche claims to have seen in the unegoistic instincts Schopenhauer had deified "the great danger to humanity . . . the will turning itself against life, the last sickness gently and melancholically announcing itself." If such a challenge to Schopenhauer's values is present in *Human, All Too Human*, however, it is well hidden. On the surface, it appears that Nietzsche rejects Schopenhauer's view that unegoistic actions exist, but completely agrees with him about their higher value.

Consider that the book's basic strategy for exhibiting the error involved in attributing a higher value to certain types of behavior is to explain them in egoistic terms. These explanations can seem to reveal the error involved in such judgments only if one assumes that a belief in the higher value of a type of behavior depends on interpreting it as unegoistic. Yet Nietzsche offers no reason to think that it does, and never questions why unegoistic behavior should be so highly valued. He seems simply to take for granted that the unegoistic is of high value, the egoistic of low value, and therefore that demonstrating an action's egoistic nature undermines its claim to high value. Rather than challenging Schopenhauer on the value of unegoistic actions, *Human, All Too Human* seems to argue that nothing possessing the higher value that an unegoistic action would have actually makes its appearance in the human world.

In *Daybreak*, by contrast, we can begin to see the shift in Nietzsche's strategy: he explicitly raises the question about the *value* of unegoistic actions, at the same time that he begins to move away from the psychological egoism of *Human, All Too Human*. Thus, while still conceding (in the spirit of *Human, All Too Human*) that egoistic actions "have hitherto been by far the most frequent actions, and will continue to be for all future time," he suggests – contrary to Kant and Schopenhauer – that we should "restore to these actions their *value*" and thus "*deprive them of their bad conscience*" (D 148). As he explains later, the *value* of "*ideal selfishness*" (as he calls it) is a matter of its role in human flourishing: "continually to watch over and care for and to keep our soul still, so that our fruitfulness shall *come to a happy fulfillment*" (D 552). And he now treats the fact that "men today feel the sympathetic, disinterested, generally useful social actions to be the *moral* actions" as a mere artifact of Christianity, "a residuum of Christian states of mind" (D 132).

Daybreak's repudiation of the thoroughgoing psychological egoism of *Human, All Too Human* is clearest in the important passage on "two ways of denying morality" (D 103), quoted earlier. As we saw, the denial of morality Nietzsche endorses in this passage differs from one "in the spirit of La Rochefoucauld" because Nietzsche admits that human beings do sometimes act from moral motives. In citing La Rochefoucauld, Nietzsche clearly alludes to the egoism of *Human, All Too Human* (see HA 133) which, by way of the equivalence between "moral" and "unegoistic," had implied the non-existence of moral motives. The passage (D 103) thus functions to separate Nietzsche's new position from his earlier one: he no longer denies the existence of morally motivated actions, but claims instead that these actions, when they occur, are based on erroneous presuppositions. In admitting that a suspicion in accord with La Rochefoucauld's way of denying morality is called for "*in very many cases*," the passage also indicates that Nietzsche continues to hold that morally motivated actions cannot be egoistic. Because he now wants to admit that people are sometimes morally motivated, he evidently must also admit that their actions can be in some sense unegoistic.

That *Human, All Too Human* and *Daybreak* thus involve two different ways of denying morality allows us to understand why Nietzsche calls *Daybreak* the beginning of his "campaign against morality." On the topic of morality, *Daybreak* can seem very similar to its predecessor, and Nietzsche's interpreters have seen little difference between them. The claims of HA 39–40, that morality is an "error" and a "lie," sound similar to the denial of morality announced in D 103. Yet, as D 103 also suggests, there is a crucial difference. *Human, All Too Human* labels as "lie" and "error" not morality, but the belief that human beings act from moral motives. It directs its polemic against this belief – and, ultimately, against a world it perceived as "human, alas, all-too-human." Only when *Daybreak* admits the existence of moral motivation can Nietzsche begin his actual campaign against morality. Rather than denying that morally motivated actions exist, he now claims that the presuppositions of such actions are erroneous.

MORALITY'S FALSE PRESUPPOSITIONS I

A false picture of agency

But what are these presuppositions? *Daybreak* suggests that they are of two types: first, a certain picture of human agents as free and morally responsible (a *logical* presupposition, as it were of morality and moral judgment); second, false beliefs (or superstitions) that explain the *moral* regard with which ancient practices and customs were regarded and that function as *causal* presuppositions of people's "moral" feelings in the present. We shall briefly illustrate both themes in *Daybreak*.

Recall Nietzsche's analogy between the denial of morality and alchemy (103). Nietzsche develops the same analogy several years later in *Beyond Good and Evil*, where he writes that:

morality in the traditional sense, the morality of intentions, was a prejudice, precipitate and perhaps provisional – something on the order of astrology and alchemy . . . [T]he decisive value of an action lies precisely in what is *unintentional* in it, while everything that is intentional, everything about it that can be seen, known, "conscious," still belongs to its surface and skin – which, like every skin, betrays something but *conceals* even more. (32)

Here Nietzsche agrees with one premise of the "morality of intentions" – the premise that "the origin of an action . . . allows [one] to decide its value" (*ibid.*) – but is denying the premise that the origin is to be found in the conscious intention: what people do is determined by *non-conscious* factors (psychological and physiological), rather than the conscious motives of which we are aware. Insofar as people assess the moral value of an action in terms of its conscious motives – as both Kant and Schopenhauer would have us do – they make moral judgments based on a false presupposition: the supposition that the conscious motive is the *cause* of the action.

Nietzsche makes this point several times in *Daybreak* (cf. 115, 116, 119, 129, 130). For example, he notes that,

The primeval delusion still lives on that one knows, and knows quite precisely in every case, *how human action is brought about*... "I know what I want, what I have done, I am free and responsible for it, I hold others responsible, I can call by its name every moral possibility and every inner motion which precedes action..." – that is how everyone formerly thought, that is how almost everyone still thinks... Actions are *never* what they appear to us to be! We have expended so much labour on learning that external things are not as they appear to us to be – very well! the case is the same with the inner world! Moral actions are in reality "something other than that" – more we cannot say: and all actions are essentially unknown. (116)

But if moral judgment requires that we know how human action *is* brought about, then the impossibility of doing that means that our practice of moral judgment is predicated on an error: we believe we can assess the "morality" of our own and others' actions, but in fact we cannot, because we are ignorant as to their true causes.

Yet why, for Nietzsche, is it so difficult to understand what causes us to do what we do? In this regard, it is important to appreciate Nietzsche's picture of human agency, one that very much anticipates the picture later developed with great precision by Freud. As Nietzsche writes:

However far a man may go in self-knowledge, nothing however can be more incomplete than his image of the totality of *drives* which constitute his being. He can scarcely name even the cruder ones: their number and strength, their ebb and flood, their play and counterplay among one another and above all the laws of their *nutriment* remain wholly unknown to him. (119)

Who we are is a "totality of drives" and what we do is a function of "their play and counterplay." But these drives are so various, so deeply seated, and their triggers (their "nutriments") so poorly understood that who we are and why we do what we do must remain largely mysterious to us. That this is Nietzsche's view is strikingly apparent a few sections earlier in his discussion of the different ways in which a person might attain "mastery" of a drive or instinct (e.g. a particularly strong sex drive). After reviewing six possible "methods" for conquering such a drive, he comments as follows:

[T]hat one *desires* to combat the vehemence of a drive at all, however, does not stand within our own power; nor does the choice of any particular method; nor does the success or failure of this method. What is clearly the case is that in this entire procedure our intellect is only the blind instrument of *another drive* which is a *rival* of the drive whose vehemence is tormenting us: whether it be the drive

to restfulness, or the fear of disgrace and other evil consequences, or love. While "we" believe we are complaining about the vehemence of a drive, at bottom it is one drive *which is complaining about another*, that is to say: for us to become aware that we are suffering from the *vehemence* of a drive presupposes the existence of another equally vehement or even more vehement drive, and that a *struggle* is in prospect in which our intellect is going to have to take sides. (109)

Whereas the conventional "moralist" believes that we freely choose our actions, that the motives for which we choose these actions are known, and that, accordingly, the moral worth of our actions can be assessed, Nietzsche suggests that this entire picture of action is a false one: we do not freely choose our action (we are mere "spectators" on the struggle between drives); we do not know the "motives" for which we act (what determines our actions are the underlying drives and the outcome of their "struggle"); and thus, insofar as moral worth depends on this (discredited) picture of action, the presuppositions of morality are false. This is not to deny that there might be good reasons to condemn those who, e.g., murder (cf. 103); Nietzsche's point is just that condemning them because they freely chose to act on the basis of an immoral motive is *not* a good reason, supposing as it does an utterly fictitious picture of human action.

MORALITY'S FALSE PRESUPPOSITIONS II

The morality of custom

There is another way, though, in which the "presuppositions" of morality are errors, one somewhat more complex than the first. This also marks the new element in *Daybreak*. In *Human, All Too Human*, Nietzsche had already denied that human agents are free and morally responsible, and had taken this to undermine judgments of moral worth (HA 39, 107). But recall that he had also denied that anyone is ever morally motivated, and that *Daybreak's* new "denial of morality" is predicated upon his changing his mind on this issue. He now admits that human beings are sometimes morally motivated, but insists that when they are, errors move them to their actions (D 103). The key to understanding Nietzsche's new view is to appreciate the important role he now finds for "custom" (*Sitte*) in the phenomenon of morality. Early on in *Daybreak*, he broaches this theme:

In comparison with the mode of life of whole millennia we present-day men live in a very immoral [*unsittlich*] age: the power of custom [*Sitte*] is astonishingly enfeebled and the sense of morality [*Sittlichkeit*] so rarefied and lofty it may be described as having more or less evaporated. This is why the fundamental insights into the origins of morality [*Moral*] are so difficult for us latecomers . . . This is, for example, already the case with the *chief proposition*: morality [*Sittlichkeit*] is nothing other (therefore *no more!*) than obedience to customs [*Sitten*], of whatever kind they may be; customs, however, are the *traditional* way of behaving and evaluating. In things in which no tradition commands there is no morality . . .

The free human being is immoral because in all things he *is determined* to depend upon himself and not upon a tradition . . . Judged by the standards of these conditions, if an action is performed *not* because tradition commands it, but for other motives (because of its usefulness to the individual, for instance) . . . it is called immoral and felt to be so by the individual who performed it . . .

What is tradition? A higher authority which one obeys, not because it commands what is *useful* to us, but simply because it *commands*. – What distinguishes this feeling in the presence of tradition from the feeling of fear in general? It is fear in the presence of a higher intellect which here commands, of an incomprehensible, indefinite power, of something more than personal – there is *superstition* in this fear. (D 9)

Here we have an account of the origin of morality (*Moral*) inspired by the etymological connection between "*Sittlichkeit*" (morality) and "*Sitte*" (custom). This connection suggests to Nietzsche the plausible hypothesis that customs constituted the first morality, that traditional ways of acting played the same role during early human life that "rarefied and lofty" moral codes, rules, and principles play today: that is, they provided the criteria for moral right and wrong. But being moral, Nietzsche emphasizes, required acting from a specific motive: the motive of "obedience to tradition."

There is a striking resonance here with Kant's notion that actions possessing moral worth are done out of respect or reverence for the moral law:

What I recognize immediately as law for me, I recognize with reverence, which means merely *subordination* of my will to a law without mediation of external influences on my senses. Immediate determination by the law and consciousness of this determination is called "*reverence*" . . . Reverence is properly awareness of a value that demolishes my self-love. Hence there is something which is regarded neither as an object of inclination nor as an object of fear, though it has at the same time some analogy with both . . . All moral *interest*, so-called, consists solely in reverence for the law. (G 401/69)

Despite a slight difference in terminology, Nietzsche's description of the most primitive form of moral motivation closely follows Kant's description of reverence. Kant's "reverence for the law" in effect becomes "obedience to tradition," while Kant's "immediate determination by" and "subordination of my will to a law without mediation" becomes obedience to "a higher authority... not because it commands what it would be *useful* for one to do, but simply because it commands." The difference in terminology, importantly, is traceable to Schopenhauer's critique of Kant. For among Schopenhauer's many formulations of his basic objection to Kant's account of moral worth, we find the complaint that what Kant calls "reverence" [*Achtung*] is in German called "obedience" [*Gehorsam*], and the claim that only fear can induce human beings "to obey some absolute command that comes from an admittedly unknown but obviously superior authority" (BM 67, 142). In these terms Schopenhauer had already stripped Kant's reverence for the law of its metaphysical connections. That Nietzsche uses almost exactly the same terms to describe what he takes to be the earliest form of moral motivation provides overwhelming evidence that he is taking Kant's conception of morality and, as it were, *naturalizing* it, so that he can tell a story about the origin of morality *without* invoking a "noumenal" world or any other suspect metaphysical categories. Morality consists, in effect, of "categorical imperatives" – imperatives that apply regardless of the agent's particular ends – but these imperatives are originally found, Nietzsche thinks, in the customary practices and obedience to a "higher authority" that constitute a tradition.[5]

But why does Nietzsche claim that the presuppositions of the morality of custom are false? On his picture, an imperative commanded by "tradition" has "categorical" or "moral" force only for those persons who have a suitably reverent or submissive attitude toward the tradition. The question then is: what sustains such an attitude? In D 9, Nietzsche suggests it is a certain sort of superstitious "fear" – not the fear of specific punishment that Schopenhauer imagines to lie at the root of all imperatives, but perhaps something more like the "irresistible fear" that Freud claims maintains both primitive taboos and the obsessional prohibitions of neurotics: "No external threat of punishment is required, for there is an internal certainty, a moral conviction, that any violation will lead to intolerable disaster." If the individual is able to articulate anything about this disaster, Freud adds, it is at most "the undefined feeling that some particular person in his

---

[5] Notice that this naturalization of Kant leads Nietzsche to part company with Schopenhauer's critique of Kant. For Schopenhauer, as we saw earlier, claimed that the real motive for obedience to an imperative was always egoistic, e.g., fear of punishment. Yet in the "morality of custom" (as described in D 9), moral behavior involves obedience to custom; it is precisely the *egoist*, from this perspective, who is *immoral*, who acts not out of "reverence" for the tradition but based on considerations of "usefulness to the individual." So Nietzsche's naturalized version of Kant's reverence for the law is *not* an egoistic motive, contrary to Schopenhauer.

environment will be injured as a result of the violation."[6] In D 9, Nietzsche similarly remarks that in a morality of custom, "punishment for breaches of custom will fall before all on the community: that supernatural punishment whose forms of expression and limitations are so hard to comprehend and are explored with so much superstitious fear."

Importantly, Nietzsche continues in the very next passage (D 10) by observing that:

> In the same measure as the sense for causality increases, the extent of the domain of morality [*Sittlichkeit*] decreases: for each time one has understood the necessary effects and has learned how to segregate them from all the accidental effects and incidental consequences (*post hoc*), one has destroyed a countless number of *imaginary causalities* hitherto believed in as the foundation of customs – the real world is much smaller than the imaginary – and each time a piece of anxiety and constraint has vanished from the world, each time too a piece of respect [*Achtung*] for the authority of custom; morality as a whole has suffered a diminution. Whoever wants to increase it must know how to prevent the results from being *subject to control.* (D 10)

Nietzsche thus claims that "respect for the authority of customs" is maintained by a belief in "*imaginary causalities*" – an irrational belief or superstition, as in the case of Freud's obsessional neurotics, that something bad will happen if customs are not followed, unaccompanied by any specific idea of what will happen or how it is related to the violation of custom. Reverence for the authority of customs depends on a belief in supernatural connections, on the "outcome of an action [being] not a consequence but a free supplement – [ultimately] God's . . . The action and its outcome had to be worked at separately, with quite different means and practices!" (D 12)

But once the natural causal connection between a proscribed action and its result is discovered, the proscription loses its higher authority. If the individual recognizes that an action is to be avoided because of a harmful consequence, the latter is regarded as the action's own result, rather than something added on to it by a supernatural power. In that case, Nietzsche agrees with Schopenhauer that the agent acts from an egoistic fear of consequences, not from a moral motive. No longer regarded as the command of a higher power, the custom has lost it moral force, and the agent no longer acts from the moral motive that Kant called "reverence," which, on Nietzsche's account, is a superstitious fear not of specific consequences, but of a higher power that controls all consequences.

---

[6] Sigmund Freud, *Totem and Taboo: Some Points of Agreement between the Mental Lives of Savages and Neurotics,* James Strachey, tr. (New York: W. W. Norton and Company, 1950), pp. 26–27.

The false presuppositions of this "morality of custom," then, are beliefs in imaginary causalities and supernatural powers which confer on customs "moral" or "categorical" status by inducing a feeling of reverence toward them: so morality depends, *causally* as it were, on these psychological facts about human beings (i.e., their being in the grip of superstitious beliefs and fears).

But does Nietzsche believe that such superstitious beliefs have anything to do with the "rarefied and lofty" version of the "moral sense" we find today? Much suggests that he does. Since he claims that the morality of custom is the origin of our more "lofty" morality, he must think that some kind of continuity exists between them. One possibility is that current morality is structurally similar to the morality of custom, but that more "lofty" authorities have replaced tradition as the source of its higher authority: while some maintain a moral or reverent attitude toward traditional practices, the more "enlightened" substitute the authority of God, conscience, or the noumenal self for that of tradition, which now becomes "mere custom." Nietzsche may well think that these new commanding authorities are also maintained as such by a belief in "imaginary causalities." That seems a plausible inference to draw from his claim that the "logic of feelings" has changed little since the morality of custom (D 18), and from his focus on a particular "imaginary causality," which certainly exists beyond the morality of custom – namely, the alleged connection between guilt and suffering, which is equivalent to the conception of suffering as a punishment. In a section on *"the re-education of the human race,"* he pleads with us to help "in this one work: to take the concept of punishment which has overrun the whole world and root it out! There exists no more noxious weed" (D 13). A later section confirms that the tendency to take natural effects as punishments is central to *Daybreak*'s understanding of current morality: "And in *summa*: what is it you really want changed? We want to cease making causes into sinners and consequences into executioners" (D 208). It would hardly be strange for Nietzsche to think that the "imaginary causality" of guilt plays a role in the modern moral conscience – for Schopenhauer, who did not even believe in God, did believe that *all* suffering results from guilt (e.g., WW II.603–05). Accordingly, Nietzsche might well think that our perception of suffering as following from guilt induces us to experience the dictates of conscience with a primitive feeling of dread or reverence, and that this gives our judgments of right and wrong their moral or categorical force.

But how can he explain the authority many people still grant morality even though they reject any causality that is not scientifically respectable, including that of guilt? Nietzsche provides an answer shortly before he explains his "denial of morality": "*Wherein we are all irrational.* – We still draw conclusions from judgments we consider false, from teachings in which we no longer believe – through our feelings" (D 99). This explains the ending of the passage on the denial of morality: "We have to *learn to think differently* – in order at least, perhaps very late on, to achieve even more: *to feel differently* (D 103). Nietzsche presumably believes that even those who no longer accept superstitious or unscientific beliefs retain *feelings* of reverence that were originally produced by these erroneous beliefs, which therefore function even now as *causal* presuppositions of people's "moral" feelings. Learning thus to think differently, to recognize our moral feelings as results of beliefs we no longer hold, Nietzsche seems to suppose, will eventually free us from these feelings, and free us to take seriously other values, as he himself was beginning to do in *Daybreak*.

CONCLUSION

Daybreak's "denial of morality" is very far from Nietzsche's last word on the subject. His later works, especially *On the Genealogy of Morality*, replace *Daybreak*'s account of the origins of morality with a much more sophisticated and complex one, and his "denial of morality" undergoes a corresponding transformation. Too often paired with *Human, All Too Human*, *Daybreak* has been too little appreciated as the real beginning of Nietzsche's own path on the topic of morality. *Human, All Too Human* lies too much under the shadow of Schopenhauer's values; only in *Daybreak* does Nietzsche break free and begin to raise his characteristic questions about the value of the unegoistic and, ultimately, of morality. The means he found to do so, his naturalized Kantian interpretation of the morality of custom, did not in fact satisfy him for long (see GM II.1–3 for his later account), and it is worth trying to figure out why as one reads *Daybreak*. For Nietzsche himself reached the perspective of his *Genealogy* only by overcoming the account of the origins of morality offered here. *Daybreak*'s importance to him lay in the fact that it gave him an initial set of hypotheses about the origins of morality as a phenomenon of nature that he could then go on to revise and refine. *Daybreak*'s importance to us may lie primarily in its ability to show that his later genealogy of morality did not emerge from thin air nor spring full-blown from Nietzsche's head, but was the product of a serious and sustained effort to understand what morality is and how it could have arisen on the assumption that it is a purely natural phenomenon.

CHAPTER 6

Nietzsche: The Gay Science

Bernard Williams

The Gay Science is a remarkable book, both in itself and as offering a way into some of Nietzsche's most important ideas. The history of its publication is rather complex, and it throws some light on the development of his thought and of his methods as a writer. He published the first edition of it in 1882. In that version, it consisted of only four books, and had no Preface, though it did have the 'Prelude in Rhymes'. A second edition appeared in 1887, which added a fifth book, the Preface, and an Appendix of further poems. This is the work as we now know it, and which is translated here.

Between the two editions of The Gay Science, Nietzsche wrote two of his best-known works, Thus Spoke Zarathustra (1883–5) and Beyond Good and Evil (1886); the last section of Book Four of The Gay Science (342)[1] is indeed virtually the same as the first section of Zarathustra. So the complete Gay Science brackets these two books, which are different from it and from each other. (Zarathustra, which is a peculiar literary experiment in a rhetoric drawn from the Bible, was once one of Nietzsche's most popular works, but it has worn less well than the others.) Book Five of The Gay Science anticipates, in turn, some of the themes of another famous book which was to follow in 1887, On the Genealogy of Morality, which is again different in tone, sustaining a more continuous theoretical argument.

The Gay Science is a prime example of what is often called Nietzsche's 'aphoristic' style. It consists of a sequence of sections which are not obviously tied to one another except, sometimes, in general content, and which do not offer a connected argument. The second half of Book Three, in particular, consists of many very short paragraphs of this kind. Elsewhere, however, there are longer passages, and in fact the arrangement of the shorter sections is not as fortuitous as it may look. It is often designed to

---

[1] References to The Gay Science, and to other works by Nietzsche, are to numbered sections.

gather thoughts which will, so to speak, circle in on some central theme or problem.

In his earlier works, Nietzsche had moved gradually towards this style. He had been appointed in 1869 as a professor of classical philology at the University of Basel, at the extraordinarily early age of twenty-four. He served in this position for ten years, resigning in 1879 because of the ill health which was to persist throughout his life. (The last letter he wrote, when in 1889 he broke down into insanity and a silence which lasted until his death in 1900, was to his distinguished colleague at Basel, Jacob Burckhardt, in which he said that he would rather have been a Swiss professor than God, but he had not dared to push egoism so far.) In his years at Basel he published first *The Birth of Tragedy*, which has the form, if not the content or the tone, of a treatise, and a set of four long essays collected as *Untimely Meditations*. In 1878–9 he brought out two books forming *Human, All Too Human*, followed in 1880 by a further part called 'The Wanderer and his Shadow', and in these writings he moved from continuous exposition and argument to setting out a sequence of thoughts which were not necessarily tied discursively to their neighbours, a style that allowed him to approach a question from many different directions. In *Daybreak*, which came out in 1881, the style is fully developed. As late as 25 January 1882 he still referred to what were to be the first books of *The Gay Science* as a continuation of *Daybreak*; by June they had acquired their separate title.

When he made that decision, he sensed that Book Four, which is called 'Sanctus Januarius' and invokes the spirit of the New Year, might be found obscure, and he was anxious about whether his correspondent, Peter Gast, would understand it. He knew that this was not just a set of penetrating, perhaps rather cynical, *aperçus*. 'Aphorism', the standard term which I have already mentioned, implies too strongly that each is supposed to be a squib, or a compact expression of a truth (often in the form of an exaggerated falsehood) in the style of the French writers La Rochefoucauld and Chamfort, whom Nietzsche indeed admired, but whom he did not simply follow in giving a self-conscious exposé of some human failing, foible or piece of self-deception. There is a certain amount of that, particularly in the earlier books, but he was very aware of the risk that such aphorisms run of sliding from the daring through the knowing to the self-satisfied (it is not merely cynicism that he intends when he says in 379 that 'we are artists of contempt'). His ambitions are deeper; the effect is meant to be cumulative, and its aim is more systematically subversive. A philosopher who had a similar intention, though in totally different connections, is the later Wittgenstein, and Nietzsche might have called the sections of this book, as Wittgenstein called the paragraphs of his manuscripts, 'remarks'.

His remarks cover very various subjects. Many of them touch on what may be called moral psychology, and sometimes he does claim to detect an egoistic origin of some ethically approved reaction (as he does, for example, in the shrewd observation about magnanimity and revenge at section 49). The search for the 'shameful origin' of our moral sentiments was later to become an important principle of his genealogical method. But he is very clear that mere reductionism, the readily cynical explanation of all such attitudes in terms of self-interest, is a mistake. Partly this is because he does not think that self-interest is an individual's basic motive anyway, and this book contains some quite complex, if unresolved, reflections on that question, in particular when he considers whether the virtues have a value for the individual who possesses them, or for the group. But, more broadly, Nietzsche thinks that the reductive spirit itself can be in error, a form of vulgarity (3), and that the 'realists' who congratulate themselves on having the measure of human unreason and self-deception are usually themselves in the grip of some ancient fantasy (57).

Above all, it is simply not enough, in Nietzsche's view, to 'unmask' some supposedly honourable sentiment or opinion and leave it at that. 'Only as creators can we destroy', he very significantly says (58). What things are *called* is fundamentally important, but a conventional set of names – as we may say, an interpretation – can be replaced only by another, more powerful, interpretation. When we say that one interpretation is more powerful than another, it is vitally important what counts as 'power'. It is often said that Nietzsche explains everything in terms of power. This says something about the way in which he saw these problems, but it is wrong if it is supposed to state his solution to it. The point is very clear in *On the Genealogy of Morality*. There he tells a story of how a certain outlook or interpretation, embodying metaphysical illusions, came into existence as a psychological compensation for the weakness of people who were powerless, and how this outlook triumphed over the conventionally strong and their view of the world. The question must be, how could this have come about? What was the source of this new power? There had to be *something to* this new way of describing the world which accounted in naturalistic terms for its triumph, and Nietzsche fully accepts this, even if he does not have a very rich vocabulary of social explanation in which he can discuss what it might be. 'Let us . . . not forget', he goes on in section 58 of *The Gay Science*, 'that in the long run it is enough to create new names and valuations and appearances of truth in order to create new "things"'.

Indeed, but this immediately raises the question, one to which Nietzsche returned in many different connections: what must someone do to 'create' new names?

The words 'The Gay Science' translate the German title 'Die Fröhliche Wissenschaft'. No one, presumably, is going to be misled by the more recent associations of the word 'gay' – it simply means joyful, light-hearted, and above all, lacking in solemnity (section 327, on taking things seriously, says something about this). 'Science' has its own difficulties. The word 'Wissenschaft', unlike the English word 'science' in its modern use, does not mean simply the natural and biological sciences – they are, more specifically, 'Naturwissenschaft'. It means any organized study or body of knowledge, including history, philology, criticism and generally what we call 'the humanities', and that is often what Nietzsche has in mind when he uses the word in the text (it is often translated as 'science', for want of a brief alternative). But in the title itself there is an idea still broader than this. It translates a phrase, 'gai saber', or, as Nietzsche writes on his title page, 'gaya scienza', which referred to the art of song cultivated by the medieval troubadours of Provence, and with that, as he explains in *Beyond Good and Evil* (260), it invokes an aristocratic culture of courtly love. As he made clear, this association comes out in the fact that the book contains poems. But the title has other implications as well. One – particularly important to understanding this book and Nietzsche more generally – is that, just as the troubadours possessed not so much a body of information as an art, so Nietzsche's 'gay science' does not in the first place consist of a doctrine, a theory or body of knowledge. While it involves and encourages hard and rigorous thought, and to this extent the standard implications of 'Wissenschaft' are in place, it is meant to convey a certain spirit, one that in relation to understanding and criticism could defy the 'spirit of gravity' as lightly as the troubadours, supposedly, celebrated their loves. This is why the original publisher could announce at the beginning of the book that it brought to a conclusion a series of Nietzsche's writings (including *Human, All Too Human* and *Daybreak*) which shared the aim of setting out 'a new image and ideal of the free spirit'.

He said that it was the most personal of his books, meaning that in part it was explicitly about his own life: some of it is like a diary. It is not irrelevant that the 'gai saber' belonged to the south of Europe, to the Mediterranean. Nietzsche spent much of his time in the last years of his working life in Italy (in places such as those he praises in sections 281 and 291), and he was very conscious of the contrast between overcast German earnestness and Southern sun and freedom, an idea which had a long literary history and had been most famously expressed, perhaps, in Goethe's *Italian Journey*. That is a recurrent contrast in *The Gay Science*, but, as so often with Nietzsche, it is not one contrast, and his reflections on the German spirit in philosophy and religion are specially nuanced in this book, for instance in his discussion (357) of 'What is German?'

Nietzsche's general reflections, here as elsewhere, have some recurrent weaknesses. There are cranky reflections on diet and climate. His opinions about women and sex, even if they include (as at 71) one or two shrewd and compassionate insights into the conventions of his time, are often shallow and sometimes embarrassing; they were, biographically, the product of an experience which had been drastically limited and disappointing. However, what is most significant for his thought as a whole is the fact that his resources for thinking about modern society and politics, in particular about the modern state, were very thin. The point is not that he was opposed to a free society, equal rights, and other typically modern aspirations (though he certainly was, as section 377, for instance, makes clear). In fact, Nietzsche has by no means been a hero exclusively of the political Right, and many radical, socialist and even feminist groups in the last century found support in his writings.[2] This was possible just because the deeply radical spirit of his work was combined with a lack of effective political and social ideas, leaving a blank on which many different aspirations could be projected. His clearly aristocratic sympathies are, in political connections, not so much reactionary as archaic, and while he has many illuminating things to say about the religious and cultural history of Europe, his conception of social relations owes more to his understanding of the ancient world than to a grasp of modernity. The idea of nihilism which is so important in his later works is undeniably relevant to modern conditions, but his discussions of such subjects as 'corruption' (in section 23 of this book) borrow a lot from the rhetoric of the Roman Empire and the disposition of its writers to praise the largely imaginary virtues of the vanished Republic.

The Gay Science marks a decisive step beyond the books that came before it because it introduces two of what were to become Nietzsche's best-known themes, the Death of God and the Eternal Recurrence. The

---

[2] A very interesting study in this connection is Steven E. Ascheim, *The Nietzsche Legacy in Germany 1890–1990* (Berkeley: University of California Press, 1992). A helpful discussion of Nietzsche's political thought is Bruce Detwiler, *Nietzsche and the Politics of Aristocratic Radicalism* (University of Chicago Press, 1990). Mark Warren, in *Nietzsche and Political Thought* (Boston: MIT Press, 1988), well brings out the limitations of Nietzsche's social ideas, but is over-optimistic in thinking that if his philosophy were true to itself, it would offer a basis for liberalism.

idea that God is dead occurs first at 108, in association with the image of
the Buddha's shadow, still to be seen in a cave for centuries after his death.
This is followed at 125 by the haunting story of a madman with a lantern
in the bright morning, looking for God. He is met by ridicule, and he
concludes that he has 'come too early', that the news of God's death has
not yet reached humanity, even though they have killed him themselves.
This idea recurs in more literal terms in 343, the first section of Book Five
(published, we may recall, five years later). The death of God is identified
there as the fact that 'the belief in . . . God has become unbelievable': this,
'the greatest recent event', is beginning to cast its shadow across Europe.
Once this event is fully recognized, it will have incalculable consequences,
in particular for European morality. Some of these consequences will be
melancholy, and indeed elsewhere Nietzsche struggles with the question of
what act of creation, by whom, might overcome the emptiness left by the
collapse of traditional illusions. But here the news brings, at least in the
short term, only joy, a sense of daybreak and freedom, the promise of an
open sea: 'maybe there has never been such an "open sea"'.

Nietzsche continued to think that the death of God would have vast
and catastrophic consequences. But on the account that he himself gave of
Christian belief and its origins (in this book and in *Beyond Good and Evil*,
but above all in *On the Genealogy of Morality*), should he really have thought
this? He believed that the faith in the Christian God, and more generally
in a reassuring metaphysical structure of the world, was a projection of
fear and resentment, representing a victory of the weak over the strong.
That metaphysical belief has died; it has been destroyed, as Nietzsche often
points out, by itself, by the belief in truthfulness – and we shall come back
to that – which was itself part of the metaphysical faith. But how much
difference should he expect its death to make? He shares with another
nineteenth-century subverter, Marx (with whom he shares little else), the
idea that religious belief is a consequence, an expression of social and
psychological forces. If those forces remain, and the Christian expression
of them collapses, then surely other expressions will take its place. If need
secretes thought, and the need remains, then it will secrete new thoughts.

Indeed, Nietzsche does think this: he thinks that liberalism, socialism,
Utilitarianism and so on are just secularized expressions of those same
forces. But he thinks that they are too manifestly close to the original,
and that our growing understanding that the world has no metaphysical
structure whatsoever must discredit them as well. The death of God is
the death of those gods, too. He has a particular contempt for benign
freethinkers who hope to keep all the ethical content of Christianity without

its theology: George Eliot is the unlucky target when the point is spelled out very clearly in *The Twilight of the Idols* (the section called 'Expeditions of an Untimely Man'). But that is not the most important point. Even if the content of our morality changes noticeably, as for instance attitudes towards sex have done in recent times, much more basic and structural elements of it, its humanitarianism and its professed belief in equal respect for everyone, are in Nietzsche's view too bound up with the mechanisms that generated Christianity, and will inevitably go the same way that it has gone. It is too soon, surely, to say that he was wrong.

For Nietzsche himself there was another dimension as well, one immediately connected with his own values. He saw the unravelling of Christianity as part of the phenomenon that he called European nihilism, the loss of any sense of depth or significance to life. The world might conceivably avoid destruction and overt hatred by organizing a pleasantly undemanding and unreflective way of life, a dazed but adequately efficient consumerism. Nietzsche probably did not think that such a society could survive in the long run, but in any case he could not reconcile himself to such a prospect or regard it as anything but loathsome. Contempt was one of his readier emotions, and nothing elicited it more than what he sometimes calls 'the last man', the contented, unadventurous, philistine product of such a culture. This book, like all his others, makes it clear that any life worth living must involve daring, individuality and creative bloody-mindedness. This is indeed expressed in the 'gaiety' of its title. Gaiety can encompass contentment, as it does on New Year's Day at the beginning of Book Four, but when that is so, it is a particular achievement and a piece of good luck. Gaiety is not itself contentment, and while it rejects solemnity and the spirit of gravity, it does so precisely because it is the only way of taking life seriously.

Nietzsche has been thought by some people to have had a brutal and ruthless attitude to the world; sometimes, perhaps, he wished that he had. But in fact, one personal feature which, together with his illness and his loneliness, contributed to his outlook was a hyper-sensitivity to suffering. It was linked to a total refusal to forget, not only the existence of suffering, but the fact that suffering was necessary to everything that he and anyone else valued. 'All good things come from bad things' is one of his fundamental tenets: it signals his rejection of what he calls 'the fundamental belief of the metaphysicians, *the belief in the opposition of values*' (*Beyond Good and Evil*, 2). This is, for him, a principle of interpretation, but it presents itself in the first instance simply as a fact, which he thought no honest understanding of the world could evade. If a sense of the world's achievements and glories – art, self-understanding, nobility of character – cannot in common honesty be separated from the knowledge of the horrors that have been involved in bringing these things about, then there is a question that cannot, Nietzsche supposed, simply be ignored: whether it has all been worth it.

Thinkers in the past have supposed that the question could be answered, and answered positively. Leibniz, with his famous doctrine that this is the best of all possible worlds, believed in a cosmic cost-benefit analysis which would vindicate God's mysterious management. Hegel had told a pro-gressive metaphysical story of the historical development of freedom and reason, which represented the horrors as all dialectically necessary to the eventual outcome, so that we could be sure that none of them was mean-ingless. Neither of these fantasies, Nietzsche reasonably thought, could be taken seriously in the late 19th century. Nor, he came to think, could one take altogether seriously someone who answered the same question, but in the negative. In his earlier years he had been very impressed, as Wagner was, by the philosophy of Schopenhauer, and his references to Schopenhauer in this book are mostly respectful (more so than those to Wagner), but he came to be very sceptical about Schopenhauer's so-called pessimism, which had been expressed in the judgement (for instance) that the world's 'non-existence would be preferable to its existence'.[3] 'We take care not to say that the world is worth *less*', he says at 346:

The whole attitude of man ... as judge of the world who finally places existence itself on his scales and finds it too light – the monstrous stupidity of this attitude has finally dawned on us and we are sick of it.

Nietzsche recognizes that his own *Birth of Tragedy* had been full of the Schopenhauerian spirit. Taken in that spirit, the question of 'the value of life', he came to think, had no answer and was indeed not a question. Yet it did not simply go away, because there remained what seemed to Nietzsche, at least, to be a fact, that anyone who really understood and held in his mind the horrors of the world would be crushed or choked by them. That fact left, if not a question to be answered, at least a problem to be overcome. Nietzsche presents the problem, and his way of overcoming it, in the form of the thought-experiment of the Eternal Recurrence, which appears for the first time in *The Gay Science*.[4] In the startling words of 341, what would

[3] *The World as Will and Representation*, trans. E. F. J. Payne (2 vols., New York: Dover, 1969), vol. II, chapter 46, p. 576.

[4] The *phrase* 'eternal recurrence' occurs first at sec 285, but in a more limited connection, of recognizing that there is no perpetual peace, but only (as the pre-Socratic philosopher Heraclitus taught) a cycle of war and peace.

you think if a demon told you that everything in life would recur over and over again eternally? How would you answer the question 'Do you want this again and innumerable times again?' This question, Nietzsche says, 'would lie on your actions as the heaviest weight'. It tests your ability not to be overcome by the world's horror and meaninglessness. There is no *belief* which could 'justify the world': confronted with the question of its value, or rather with the replacement for that question, which is the prospect of being crushed by the consciousness of what the world is like, the only issue is (as Nietzsche also puts it) whether one can say 'yes' to it, and the test of that is whether seriously and in the fullest consciousness you could will that the course of everything should happen over and over again, including not just its pain and cruelty and humiliation, but also its triviality, emptiness and ugliness, the last man and everything that goes with him.

This is an entirely hypothetical question, a thought-experiment. It is not a matter, as I read him, of Nietzsche's believing in a *theory* of eternal recurrence. The idea (which does not occur in *Beyond Good and Evil* or *The Genealogy of Morality*) appears in *Zarathustra* in a form similar to that of *The Gay Science*, and Nietzsche mentions its importance in *The Twilight of the Idols* and in *Ecce Homo* (the intellectual autobiography that he wrote on the verge of insanity). There are some places in which it is treated as a theoretical idea, but they are largely confined to his unpublished notes (his *Nachlass*), some of which, particularly from his last years, were published in *The Will to Power*, which is not a book by Nietzsche at all, but a selection from these notes tendentiously put together by his sister.

But if the idea of the Eternal Recurrence is a thought-experiment, how can answering its question lie on our actions 'as the heaviest weight'? If it is a mere fantasy, then how can 'willing' the Eternal Recurrence cost one anything at all? It seems as simple as saying 'yes'. But one has to recall that in facing the question one is supposed to have a real and live consciousness of everything that has led to this moment, in particular to what we value. We would have to think in vivid detail, if we could, of every dreadful happening that has been necessary to create Venice, or Newton's science, or whatever one thinks best of in our morality. Then we would have not simply to say 'yes', but to say 'yes' and mean it. That does not seem exactly weightless. What perhaps does less work in the thought-experiment is the element, which Nietzsche certainly thought essential to it, of *eternity*. If there is anything in this test at all, why would willing one recurrence not be enough? If you could overcome the 'nausea', as Zarathustra repeatedly puts it, of the prospect that the horrors and the last man and all the rest will come round again *even once*, and say 'yes' to it, you would have taken the essential step: could willing all those further recurrences cost you very much more?

There is another, very natural, reaction to the problem, which is almost everyone's reaction: to forget about it. One can forget that the horrors exist, and also, if one has a taste for metaphysical consolations, that God is dead. The narrator of Scott Fitzgerald's *The Great Gatsby* says of Tom and Daisy that they 'retreated back into their money and their vast carelessness, or whatever it was that held them together', and that is, roughly speaking, the remedy that the 'last man' finds for Nietzsche's problem. David Hume spoke of 'carelessness and inattention' as the only remedy for sceptical doubts; but that is not the same, because Hume thought that sceptical doubts were *unreal*. Nietzsche knew that the considerations we all forget were not unreal, and he held obstinately to an idea of truthfulness that would not allow us to falsify them. In this book, he calls on honesty and intellectual conscience at 319 and (as we shall see) at 344; at 284 he speaks of those who have to have an argument against the sceptic inside themselves – 'the great self-dissatisfied people'. In *The Anti-Christ* (50), at the very end of his active life, he wrote:

Truth has had to be fought for every step of the way, almost everything else dear to our hearts, on which our love and our trust in life depend, has had to be sacrificed to it. Greatness of soul is needed for it, the service of truth is the hardest service. – For what does it mean to be *honest* in intellectual things? That one is stern towards one's heart, that one despises 'fine feelings', that one makes every Yes and No a question of conscience!

The value of truthfulness embraces the need to find out the truth, to hold on to it, and to tell it – in particular, to oneself. But Nietzsche's own dedication to this value, he saw, immediately raised the question of what this value is. We have taken it for granted, he thinks, and we have seriously misunderstood it: as he says in *Beyond Good and Evil* (177), 'Perhaps nobody yet has been truthful enough about what "truthfulness" is.'

Section 344 of *The Gay Science* (the second section of Book Five) gives one of Nietzsche's most important and illuminating statements of this question:

This unconditional will to truth – what is it? Is it the will not to let oneself be deceived? Is it the will *not to deceive*? For the will to truth could be interpreted in this second way, too – if 'I do not want to deceive *myself*' is included as a special case under the generalization 'I do not want to deceive'. But why not deceive? But why not allow oneself to be deceived?

The reasons for not wanting to be deceived, he goes on to say, are prudential; seen in that light, wanting to get things right in our intellectual studies and in practical life will be a matter of utility. But those considerations cannot possibly sustain an *unconditional* value for truth: much of the time it is more useful to believe falsehoods. Our belief in the unconditional will to truth

must have originated *in spite of* the fact that the disutility and dangerousness of 'the will to truth' or 'truth at any price' is proved to it constantly. 'At any price': we understand this well enough once we have offered and slaughtered one faith after another on this altar! Consequently, 'will to truth' does *not* mean 'I do not want to let myself be deceived' but – there is no alternative – 'I will not deceive, not even myself'; *and with that we stand on moral ground.*

. . . you will have gathered what I am getting at, namely, that it is still a *metaphysical faith* upon which our faith in science rests – that even we knowers of today, we godless anti-metaphysicians, still take *our* fire, too, from the flame lit by the thousand-year-old faith, the Christian faith which was also Plato's faith, that God is truth; that truth is divine . . .

The title of the section is 'In what way we, too, are still pious'. The idea is developed further in Book III of *On the Genealogy of Morality*, where the 'ascetic ideal' which has received an unflattering genealogical explanation is discovered to lie at the root of the will to truth, which powered the need to discover that very explanation. But that does not overthrow the will to truth: 'I have every respect for the ascetic ideal *in so far as it is honest!*' (III.26).

The 'unconditional will to truth' does not mean that we want to believe any and every truth. It does mean that we want to understand who we are, to correct error, to avoid deceiving ourselves, to get beyond comfortable falsehood. The value of truthfulness, so understood, cannot lie just in its consequences, as Nietzsche repeatedly points out. Earlier in this book (121), he says that various beliefs may be necessary for our life, but that does not show them to be true: 'life is not an argument'. Already in *Human, All Too Human* (517) he had noted: '*Fundamental Insight*: There is no pre-established harmony between the furthering of truth and the well-being of humanity.' Again, in *Beyond Good and Evil* (11) he says that we must understand that there are some judgements which 'must be *believed* to be true, for the sake of preservation of creatures like ourselves, though they might, of course, be false judgements for all that'.

Truth may be not just unhelpful, but destructive. In particular the truths of Nietzsche's own philosophy, which discredit the metaphysical world, can (as we have seen) destructively lead to nihilism if they come to be accepted.

In the *Nachlass* (*The Will to Power* 5) there is a revealing note, which mentions the way in which the idea of truthfulness has turned against the morality which fostered it, and ends with the remark:

This antagonism – *not* to esteem what we know, and not to be *allowed* any longer to esteem the lies we should like to tell ourselves – results in a process of dissolution.

In what ways are we 'not allowed' to esteem these lies? To some degree, Nietzsche thought that this was already in his time a historical or social necessity: that, at least among thoughtful people, these beliefs simply could not stand up much longer or have much life to them. It is a good question whether this was right, indeed whether it is right today – particularly when we recall the secularized, political, forms which are now taken, as Nietzsche supposed, by the same illusions. What is certainly true is that Nietzsche took it to be an *ethical* necessity, for himself and anyone he was disposed to respect, not to esteem these illusions. He did think that there were things which, even for honest and reflective people, could rightly compensate in some ways for the loss of the illusions; it is in this spirit that he remarks elsewhere in the *Nachlass* (*The Will to Power* 822): 'We possess *art* lest *we perish of the truth.*' He does not mean that we possess art in place of the truth; he means that we possess art so that we can possess the truth and not perish of it.

There continue to be complex debates about what Nietzsche understood truth to be. Quite certainly, he did not think, in pragmatist spirit, that beliefs are true if they serve our interests or welfare: we have already seen some of his repeated denials of this idea. A more recently fashionable view of him is that he shared, perhaps founded, a kind of deconstructive scepticism to the effect that there is no such thing as truth, or that truth is what anyone thinks it is, or that it is a boring category that we can do without. This is also wrong, and more deeply so. As we have seen, Nietzsche did not think that the ideal of truthfulness went into retirement when its metaphysical origins were discovered, and he did not suppose, either, that truthfulness could be detached from a concern for the truth. Truthfulness as an ideal retains its power, and so far from truth being dispensable or malleable, his main question is how it can be made bearable. Repeatedly Nietzsche – the 'old philologist', as he called himself – reminds us that, quite apart from any question about philosophical interpretations, including his own, there are facts to be respected. In *The Anti-Christ* (59) he praises the ancient world for having invented 'the incomparable art of reading well, the prerequisite for all systematic knowledge', and with that 'the *sense for facts*, the last-developed and most valuable of all the senses'. At the beginning of *On the*

Genealogy of Morality, he tells us that 'the English psychologists' should not
be dismissed as old, cold, boring frogs; rather, they are brave animals,

who have been taught to sacrifice desirability to truth, every truth, even a plain,
bitter, ugly, foul, unchristian, immoral truth . . . Because there are such truths –

He keenly detects elements in our intellectual structures which we mistake for truths. In *The Gay Science* he stresses the importance of 'a law
of agreement', which regulates people's thoughts and provides intellectual
security (76). He stresses the historical, indeed the continuing, importance
of these conceptions, but he does not think that they are the truth, or that
they are immune to the discovery of truth. They are *contrasted* with the
truth, and the question is, what will emerge from a battle between them
and a growing awareness of the truth: as he asks at 110, 'to what extent can
truth stand to be incorporated?'

In his earliest writings about truth and error, Nietzsche sometimes spoke
as though he could compare the entire structure of our thought to the 'real'
nature of things and find our thought defective. It is as though the business
of using concepts at all falsified a reality which in itself was – what? Formless, perhaps, or chaotic, or utterly unstructured. Later, he rightly rejected
this picture, with its implication that we can somehow look round the edge
of our concepts at the world to which we are applying them and grasp it
as entirely unaffected by any descriptions (including, we would be forced
to admit, the descriptions 'formless', 'chaotic', and so on).[5] There are passages in *The Gay Science* where it is unclear whether he is still attached to
this picture. He discusses fictions, the practice of regarding things as equal
or identical or mathematically structured when they are not so or only
approximately so (110, 121). He is making the point, certainly, that math-
ematical representations which are offered by the sciences are in various
ways idealizations, and this is entirely intelligible. There is greater ambiguity when he suggests that nothing is really 'identical' or 'the same'. To
take an example: the concept 'snake' allows us to classify various individual
things as 'the same animal', and to recognize one individual thing as 'the
same snake'. It is trivially true that 'snake' is a human concept, a cultural
product. But it is a much murkier proposition that its use somehow *falsifies* reality – that 'in itself' the world does not contain snakes, or indeed
anything else you might mention. Nietzsche came to see that this idea of
the world 'in itself' was precisely a relic of the kind of metaphysics that he

---

[5] This is well argued by Maudemarie Clark, *Nietzsche on Truth and Philosophy* (Cambridge University
Press, 1991).

wanted to overcome. As a remark in the *Nachlass* puts it (*The Will to Power* 567): 'The antithesis of the apparent world and the true world is reduced to the antithesis "world" and "nothing".'

It is less than clear, and also well worth considering, how far the formulations of *The Gay Science* still commit him to the murky metaphysical picture. Some of the same problems affect another idea which appears in the book, and which was to be important in works he wrote after it, the idea of 'a perspective'. Our interpretative outlook, our particular 'take' on the world, is modelled on the analogy of a literal, visual, perspective, and this analogy has two implications: that we understand that there can be alternative perspectives, and, importantly, that these will be alternative perspectives *on the same reality*. In later works, Nietzsche is often less than definite about what is involved in this second implication, but he is very clear about the first implication, and indeed urges us to combine perspectives, or move between them, which shows that we not only know *that* there are other perspectival views, but that we know what some of them are. In *The Gay Science*, he seems on the very edge of stepping into this problem. Section 299, for instance, suggests that we can make use of different perspectives. But at 374, where he says 'we cannot reject the possibility that it [the world] includes infinite interpretations', the idea of the 'alternatives' seems to remain an entirely abstract possibility: 'we cannot look around our corner'.

The 'Greeks were superficial – out of profundity', he says in the Preface (and he repeated the remark later, in the epilogue to *Nietzsche Contra Wagner*). But the Greeks in their time could straightforwardly display a delight in surfaces and appearances which was indeed profound. That is not possible for us, after so much history: any such attitude for us will be a different and more sophisticated thing, and it will represent an achievement. At the very end of the book, he returns to the gaiety of the gay science, and calls up the ideal of 'a spirit that plays naively, i.e. not deliberately but from overflowing abundance and power, with everything that was hitherto called holy, good, untouchable, divine...' This might seem even inhuman in comparison to conventional forms of seriousness, that is to say, solemnity,

and in spite of all this, it is perhaps only with it that *the great seriousness* really emerges; that the real question mark is posed for the first time; that the destiny of the soul changes; the hand of the clock moves forward...

Then he adds, at the end of that section, '... the tragedy begins'. But immediately there comes the last section of all, *Epilogue*, in which the spirits of his own book tell him to stop these gloomy noises, these 'voices from the crypt, and marmot whistles'. 'Nicht solche Töne!' they cry in an echo of Schiller's *Ode to Joy*, 'Not such sounds!' He says he will give them something else – the poems, presumably, with which he ends the book. But he does so with a final question, and it is a question which he wanted his readers to ask themselves not just at the end of this book, but throughout it and indeed throughout all his books – 'Is that what you *want*?'

CHAPTER 7

Nietzsche: Thus Spoke Zarathustra

Robert Pippin

THE TEXT

Nietzsche published each of the first three parts of *Thus Spoke Zarathustra* (TSZ hereafter) separately between 1883 and 1885, during one of his most productive and interesting periods, in between the appearance of *The Gay Science* (which he noted had itself marked a new beginning of his thought) and *Beyond Good and Evil*. As with the rest of his books, very few copies were sold. He later wrote a fourth part (called "Fourth and Final Part") which was not published until 1892, and then privately, only for a few friends, by which time Nietzsche had slipped into the insanity that marked the last decade of his life.[1] Not long afterwards an edition with all four parts published together appeared, and most editions and translations have followed suit, treating the four parts as somehow belonging in one book, although many scholars see a natural ending of sorts after Part III and regard Part IV as more of an appendix than a central element in the drama narrated by the work. Nietzsche, who was trained as a classicist, may have been thinking of the traditional tragedy competitions in ancient Greece, where entrants submitted three tragedies and a fourth play, a comic and somewhat bawdy satyr play. At any event, he thought of this final section as in some sense the "Fourth Part" and any interpretation must come to terms with it.

TSZ is unlike any of Nietzsche's other works, which themselves are unlike virtually anything else in the history of philosophy. Nietzsche himself provides no preface or introduction, although the section on TSZ in his late book, *Ecce Homo*, and especially its last section, "Why I am a Destiny," are invaluable guides to what he might have been up to. Zarathustra seems to

---

[1] Nietzsche went mad in January 1889. For more on the problem of Part IV, see Laurence Lampert's discussion in *Nietzsche's Teaching: An Interpretation of "Thus Spoke Zarathustra"* (New Haven: Yale University Press, 1986), pp. 287–91. For a contrasting view (that Part IV is integral to the work and a genuine conclusion), see Robert Gooding-Williams, *Zarathustra's Dionysian Modernism* (Stanford: Stanford University Press, 2001).

be some sort of prophet, calling people, modern European Christian people especially, to account for their failings and encouraging them to pursue a new way of life. (As we shall discuss in a moment, even this simple characterization is immediately complicated by the fact that Nietzsche insists that this has nothing to do with a "replacement" religion, and that the book is as much a parody of a prophetic view as it is an instance of it.)[2] In *Ecce Homo* Nietzsche expresses some irritation that no one has wondered about the odd name of this prophet. Zarathustra was a Persian prophet (known to the Greeks as Zoroaster)[3] and he is important for Nietzsche because he originally established that the central struggle in human life (even cosmic life) was between two absolutely distinct principles, between good and evil, which Nietzsche interpreted in Christian and humanist terms as the opposition between selflessness and benevolence on the one hand and egoism and self-interest on the other. Nietzsche tells us two things about this prophet:

Zarathustra created this fateful error of morality: this means he has to be the first to recognize it.[4]

(Nietzsche means that Zarathustra was the first to recognize its calamitous consequences.) And:

[t]he self-overcoming of morality from out of truthfulness; the self-overcoming of the moralists into their opposite – into me – that is what the name Zarathustra means coming from my mouth.[5]

That is, we can now live, Zarathustra attempts to teach, freed from the picture of this absolute dualism, but without moral anarchy and without sliding into a bovine contentment or a violent primitivism. Sometimes, especially in the first two parts, this new way of living is presented in sweeping and collective, historical terms, as an epochal transition from mere human being to an "overman," virtually a new species. This way of characterizing the problem tends to drop out after Part II, and Zarathustra focuses his attention on what he often calls the problem of self-overcoming: how each of us, as individuals, might come to be dissatisfied with our way of living and so be able to strive for something better, even if the traditional supports for and guidance toward such a goal seem no longer credible (e.g.

[2] Cf. Friedrich Nietzsche, *Ecce Homo* (hereafter EH), in *The Anti-Christ, Ecce Homo, Twilight of the Idols*, trans. Judith Norman (Cambridge: Cambridge University Press, 2005), §6, pp. 129–31.
[3] Estimates about when Zarathustra actually lived vary from 6000 BCE to 600 BCE. Somewhere between 1500 BCE and 1000 BCE would appear the safest guess. Nietzsche, however, evinces virtually no interest in the historical Zarathustra or the actual religion of Zoroastrianism.
[4] EH, §3, p. 145.   [5] Ibid.

the idea of *the* purpose of human nature, or what is revealed by religion, or any objective view of human happiness and so forth). And in Part III Zarathustra asks much more broadly about a whole new way of thinking about or imagining ourselves that he believes is necessary for this sort of re-orientation. He suggests that such a possibility depends on how we come to understand and experience temporality at a very basic level, and he introduces a famous image, "the eternal return of the same" (which he elsewhere calls Zarathustra's central teaching), to begin to grapple with the problem. He himself becomes deathly ill in contemplating this cyclical picture; not surprisingly since it seems to deny a possibility he himself had hoped for at the outset – a *decisive* historical revolution, a time after which all would be different from the time before. Many of the basic issues in the book are raised by considering what it means for Zarathustra to suffer from and then "recover" from such an "illness."

THE INTERPRETIVE PROBLEM

TSZ is often reported to be Nietzsche's most popular and most read book, but the fact that the book is so unusual and often hermetic has made for wildly different sorts of reception. Here is one that is typical of the kind of popular reputation Nietzsche has in modern culture:

Together with Goethe's *Faust* and the New Testament, *Zarathustra* was the most popular work that literate soldiers took into battle for inspiration and consolation [in WW I – RP]. The "beautiful words" of Zarathustra, one author wrote, were especially apt for the Germans who "more than any other Volk possessed fighting natures in Zarathustra's sense." About 150,000 copies of a specially durable wartime *Zarathustra* were distributed to the troops.[6]

Now it is hard to imagine a book less suitable for such a purpose than Nietzsche's *Thus Spoke Zarathustra*. It is true that Zarathustra had famously said, "You say it is the good cause that hallows even war? I tell you: it is the good war that hallows any cause" (p. 33), but even that passage is surrounded by claims that the highest aspiration is actually to be a "saint of knowledge," and that only failing that should one become a warrior (what sort of continuum could this be?), and that the "highest thought" of such warriors should be one commanded by Zarathustra, and it should have nothing to do with states and territory but with the injunction that human

---

[6] Steven Aschheim, *The Nietzsche Legacy in Germany, 1890–1990* (Berkeley: University of California Press, 1992), p. 135. The quotation cited is from Rektor P. Hoche, "Nietzsche und der deutsche Kampf," *Zeitung für Literatur, Kunst und Wissenschaft* 39:6 (12 March 1916).

being shall be overcome. (What armies would be fighting whom in such a cause?)[7] Moreover one wonders what "inspiration and consolation" our "literate soldiers" could have found in the Fellini-esque title character,[8] himself hardly possessed of a "warlike nature," chronically indecisive, sometimes self-pitying, wandering, speechifying, dancing about and encouraging others to dance, consorting mostly with animals, confused disciples, a dwarf, and his two mistresses. And what could they have made of the speeches, with those references to bees overloaded with honey, soothsayers, gravediggers, bursting coffins, pale criminals, red judges, self-propelling wheels, shepherds choking on snakes, tarantulas, "little golden fishing rods of wisdom," Zarathustra's ape, Zarathustra speaking too "crudely and sincerely" for "Angora rabbits," and the worship of a jackass in Part IV, with that circle of an old king, a magician, the last pope, a beggar, a shadow, the conscientious of spirit, and a sad soothsayer?

What in fact could *anyone* make of this bewildering work, parts of which seem more hermetic than Celan, parts more self-indulgent and bizarre than bad Bob Dylan lyrics? Do we know what we are *meant* to make of it? Nietzsche himself, in *Ecce Homo*, was willing to say a number of things about the work, that in it he is the "inventor of the dithyramb,"[9] that with TSZ he became the "first tragic philosopher," and that TSZ should be understood as "music." When it is announced, as the work to follow *The Gay Science*, we are clearly warned of the difficulty that will challenge any reader. Section §342 had concluded the original version of *The Gay Science* with "Incipit tragoedia," and then the first paragraph of TSZ's Prologue. Nietzsche's warning comes in the second edition Preface:

"*Incipit tragoedia*" [tragedy begins] we read at the end of this suspiciously innocent book. Beware! Something utterly wicked and mischievous is being announced here: *incipit parodia* [parody begins], no doubt."[10]

Are there other works that could be said to be both tragedies and parodies? *Don Quixote*, perhaps, a work in many other ways also quite similar

---

7 In EH, §1, p. 144 when Nietzsche says that after Zarathustra "the concept of politics will have then merged entirely into a war of spirits" he does not pause to tell us what a war, not of bodies, but of *spirits* might be. And he goes on to say "there will be wars such as the earth has never seen," and we might note that he seems to mean that different sorts, *types* of "wars" will make up "great politics."

8 Cf. EH, §1, p. 144: "I do not want to be a saint, I would rather be a buffoon . . . Perhaps I am a buffoon . . . And yet in spite of this or rather not in spite of this – because nothing to date has been more hypocritical than saints – the truth speaks from out of me. – But the truth is *terrible*: because *lies* have been called truth so far."

9 A dithyramb was a choral hymn sung in the classical period in Greece by fifty men or boys to honor the god Dionysus.

10 Friedrich Nietzsche, *The Gay Science* (hereafter GS), edited by Bernard Williams (Cambridge: Cambridge University Press), §1, p. 4.

to TSZ?[11] If Nietzsche announced that his TSZ can and should be read as a parody, what exactly would that mean? I do not mean what it would mean to find parts of it funny; I mean trying to understand *how* it could be both a prophetic book and a kind of send-up of a prophetic book. How it could both present Zarathustra as a teacher and parody his attempt to play that role? Why has the work remained for the most part a place simply to mine for quotations in support of Nietzschean "theories" of the overman, the Eternal Return of the Same, and the "last human beings"; all as if the theories were contained inside an ornate literary form, delivered by Nietzsche's surrogate, an ancient Persian prophet? At the very least, especially when we look also to virtually everything written after the later 1870s, when Nietzsche in effect abandoned the traditional essay form in favor of less continuous, more aphoristic, and here parabolic forms, it is clear that Nietzsche wanted to resist incorporation into traditional philosophy, to escape traditional assumptions about the writing of philosophy. In a way that point is obvious, nowhere more obvious than in the form of TSZ, even if the steady stream of books about Nietzsche's metaphysics, or value theory, or even epistemology shows no sign of abating. The two more interesting questions are rather, first, what one takes such resistance to mean, what the practical point is, we might say, of the act of so resisting, what Nietzsche is trying to *do* with his books, as much as what his books mean, if we are not to understand them in the traditional philosophical sense. (It would have been helpful if, in *Ecce Homo*, Nietzsche had not just written the chapter "Why I Write Such Good Books," but "Why I Write Books At All.") Secondly, why has this resistance been so resisted, to the point that there are not even many disputes about TSZ, no contesting views about what *parodia* might have meant?

One obvious answer should be addressed immediately. It may be so hard to know what TSZ is for, and so easy simply to plunder it unsystematically, because the work is in large part a failure. TSZ echoes Romantic attempts at created mythologies, such as William Blake's, as well as Wagner's attempt to re-work Teutonic myth, but it remains so sui generis and unclassifiable that it resists even the broadest sort of category and does not itself instruct us, at least not very clearly or very well, about how to read it. That it is both

---

[11] The intertwining of the two dramatic modes of tragedy and comic parody appear throughout the text. A typical example is at the end of "The Wanderer" in Part III, when Zarathustra laughs in a kind of self-mocking and then weeps as he remembers the friends he has had to leave behind (p. 123). It is also very likely that Nietzsche, the "old philologist," is referring to the end of Plato's *Symposium*, where Socrates claims that what we need is someone who can write both tragedies and comedies, that the tragic poet might also be comic (*Symposium*, 223c–d).

a tragedy and a parody helps little with the details. Large stretches of it seem ponderous and turgid, mysteriously abandoning Nietzsche's characteristic light touch and pithy wit. The many dreams and dream images appealed to by Zarathustra jumble together so much (in one case, grimacing children, angels, owls, fools, and butterflies as big as children tumble out of a broken coffin) that an attempt at interpretation seems beside the point. (When a disciple tries to offer a reading of this dream – and seems to do a pretty fair job of it – Zarathustra ultimately just stares into this disciple's face and shakes his head with apparent deep disappointment.) These difficulties have all insured that TSZ is not read or studied in university philosophy departments anywhere near as often as the Nietzschean standards, *The Birth of Tragedy*, *The Uses and Disadvantages of History*, *Beyond Good and Evil*, and *The Genealogy of Morals*.

This is understandable, but such judgments may be quite premature. Throughout the short and extremely volatile reception of his work, Nietzsche may not yet have been given enough leeway with his various experiments in a new kind of philosophical writing, may have been subject much too quickly to philosophical "translations." This is an issue – how to write philosophy under contemporary historical conditions, or even how to write "philosophically" now that much of traditional philosophy itself is no longer historically credible – that Nietzsche obviously devoted a great deal of thought to, and it is extremely unlikely that his conclusions would not show up in worked out, highly crafted forms. They ask of the reader something different than traditional reading and understanding, but they are asking for some effort, even demanding it, from readers. This is especially at issue in TSZ since insofar as it could be said to have a dominant theme, it is *this* problem, Zarathustra's problem: who is his audience? What is he trying to accomplish? How does he think he should go about this? While it is pretty clear what it means for his teaching to be rejected, he seems himself very unsure of what would count as having that teaching understood and accepted. (The theme – the question we have to understand first before anything in the work can be addressed – is clearly announced in the subtitle: *A Book for All and None*. How *could* a book be for all and none?)

THUS SPOKE ZARATHUSTRA AS A WORK OF LITERATURE?

On the face of it at least some answers seem accessible from the plot of the work. Zarathustra leaves his cave to revisit the human world because he wants both to prophesy and help hasten the advent of something like a new "attempt" on the part of mankind, a post "beyond" or "over the human" (*Übermensch*) aspiration. Such a goal would be free of the psychological dimensions that have led the human type into a state of some crisis (made worse by the fact that most do not think a crisis has occurred or that any new attempt is necessary). Much of the first two parts is thus occupied with setting out these failings, and the various human types who most embody them, railing against them by showing what they have cost us, and intimating how things might be different. Some such failings, like having the wrong sort of relation to oneself, or being burdened with a spirit of revenge against time itself, are particularly important. So we are treated to brief characterizations of the despisers of the body, the pale criminal, the preachers of death, warriors, chastity, the pitying, the hinterworldly, the bestowers of virtue, women, priests, the virtuous, the rabble, the sublime ones, poets, and scholars. Along the way these typologies, one might call them, are interrupted by even more figurative parables (On the Adder's Bite, the Blessed Isles, Tarantulas, the Stillest Hour), by highly figurative homilies on such topics as friends, marriage, a free death, self-overcoming, redemption, and prudence, as well as by three songs, Night Song, Dance Song, and Grave Song.

However, we encounter a very difficult issue right away when we try to take account of the fact that in all these discussions, Zarathustra's account is throughout so highly parabolic, metaphorical, and aphoristic. Rather than state various claims about virtues and the present age and religion and aspirations, Zarathustra speaks about stars, animals, trees, tarantulas, dreams, and so forth. Explanations and claims are almost always analogical and figurative. (In his discussion of TSZ in *Ecce Homo*, Nietzsche wrote, "The most powerful force of metaphor that has ever existed is poor and trivial compared with the return of language to the nature of imagery.")[12] Why is his message given in such a highly figurative, literary way? It is an important question because it goes to the heart of Nietzsche's own view of his relation to traditional philosophy, and how the literary and rhetorical form of his books marks whatever sort of new beginning he thinks he has made. Philosophy after all has traditionally thought of itself as clarifying what is unclear, and as attempting to justify what in the everyday world too often passes without challenge. Philosophy tries to reveal, we might say in general, what is hidden (in presuppositions, commitments, folk wisdom,

---

[12] EH, §6, p. 130.

etc.). If we think of literature in such traditional ways, though, then there is a clear contrast. A literary work does not assert anything. "Meaning" in a poem or play or novel is not only hidden, and requires effort to find; our sense of the greatness of great literature is bound up with our sense that the credibility and authority of such works rests on how much and how complexly meaning is both profoundly and unavoidably hidden and enticingly intimated, promised; how difficult to discern, but "there," extractable in prosaic summaries only with great distortion. Contrary to the philosophical attempt (or fantasy) of freeing ordinary life from illusions, confusions and unjustified presuppositions, one way in which a literary treatment departs from ordinary life lies in its great compression of possible meanings, defamiliarization, "showing" paradoxically how much *more* is hidden, mysterious, sublime in ordinary life than is ordinarily understood. (One thinks of Emily Dickinson's pithy summary: "Nature is a haunted house, but art is a house that wants to be haunted.")[13]

What would it mean to present a "teaching" with so many philosophical resonances, so close to the philosophy we might call "value theory," in a way that not only leaves so much hidden, but that in effect heightens our sense of the interpretive work that must be done before philosophical reflection can hope to begin (if even then), and even further impedes any hermeneutic response by inventing a context so unfamiliar and often bizarre? There is

---

[13] Emily Dickinson, *Emily Dickinson: Selected Letters*, ed. T. H. Johnson (Cambridge: Harvard University Press, 1958), p. 236. There is another text by a "Nietzschean" author that might also serve as, might even have been, a commentary on this aspect of TSZ – Kafka's famous parable, "On Parables":

Many complain that the words of the wise are always merely parables and of no use in daily life, which is the only life we have. When the sage says, "Go over," he does not mean that we should cross to some actual place, which we could do anyhow if the labor were worth it; he means some fabulous yonder [Drüben], something unknown to us, something that he cannot designate more precisely either, and therefore cannot help us here in the very least. All these parables set out to say merely that the incomprehensible is incomprehensible, and we know that already. But the cares we have to struggle with every day; that is a different matter.

Concerning this a man once said: Why such reluctance? If you only followed the parables you yourselves would become parables and with that rid of all your daily cares.

Another said: I bet that is also a parable.

The first said: You have won.

The second said: But unfortunately only in parable.

The first said: No, in reality; in parable you have lost.

Franz Kafka, *The Basic Kafka* (New York: Pocket Books, 1979), p. 58. It is well known that Kafka read and admired Nietzsche. The story about his vigorous defense of Nietzsche against Max Brod's charge that Nietzsche was a "fraud" is often cited. See Klaus Wagenbach, *Kafka*, trans. Ewald Osers (Cambridge: Harvard University Press, 2003), p. 41.

a famous claim concerning truth and appearance and a set of complex images that are both relevant to this question.[14]

TRUTH, APPEARANCE, AND THE FAILURE OF DESIRE

In more traditional philosophical terms, Nietzsche often stresses that we start going wrong when we become captured by the picture of revealing "reality," the "truth," beneath appearances, in mere opinions. This can be particularly misleading, Nietzsche often states, when we think of ourselves in post-Kantian modernity as having exposed the supposed groundlessness "underneath" the deceptive appearances of value and purpose, when we think that we have rendered impossible any continuation of Zarathustra's pronounced love of human beings, life, and the earth. Some impasse in the possible affirmation of value (what Zarathustra calls "esteeming") *has* been reached ("nihilism") but this "radical enlightenment" picture is not the right description. (See Zarathustra's attack on the "preachers of death" and his rejection there of the melancholy that might result when "they encounter a sick or a very old person or a corpse, and right away they say, 'life is refuted'" (p. 32).) And Nietzsche clearly wants to discard as misleading that simple distinction between appearance and reality itself. He is well known for claiming, in his own mini-version of the self-education of the human spirit in *The Twilight of the Idols*, that

We have abolished the real world: what world is left? The apparent world perhaps? . . . But no! *with the real world we have also abolished the apparent world.*[15]

However, even if this sort of suspicion of the everyday appearances (that they are merely a pale copy of the true world, the true ideal, etc.) is rejected, it is very much not the case that Nietzsche wants to infer that we are therefore left merely to achieve as much subjectively measured happiness as possible, nor does he intend to open the door to a measureless, wildly tolerant pluralism. As he has set it out, Nietzsche's new philosophers (or post-philosophers) are still driven by what he calls a modern

---

[14] I pass over here another complex dimension of Nietzsche's literary style. Zarathustra is not Nietzsche, any more than Prospero is Shakespeare, and appreciating the literary irony of the work is indispensable to a full reading. I have tried to sketch an interpretation along these lines in "Irony and Affirmation in Nietzsche's *Thus Spoke Zarathustra*," in *Nietzsche's New Seas: Explorations in Philosophy, Aesthetics, and Politics*, ed. Michael Allen Gillespie and Tracy Strong (Chicago: University of Chicago Press, 1988), pp. 45–74.

[15] Friedrich Nietzsche, *Twilight of the Idols*, in *Twilight of the Idols and The Anti-Christ*, trans. R. J. Hollingdale (Harmondsworth: Penguin Books, 1968), p. 50.

"intellectual conscience":[16] they want to know if what matters to them now ought to matter, whether there might be more important things to care about. Even though not driven by an otherworldly or transcendent or even "objective" ideal beneath or above the appearances, they should still be able to "overcome themselves" and in this way, to escape "wretched contentment." That is, they cannot orient themselves from the question, "What matters *in itself*?" as if a reality beneath the appearances, but even without reliance on such a reality, a possible self-dissatisfaction and striving must still be possible if an affirmable, especially what Nietzsche sometimes calls a "noble" life, is still to be possible. And he clearly believes that the major element of this possibility is *his* own effect on his listeners. A great deal depends *on him* (just as in the "tragic age of the Greeks," Socrates was able to create, to legislate a new form of life). In what way, goes the implied question or experiment, can a human being now tied to the "earth" still aspire to be ultimately "overman," *Übermensch*? How could one come to *want* such an earthly self-overcoming in these post-death-of-God conditions? Whence the right sort of contempt for one's present state, and aspiration for some future goal? Whatever the answer to such questions, Nietzsche clearly thinks that the character of Zarathustra's literary rhetoric must be understood in terms of this goal.

Parallel to the paradox of a book for all and none, this problem suggests the paradox of how Zarathustra by "going *under*" and by destroying hopes for a "hinterworld" in the names of "earth" and "life" can prepare the way for a new form of "going *over*," can prepare the transition between human beings as they now are and an "overman." One final version of essentially the same paradox: how can Zarathustra inspire and shame without being imitated, without creating disciples?[17]

---

[16] GS, §2, p. 29. See also the remark in *Daybreak*, about how the drive to knowledge

"has become too strong for us to be able to want happiness without knowledge or [to be able to want the happiness] of a strong, firmly rooted delusion; even to imagine such a state of things is painful to us! Restless discovering and divining has such an attraction for us, and has grown as indispensable to us as is to the lover his unrequited love, which he would at no price relinquish for a state of indifference – perhaps, indeed, we too are unrequited lovers" (Friedrich Nietzsche, *Daybreak: Thoughts on the Prejudices of Morality*, trans. R. J. Hollingdale and ed. Maudemarie Clark and Brian Leiter (Cambridge: Cambridge University Press, 1997), §429, p. 184).

[17] In EH, what distinguishes Zarathustra is said to be his capacity for contradictions like this (EH, §6, pp. 129–130). See also section 1, "On Great Longing," references to "loving contempt" (p. 179) and to the intertwining of love and hate for life in "The Other Dance Song" (p. 181). This is also the problem of "exemplarity" in Nietzsche's *Schopenhauer as Educator* essay. There is an illuminating essay on this issue, "Nietzsche's Perfectionism: A Reading of *Schopenhauer as Educator*," of great relevance to TSZ, by James Conant in *Nietzsche's Postmoralism: Essays on Nietzsche's Prelude to Philosophy*, ed. R. Schacht (Cambridge: Cambridge University Press, 2001), pp. 180–257.

For example, in the Preface to *Beyond Good and Evil*, Nietzsche notes that our long struggle with and often opposition to and dissatisfaction with our own moral tradition, European Christianity, has created a "magnificent tension (*Spannung*) of the spirit in Europe, the likes of which the earth has never known: with such a tension in our bow we can now shoot at the furthest goals." But, he goes on, the "democratic Enlightenment" also sought to "unbend" such a bow, to "make sure that spirit does not experience itself so readily as 'need.'"[18] This latter formulation coincides with a wonderfully lapidary expression in *The Gay Science*. In discussing "the millions of Europeans who cannot endure their boredom and themselves," he notes that they would even welcome "a craving to suffer" and so "to find in their suffering a probable reason for action, for deeds." In sum: "neediness is needed!" ("Not ist nötig").[19] In TSZ, the point is formulated in a similar way:

Beware! The time approaches when human beings no longer launch the arrow of their longing beyond the human, and the string of their bow will have forgotten how to whir!

Beware! The time approaches when human beings will no longer give birth to a dancing star. Beware! The time of the most contemptible human is coming, the one who can no longer have contempt for himself. [p. 9][20]

In these terms Nietzsche is trying to create something like a living model for a new, heroic form of affirmation of life (something like the way Montaigne simply offered himself to his readers),[21] and by means of this model to re-introduce this "tension" of spirit so necessary for self-overcoming. This picture of a living, complex Zarathustra and his unsettledness, his inability to rest content either in isolation or in society, his uncertainty about a form of address, his apostrophes to various dimensions of himself, his illness and recovery, are all supposed to provide us with both an archetypal picture of the great dilemma of modernity itself (the problem of affirmation, a new striving to be "higher"), but also to inspire the kind of thoughtfulness and risk-taking Zarathustra embodies. In his more grandiose moments Nietzsche no doubt thought of Zarathustra's struggles and explorations as

[18] Friedrich Nietzsche, *Beyond Good and Evil*, trans. Judith Norman, ed. Rolf-Peter Horstmann and Judith Norman (Cambridge: Cambridge University Press, 2002), Preface, p. 4.

[19] GS, §56.

[20] See also "On Unwilling Bliss" in the third part, where Zarathustra speaks of the "desire for love" (pp. 127–30).

[21] For more on Nietzsche's relation to Montaigne and the French psychological tradition, see my *Nietzsche moraliste français. La conception nietzschéenne d'une psychologie philosophique*, forthcoming, 2005, Odile Jacob. Emerson is also clearly a model as well. See Conant, *Nietzsche's Postmoralism*.

reaching for us the same fundamental level as Homer's Odysseus, as Moses, as Virgil's Aeneas, as Christ. TSZ is somehow to be addressed to the source of whatever longing, striving, desire gives life a direction, inspires sacrifice and dedication. And it will be a very difficult task. There is a clear account of the basic issue in *Ecce Homo*:

The psychological problem apparent in the Zarathustra type is how someone who to an unprecedented degree says no and *does* no to everything everyone has said yes to so far, – how somebody like this can nevertheless be the opposite of a no-saying spirit.[22]

And this way of putting the point makes it clear that Nietzsche also imagines that the experiment in so addressing each other might easily and contingently fail and fail catastrophically; it may just be the case that a sustainable attachment to life and to each other requires the kind of more standard, prosaic "illusion" (a lie) that we have also rendered impossible. The possibility of such a failure is also an issue that worries Zarathustra a great deal, as we shall see.

The problem, then, that Zarathustra must address, the problem of "nihilism," is a kind of collective failure of desire, bows that have lost their tension, the absence of "need" or of any fruitful self-contempt, the presence of wretched contentment, "settling" for too little. And these discussions of desire and meaning throw into a different light how he means to address such a failure. As we have seen, even texts other than TSZ are overwhelmingly literary, rhetorically complex, elliptical, and always a matter of adopting personae and "masks," often the mask of a historian or scientist.[23] He appears to believe that this is the only effective way to reach the level of such concern – to address an audience suffering from failed desire (without knowing it). Nietzsche clearly thinks we cannot understand such a possibility, much less be both shamed and inspired by it, except by a literary and so "living" treatment of such an existential possibility. And Nietzsche clearly thinks he has such a chance, in the current historical context of crisis, collapse, boredom, and confusion, a chance of shaming and cajoling us away from commitments that will condemn us to a "last man" or "pale atheist" sort of existence, and of inspiring a new desire, a new "tension" of the spirit. Hence the importance of these endless pictures and images: truth as a woman, science as gay, troubadours, tomb robbers,

---

[22] EH, §6, pp. 130–131.
[23] For an extensive discussion of the issue of masks in TSZ see Stanley Rosen, *The Mask of Enlightenment: Nietzsche's Zarathustra* (Cambridge: Cambridge University Press, 1995).

seduction, romance, prophets, animals, tightrope walkers, dwarves, bee-
hives, crazy men, sleep, dreams, breeding, blonde beasts, twilight of the
gods, and on and on. (It makes *all* the difference in the world if, having
appreciated this point, we then appreciate that such notions as "the will
to power" and "the eternal return of the same" *belong on this list*, are not
independent "philosophical" explanations of the meaning of the list. It is
not an accident that Nietzsche often introduces these notions with the
same hypothetical indirectness that he uses for the other images.)

THE DRAMATIC ACTION (PROLOGUE AND PART I)

However, as in many dramatic and literary presentations of philosophy
(such as Platonic dialogues, Proust's novel, Beckett's plays, and so forth)
there are not only things said, but things done, and said and done by
characters located somewhere and at a time, usually within a narrative
time that is constantly changing contexts, conditions of appropriateness,
aspects of relevance, and the like. On the face of it this means that one
ought to be aware of who says what to whom when, and what is shown
rather than said by what they do and what happens to them. In this case,
Zarathustra had left the human world when he was thirty and stayed ten
years in the mountains. We are not told why, although it is implied that
he had psychologically "burned up"; he carried his own "ashes" up to the
mountain. In the section "The Hinterworldly" he also tells us that he
managed to free himself (he does not tell us how) from the view that the
finite human world was an imperfect copy of something better, "the work
of a suffering and tortured god," that such views were a kind of disease
he had recovered from, and that he now speaks of "the meaning of the
earth" (p. 6). But we are not told exactly when this event occurred, before
or after his voluntary exile, and the speech can be misleading unless, as
just discussed above, it is read together with a number of others about self-
overcoming. That is, it turns out not at all to be *easy*, having abandoned a
transcendent source of ideals, to live in a way true to this meaning of the
earth or to understand in what sense this is a "self-overcoming" way. The
latter is not a mere "liberationist" project, but one that in some ways is
even more difficult than traditional self-denying virtue.

We also have no clear sense of what Zarathustra did all day, every day
for ten years; he seemed mostly to think, contemplate, and talk to animals, especially his favorites, his snake and eagle (already an indication of
a link between the low and the high in all things human). But we do know
that something happened to him one day, his "heart transformed," and he

resolved to re-enter the human world. We might assume, given Nietzsche's own diagnosis of the age, that this change was brought about by a sense of some coming crisis among humans. That is, Nietzsche is well known for calling this crisis "nihilism," and eventually many of Zarathustra's speeches express this urgency about our becoming the "last human beings," humans who can no longer "overcome themselves." But initially Zarathustra's return is promoted by motives that are explicit and somewhat harder to understand. He had become "weary" of the wisdom gained while in isolation and needs to distribute it, much as the sun gratuitously "overflows" with warmth and light for humans; he would be in some way fatigued or frustrated by not being able to share this overflow. In a brief exchange with a hermit on the way down, we learn two further things about Zarathustra's motives. His generosity is prompted by *a love of human beings*, and those who remain in hermit-like isolation can do so only because they have not heard that "God is dead."

These references to love, gift-giving, and Zarathustra's potential weariness are quite important since they amount to his further figurative answers to questions about the intended function and purpose of TSZ; it is a gift of love and meant to inspire some erotic longing as well. (This assumes that Zarathustra's fate in some way allegorizes what Nietzsche expects the fate of TSZ to be and, while this seems credible, Nietzsche also ironicizes Zarathustra enough to give one pause about such an allegory.) The images suggest that the lassitude, smug self-satisfaction, and complacency that Zarathustra finds around him in the market place and later in the city define the problem he faces in the unusual way suggested above. It again suggests that what in other contexts he could call the problem of nihilism is not so much the result of some discovery, a new piece of knowledge (that God is dead, or that values are ungrounded, contingent psychological projections), nor merely a fearful failure of will, a failing that requires the rhetoric of courage, a call to a new kind of strength. As noted, the problem Zarathustra confronts seems to be a failure of desire; nobody wants what he is offering, and they seem to want very little other than a rather bovine version of happiness. It is that sort of failure that proves particularly difficult to address, and that cannot be corrected by thinking up a "better argument" against such a failure.

The events that are narrated are also clearly tied to the question of what it means for Zarathustra to have a teaching, to try to impart it to an audience suffering in this unusual way, suffering from complacency or dead desire. Only at the very beginning, in the Prologue, does he try to "lecture publicly," one might say, and this is a pretty unambiguous failure.

He is jeered at and mocked and he leaves, saying "I am not the mouth for these ears" (p. 9). The meaning of his attempt, however, seems to be acted out in an unusual drama about a tightrope walker who mistakenly thinks he is being called to start his act, does so, and then is frightened into a fall by a "jester" who had attempted to leap over the tightrope walker. It is not uncommon in TSZ that Zarathustra later returns to some of these early images and offers an interpretation. In Part III, in the section called "On Old and New Tablets," Zarathustra remarks,

This is what my great love of the farthest demands: *do not spare your neighbor*! Human being is something that must be overcome.
    There are manifold ways and means of overcoming: *you* see to it! But only a jester thinks: "human being can also be *leaped over*." (p. 159)

This is only one of many manifestations of the importance of understanding Zarathustra's "love" and his intimations of the great difficulty involved in his new doctrine of self-overcoming. Here it is something that must be accomplished by each ("*you* see to it!") and even more strikingly, the reminder here of the Prologue appears to indicate that Zarathustra himself had portrayed his own teaching in a comically inadequate way, preaching to the multitudes as if people could simply begin to overcome themselves by some revolutionary act of will, as if the overman were a new species to be arrived at by "overleaping" the current one. We come closer here to the parodic elements of the text; in this case a kind of self-parody.

THE WANDERING ZARATHUSTRA (PART II)

The other plot events in the book also continue to suggest a great unsettledness in Zarathustra's conception and execution of his project, rather than a confident manifesto by Nietzsche through the persona of Zarathustra. He had shifted from market place preaching to conversations with disciples in Part I, and at the end of that Part he decides to forgo even that and to go back to his cave alone, and warns his disciples to "guard" themselves against him, and even "to be ashamed of him" (p. 59). At the beginning of Part II he begins to descend again, and again we hear that he is overfull and weary with his gifts and with love (the image of love has changed into something more dramatic: "And may my torrent of love plunge into impasses!"), but now we hear something new, something absent from his first descent: he is also concerned and impatient. "My enemies have become powerful and have distorted the image of my teaching." He will seek out his friends and disciples again (as well as his enemies this time, he notes) but he seems to have realized that part of the problem with the dissemination of his teachings and warnings lies in him, and not just the audience. He admits that his wisdom is a "wild" wisdom that frightens, and that he might scare everyone off, even his friends. "If only my lioness-wisdom could learn to roar tenderly!" he laments, a lesson he clearly thinks he has not yet learned.

The crucial dramatic event in Part II is what occurs near the end. Until then many of Zarathustra's themes had been similar to, or extensions of, what he had already said. Again he seeks to understand the possibility of a form of self-dissatisfaction and even self-contempt that is not based on some sense of *absence* or incompleteness, a natural gap or imperfection that needs to be filled or completed, and so a new goal that can be linked with a new *kind* of desire to "overcome." He discusses that issue here in terms of "revenge," especially against time, and he begins to worry that, with no redemptive revolutionary hope in human life, no ultimate justice in the after-life, and no realm of objective "goods in themselves" or any natural right, human beings will come to see a finite, temporally mutable, contingent life as a kind of burden, or curse, or purposeless play, and they will exact revenge for having been arbitrarily thrown into this condition. What he means to say in the important section "On the Tarantulas" is something he had not made clear before, least of all to himself. Indeed, he had helped create the illusion he wants to dispel. He now denies that he, Zarathustra, is a historical or revolutionary figure who will somehow save all of us from this fate, and he denies that the overman is a historical goal (in the way a prophet would foretell the coming of *the* redeemer) but a personal and quite elusive, very difficult new kind of ideal for each individual. In this sense TSZ can be a book for all, for anyone who is responsive to the call to self-overcoming, but for none, in the sense that it cannot offer a comprehensive reason (for anyone) to overcome themselves and cannot offer specific prescriptions. (It is striking that, although Zarathustra opens his speeches with the call for an overman, that aspect of his message virtually drops out after Part II.)[24] Indeed Zarathustra's role as such an early prophet is again part of what makes his early manifestation comic, a *parodia*. He is clearly pulling back from such a role:

But so that I do *not* whirl, my friends, bind me fast to the pillar here! I would rather be a stylite than a whirlwind of revenge!

Indeed, Zarathustra is no tornado or whirlwind; and if he is a dancer, nevermore a tarantella dancer! (p. 79)

---

[24] For more detail on the relation between the first two parts and the last two, see Pippin, "Irony and Affirmation."

Even so, this dance of some escape from revenge is hardly an automatic affirmation of existence as such. Throughout Part II, there are constant reminders of how *hard* this new sort of self-overcoming will be. The "Famous Wise Men" did not know the first thing about what "spirit" truly was:

Spirit is life that itself cuts into life; by its own agony it increases its own knowledge – did you know that?

And the happiness of spirit is this: to be anointed and consecrated by tears to serve as a sacrificial animal – did you know that? (p. 80)

Other dimensions of this "agony," and the failed hopes of the beginning of his project start appearing. He says that "My happiness in bestowing died in bestowing, my virtue wearied of itself in its superabundance" (p. 82). Paradoxical (to say the least) formulations arise. "At bottom I love only life – and verily, most when I hate it!"

THE PROBLEM OF SELF-OVERCOMING

But he seems also to be gaining some clarity about his earlier aspirations and about the nature of the theme that plays the most important role in TSZ, "self-overcoming." In a passage with that name, he comments on the doctrine most associated with Nietzsche, "the will to power." But again everything is expressed figuratively. He says that all prior values had been placed in a "skiff" as a result of the "dominating will" of the inventors of such values and he suggests that this "river of becoming" has carried those values to a disturbingly unexpected fate. He counsels these "wisest ones" not to think of this historical and largely uncontrollable fate as dangerous and the end of good and evil; rather the river itself (not a psychological will for power on the part of the creators) is the will to power, the "unexhausted begetting will of life," the current of radical historical change "upon" which or in terms of which obeying and esteeming and committing must always go on. And he notes that he has learned three things about this process. (1) Life itself (that is the possibility of *leading* a life) always requires "obedience," that is, the possibility of commitment to a norm or goal and the capacity to sustain such commitment. (2) "The one who cannot obey himself is commanded." (If we do not find a way of leading our life, it will be led for us one way or another.) And (3) "Commanding is harder than obeying." He then adds what is in effect a fourth point to these, that the attempt to exercise such command is "an experiment and a risk"; indeed a risk of life. He tells us that with these questions he is at the very "heart of life and into the roots of its heart" (p. 89). There, in this heartland, he again confronts the problem he had discussed earlier in many different ways, the wrong sort of self-contempt, the absence of any arrows shot beyond man, no giving birth to stars, the bovine complacency of the last human beings. He asks again, that is, *the* question: without possible reliance on a faith in divine purposes or natural perfections (that river has "carried" us beyond such options), how should we now understand the possibility of the "intellectual conscience" without which we would be beneath contempt? That is, whence the experience that we are *not* as we could be, that what matters to me now might not be what should matter most, that our present state, for each individual, must be "overcome"? Why? Since the summary "secret" that Zarathustra has learned from life is expressed this way – "And this secret life itself spoke to me: 'Behold,' it said, 'I am that *which must always overcome itself*,'" – it appears that what is at stake for him is the possibility of coming to exercise power *over oneself*; that is, to lead one's life both by sustaining commitments (right "to the death," he often implies, suggesting that being able to lead a life in such a whole-hearted way is much more to be esteemed than merely staying alive) and by finding some way to endure the altering historical conditions of valuing, esteeming, such that one can "overcome" the self so committed to prior values and find a way to "will" again. One could say that what makes the "overman" (*Übermensch*) genuinely self-transcending is that he can over-come himself, accomplish when necessary this self-transcending (*Selbst-Überwindung*.) He thereby has gained power "over" himself and so realized his will to power:

That I must be struggle and becoming and purpose and the contradiction of purposes – alas, whoever guesses my will guesses also on what *crooked* paths it must walk!
   Whatever I may create and however I may love it – soon I must oppose it and my love, thus my will wants it. (pp. 89–90)

Likewise, Zarathustra stresses that good and evil, any life-orienting normative distinctions, are hardly everlasting; rather they "must overcome themselves out of themselves again and again." That is, self-overcoming is not transcending a present state for the sake of an ideal, stable higher state (as in a naturally perfected state or any other kind of fixed telos). All aspirations to be more, better than one is, if they are possible at all in present conditions, are provisional, will always give rise to further transformed aspirations. Zarathustra's questions about this do not so much concern traditional philosophical questions about such a form of life but a much more difficult one to address: could we *bear, endure* such a fate? Clearly

Zarathustra's own starts and stops, and the effect these have on him, are meant to raise such an issue dramatically. (And it is not at all clear that this issue is in any way resolved, or that a resolution is even relevant.)

Two other things are quite striking about these formulations. The first, as the autobiographical inflection of such passages makes clear, is that we have to see Zarathustra as embodying this struggle, and thus must note that this possibility – the heart of everything, the possibility of self-overcoming – seems thereby also tied somehow to *his* problems of rhetoric, language, of audience, friends, his own loneliness, and occasional bitterness and pity. Some condition of success in self-overcoming is linked to achieving the right relation to others (and so, by implication, is inconsistent with a hermit-like, isolated life). The second emerges quickly from the first. We have to note that Zarathustra, as the embodiment of this struggle, whatever this relation to others turns out to be, is completely uninterested in gaining power *over others*, subjecting as much or as many as possible to his control or command. ("I lack the lion's voice for all commanding" (p. 116).) *Self-*commanding (and, dialectically, self-obeying) are the great problems. (In fact he keeps insisting that the *last* thing he wants is the ability to command them. His chief problem is that whenever he hears them re-formulate what he thinks he has said or dreamt, he is either disappointed, or perhaps anxious that he does not understand his own "doctrine"; they may be right, he may be wrong, and no intellectual conscience could sustain a commitment that was suspected of being delusory.) Even when he appears to discuss serving or mastering others, he treats it as in the service of self-mastery and so again possible self-overcoming. ("[A]nd even in the will of the serving I found the will to be master" (p. 89).)[25]

These are less formulations of a position than fragmentary and largely programmatic aspects of Zarathustra's self-diagnosis and the cure he at least aspires to. Many philosophical questions arise inevitably. *What* would be amiss, lost, wrong in a life not fully or not at all "led" by a subject? How could this aspiration towards something believed to be higher or more worthy than what one is or has now *be directed*, if all the old language of external or objective forms of normative authority is now impossible? On what grounds can one say that a desire to cultivate a different sort of self, to

---

[25] There are of course other passages in Nietzsche which seem to encourage a violent upheaval, all so that the strong can rule over the weak and so forth. I have only space to say that if we use TSZ as a model for reading Nietzsche, and attend to issues like voice, persona, irony, and context, we will see a Nietzsche very different from the traditional one. For more on the political issues in Nietzsche, see my "Deceit, Desire, and Democracy: Nietzsche on Modern Eros," *International Studies in Philosophy*, 32:3 (March, 2000), pp. 63–70.

overcome oneself, is really in the service of a "higher" self? Higher in what sense? What could be said to be responsible for (relied on for) securing this obedience, for helping to ward off skepticism when it arises? Under what conditions can such commitments and projects be said to lose their grip on a subject, fail, or die?

In general Zarathustra does not fully accept the burden of these questions as ones he must assume. For one thing he clearly does not believe that the inspiration for such an attempt at self-direction and something like "becoming better at becoming who one is"[26] can be provided by an argument or a revelation or a command. One would already have had to measure oneself and one's worth against "arguments" or "revelation" or "authoritative commands" for such different calls to be effective and it is to *that* prior, deepest level of commitment that Zarathustra, however indirectly and figuratively, is directing his rhetoric. And given the great indeterminateness of his approach, he is clearly much more interested in the qualitative characteristics of such commitments than with their content. The quality he is most interested in turns out to be extremely complex: on the one hand, "whole-heartedness" and an absorbed or passionate "identification" with one's higher ideal; on the other hand, a paradoxical capacity to "let go" of such commitments and pursue other ideals when the originals (somehow) cease to serve self-overcoming and self-transcendence, when they lead to complacency and contentment.

However, to come to by far the most complicated issue introduced by Zarathustra's speeches, he clearly also thinks that such qualitative considerations – the chief topic of the book, the qualitative dimensions of a self-relation that will in the present circumstances make possible a yearning for a self-overcoming and escape from mere contentment – will also *rule out various contents*. It is clear that he, and in this case Nietzsche as well, thinks that one cannot whole-heartedly and "self-overcomingly" *be* a "last human being" or any of its many manifestations (a petty tyrant, a pale atheist, a "reactive" type, a modern ascetic). Such types embody forms of a "negative" self-relation that are "reactive" and self-denying in a way that makes true self-overcoming and self-affirmation impossible and so will not allow that form of identification with one's deeds that Zarathustra suggests should be like the way a "mother" sees herself in her "child." ("I wish *your* self were in the deed like the mother is in the child; let that be *your* word on virtue" (p. 74).) Yet it is also clear that one cannot simply *will* "to have contempt for oneself as Zarathustra recommends." The right relation

---

[26] That is, better at becoming who one truly is, beyond or over one's present state.

between shame and yearning is as delicate and elusive as are Zarathustra's strange speeches and dreams and visions. And, as we have been seeing, he also clearly thinks (or he experiences in his own adventures) that only *some kinds of relations to others* are consistent with the possibility of such genuine self-direction. Merely commanding others, discipleship, indifference, or isolation are all ruled out. Since we also do not ever get from Nietzsche a discursive account of what distinguishes a genuine form of self-direction and self-overcoming from an illusory or self-deceived one (whatever such a distinction amounts to, it is not of the kind that could be helped, would be better realized, by such a theory), elements of how he understands that distinction emerge only indirectly and, together with a clearer understanding of self-overcoming and the social relations it requires, would all have to be reconstructed from a wide variety of contexts and passages. Moreover, to make everything even more complicated, Nietzsche also clearly believes that such a whole-hearted aspiration to self-overcoming is also consistent with a certain level of *irony*, some distance from one's ideals, the adoption of personae and masks, and even a kind of esotericism when addressing different audiences.

ILLNESS AND CONVALESCENCE (PART III)

But while Zarathustra does not treat these issues as discursive problems, as if they were problems about skepticism or justification, he does *suffer* from them, suffer from the burden that the thought of such contingency imposes on any possibly worthy life. He becomes ill, apparently ill with the human condition as such, even disgusted by it, and a great deal of the latter four speeches of Part II and the majority of Part III involve his possible recovery from such an illness, his "convalescing." There is in effect a kind of mini-narrative from the speech called "The Soothsayer" in Part II until the speech "On Unwilling Bliss" in Part III that is at the center of the work's drama, and the re-orientation effected there is played out throughout the rest of Part III, especially in "The Convalescent." Dramatically, at the end of Part II Zarathustra again resolves to return home, and in Part III he is underway back there, and finally reaches his cave and his animals.

"The Soothsayer" begins with remarks about the famous doctrine mostly attributed to Nietzsche, but here expressed by a soothsayer and quoted by Zarathustra. (In *Ecce Homo*, the idea is called the "basic idea" and "fundamental thought" of the work.)[27] This notion, that "Everything is

---

[27] EH, §1, pp. 123 and 124.

empty, everything is the same, everything was!" is promptly interpreted in a melancholic way, such that "We have become too weary to die; now we continue to wake and we live on – in burial chambers" (p. 106). It is this prophecy that "went straight to his [Zarathustra's] heart and transformed him." He does not eat or drink for three days, does not speak, and does not sleep. In typically figurative language he explains the source of his despair in a way that suggests a kind of self-critique. He had clearly earlier placed his hopes for mankind in a dramatic historical, epochal moment, the bridge from man to the overman, and he now realizes that it was a mistake to consider this a historical goal or broad civilizational ideal, that such a teleology is a fantasy, that rather "all recurs eternally," that the last human being cannot be overcome in some revolutionary moment. In the language of his strange dream he finds that he does not, after all, have the "keys" to open the relevant historical gate (he thought he did, thought he need not only keep watch over, but could open up, what had gone dead), that it is a matter of chance or a sudden wind whether or not a historical change will occur within individuals, and if it does, it might be nothing but the release of what had been dead. His disciples promptly interpret the dream in exactly the opposite way, as if Zarathustra himself were "the [liberating] wind." Zarathustra merely shakes his head in disappointment and continues his wandering home.

The details of Zarathustra's re-evaluation of what is required now of him and his addressees in order, in effect, to "take up the reins" of a life and live it better, to embody a commitment to constant self-transcendence, instead of merely suffering existence, involve scores of images and parables. Zarathustra will not now see himself as removing the deformity from "cripples." That is useless, he implies; they must do that for themselves. Or Zarathustra must learn to be silent often, to teach by not teaching, and this occasions the clearest expressions, even at this late date, of the ambiguities in Zarathustra's role and self-understanding:

Is he a promiser? Or a fulfiller? A conqueror? Or an inheritor? An autumn? Or a plow? A physician? Or a convalescent?

Is he a poet? Or a truthful man? A liberator? Or a tamer? A good man? Or an evil man?

I walk among human beings as among fragments of the future; the future that I see. (p. 110)

Yet again, the question of who Zarathustra is, what he stands for, what his purpose is, remains a puzzling question *for Zarathustra himself*. Zarathustra, in other words, cannot understand what it means to be a "spokesman" for

Zarathustra. We are obviously very far from being able to see him as a spokesman for Nietzsche.

This is all also said to effect a kind of "reconciliation" with circular, repetitive time. He will encourage a liberation in which what we took to be what merely happened to us in the past can be assumed as the burden of one's own doing, that one will heroically take on what merely "was" as one's own and so transform it into "thus I willed it." (This might be likened to a Greek tragic hero who takes on more of a burden of what was done than can be strictly attributed to his deed, someone like Oedipus or Ajax.[28]) He does not need the "lion's voice" of commanding: "The stillest words are those that bring the storm. Thoughts that come on the feet of doves steer the world" (p. 117).

Throughout Part III, Zarathustra speaks mostly to himself; he learns that his greatest danger is "love," "the danger of the loneliest one, love of everything *if only it lives*!" (p. 123). He must struggle with a "spirit of gravity," his own reflective doubt that he will be "dragged down" by the "abysmal thought" of the Eternal Return. It is in this struggle that he realizes that the way in which the meaning of the absence of historical revolution or redemption is lived out or embodied in a life is not something that can be easily read off from the mere doctrine itself. There is no clear, unavoidable inference either to despair, indifference, or affirmation. The dwarf, the spirit of gravity, does that (reads despair as the implication) and "makes it too easy on himself" (p. 126). And Zarathustra again tries to "dream" his way out of his sadness by dreaming himself as a young shepherd "choking" on his own "circular" doctrine, the Eternal Return, but one who succeeds in "biting off the head of the snake" that had crawled into his throat, and so emerged "a transformed, illuminated, laughing" being (p. 127). Just how exactly the despair-inducing features of there being no temporal redemption and a ceaseless return of even the last men are transformed into an affirmative vision, and just how *this* is captured by "biting the head off the snake" is not clear. When that very question comes up much more explicitly in "The Convalescent" (Zarathustra fasts again for seven days and when he resumes speaking he mentions again the "nausea" that the thought of the Eternal Return occasioned), the attempt by his animals to attribute the Eternal Return to Zarathustra as a "teaching" is met first by his complaint that they are turning him and his struggle into a "hurdy-gurdy song" and when they go on and interpret the doctrine as a kind of immortality teaching (that Zarathustra will return), Zarathustra ignores them, communes only

---

[28] See Bernard Williams, *Shame and Necessity* (Berkeley: University of California Press, 1994).

with his soul. Also, given that aspects of Zarathustra's own despair *return* after this, the image of recovery might be as much wishful thinking, or at least the expression of a mere faint hope as it is a settled event.

ZARATHUSTRA'S TRAGIC END? PARABLES AND PARODY (PART IV)

This dialogue with his disciples also shows that one of the things that recurs repeatedly for Zarathustra are his own words; that he cannot prevent the "literalization" of his parabolic speech. His disciples are not dense or merely mistaken; they are simply trying to understand what Zarathustra means. When repeated as a teaching or a doctrine, Zarathustra's parabolic speech becomes parodic, comic. But he has no option other than saying nothing (and he has found that he cannot live in such isolation) or preaching more directly, in which case his disciples would be (even more than they already are) following him, not themselves. The parodic return of his own words is thus the heart of his tragedy.[29]

After this expression of his putative, perhaps short-lived new self-understanding, he believes he can say such things as "I gave it [chance] back to all things, I redeemed them from their servitude under purpose" (p. 132). Having done so, a "homecoming" back with his animals is now possible, he thinks, and he expresses the relation to others, here his animals, that he would have wanted "down there," but failed to achieve: "We do not implore one another, we do not deplore one another, we walk openly with one another through open doors" (p. 147). Thus, as we drift towards the end of Part III, which Nietzsche at one time clearly conceived as the end of the book, Zarathustra's despair at any change in the collective or individual lives of human beings seems at its darkest. However, as is so typical of the wandering eros of Zarathustra, within a few speeches he announces yet again "I want to return to mankind once more" (p. 156).

He does not, however, and at the beginning of Part IV, Zarathustra is still alone, and he is old now. He re-encounters the soothsayer but one cannot see in their confrontation that anything decisive is settled. And, although Zarathustra begins to talk with and assemble a wide variety of what are called "higher human beings" (kings, an old magician, the pope, the voluntary beggar, the shadow, the conscientious of spirit, the sad soothsayer, and the ass), his own "teaching" about overcoming and the higher seems here yet again parodied rather than celebrated. As noted, Part IV reads more like a comic, concluding satyr play to a tragic trilogy

---

[29] On this point I am grateful to conversations with David Wellbery.

than a real conclusion. It is especially self-parodic when all these so-called higher types end up worshipping a jackass, presumably because the ass can at least make a sound that articulates what all have been seeking, a mode of affirmation and commitment. The ass can say Hee-yaw, that is, ja, or Yes!

So we end with the same problem. Zarathustra must report, "But I still lack the proper human beings." However, when a "cloud of love" descends around him,[30] and he hears a lion's roar (a "sign" that takes us back to the three metamorphoses of the first speech), he also believes that "My children are near, my children," and yet again he leaves his cave, "glowing and strong, like a morning sun that emerges from dark mountains" (p. 266). But by this point we are experiencing as readers our own eternal return, the cycle of hope and despair, descent and return, sociality and isolation, love and contempt, parable and parody, lower and higher, earth and heaven, snake and eagle, that we have been reading about throughout. The "ending" in other words is meant to suggest a cyclical temporality, as if to pose for us the question Zarathustra continually has to ask himself. The question is oriented from the now familiar assumptions: no redemptive or revolutionary moment in human time, no re-assurance about or reliance on the naturally right or good; no revelations from God; and the eventual return of everything we have tried to overcome. Given such assumptions, the question is whether the self-overcoming Zarathustra encourages, the desire for some greater or better form of self-direction, assuming the full burden of leading a life, is practically possible, from the lived viewpoint of the agent.

In keeping with the unsystematic form of the clear models for TSZ – biblical wisdom literature, the French moral psychologists of the sixteenth and seventeenth centuries (Montaigne, Pascal, La Rochefoucauld), Emerson, Goethe – it is of course appropriate that we be "taught" nothing about this by Zarathustra, "taught" if at all only by his ultimate silence about this new possibility and so its challenge to us, to make it "our own." No lessons can be drawn from it, no summary credo articulated, no justification for a position formulated, any more than any "gift of love" like this, any image of a life worth living under these conditions, can be interrogated in this way. The work seems to function as the same kind of "test" for the reader as the soothsayer's doctrine for Zarathustra. Either the temper and credibility of Zarathustra's constant return to the ultimately unredeemable human world

---

[30] Compare, "*it is only in love*, only when shaded by the illusions produced by love, that is to say in the unconditional faith in right and perfection, that man is creative." Friedrich Nietzsche, "On the Uses and Disadvantages of History for Life," in *Untimely Meditations*, trans. R. J. Hollingdale, ed. Daniel Breazeale (Cambridge: Cambridge University Press, 1997), §7, p. 95.

will strike the chord Nietzsche hoped still existed, or it will not; either there
are such "children" as Zarathustra sees in his final vision, or they will seem
like the illusions that so many of Zarathustra's hopes have proven to be
from the beginning. Or to adopt the language of Zarathustra, and in this
case at least, Nietzsche himself, perhaps such children do have the status
of mere dreams, but they thereby also might satisfy what Nietzsche once
described as the conditions of contemporary self-overcoming: the ability
to "dream" without first having to "sleep."[31]

[31] GS, §59. A re-orientation of some sort that would permit the entertaining of some aspiration or
ideal, some inspiring picture that would not (given our intellectual conscience) have to be treated as
a distortion or fantasy or merely utopian (that we would not have to "sleep," shut off our conscience)
in order to dream in this way, is at the heart of the Kafka fable cited in n. 13 above. From what
has become the ordinary viewpoint, parables are a waste of time (What is Nietzsche's proposal? His
plan? How does he want us to live?), and the right understanding would be to *live out* the parable;
but, paradoxically, not "*as* a parable," as if a self-conscious idealization. That would be "correct,"
from the viewpoint of reality, but a destruction of the parable's function; one would have "lost."

CHAPTER 8

Nietzsche: Beyond Good and Evil

Rolf-Peter Horstmann

I

Beyond Good and Evil (*BGE*) is often considered to be one of Friedrich Nietzsche's greatest books.[1] Though it is by no means clear what criteria this assessment is based on, it is easy to understand how it comes about. It seems to be an expression of the feeling that in this book Nietzsche gives the most comprehensible and detached account of the major themes that concerned him throughout his life. Nietzsche was suspicious of almost everything addressed in this book – whether it be knowledge, truth, philosophy, or morality and religion. He regarded them as the source, or at least the effect, of a misguided tendency in the development of human nature: one that has led to disastrous cultural, social, and psychological consequences. At the same time he lets us share his more constructive views as well, mainly his views on how he wants us to perceive the world and to change our lives in order to live up to this new perception. He speaks of perspectivism, the will to power, of human nobility (*Vornehmheit*) and of the conditions of a life liberated from the constraints of oppressive tradition. In the middle of the book, he even adds a number of short aphorisms, and he ends the book with a poem that hints at the artistic background to his concern with decadence and the means for overcoming it. Thus it would seem that the whole range of Nietzsche's interests, his prejudices and his preferences, his loathings and his hopes, and above all his deep insights into our situation

I thank Dartmouth College and especially Sally Sedgwick and Margaret Robinson, whose generous hospitality gave me the opportunity to write this text. Special thanks to Karl Ameriks and Gary Hatfield for transforming my "English" into English and to Andreas Kemmerling for helpful suggestions. Very special thanks to Dina Emundts for all sorts of comments. The version printed here owes much to careful editing by Hilary Gaskin.

[1] See, for example, the Introductions to *BGE* by Walter Kaufmann (Vintage: New York, 1966) and Michael Tanner (Penguin: Harmondsworth, 1999; translation R. Hollingdale), and also Kaufmann, *Nietzsche: Philosopher, Psychologist, Antichrist* (Meridian Books: New York, 1956), and Tanner, *Nietzsche* (Oxford University Press: Oxford/New York, 1994). References for all quotations from *BGE* are to section numbers.

in the modern world, are united in an exemplary way in *BGE*, and for this reason it is a great book.

Although there is something to be said for this view, it is not the only view that is possible. There are quite a number of thinkers who would insist that it makes no sense at all to attribute greatness to any of Nietzsche's works. For these readers, all of Nietzsche's writings are flawed by serious shortcomings that justify fundamental complaints, ranging from accusations that they are utterly irrational, or devoid of informative content, to the conviction that they contain nothing but silly proclamations based on unwarranted generalizations – or a mixture of both. According to proponents of this view, the best way to think of Nietzsche's works is as the disturbing documents of the creative process of someone who was on the verge of madness. To call any of his works great would therefore amount to a categorical mistake. Interestingly enough, this bleak evaluation is not based on any disagreement with what the work's admirers tell us we will find in it, or even any disagreement with the claim that it gives us the quintessential Nietzsche.

It is a perplexing fact that it is by no means easy to decide which of these two conflicting attitudes towards *BGE* should prevail, and in the end it may be a rather personal matter. Nevertheless it is possible to identify some conditions that will influence how we are likely to think about the merits of this work. Three main factors should be taken into consideration. First, much depends on how we interpret the aims pursued by Nietzsche's work in general and *BGE* in particular. Second, our evaluation will depend on the amount of tolerance and sympathy that we are prepared to mobilize towards Nietzsche the person, and also towards certain tendencies in bourgeois culture in Germany in the second half of the nineteenth century. The third and most important factor, however, is the way that we feel about the very framework in which all our dealings with what we take to be reality are embedded: if we are confident that our normal outlook on whatever concerns us has been proven to be ultimately right, or at least on the right track, then chances are high that we will end up thinking of Nietzsche and *BGE* as a nuisance. If we are not convinced of the soundness of our normal views, then we might have second thoughts about things, and in that case a book like *BGE* might be considered illuminating and even helpful.

II

Let us start with Nietzsche the person. In the history of art, science, philosophy, and even literature one very often finds that in order to appreciate or to evaluate a work it is not much of an advantage to be familiar with its author and his life: an intellectual or artistic product is better judged on its own merits than on the basis of uncertain knowledge about the idiosyncratic features and muddled purposes of its author. Moreover, in some cases authors intentionally withdraw from their products in an attempt to become invisible and to let the work speak for itself, and thus leave us very few personal clues in their works. Rousseau could serve as an example of the first kind of case and Kant of the second; Kant goes so far as to use the phrase *de nobis ipsis silemus* ("of our own person we will say nothing") as a motto for his main work. We therefore tend to believe that a distinction can be drawn between the private views of the author and the meaning of the work which the author produces.

Yet there are some works with respect to which such a consideration does not so easily apply. These are works whose very meaning is tied intrinsically to the person of their author, as is the case with diaries, letters, personal notes, or autobiographies. Here our knowledge about the author, or perhaps an understanding of the situation the author is in, are necessary ingredients for an appreciation of the text. There are many reasons to presume that Nietzsche thought of many of his texts as being like diaries or personal notes that tell us something about himself and about his perspective on the matters they address, rather than as products that aim at objective, non-personal results. Hence, his biography may be of interest in any attempt to assess his work.

Nietzsche's life is surely not a success story; on the contrary, it is a rather sad story of misery and failure. It is the story of a man who from the beginning of his adult life, until the sudden and catastrophic end of his productive period, was confronted with embarrassing and humiliating experiences. This is true of his private life as well as of his relations with the intellectual community of his time. He was plagued by ill health, a psychosomatic wreck, suffering from all sorts of diseases ranging from chronic nervous ailments and severe eye problems, which left him almost blind, to extremely exhausting states of prolonged migraine. These conditions made life tolerable for him only in a few places in northern Italy (in the winter) and the Swiss Engadine (in the summer), and it is in these places that he spent most of his time in the 1880s. His social relations were always, to put it mildly, somewhat complicated. Those who apparently cared most about him, his mother and his sister, he found oppressive and distasteful because they represented a type of personality he deeply despised.[2] Though

---

[2] See the annihilating remark aimed at both of them in *Ecce Homo* which culminates in Nietzsche's pronouncement: "I confess that the deepest objection to the Eternal Recurrence, my real idea from

he prided himself on being comfortable with women, he does not seem to have been very successful in establishing emotionally satisfying relationships with them, which is hardly surprising given his views on women and on femininity (*Weiblichkeit*) in general.[3] Things did not go much better with his friends. The people whom he called "friends" he quite often spoke of with great resentment: he charged all of them with a lack of sensitivity toward him, he complained that none of them ever bothered to study his works, and he accused them of failing to defend him against public neglect.[4] In short, he suffered deeply from a sense of solitude and isolation, from not being appropriately acknowledged because of the supposed imperfections of the people around him.

To make things even worse, Nietzsche was not given the opportunity to compensate for the shortcomings of his private life by enjoying institutional and public success in his roles as a university teacher and author. Although he made a very promising start – he was appointed professor of classics at Basel university at the early age of twenty-four – his academic career disintegrated rapidly, in part because of his poor health and in part because he became annoyed with his teaching duties. As for his fortunes as an author, not much can be said that is positive. His first book, the now highly acclaimed treatise *The Birth of Tragedy*, did at least attract the attention of classicists (though their reaction to it was for the most part emphatically negative) and of members of the Wagnerian community (including Wagner himself).[5] But soon he had to realize that there was only a marginal interest among the public in his way of dealing with issues, whether they were philosophical topics such as truth and the metaphysical foundations of knowledge, topics concerning the history and value of religion and morality, or topics such as the critical assessment of modern culture and ideas about how to overcome what he considered to be the fundamental problems of modernity.

---

the abyss, is always my mother and my sister" (*KSA* VI, § 267, translation from Tanner, *Nietzsche*, p. 68). *KSA* refers to *Sämtliche Werke: Kritische Studienausgabe*, ed. G. Colli and M. Montinari, 15 vols. (de Gruyter: Berlin, 1980); this edition is based on the critical edition of Nietzsche's works, *Werke: Kritische Gesamtausgabe*, ed. G. Colli and M. Montinari, 28 vols. to date (de Gruyter: Berlin, 1967–).

[3] Though Nietzsche addresses this topic in *BGE* as well (§ 232 *et seq.*), the general tendency of his outlook on women is documented most succinctly in the relevant passage of *Ecce Homo* ("Why I Write Such Good Books," § 5).

[4] A good example of this assessment of his friends is again to be found in *Ecce Homo* ("The Case of Wagner," § 4).

[5] See the Introduction by Raymond Geuss to the edition of *The Birth of Tragedy* in this series (Cambridge University Press, 1999).

This lack of interest showed in the dismal number of copies sold of his books.[6]

The most discouraging experience for Nietzsche, however, may not have been this failure to gain a wider recognition. If he could have believed that his few readers represented some sort of elite, perhaps a group of distinguished intellectuals, then their taking notice of his writings would have been of importance to him and this might have counterbalanced his lack of public success. Unfortunately he could not entertain even that belief. From the very few reactions he became aware of – mostly reviews of his books in more or less obscure journals – he had to conclude that he was read by only a few readers – and the wrong ones. In his view, his readership consisted of people either unable or unwilling (or both) to understand him adequately. He blamed his readers for not being in the least prepared to give credit to his intentions and for being attentive only to those points which conveniently confirmed them in their own negative preconceptions. What he was missing on a fundamental level was a readiness on the part of readers to explore things his way, a feeling of intellectual kinship between author and audience, or, to put it another way, he deeply craved recognition from an audience that he thought fitting. This is touchingly expressed in two short remarks from *Ecce Homo*. The first relates explicitly only to his *Zarathustra*, though it is quite likely that Nietzsche thought it true of his other writings as well: "In order to understand anything at all from my *Zarathustra*, you might need to be conditioned as I am – with one foot *beyond* life."[7] The second remark delineates what he takes to be his ideal reader, and there is no doubt that he meant what he says: "When I call up the image of a perfect reader, what emerges is a monster of courage and curiosity, who is also supple, clever, cautious, a born adventurer and discoverer."[8]

---

[6] Of the book Nietzsche valued most, *Zarathustra*, whose first three parts were published separately in 1883 and 1884, only about sixty to seventy copies each were sold within the first three years after their appearance (see letter to Franz Overbeck, summer 1886: *KSB* VII, pp. 206–9). The fourth part of the *Zarathustra* was published in 1885 in a private edition of only forty copies and was not accessible to a wider public before 1892. *BGE* did not fare much better: 114 copies were sold within a year (see letter to Peter Gast, 8 June 1887: *KSB* VIII, pp. 86–8). Nietzsche comments (in the same letter to Gast): "Instructive! Namely, they simply don't want my literature." It seems that most of his other books had the same fate – they too were utterly neglected during the period in his life when he would still have cared about their success.

[7] *Ecce Homo* ("Why I Am so Wise," end of § 3).

[8] *Ibid.* ("Why I Write Such Good Books," end of § 3). In the same text he mentions explicitly the reactions to *BGE* as an example of how severely it was misunderstood or, to use his terminology, how gravely this book was sinned against because its readers were not up to its challenge ("Why I Write Such Good Books," end of § 1).

What emerges is a picture of a totally isolated, highly neurotic man who had to try hard to avoid thinking of himself as a complete failure. His way of dealing with this situation seems to have been simply not to accept the idea that all these annoying circumstances might have been brought about partly by particularities or deficiencies that could be traced back to his own person, so he managed to combine a perfectly clear and even realistic assessment of what was happening to him with an unshakeable conviction that all this had nothing to do with him and revealed nothing about him. It is this ability which, in my view, accounts for two dominant traits that appear in his published works. The first is that he never even came close to considering the possibility that – given the general intellectual climate of his time – his lack of success as an author might have something to do with his pursuing the "wrong" topics in a "wrong" way. It never crossed his mind that what he thought to be an interesting, novel, and valuable insight might indeed have been exactly what it seemed to be to almost all of his contemporaries – an overstated triviality, an extremely one-sided exaggeration or an embarrassing piece of bad reasoning. He simply stuck to the points he felt he had to make, deeply convinced of being on the right track, and fending off all signs of criticism or neglect with the maxim "so much the worse for the critic."[9]

This attitude becomes increasingly visible in his writings after *Zarathustra* and culminates in his late texts of 1888, especially in *Ecce Homo*. Here we find brilliant and witty remarks which rightly became notorious (though Nietzsche himself might not have found them very amusing, because they can also be read as documents of despair). I quote two of them: "We all know, several of us even know from experience, what it is to have long ears. Well then, I will dare to claim that I have the smallest ears. This is of no little interest to women – it seems they think I understand them better? . . . I am the *anti-ass par excellence* and this makes me a world-historical monster – I am, in Greek, but not only in Greek, the *Antichrist*."[10] The other is: "I know my fate. One day, my name will be associated with

---

[9] In *Ecce Homo* Nietzsche even presents an explanation as to why he believes this stance to be perfectly reasonable: "Ultimately, nobody can get more out of things, including books, than he already knows. For what one lacks access to from experience one will have no ear. Now let us imagine an extreme case: that a book speaks of nothing but events that lie altogether beyond the possibility of any frequent or even rare experience – that it is the first language for a new series of experiences. In that case, simply nothing will be heard, but there will be the acoustic illusion that where nothing is heard, nothing is there . . . Whoever thought he had understood something of me, had made up something out of me after his own image . . . and whoever had understood nothing of me, denied that I need to be considered at all." "Why I Write Such Good Books," § 1, translation from W. Kaufmann, *On the Genealogy of Morals and Ecce Homo* (Vintage: New York, 1967), p. 261.

[10] *Ecce Homo*, "Why I Write Such Good Books," end of § 2, translation Kaufmann, p. 263.

the memory of something tremendous – a crisis the like of which the world has never seen, the most profound collision of conscience, of a decision brought about *against* everything that has ever been believed, demanded, or held holy so far. I am not a man. I am dynamite."[11]

The second trait which we find in Nietzsche's writings is closely connected to his inability to assess himself in the light of others' reactions. It consists in his total unconcern about the tenability of his views when judged according to standards that he thinks are alien to his approach. Starting from the conviction that there is no common ground between him and his reader, that what he has to say is most likely incomprehensible to almost everybody else, he does not feel obliged to enter the social game of competitive discourse. He refuses to try to convince people by somehow connecting to their way of thinking; he does not refute possible arguments against the points he wants to make by giving reasons in their favor. Instead, he makes abundantly clear his contempt for "normal" thinking and his impatience with the evaluations of others. It is this stance which gives so many readers the impression of an overwhelming polemical element in Nietzsche's literary presentation of his views. He reinforces it by insisting over and over again that what he has to tell us are above all *his* truths. The claim to exclusivity is meant to imply both that his main concern is not whether we find these truths convincing, and that he does not pretend to have found *the* Truth, for he thinks this is a metaphysical illusion anyway.

Thus we find embedded in Nietzsche's basic view of himself the recommendation not that we read his texts as aiming at "objectively valid" judgments, at judgments that are (metaphysically) true irrespective of the cultural and psychological context in which they are made (whatever that may be), but that we think of them as narratives that he invites us to listen to, without really obliging us to believe them if we are not the right kind of person. This does not mean that the stories he has to tell us about, say, truth, morality, the will to power, or culture are, in his view, on a par with fictions, pleasant or otherwise. On the contrary, he believed his stories to be the ultimate stories, the stories that are destined to become the standard versions of our assessment of these phenomena. This is not because his narratives are objectively, or in a context-free sense, the most fitting; rather, they will succeed because eventually people will change to a condition where they appreciate the fact that these narratives are best suited to capture their sense of the right perspective on phenomena if they

---

[11] *Ibid.*, "Why I Am a Destiny," beginning of § 1, translation Kaufmann, p. 326.

are considered against the background of what for them is the real meaning of life.

Before looking more closely at some aspects of *BGE* itself, let me summarize what I take to be the lessons for approaching Nietzsche's writings that can be learned from his personal situation and his way of dealing with it. They take the form of three warnings: (1) do not expect these writings to express impartial views on whatever subject they address – they express, in an emphatic sense, Nietzsche's own views; (2) do not be annoyed by his obsession with apodictic statements whose immense generality very often contradicts both normal expectations of modesty and the most obvious requirements of common sense – these stylistic eccentricities reflect his resolute disdain for what most people cherish, especially people who he suspects are not willing to listen to him; (3) never forget that the author does not want to get mixed up with "us," his normal insensitive "academic" readers. He does not want to be "one of us" – instead he insists on what he calls "distance," in order to uphold his view of himself and to remind us of his uniqueness. A last quotation from *Ecce Homo* may highlight these points: "*Listen to me* [the emphasis is on the 'me']. *For I am thus and thus. Do not, above all, confound me.*"[12]

III

BGE is the first book Nietzsche published after *Thus Spoke Zarathustra*. He never gave up on the notion that all he really wanted to say is contained in *Zarathustra*, and this led him to claim that the works he wrote after *Zarathustra* are essentially nothing but elaborations and explications of ideas already present in his *opus magnum*. This claim has been disputed by quite a number of his commentators, firstly because many of the most central ideas in *Zarathustra* cease to play an important role in his later writings, and secondly because the literary form of the later writings connects them much more closely to his books prior to *Zarathustra* than to *Zarathustra* itself.[13] However that may be, Nietzsche himself was of the opinion that *Zarathustra* set the stage for everything he had to do subsequently. He writes: "The task for the years that followed [i.e. the years after *Zarathustra*] was mapped out as clearly as possible. Once the yes-saying part of my task had been solved [by means of *Zarathustra*], it was time for the no-saying, no-doing part."[14] This seems to imply that he regarded his post-*Zarathustra* writings as consisting of predominantly critical essays.

---

[12] *Ibid.*, Preface, § 1.   [13] See, e.g., M. Tanner, Introduction to *BGE* and *Nietzsche*, p. 59.
[14] *Ecce Homo*, '*Beyond Good and Evil*', § 1, translation Kaufmann, p. 310.

BGE is best known to a wider public for its proverbs. Indeed, some of Nietzsche's best-known maxims are assembled in this text, ranging from perspicuous insights to highly controversial statements. Starting with the Preface, where we find his much used and misused saying, "Christianity is Platonism for the 'people,'" almost every one of the nine parts of the book contains lines that have entered the repertoire of educated or polemical discourse: "life as such is will to power" (§ 13); "humans are *the still undetermined [nicht festgestellte] animals*" (§ 62); "When a woman has scholarly inclinations, there is usually something wrong with her sexuality" (§ 144); "*Morality in Europe these days is the morality of herd animals*" (§ 202); and (slightly paraphrased here): "saintliness – the highest spiritualization of the instinct of cleanliness" (§ 271).

These proverbs are in a way the least of what *BGE* has to offer. Its primary fascination lies on a deeper level: this book introduces us into a world of remarkable conjectures, suspicions, and implications. Though one might say this is true of most of Nietzsche's other published works as well, with the exception of *Zarathustra*, there is nevertheless a difference in emphasis between *BGE* and the other writings. Whereas the other texts pursue their subjects from many different angles, *BGE* (like *The Genealogy of Morals*, which Nietzsche announced on the back of its title page as "a sequel to my last book, *Beyond Good and Evil*, which it is meant to supplement and clarify") is highly focused on the psychological aspects of its topics. In *BGE* Nietzsche confronts us primarily (though not exclusively) with a dimension of his thought that he was particularly proud of – his psychological stance. This integration of what he calls a psychological point of view into his general practice of casting doubts on received convictions by tracing their origins, of throwing into question our most fundamental beliefs by pointing out their shakiness, and of scrutinizing available alternatives in the light of a new vision of the value of life – this I take to be the most distinctive feature of *BGE*.

Nietzsche himself gives the following account of what he is doing in *BGE*: "This book (1886) is in every essential a *critique of modernity*; modern sciences, modern arts, even modern politics are not excluded. Besides this, it is an indication of an opposing type, which is as un-modern as possible, a noble, yes-saying type."[15] Though this characterization is accurate and confirms the view that Nietzsche considers his task to be mainly a critical one, it is by no means complete. Interestingly enough, it does not mention two topics which some readers take to be the subject of the most

[15] *Ibid.*

disturbing reflections in the book: morality and religion. This is surprising because these are the topics which seem to emerge most strongly in any consideration of its main message.

In order to appreciate the distinctive approach which Nietzsche favors in *BGE* in his dealings with what he calls "modernity," it might be worthwhile to say a few words about his more general outlook. The starting point for almost everything Nietzsche is interested in throughout his entire intellectual career can be nicely summarized in the form of the question "how are we to live?" or, more poignantly, "how are we to endure life?" He considered this question to be of the utmost importance, because of three interconnected convictions that he treated virtually as facts. His first conviction was that life is best conceived of as a chaotic dynamic process without any stability or direction. The second is articulated in the claim that we have no reason whatsoever to believe in any such thing as the "sense" or the "value" of life, insofar as these terms imply the idea of an "objective" or "natural" purpose of life. The third is that human life is value-oriented in its very essence – that is, without adherence to some set of values or other, human life would be virtually impossible. Whereas the first conviction is supposed to state an ontological fact, the second is meant to be an application of the ontological point to the normative aspects of human life in particular. The third conviction, though somewhat at odds with the other two, is taken by Nietzsche to reveal a psychological necessity. (How Nietzsche came to hold these convictions, and whether they can be supported, there is not space to examine here, although a closer look would no doubt lead back to his use of some of Schopenhauer's ideas and to his picture of what constituted the cultural life of pre-Socratic ancient Greece.)

Against the background of these convictions, Nietzsche became interested in the question of the origin of values, a question that eventually led him to a whole array of unorthodox and original answers. All his answers ultimately follow from a pattern of reasoning which in its most basic structure is quite simple and straightforward: if there are no values "out there," in the sense in which we believe stars and other physical objects to be "out there" and if, at the same time, we cannot do without values, then there must be some value-creating capacity within ourselves which is responsible for the values we cherish and which organizes our lives. Though presumably we are all endowed with this capacity,[16] there are very few of us who manage to create values powerful enough to force people into acceptance and to

---

[16] For, after all, there seems to be no reason to think that Nietzsche would not allow in principle that each of us could be transformed into a "free spirit," i.e., a person who has the capacity and strength to create and stick to the "right" values.

constitute cultural and social profiles. To create such constitutive values seems to be, according to Nietzsche, the prerogative of real philosophers (not philosophy professors), of unique artists (if there are any), of even rarer founders of religions, and, above all, of institutions that develop out of the teaching of creative individuals, i.e., of science, philosophy, and theology. Thus, anyone interested in the function and the origin of values should scrutinize the processes which enabled these persons and institutions to create values.

At this point Nietzsche's more detailed investigations tend to start spreading out in a remarkable number of different directions. It is here, too, that in one sense we should take *BGE* to have its point of departure. That the detailed analysis of all the phenomena connected with the concept of value is a very tricky task methodologically is documented not only in *BGE* but also in almost all of Nietzsche's other writings. Acknowledging the fact that the different features of the value-creating processes are much too complex to be accessible by means of a single explanatory scheme, Nietzsche tentatively pursues several different approaches. He merges psychological hypotheses with causal explanations, and combines them with historical observations and linguistic considerations into a multi-perspectival technique that he fondly refers to as his "genealogical method." In *BGE*, where he is occupied mainly with the psychological dimension of the process of value formation, he applies this method primarily in an attempt to come to an understanding of those aspects of the value problem that pertain to its normative elements, that is, to the question of good and bad.

At the risk of oversimplification one can say the bulk of this work addresses three topics, each one of which can be expressed best in terms of a question. The first is this: why is it impossible for us to live without values, why do we need values at all, or, more in line with Nietzsche's terminology, what is the value of values? The second is this: how does it happen that the values we and the overwhelming majority of the members of our culture subscribe to have either been bad from the beginning or have degenerated into bad values? The third topic is this: what is the right perspective on values; what should we expect values to be? Though these three questions are in a certain sense perennial, Nietzsche relates them directly to what he saw as the manifest historical situation of his age and the prevailing conditions of the cultural tradition he lived in, so much of what he has to say is deeply rooted in his response to late nineteenth-century central European conceptions. This is something we should never forget when we confront his texts. Nietzsche speaks to us from the past, and this fact alone might account for some features of his writing that we would now consider idiosyncratic – for example, his way of talking about women and about national characteristics.

IV

At this point we face a problem that I take to be crucial for any adequate assessment of Nietzsche's project. It concerns the manner in which we are to comprehend his approach to the topics under examination. Now that we have identified a number of central questions that he discusses in *BGE*, it is tempting to proceed in the way normally used in dealing with philosophical texts: stating the questions addressed, and then trying to line up the arguments that the advocate of a position puts forward in favor of the answers he comes up with. However, in the case of Nietzsche and *BGE* it is by no means evident that such a procedure would capture what Nietzsche is doing and what *BGE* is all about. There are few arguments to be found in *BGE*, and those which can be extracted are seldom of the most convincing kind. Following the normal procedure would also encourage the illusion that Nietzsche designed *BGE* to be understood simply in terms of arguments, whether good or bad, and I cannot find anything in *BGE* which would encourage such an illusion.[17]

There is considerable evidence that we should try a different approach, and the clue lies in Nietzsche's numerous allusions to the practices of what he calls the "new philosophers." To be the type of philosopher Nietzsche values is to follow hunches, to think at a "presto" pace (§ 213), to embark on experiments both intellectual and existential (§§ 205, 210),[18] to transform and to create values (§§ 203, 211), to put forward hypotheses that are risky: in short, to be interested in what he calls "dangerous perhapses" (§ 2). One would not expect a person with this conception of philosophy to hold the idea that what counts most in the endeavor to reach highly unorthodox and sometimes even shocking insights is to be in possession of a "good argument," and that one could or should present one's views in compliance

---

[17] There are passages that make it very hard to believe in this illusion. See, e.g., remarks in § 5 that the activity of reason-giving is a *post hoc* affair intended to justify "some fervent wish that they have sifted through and made properly abstract," or (in the same section) his making fun of Spinoza's *mos geometricus* as a masquerade. In my eyes, the most striking passage for discouraging this illusion is to be found in § 213, where Nietzsche talks about what he calls philosophical states or moods. Here he compares the "right" way of doing philosophy with the "normal" attitude and writes concerning the latter: "You ['normal' philosophers] imagine every necessity is a need, a painful having to follow and being compelled." This "having to follow" and "being compelled" I read as a reference to the procedure of establishing results via sound arguments.

[18] Nietzsche uses the German word *Versuch* (attempt, experiment) in a broad way which makes that term cover the connotations of *Versuchung* (temptation) and *Versucher* (tempter) as well. Cf. § 42.

with this idea. Rather, one would expect such a person to pursue a very different path in expressing his views, which would involve starting with a bold claim or striking observation and then using it in a variety of different ways. It might form the basis for an analysis of something in terms of that claim or observation, or it might point to a symptom, presupposition, or consequence of a very general or a very particular state of affairs. It even might be related tentatively to topics which at first sight have nothing to do with what the original claim or the first observation was about. In short, one could envision a philosopher under the spell of Nietzschean "new philosophy" as someone whose methodology is deeply entangled in and in thrall to what could be called "what if" scenarios.[19]

If this is how a "new philosopher" approaches problems, it seems beside the point to treat Nietzsche's proclaimed insights as based on arguments. The concept of a "result" or a "solution" also becomes obsolete, since this type of philosophy is obviously not oriented towards results and solutions understood in the sense of statements which can be defended against thorough critical resistance. Its aim consists instead in the uncovering of surprising possibilities and the playful presentation of innovative perspectives that do not aspire to the status of rock-hard "truths" but are meant to be offerings or propositions for a like-minded spirit.[20]

Nietzsche obviously intended *BGE* to exemplify as clearly as possible all the characteristics he attributes to the style, the method, and the intentions of the "new philosophers" – and yet it is remarkable how often this fact is not sufficiently acknowledged by his interpreters. This oversight is remarkable not only because it seems to be in part responsible for awkward attempts to integrate Nietzsche's intellectual products into traditional academic philosophy,[21] but above all because it tends to miss what might be

---

[19] It should go without saying that this imagined scenario does not exclude "good arguments." Rather, the scenario is meant to show that if one deals with topics in the way outlined above, the guiding intention is not to give or to find "good arguments." In Nietzsche's terminology, this amounts to the claim that a "good argument" is not an overriding methodological "value." Invoking his polemical inventory, one could say, in his spirit: to be obsessed by "the will to a good argument" indicates bad taste.

[20] Again, this characterization is not meant to suggest that what these "new philosophers" are proclaiming is something they are not serious about or do not want us to take seriously. It is only meant to emphasize that what they put forward is connected very intimately with their personal point of view, and hence it is nothing that they can force on someone if there is no shared basis of experience, of resentment (*ressentiment*), or suffering. See *BGE* § 43, where Nietzsche expresses this point in an especially belligerent fashion.

[21] These attempts do not necessarily result in uninformative or misleading accounts of aspects of Nietzsche's thought. On the contrary, many of them shed considerable light on the historical background of his ideas and on the impact they could have on various discussions that happen to take place within the framework of academic philosophy. They are, however, operating under

called, for want of a better term, the "socio-hermeneutical" dimension of what has become known as his doctrine of "perspectivism." This doctrine in its most trivial reading amounts to the claim that our view of the world and, consequently, the statements we take to be true, depend on our situation, on our "perspective" on the world. Perspectivism thus understood gives rise to the epistemological thesis that our knowledge claims can never be true in an absolute or an objective sense, partly because of the necessary spatial and temporal differences between the viewpoints that each knower is bound to occupy when relating to an object, and also because of the fact that we can never be certain that what appears to us to be the case really is the case. Though it is true that in some of his more conventional moods Nietzsche seems to have thought about perspectivism along these lines, this reading gives no hint whatsoever of why he should have been attracted to such a doctrine in his more inspired moments. In this epistemological version the doctrine is neither original nor interesting, but merely a version of skeptical or idealist claims that used to be connected in popular writings with names like Berkeley and Kant.[22]

However, perspectivism takes on a much more promising dimension if it is put into the broader context of the problem of justifying or at least of making plausible an insistence on integrating a personal or subjective element into the expression of one's views as a condition of their making sense at all. By looking at this doctrine in this context, we can appreciate it as stating conditions for understanding an expression that purports to express something true, be it a text, a statement, or a confession. These conditions can be summarized in terms of two essential convictions. (1) In order to understand a claim for truth embodied in an expression, one has

the unavoidable (and, perhaps, reasonable) restrictions of that framework. This puts them in the position of having to abstract from the personal or "perspectival" features essential to Nietzsche's conceptions. That there is a price to be paid for this "academization" is obvious. It is revealed in the difference between the excitement and fun that one can have in reading Nietzsche and the boredom that one sometimes experiences when reading the literature on him.

[22] Here I have to confess that this sketch of the epistemological interpretation of Nietzsche's perspectivism may not be the most sympathetic one, and no doubt one can find in the literature much more sophisticated versions of this doctrine. However, this does not affect the main point I want to make, which consists in the claim that the epistemological reading misses the central feature of Nietzsche's doctrine. There are some other misgivings concerning the reading that deserve mention. The first consists in the fact that Nietzsche – especially in *BGE* – is not in sympathy with skepticism (see § 208). Hence, why should he be interested in putting forward a doctrine containing skeptical implications? A further reservation about the feasibility of the epistemological reading can be seen in the annoying consequence of having to credit Nietzsche with all sorts of paradoxical and self-refuting claims such as "If perspectivism is true we cannot know it to be true." It should be noted that the "German form of skepticism" discussed approvingly in § 209 has nothing to do with epistemological skepticism.

to have an understanding of the situation from which that claim originates, and this presupposes being acquainted with and involved in the personal attitudes, subjective experiences, and private evaluations which form the basis of the view expressed. (2) In order to judge the correctness, or perhaps merely the plausibility, of such a claim, one has to have an experiential or existential background similar to that of the person who made the claim. It is because of this insistence on integrating subjective aspects into the process of understanding, and because of the idea that judging the truth of a view presupposes shared experiences, that I call this the "socio-hermeneutical" reading of perspectivism.

If perspectivism is understood in these terms, then much of what is going on in *BGE* and other texts by Nietzsche begins to look considerably less arbitrary and idiosyncratic than has been claimed. For example, his so-called "theory of truth" which he alludes to quite often in the first two books of *BGE*, seems less absurd than many commentators have taken it to be. According to these critics Nietzsche's perspectival conception of truth endorses the following three statements: (1) there is no absolute or objective truth; (2) what is taken to be truth is nothing but a fiction, that is, a perspectival counterfeit or forgery (*Fälschung*) of what really is the case; and (3) claims (1) and (2) are true. These three statements together seem to imply the paradoxical claim that it is true that there is no truth. So the critic argues.[23] However, when read in the light of the preceding remarks a much less extravagant interpretation of Nietzsche's theory of truth suggests itself which is completely independent of the issue of whether he really subscribes to these three statements. On this interpretation, Nietzsche's theory claims only (1) that there are no context-free truths, where a context is to be defined as the set of subjective conditions that the utterer of a truth is governed by and that anyone who wishes correctly to judge it is able to apprehend.[24] It also claims (2) that as an utterer or judger of a truth we are never in a position to be familiar with a context in its entirety, that is, with all the conditions that define it, and therefore we have to settle for an incomplete version of a context where the degree of incompleteness depends on differences between our capacities to understand ourselves and others. From this it follows (3) that, given our situation, every truth is

---

[23] That there are many epistemological and logical problems connected with holding such a para-doxical claim is not difficult to point out. The most comprehensive discussion of these problems with reference to Nietzsche that I know of is by M. Clark, *Nietzsche on Truth and Philosophy* (Cambridge University Press: Cambridge, 1990).

[24] Put a bit more bluntly, this claim amounts to the assertion that the concept "objective or absolute truth" is an empty concept when understood in contraposition to "perspectival truth."

defined by this necessarily incomplete context. Thus every truth is a partial truth or a perspectival fiction.[25]

This "socio-hermeneutical" reading of perspectivism points to a more commonsensical understanding of Nietzsche's claims regarding truth. It also suggests that some of the stylistic peculiarities of *BGE* and other texts had a methodological function. *BGE*, like most of Nietzsche's other texts, has an aphoristic form.[26] It looks like a collection of impromptu remarks, each of which explores to a different degree of depth some aspect or other of a particular observation, specific claim, or surprising phenomenon. These remarks are numbered and loosely organized into topic-related groups, each one of which carries a short descriptive phrase that functions as its title. The impression is of an apparently arbitrary compilation of notes which are actually presented in an artful, though idiosyncratic way. Thus it has been maintained that we should approach *BGE* as we would a work of literature rather than strictly in terms of philosophical text. Though this impression is by no means misleading, it fails to be sensitive to the intentions guiding the architectonic of this text. If a claim is fully comprehensible only when placed in its appropriate subjective and existential context, then it is incumbent on an author to convey as much information about this context as possible. One way of doing this consists in presenting a whole array of thoughts which are designed primarily to inform us about the various subjective stances characteristic of the individual making the claim. The resulting collection may seem random because it can include almost any conceivable digression under the pretense of being informative about the subjective context. However, if the socio-hermeneutical interpretation is correct, the seeming randomness of Nietzsche's aphorisms can equally well be taken as a calculated and methodologically appropriate consequence of his perspectivism. In Nietzsche's writings, as in life, randomness can turn out to be an applied method in disguise.

---

[25] It should be noticed that this reading is compatible with some of the most disturbing features of Nietzsche's talk about truth. It allows us to make sense of his insistence that there are degrees of truth, which is exhibited most clearly in *BGE* in his reflection on how much "truth" one can take (§ 39). It also makes understandable the idea, very important to him, that truth is just a special case of error. And it allows for the use of personal pronouns in connection with truth, a habit Nietzsche is very fond of (cf. §§ 5, 43, 231).

[26] Though there is some question as to the applicability of terms such as "aphorism" or "aphoristic form" to Nietzsche's texts, he himself does not seem to have problems with such a characterization. His own use of these terms in reference to his writings is documented in *On the Genealogy of Morals*, Preface § 2 (*KSA* V, p. 248) and § 8 (*KSA* V, p. 255) and in *Twilight of Idols*, §§ 9, 51 (*KSA* VI, p. 153).

V

BGE deals with questions of how values arise psychologically and how we should evaluate them. It discusses the origin and the meaning of philosophical values such as truth, the religious practice of establishing and enforcing specific values such as faith, piety, and love of man, and the motives and mechanisms involved in our cultivation of moral values such as pity, fairness, and willingness to help each other. It also treats such political and social values as democracy, equality, and progress, seeing them as means of oppression and as indicators of decay and degeneration. Most of this is done with the aim of finding out what brought about the modern way of life, and what made modern culture such a doomed enterprise. The general tendency of the book is to claim that at the base of the most deeply habitualized normative evaluations that modern people take for granted, their most fundamental judgments about what has to be considered "good" or "bad" in almost every sphere of human activity, there ultimately lies a mixture of appalling character traits, ranging from weakness and fear to wishful thinking and self-betrayal, and all these find their symptomatic expression in the modern condition.

Neither this critical message nor the material Nietzsche relies upon in order to substantiate his assessment of modernity is peculiar to *BGE*. In almost all his other writings,[27] he discusses the shortcomings of philosophy, the dangers of religion, the built-in biases of science, and the damaging consequences of institutionalized moral and cultural values, and he arrives at similar bleak conclusions. Thus, the message of *BGE* is just another version of Nietzsche's general project. However, *BGE* is distinctive not only in its emphasis on a psychological explanation of the rise to dominance of specific values, but also in two further respects. The first relates to the doctrine of the "will to power," the second to his views on what might be called "good" or "adequate" ways of confronting reality. Both topics belong to his relatively rare excursions into the world of "positive" thinking.

---

[27] Obviously this overlap is intended by Nietzsche. It seems to be an architectonic device, for he frequently quotes from and alludes to his other texts. The best example of this practice is to be found right at the beginning (§ 2) of *BGE* where he cites almost verbatim from the beginning of *Human, All Too Human*. This quotation refers to his diagnosis of the most fundamental mistake of traditional metaphysicians, i.e., their conception of the origin of oppositions. Cf. B. Glatzeder: *'Perspektiven der Wünschbarkeit'. Nietzsches Metaphysikkritik in Menschliches Allzumenschliches* (Philo Verlag: Berlin, 2000). In quoting this appraisal, which forms the basis of his far reaching criticism of metaphysics and its notion of "objective" truth, he can treat it like a result whose justification is already given elsewhere.

The "will to power" makes its first public appearance in *Thus Spoke Zarathustra*. There it is introduced as one of the three major teachings Zarathustra has to offer, the other two being his advocacy of the overman (*Übermensch*) and the conception of the Eternal Recurrence. It is somewhat surprising that in *Zarathustra* Nietzsche has little to say about what the "will to power" means. Fortunately he is a bit more explicit in *BGE*, although here too the doctrine receives what is by no means an exhaustive treatment.[28] There is, however, some evidence that he wants us to think of this doctrine as advancing or at least implying an ontological hypothesis. Focusing on the hints he gives in *BGE*, the following picture emerges: if we look at the phenomenon of organic life as an integral part of reality, we find that it consists not in a static condition but in a dynamic and chaotic process of creation and decay, of overpowering and becoming overpowered, of suppressing and being suppressed. This suggests that what governs these processes is some sort of power struggle where every single form of life has a tendency to overpower every other form. However, to think of life in this way we have to assume that each living particle is endowed with a certain amount of power that it has a will to realize. This amount is supposed to define its "will to power" and thus is ultimately decisive for its ability to develop itself and to survive, or, to use a famous Nietzschean phrase, for its potential to become what it is. It is this line of thought which led Nietzsche to the assertion that life is "will to power" (§§ 13, 259).

But this is merely one part of the story. In *BGE* Nietzsche tentatively tries to pursue the conception of a "will to power" in a further direction. He aims at a broader application of the conception by transforming it from a principle of organic life into a much broader axiom pertaining to the essence of nature in general. It is here that it acquires an ontological meaning. The main motive for his attempt to conceive of the "will to power" as a general ontological principle seems to be that there is no reason to restrict the explanatory force of that concept to organic life. Why not think of inorganic matter, of the material world, in terms of "will to power" as well? Matter would then have to be conceived as "will to power" paralyzed, as

---

[28] It is because of the relatively superficial and vague treatment of this doctrine in his published writings that many interpretations of the meaning and function of "will to power" rely heavily on Nietzsche's *Nachlass*, the voluminous collection of his unpublished notes. However, though the *Nachlass* indeed contains a considerable amount of material pertaining to that conception, it has the disadvantage of giving support to widely divergent, if not contradictory, interpretations. This is due to the fact that Nietzsche seems to have been experimenting with different meanings of this concept without reaching a definite position. To appreciate the whole range of readings possible see, for example, G. Abel, *Nietzsche: Die Dynamik der Willen zur Macht und die ewige Wiederkehr* (de Gruyter: Berlin, 1998, 2nd edn), and V. Gerhardt, *Vom Willen zur Macht: Anthropologie und Metaphysik der Macht am exemplarischen Fall Friedrich Nietzsches* (de Gruyter: Berlin, 1996).

"will to power" in a state of potentiality. According to Nietzsche this view would allow for a unified account of the world in its totality: "The world seen from inside, the world determined and described with respect to its 'intelligible character' – would be just this will to power and nothing else" (§ 36). This view would also have the advantage of overcoming the basic bias of traditional metaphysics that there is a difference in kind between being and becoming, because it implies that being static and stable is in the end nothing but a degenerative form of becoming, or nothing but an unactualized power process. It goes without saying that Nietzsche is very much in favor of this claim.

Even if it is conceded that Nietzsche never really elaborated his concept of the "will to power" sufficiently, it does not appear to be one of his more attractive ideas. The reason for this is that it purports to give us insight into the essence of nature, what nature is "in itself," but this does not square well with his emphatic criticism, put forward in *BGE* and elsewhere, of the very notion of an "in itself." According to Nietzsche there is no "in itself," no essence, no fixed nature of things, and all beliefs to the contrary are founded on deep and far-reaching metaphysical illusions. It seems therefore that one cannot avoid the unsettling conclusion that the doctrine of a "will to power" shares all the vices which Nietzsche attributes to metaphysical thinking in general.

There are no such untoward consequences of the second piece of "positive" thinking in *BGE*, but this is because it scarcely qualifies as thinking at all, consisting instead of fantasies about what the ideal conditions would be for a person to be able to participate in productive thinking. Here productive thinking seems to mean the capacity to live up to the task of enduring an unbiased assessment of reality. Nietzsche summarizes these fantasies in the picture he gives of the "new philosophers" and in remarks on what it means to be noble. Nobility, for him, has to do with putting oneself at a distance from people and things. It is rooted in and is the product of the "pathos of distance," to use his influential formula (§ 257). This pathos has to be conceived as the socially inherited ability (1) to have a sense for differences in rank between persons, (2) to accept these differences as pointing to differences in distinction (defined as a positive quality of worthiness), and (3) to strive for higher distinction. A person possessing this ability is able to strive for unique states of awareness: "Without the *pathos of distance* . . . that *other* more mysterious pathos could not have grown at all, that demand for new expansions of distance within the soul itself, the development of states that are increasingly high, rare, distant, tautly drawn and comprehensive, and, in short, the enhancement of the type 'man,' the constant 'self-overcoming of man' (to use a moral formula in a supra-moral sense)" (§ 257). The ability to achieve such states seems to function as a condition of gaining important insights and having the psychological resources needed to live with them, and it indicates a certain stance towards reality superior to "normal" or "common" attitudes (cf. § 268).

With this plea for nobility Nietzsche states again his conviction that what ultimately counts in our epistemic dealings with reality is not knowledge *per se*, that is, knowledge detached from the knower. What deserves the title of knowledge has to be intimately connected with the special and unique situation a knowing subject is in. This is so not only because according to Nietzsche knowledge is not an "objective" or impersonal affair, something one can have like a detached thing that one possesses, but above all because the knowing subject has to *live* his knowledge. The extent to which a subject can do this depends on personal constitution, character traits, and intellectual robustness. Knowledge thus becomes associated with the question of how much truth one can endure (cf. § 39). It is in this context that the concept of nobility reveals itself to be part of a "positive" teaching: nobility that is the product of the social pathos of distance increases the potential of a subject for enduring "uncommon" knowledge because it promotes more comprehensive states, and these in turn indicate a growing strength in the subject's character that enables it to cope with more of "the truth." This at least seems to be Nietzsche's message.

What is it that makes reading *BGE* and other writings of Nietzsche such an attractive and stimulating experience? The main reason, I believe, has little to do with the plausibility, let alone the correctness, of his views. On the contrary, we like many of his ideas precisely because of their pointed one-sidedness, their extravagance, and their eccentricity. Nor, I suspect, are we now especially preoccupied with the topics which he obviously took to be decisive for an evaluation of our way of living under modern conditions. Many of his themes we now consider rather obsolete, and to some of them we no longer have any immediate access because they are deeply rooted in their nineteenth-century contexts. The fascination his works still have must therefore originate from somewhere else. If one wants to account for the appeal of his writings, it is perhaps advisable not to look too closely at his actual teachings, but to think of his texts as a kind of mental tonic designed to encourage his readers to continue to confront their doubts and suspicions about the well-foundedness of many of their most fundamental ideas about themselves and their world. This would suggest that Nietzsche's works may still be captivating because they confront a concern that is not restricted to modern times. They address our uncomfortable feeling that our awareness of ourselves and of the world depends on conceptions that we ultimately do not understand. We conceive of ourselves as subjects trying to live a decent life, guided in our doings by aims that fit the normal expectations of our social and cultural environment; we believe certain things to be true beyond any doubt, and we hold others and ourselves to many moral obligations. Although all this is constitutive of a normal way of life, we have only a vague idea of why we have to deal with things in this way; we do not really know what in the end justifies these practices. In questioning not the normality but the objectivity or truth of such a normal world view, Nietzsche's writings can have the effect of making us feel less worried about our inability to account for some of our central convictions in an "absolute" way. It is up to each of us to decide whether to be grateful for this reminder or to loathe it.

CHAPTER 9

Nietzsche: On the Genealogy of Morality

Keith Ansell-Pearson

INTRODUCTION TO NIETZSCHE'S TEXT

Although it has come to be prized by commentators as his most important and systematic work, Nietzsche conceived *On the Genealogy of Morality* as a 'small polemical pamphlet' that might help him sell more copies of his earlier writings.[1] It clearly merits, though, the level of attention it receives and can justifiably be regarded as one of the key texts of European intellectual modernity. It is a deeply disturbing book that retains its capacity to shock and disconcert the modern reader. Nietzsche himself was well aware of the character of the book. There are moments in the text where he reveals his own sense of alarm at what he is discovering about human origins and development, especially the perverse nature of the human animal, the being he calls 'the sick animal' (*GM*, III, 14). Although the *Genealogy* is one of the darkest books ever written, it is also, paradoxically, a book full of hope and anticipation. Nietzsche provides us with a stunning story about man's monstrous moral past, which tells the history of the deformation of the human animal in the hands of civilization and Christian moralization; but also hints at a new kind of humanity coming into existence in the wake of the death of God and the demise of a Christian-moral culture.

On the Genealogy of Morality belongs to the late period of Nietzsche's writings (1886–8). It was composed in July and August of 1887 and published in November of that year. Nietzsche intended it as a 'supplement' to and 'clarification' of *Beyond Good and Evil*, said by him to be 'in all essentials' a critique of modernity that includes within its range of attack modern science, modern art and modern politics. In a letter to his former Basel colleague Jacob Burckhardt dated 22 September 1886, Nietzsche stresses that *Beyond Good and Evil* says the same things as *Zarathustra* 'only in a way that is different – very different'. In this letter he draws attention

---

[1] Letter to Peter Gast, 18 July 1887, in *Selected Letters of Friedrich Nietzsche*, ed. Christopher Middleton (London and Chicago: University of Chicago Press, 1999), p. 269.

to the book's chief preoccupations and mentions the 'mysterious conditions of any growth in culture', the 'extremely dubious relation between what is called the "improvement" of man (or even "humanisation") and the enlargement of the human type', and 'above all the contradiction between every moral concept and every scientific concept of *life*'. *On the Genealogy of Morality* closely echoes these themes and concerns. Nietzsche finds that 'all modern judgments about men and things' are smeared with an over-moralistic language; the characteristic feature of modern souls and modern books is to be found in their 'moralistic mendaciousness' (*GM*, III, 19).

In *Ecce Homo* Nietzsche describes the *Genealogy* as consisting of 'three decisive preliminary studies by a psychologist for a revaluation of values'. The First Essay probes the 'psychology of Christianity' and traces the birth of Christianity not out of the 'spirit' *per se* but out of a particular kind of spirit, namely, *ressentiment*; the Second Essay provides a 'psychology of the conscience', where it is conceived not as the voice of God in man but as the instinct of cruelty that has been internalized after it can no longer discharge itself externally; the Third Essay inquires into the meaning of ascetic ideals, examines the perversion of the human will, and explores the possibility of a counter-ideal. Nietzsche says that he provides an answer to the question where the power of the ascetic ideal, 'the *harmful* ideal *par excellence*', comes from, and he argues that this is simply because to date it has been the *only* ideal; no counter-ideal has been made available '*until the advent of Zarathustra*'.

The *Genealogy* is a subversive book that needs to be read with great care. It contains provocative imagery of 'blond beasts of prey' and of the Jewish 'slave revolt in morality' which can easily mislead the unwary reader about the nature of Nietzsche's immoralism. In the preface, Nietzsche mentions the importance of readers familiarizing themselves with his previous books – throughout the book he refers to various sections and aphorisms from them, and occasionally he makes partial citations from them. The critique of morality Nietzsche carries out in the book is a complex one; its nuances are lost if one extracts isolated images and concepts from the argument of the book as a whole. His contribution to the study of 'morality' has three essential aspects: first, a criticism of moral genealogists for bungling the object of their study through the lack of a genuine historical sense; second, a criticism of modern evolutionary theory as a basis for the study of morality; and third, a critique of moral values that demands a thorough revaluation of them. Nietzsche's polemical contribution is intended to question the so-called self-evident 'facts' about morality and it has lost none of its force today.

READING NIETZSCHE

Nietzsche is often referred to as an 'aphoristic' writer, but this falls short of capturing the sheer variety of forms and styles he adopted. In fact, the number of genuine aphorisms in his works is relatively small; instead, most of what are called Nietzsche's 'aphorisms' are more substantial paragraphs which exhibit a unified train of thought (frequently encapsulated in a paragraph heading indicating the subject matter), and it is from these building blocks that the other, larger structures are built in more or less extended sequences. Nietzsche's style, then, is very different from standard academic writing, from that of the 'philosophical workers' he describes so condescendingly in *Beyond Good and Evil* (*BGE*, 211). His aim is always to energize and enliven philosophical style through an admixture of aphoristic and, broadly speaking, 'literary' forms. His stylistic ideal, as he puts it on the title page of *The Case of Wagner* (parodying Horace), is the paradoxical one of 'ridendo dicere severum' ('saying what is sombre through what is laughable'), and these two modes, the sombre and the sunny, are mischievously intertwined in his philosophy, without the reader necessarily being sure which is uppermost at any one time.

Nietzsche lays down a challenge to his readers, and sets them a pedagogical, hermeneutic task, that of learning to read him well. He acknowledges that the aphoristic form of his writing causes difficulty, and emphasizes that an aphorism has not been 'deciphered' simply when it has been read out; rather, for full understanding to take place, an 'art of interpretation' or exegesis is required (the German word is *Auslegung*, literally a laying out). He gives the attentive reader a hint of what kind of exegesis he thinks is needed when he claims that the Third Essay of the book 'is a commentary on the aphorism that precedes it' (he intends the opening section of the essay, not the epigraph from *Zarathustra*).

GENEALOGY AND MORALITY

For Nietzsche, morality represents a system of errors that we have incorporated into our basic ways of thinking, feeling and living; it is the great symbol of our profound ignorance of ourselves and the world. In *The Gay Science* 115, it is noted how humankind has been educated by 'the four errors': we see ourselves only incompletely; we endow ourselves with fictitious attributes; we place ourselves in a 'false rank' in relation to animals and nature – that is, we see ourselves as being inherently superior to them; and, finally, we invent ever new tables of what is good and then accept them as eternal and unconditional. However, Nietzsche does not propose we should make ourselves feel guilty about our incorporated errors (they have provided us with new drives); and neither does he want us simply to accuse or blame the past. We need to strive to be more just in our evaluations of life and the living by, for example, thinking 'beyond good and evil'. For Nietzsche, it is largely the prejudices of morality that stand in the way of this; morality assumes knowledge of things it does not have.

The criticism Nietzsche levels at morality – what we moderns take it to be and to represent – is that it is a menacing and dangerous system that makes the present live at the expense of the future (*GM*, Preface, 6). Nietzsche's concern is that the human species may never attain its '*highest potential and splendour*' (ibid.). The task of culture is to produce sovereign individuals, but what we really find in history is a series of deformations and perversions of that cultural task. Thus, in the modern world the aim and meaning of culture is taken to be 'to breed a tame and civilized animal, a *household pet*, out of the beast of prey "man"' (*GM*, I, 11), so that now man strives to become 'better' all the time, meaning 'more comfortable, more mediocre, more indifferent, more Chinese, more Christian . . .' (*GM*, I, 12). This, then, is the great danger of modern culture: it will produce an animal that takes taming to be an end in itself, to the point where the free-thinker will announce that the end of history has been attained (for Nietzsche's criticism of the 'free-thinker' see *GM*, I, 9). Nietzsche argues that we moderns are in danger of being tempted by a new European type of Buddhism, united in our belief in the supreme value of a morality of communal compassion, 'as if it were morality itself, the summit, the *conquered* summit of humankind, the only hope for the future, comfort in the present, the great redemption from all past guilt . . .' (*BGE*, 202).

Nietzsche argues that in their attempts to account for morality philosophers have not developed the suspicion that morality might be 'something problematic'; in effect what they have done is to articulate 'an erudite form of true belief in the prevailing morality', and, as a result, their inquiries remain 'a part of the state of affairs within a particular morality' (*BGE*, 186). Modern European morality is 'herd animal morality' which considers itself to be the definition of morality and the only morality possible or desirable (*BGE*, 202); at work in modern thinking is the assumption that there is a single morality valid for all (*BGE*, 228). Nietzsche seeks to develop a genuinely critical approach to morality, in which all kinds of novel, surprising and daring questions are posed. Nietzsche does not so much inquire into a 'moral sense' or a moral faculty as attempt to uncover *the different senses* of morality, that is the different 'meanings' morality can be credited with in the history of human development: morality as symptom, as mask, as sickness, as stimulant, as poison, and so on. Morality, Nietzsche holds, is a surface phenomenon that requires meta-level interpretation in accordance with a different, superior set of extra-moral values 'beyond good and evil'.

On several occasions in the *Genealogy*, Nietzsche makes it clear that certain psychologists and moralists have been doing something we can call 'genealogy' (see, for example, *GM*, I, 2 and II, 4, 12). He finds all these attempts insufficiently critical. In particular, Nietzsche has in mind the books of his former friend, Paul Rée (1849–1901), to whom he refers in the book's preface. In section 4 he admits that it was Rée's book on the origin of moral sensations, published in 1877, that initially stimulated him to develop his own hypotheses on the origin of morality. Moreover, it was in this book that he 'first directly encountered the back-to-front and perverse kind of genealogical hypotheses', which he calls 'the English kind'. In section 7 Nietzsche states that he wishes to develop the sharp, unbiased eye of the critic of morality in a better direction than we find in Rée's speculations. He wants, he tells us, to think in the direction 'of a real *history of morality*' (*die wirkliche* Historie der Moral); in contrast to the 'English hypothesis-mongering *into the blue*' – that is, looking vainly into the distance as in the blue yonder – he will have recourse to the colour 'grey' to aid his genealogical inquiries, for this denotes, 'that which can be documented, which can actually be confirmed and has actually existed . . . the whole, long, hard-to-decipher hieroglyphic script of man's moral past!' (*GM*, Preface, 7). Because the moral genealogists are so caught up in 'merely "modern" experience' they are altogether lacking in knowledge; they have 'no will to know the past, still less an instinct for history . . .' (*GM*, II, 4). An examination of the books of moral genealogists would show, ultimately, that they all take it to be something given and place it beyond questioning. Although he detects a few preliminary attempts to explore the history of moral feelings and valuations, Nietzsche maintains that even among more refined researchers no attempt at critique has been made. Instead, the popular superstition of Christian Europe that selflessness and compassion are what is characteristic of morality is maintained and endorsed.

Nietzsche begins the *Genealogy* proper by paying homage to 'English psychologists', a group of researchers who have held a microscope to the soul and, in the process, pioneered the search for a new set of truths: 'plain, bitter, ugly, foul, unchristian, immoral . . .' (*GM*, I, 1). The work of these psychologists has its basis in the empiricism of John Locke, and in

David Hume's new approach to the mind that seeks to show that so-called complex, intellectual activity emerges out of processes that are, in truth, 'stupid', such as the *vis inertiae* of habit and the random coupling and mechanical association of ideas. In the attempt of 'English psychologists' to show the real mechanisms of the mind Nietzsche sees at work not a malicious and mean instinct, and not simply a pessimistic suspicion about the human animal, but the research of proud and generous spirits who have sacrificed much to the cause of truth. He admires the honest craftsmanship of their intellectual labours. He criticizes them, however, for their lack of a real historical sense and for bungling their moral genealogies as a result, and for failing to raise questions of value and future legislation. This is why he describes empiricism as being limited by a 'plebeian ambition' (*BGE*, 213). What the 'English' essentially lack, according to Nietzsche, is 'spiritual vision of real *depth* – in short, philosophy' (*BGE*, 252).

In section 12 of the Second Essay Nietzsche attempts to expose what he takes to be the fundamental naïveté of the moral genealogists. This consists in highlighting some purpose that a contemporary institution or practice purportedly has, and then placing this purpose at the start of the historical process which led to the modern phenomenon in question. In *GM*, II, 13 he says that only that which has no history can be defined, and draws attention to the 'synthesis of meanings' that accrues to any given phenomenon. His fundamental claim, one that needs, he says, to inform all kinds of historical research, is that the origin of the development of a thing and its 'ultimate usefulness' are altogether separate. This is because what exists is 'continually interpreted anew . . . transformed and redirected to a new purpose' by a superior power. Nietzsche is challenging the assumption that the manifest purpose of a thing ('its utility, form and shape') constitutes the reason for its existence, such as the view that the eye is made to see and the hand to grasp. He argues against the view that we can consider the development of a thing in terms of a 'logical *progressus*' towards a goal. This naïvely teleological conception of development ignores the random and contingent factors within evolution, be it the evolution of a tradition or an organ. However, he also claims that 'every purpose and use is just a *sign* that the will to power' is in operation in historical change. This further claim has not found favour among theorists impressed by Nietzsche's ideas on evolution because they see it as relying upon an extravagant metaphysics. It is clear from his published presentations of the theory of the will to power that Nietzsche did not intend it to be such.

Nietzsche knows that he will shock his readers with the claims he makes on behalf of the will to power, for example, that it is the '*primordial fact* of all history' (*BGE*, 259). To say that the will to power is a 'fact' is not, for Nietzsche, to be committed to any simple-minded form of philosophical empiricism. Rather, Nietzsche's training as a philologist inclined him to the view that no fact exists apart from an interpretation, just as no text speaks for itself, but always requires an interpreting reader. When those of a modern democratic disposition consider nature and regard everything in it as equally subject to a fixed set of 'laws of nature', are they not projecting on to nature their own aspirations for human society, by construing nature as a realm that exhibits the rational, well-ordered egalitarianism which they wish to impose on all the various forms of human sociability? Might they be, as Nietzsche insinuates, masking their 'plebeian enmity towards everything privileged and autocratic, as well as a new and more subtle atheism'? But if even these purported facts about nature are really a matter of interpretation and not text, would it not be possible for a thinker to deploy the opposite intention and look, with his interpretive skill, at the same nature and the same phenomena, reading 'out of it the ruthlessly tyrannical and unrelenting assertion of power claims'? Nietzsche presents his readers with a contest of interpretations. His critical claim is that, whereas the modern 'democratic' interpretation suffers from being moralistic, his does not; his interpretation of the 'text' of nature as will to power allows for a much richer appreciation of the economy of life, including its active emotions. In the *Genealogy*, Nietzsche wants the seminal role played by the active affects to be appreciated (*GM*, II, 11). We suffer from the 'democratic idiosyncrasy' that opposes in principle everything that dominates and wants to dominate (*GM*, II, 12). Against Darwinism, he argues that it is insufficient to account for life solely in terms of adaptation to external circumstances. Such a conception deprives life of its most important dimension, which he names '*Aktivität*' (activity). It does this, he contends, by overlooking the primacy of the 'spontaneous, expansive, aggressive . . . formative forces' that provide life with new directions and new interpretations, and from which adaptation takes place only once these forces have had their effect. He tells us that he lays 'stress on this major point of historical method because it runs counter to the prevailing instinct and fashion which would much rather come to terms with absolute randomness, and even the mechanistic senselessness of all events, than the theory that is *power-will* a acted out in all that happens' (*GM*, II, 12).

Nietzsche's polemic challenges the assumptions of standard genealogies, for example, that there is a line of descent that can be continuously traced from a common ancestor, and that would enable us to trace moral notions and legal practices back to a natural single and fixed origin. His emphasis is rather on fundamental transformations, on disruptions, and on psychological innovations and moral inventions that emerge in specific material and cultural contexts.

Undue emphasis should not be placed, however, on the role Nietzsche accords to contingency and discontinuity within history, as this would be to make a fetish of them as principles. Contrary to Michel Foucault's influential reading of genealogy, Nietzsche does not simply oppose himself to the search for origins, and neither is he opposed to the attempt to show that the past actively exists in the present, secretly continuing to animate it.[2] Much of what Nietzsche is doing in the book is only intelligible if we take him to be working with the idea that it does. Nietzsche opposes himself to the search for origins only where this involves what we might call a genealogical narcissism. Where it involves the discovery of difference at the origin, of the kind that surprises and disturbs us, Nietzsche is in favour of such a search. This is very much the case with his analysis of the bad conscience. For Nietzsche, this is an 'origin' (*Ursprung*) that is to be treated as a fate and as one that still lives on in human beings today.

'GOOD, BAD AND EVIL'

In the first of the three essays of which the *Genealogy* is composed, Nietzsche invites us to imagine a society which is split into two distinct groups: a militarily and politically dominant group of 'masters' exercises absolute control over a completely subordinate group of 'slaves'. The 'masters' in this model are construed as powerful, active, relatively unreflective agents who live a life of immediate physical self-affirmation: they drink, they brawl, they wench, they hunt, whenever the fancy takes them, and they are powerful enough, by and large, to succeed in most of these endeavours, and uninhibited enough to enjoy living in this way. They use the term 'good' to refer in an approving way to this life and to themselves as people who are capable of leading it. As an afterthought, they also sometimes employ the term 'bad' to refer to those people – most notably, the 'slaves' – who by virtue of their weakness are not capable of living the life of self-affirming physical exuberance. The terms 'good' and 'bad' then form the basis of a variety of different 'masters' moralities'. One of the most important events in Western history occurs when the *slaves* revolt against the masters' form of valuation. The slaves are, after all, not only physically weak and oppressed, they are also by virtue of their

---

[2] Michel Foucault, 'Nietzsche, Genealogy, and History' (1971), in *The Essential Works of Foucault*, volume II: 1954–84, ed. James Faubion, trans. Robert Hurley and others (London: Penguin Books, 2000), pp. 369–93.

very weakness debarred from spontaneously seeing themselves and their lives in an affirmative way. They develop a reactive and negative sentiment against the oppressive masters which Nietzsche calls '*ressentiment*', and this *ressentiment* eventually turns creative, allowing the slaves to take revenge in the imagination on the masters whom they are too weak to harm physically. The form this revenge takes is the invention of a new concept and an associated new form of valuation: 'evil'. 'Evil' is used to refer to the life the masters lead (which *they* call 'good') but it is used to refer to it in a *disapproving* way. In a 'slave' morality this negative term 'evil' is central, and slaves can come to a pale semblance of self-affirmation only by observing that they are *not* like the 'evil' masters. In the mouths of the slaves, 'good' comes to refer not to a life of robust vitality, but to one that is 'not-evil', i.e. not in any way like the life that the masters live. Through a variety of further conceptual inventions (notably, 'free will'), the slaves stylize their own natural weakness into the result of a choice for which they can claim moral credit. Western morality has historically been a struggle between elements that derive from a basic form of valuation derived from 'masters' and one derived from 'slaves'.

THE FATE OF BAD CONSCIENCE

In the Second Essay, Nietzsche develops a quite extraordinary story about the origins and emergence of feelings of responsibility and debt (personal obligation). He is concerned with nothing less than the evolution of the human mind and how its basic ways of thinking have come into being, such as inferring, calculating, weighing and anticipating. Indeed, he points out that our word 'man' (*manas*) denotes a being that values, measures and weighs. Nietzsche is keen to draw the reader's attention to what he regards as an important historical insight: the principal moral concept of 'guilt' (*Schuld*) descends from the material concept of 'debts' (*Schulden*). In this sphere of legal obligations, he stresses, we find the breeding-ground of the 'moral conceptual world' of guilt, conscience and duty (*GM*, II, 6).

Nietzsche opens the Second Essay by drawing attention to a paradoxical task of nature, namely, that of breeding an animal that is sanctioned to promise and so exist as a creature of time, a creature that can remember the past and anticipate the future, a creature that can in the present bind its own will relative to the future in the certain knowledge that it will in the future effectively remember that its will has been bound. For this cultivation of effective memory and imagination to be successful, culture needs to work against the active force of forgetting, which serves an important physiological function. The exercise of a memory of the will supposes that the human animal can make a distinction between what happens by accident and what happens by design or intention, and it also presupposes an ability to think causally about an anticipated future. In section 2, Nietzsche makes explicit that what he is addressing is the 'long history of the origins of *responsibility*'. The successful cultivation of an animal sanctioned to promise requires a labour by which man is made into something 'regular, reliable, and uniform'. This has been achieved by what Nietzsche calls the 'morality of custom' (*Sittlichkeit der Sitte*) and the 'social straitjacket' which it imposes. The disciplining of the human animal into an agent that has a sense of responsibility (*Verantwortlichkeit*) for its words and deeds has not taken place through gentle methods, but through the harsh and cruel measures of coercion and punishment. As Nietzsche makes clear at one point in the text: 'Each step on earth, even the smallest, was in the past a struggle that was won with spiritual and physical torment . . .' (III, 9). The problem for culture is that it has to deal with an animal that is partly dull, that has an inattentive mind and a strong propensity to active forgetfulness. In most societies and ages, this problem has not been solved by gentle methods: 'A thing must be burnt in so that it stays in the memory' (II, 3). Nietzsche's insight is that without blood, torture and sacrifice, including 'disgusting mutilations', what we know as 'modern psychology' would never have arisen. All religions are at bottom systems of cruelty, Nietzsche contends; blood and horror lies at the basis of all 'good things'. In a certain sense it is possible to locate the whole of asceticism in this sphere of torment: 'a few ideas have to be made ineradicable . . . unforgettable and fixed in order to hypnotize the whole nervous and intellectual system through these "fixed ideas" . . .' (ibid.).

The fruit of this labour of *Cultur* performed on man in the prehistorical period is the sovereign individual who is master of a strong and durable will, a will that can make and keep promises. On this account freedom of the will is an achievement of culture and operates in the context of specific material practices and social relations. Nietzsche calls this individual autonomous and supra-ethical (*übersittlich*): it is supra-ethical simply in the sense that it has gone beyond the level of custom. For Nietzsche the period of 'the morality of custom' pre-dates what we call 'world history' and is to be regarded as the 'decisive historical period' which has determined the character of man (*GM*, III, 9). The sublime work of morality can be explained as the 'natural' and necessary work of culture (of tradition and custom). The sovereign individual is the kind of self-regulating animal that is required for the essential functions of culture (for example, well-functioning creditor–debtor relations). It cannot be taken to be his ideal in any simple or straightforward sense.[3]

In *GM*, II, 16 Nietzsche advances, albeit in a preliminary fashion, his own theory on the 'origin' of the bad conscience. He looks upon it 'as a serious illness to which man was forced to succumb by the pressure of the most fundamental of all changes which he experienced'. This change refers to the establishment of society and peace and their confining spaces, which brings with it a suspension and devaluation of the instincts. Nietzsche writes of the basic instinct of freedom – the will to power – being forced back and repressed (II, 17–18). Human beings now walk as if a 'terrible heaviness' bears down on them. In this new scenario the old animal instincts, such as animosity, cruelty, the pleasure of changing and destroying, do not cease to make their demands, but have to find new and underground satisfactions. Through internalization, in which no longer dischargeable instincts turn inward, comes the invention of what is popularly called the human 'soul': 'The whole inner world, originally stretched thinly as though between two layers of skin, was expanded and extended itself and granted depth, breadth, and height in proportion to the degree that the external discharge of man's instincts was *obstructed*.' Nietzsche insists that *this* is 'the origin of "bad conscience"'. He uses striking imagery in his portrait of this momentous development.

On the one hand, Nietzsche approaches the bad conscience as the most insidious illness that has come into being and from which man has yet to recover, his sickness of himself. On the other hand, he maintains that the 'prospect of an animal soul turning against itself' is an event and a spectacle too interesting 'to be played senselessly unobserved on some ridiculous planet'. Furthermore, as a development that was prior to all *ressentiment*, and that *cannot* be said to represent any organic assimilation into new circumstances, the bad conscience contributes to the appearance of an animal on earth that 'arouses interest, tension, hope', as if through it 'something . . . were being prepared, as though man were not an end but just a path, an episode, a bridge, a great promise' (*GM*, II, 16). Nietzsche observes that although it represents a painful and ugly growth, the bad conscience is not simply to be looked upon in disparaging terms; indeed, he speaks of the '*active* bad conscience'. It can be regarded as the 'true womb of ideal and imaginative events'; through it an abundance of 'disconcerting beauty and affirmation' has been brought to light.

---

[3] Nietzsche criticizes the ideal of 'a single, rigid and unchanging *individuum*' in *Human, All Too Human* 618.

In the course of history, the illness of bad conscience reached a terrible and sublime peak. In prehistory, argues Nietzsche, the basic creditor–debtor relationship that informs human social and economic activity also finds expression in religious rites and worship, for example, the way a tribal community expresses thanks to earlier generations. Over time the ancestor is turned into a god and associated with the feeling of fear (the birth of superstition). Christianity cultivates further the moral or religious sentiment of debt, and does so in terms of a truly monstrous level of sublime feeling: God is cast as the ultimate ancestor who cannot be repaid (*GM*, II, 20).

SIN AND THE ASCETIC IDEAL

The sense of 'guilt' has evolved through several momentous and fateful events in history. In its initial expression it is to be viewed 'as a piece of animal psychology, no more...' (*GM*, III, 20). In the earliest societies, a person is held answerable for his deeds and obliged to honour his debts. In the course of history this material sense of obligation is increasingly subject to moralization, reaching its summit with guilt before the Christian God. In the Third Essay, the ascetic priest comes into his own. Nietzsche had introduced the 'priests' into his account in the First Essay as a faction of the ruling class of 'masters', who distinguish themselves from the other masters by an extreme concern for purity (*GM*, I, 6–7). Originally, this concern is no more than a variant of the superiority of the master-caste as a whole over the slaves: the priests are masters and thus can afford to wash, wear clean clothes, avoid certain malodorous or unhealthy foods, etc. Slaves have no such luxury. Priestly purity, however, has a dangerous tendency to develop into more and more extreme and more and more internalized forms. Priests become expert in asceticism, and in dealing with all forms of human suffering. It is in the hands of the priest, an artist in feelings of guilt, Nietzsche says, that guilt assumes form and shape: '"Sin" – for that is the name for the priestly reinterpretation of the animal "bad conscience" ... – has been the greatest event in the history of the sick soul up till now: with sin we have the most dangerous and disastrous trick of religious interpretation' (*GM*, III, 20). The value of the priestly type of existence, says Nietzsche, lies in the fact that it succeeds in changing the direction of *ressentiment* (*GM*, III, 15).

In the First Essay, we saw the slaves in the grip of a creative *ressentiment* directed against the masters which could be expressed in the following terms: they – the masters – are 'evil', whereas we are not-evil (therefore, good). Important as the invention of the concept of 'evil' is historically, in itself it does not yet solve the slaves' problem. In fact, in some ways it makes it more acute: If we are good, why do we suffer? The correct answer to this question, Nietzsche believes, is that the slaves suffer because they are inherently weak, and it is simply a biological fact that some humans are much weaker than others, either by nature or as a result of unfortunate circumstances. This answer, however, is one no slave can be expected to tolerate because it seems to make his situation hopeless and irremediable, which, in fact, Nietzsche thinks it is. Humans can bear suffering; what they cannot bear is seemingly senseless suffering, and this is what the slaves' suffering is. It has no meaning, it is a mere brute fact. The priests' intervention consists in giving the slaves a way of interpreting their suffering which at least allows them to make some sense of it. 'You slaves are suffering', so runs the priestly account, '*because* **you** are evil'. The *ressentiment* that was directed at the masters is now turned by the slaves on themselves. The sick, suffering slave becomes a 'sinner'. In addition to this diagnosis of the cause of suffering, the priests also have a proposed therapy. Since 'evil' designates the kind of intense vitality the masters exhibit in their lives, the way to escape it is to engage in a progressive spiral of forms of life-abnegation and self-denial. In the long run, this therapy makes the original 'disease' – the suffering that results from human weakness – worse, but in the short run of 2,000 years or so, it has mobilized what energy the slaves command in the service of creating what we know as Western culture.

The 'healing instinct of life' operates through the priest, in which ideas of guilt, sin, damnation, and so on, serve 'to make the sick *harmless* to a degree', and the instincts of the sufferer are exploited 'for the purpose of self-discipline, self-surveillance, and self-overcoming' (*GM*, III, 16). The priests' remedy for human suffering is the ascetic ideal, the ideal of a human will turned utterly against itself, or self-abnegation *for its own sake*. Such an ideal seems to express a self-contradiction in as much as we seem to encounter with it life operating against life. Nietzsche argues, however, that viewed from physiological and psychological angles this amounts to nonsense. In section 13 of the Third Essay he suggests that, on closer examination, the self-contradiction turns out to be only apparent, it is 'a psychological misunderstanding of something, the real nature of which was far from being understood . . .' His argument is that the ascetic ideal has its source or origins in what he calls 'the protective and healing instincts of a degenerating life'. The ideal indicates a partial physiological exhaustion, in the face of which 'the deepest instincts of life, which have remained intact, continually struggle with new methods and inventions'. The ascetic ideal amounts, in effect, to a trick or artifice (*Kunstgriff*) for the preservation of life. The interpretation of suffering developed by the ascetic ideal for a long time now has succeeded in shutting the door on a suicidal nihilism by giving humanity a goal: morality. The ideal has added new dimensions and layers to suffering by making it deeper and more internal, creating a suffering that gnaws more intensely at life and bringing it within the perspective of metaphysical-moral guilt. But this saving of the will has been won at the expense of the future and fostered a hatred of the conditions of human existence. It expresses a 'fear of happiness and beauty' and 'a longing to get away from appearance, transience, growth, death'.

The real problem, according to Nietzsche, is not the past, not even Christianity, but present-day Christian-moral Europe. 'After such vistas and with such a burning hunger in our conscience and science', he writes in an aphorism on the great health, 'how could we still be satisfied with *present-day man?*' (*GS*, 382). We live in an age in which the desire for man and his future – a future beyond mere self-preservation, security and comfort – seems to be disappearing from the face of the earth. Modern atheists who have emancipated themselves from the affliction of past errors – the error of God, of the world conceived as a unity, of free will, and so on – have only freed themselves from something and not for something. They either believe in nothing at all or have a blind commitment to science and uphold the unconditional nature of the will to truth. By contrast, Nietzsche commits himself to the '*supreme affirmation*' that is born out of fullness, and this is 'an affirmation without reservation even of suffering, even of guilt, even of all that is strange and questionable in existence'. Nietzsche stresses that this 'Yes to life' is both the highest and deepest insight that is 'confirmed and maintained by truth and knowledge' (*EH* 'BT', 2). It is not, then, a simple-minded, pre-cognitive 'Yes' to life that he wants us to practise, but one, as he stresses, secured by 'truth and knowledge'. The 'free spirit' knows what kind of 'you shall' he has obeyed, Nietzsche writes; and in so doing, 'he also knows what he now *can*, what only now he – *may* do . . .' (*HH*, Preface).

NIETZSCHE AND POLITICAL THOUGHT

Nietzsche's political thinking remains a source of difficulty, even embarrassment, because it fails to accord with the standard liberal ways of thinking about politics which have prevailed in the last 200 and more years. As in liberalism, Nietzsche's conception of politics is an instrumental one, but he differs radically from the liberal view in his valuation of life. For liberalism, politics is a means to the peaceful coexistence of individual agents; for Nietzsche, by contrast, it is a means to the production of human greatness. Nietzsche challenges what we might call the ontological assumptions that inform the positing of the liberal subject, chiefly that its identity is largely imaginary because it is posited only at the expense of neglecting the cultural and historical formation of the subject. The liberal formulation of the subject assumes individual identity and liberty to be a given, in which the individual exists independently of the mediations of culture and history and outside the medium of ethical contest and spiritual labour. Nietzsche is committed to the enhancement of man and this enhancement does not consist in improving the conditions of existence for the majority of human beings, but in the generation of a few, striking and superlatively vital 'highest exemplars' of the species. Nietzsche looks forward to new philosophers who will be strong and original enough to revalue and reverse so-called 'eternal values' and, in teaching human beings that the future depends on their will, 'will prepare the way for great risk-taking and joint experiments in discipline and breeding', and in this way, 'put an end to that terrible reign of nonsense and coincidence that until now has been known as "history"' (BGE, 203).

In the two early essays from 1871–2 included in this volume, 'The Greek State' and 'Homer's Contest', we see at work the stress Nietzsche places on political life not as an end in itself but as a means to the production of great human beings and an aristocratic culture. Nietzsche presents a stark choice between 'culture' and 'politics' (or the claims of justice). He argues that if we wish to promote greatness and serve the ends of culture, then it is necessary to recognize that an essential aspect of society is economic servitude for the majority of individuals. We must not let the 'urge for justice... swamp all other ideas'; or, as Nietzsche memorably puts it, the 'cry of compassion' must not be allowed to tear down the 'walls of culture'.

When Nietzsche took up his teaching appointment at Basel University, he sought to make a contribution to the so-called 'Homeric question' which was centred on issues about the authenticity, authorship and significance of the works ascribed to 'Homer'. He addressed the topic in his inaugural lecture given in 1869, which was entitled 'Homer and Classical Philology' (originally conceived as an essay on 'Homer's Personality'). He comments upon the significance of the Greek *agon* (contest) in research he had done on a neglected (and maligned) Florentine manuscript on an imaginary contest between Homer and Hesiod (the first part of this research was published in 1870 and a second part in 1873).[4] An exploration of what constitutes the kernel of the Hellenic idea of the contest (*agon*, *certamen*) becomes the major concern of Nietzsche's speculations on the 'event' of Homer in the unpublished essay 'Homer's Contest' that we publish here. Two points are worth noting about this research work by the young Nietzsche: first, that it is an early exercise in genealogy in the sense that it focuses on what it means to reclaim something from the past – in this case antiquity – for the present, and, second, that the motif of the contest is one that persists in Nietzsche and runs throughout his writings.

Nietzsche's positions on ethics and politics may not ultimately compel us but they are more instructive than is commonly supposed, and certainly not as horrific as many of his critics would have us believe.[5] He is out to disturb our satisfaction with ourselves as moderns and as knowers. Although we may find it difficult to stomach some of his specific proposals for the overcoming of man and morality, his conception of genealogy has become a constitutive feature of our efforts at self-knowledge.

[4] See Nietzsche, *Kritische Gesamtausgabe Werke*, ed. Giorgio Colli and Mazzino Montinari (Berlin and New York: Walter de Gruyter, 1967ff.), 2.1, pp. 271–339.

[5] See the fine study by John Richardson, *Nietzsche's New Darwinism* (Oxford and New York: Oxford University Press, 2004).

CHAPTER 10

Nietzsche: The Anti-Christ, Ecce Homo, Twilight of the Idols

Aaron Ridley

In Turin, on 3 January 1889, Nietzsche suffered an irrevocable mental collapse. By the time of his death, in 1900, he had become wholly physically incapacitated as well.[1] It seems probable that the cause was syphilis. It is apparently common for syphilitics to experience a period of uplift, a remarkable sense of well-being, in the months preceding the final collapse. Certainly this was so in Nietzsche's case. In the year before his breakdown his letters are increasingly touched with euphoria. His health, extremely poor for well over a decade, seems to him to be on the mend: 'I have just looked at myself in a mirror – I have never before appeared as I do now: in exemplary good spirits, well-nourished, and looking ten years younger than I ought to';[2] 'my health, like the weather, appears every day with irrepressible brightness and gaiety'.[3] He feels more equal than he has ever felt to the most demanding of intellectual tasks: 'it is my great *harvest-time.* Everything comes easily to me, everything I try succeeds, notwithstanding that no one has yet had such great matters in hand as I have';[4] 'the heaviest tasks, for which no man has yet been sufficiently strong, come easily'.[5] His estimate of himself and of his abilities acquires a megalomanic tinge: 'in two months I shall be the first name on earth'; 'What is remarkable here in Turin is the fascination I exercise on people . . . every face changes; women gaze after me in the street';[6] 'there are no longer any accidents in my life'.[7] And these remarks – and there are many like them – inevitably raise a preliminary question. Are the philosophical works that Nietzsche produced in this final year, the works collected here in this volume, the products of an already-deranged mind?

---

[1] For a sensitive account of Nietzsche's decline, see R. J. Hollingdale, *Nietzsche: The Man and his Philosophy* (Cambridge: Cambridge University Press, 1999). The letters cited in nn. 2–7 are taken from Hollingdale. See also Lesley Chamberlain, *Nietzsche in Turin* (London: Quartet, 1996).
[2] To Peter Gast, 30 October 1888.   [3] To Carl Fuchs, 18 December 1888.
[4] To Franz Overbeck, 18 October 1888.   [5] To his mother, 21 December 1888.
[6] To Franz Overbeck, 25 December 1888.   [7] To August Strindberg, 7 December 1888.

NIETZSCHE'S SANITY

The 1888 texts are certainly very diverse. One – *Twilight of the Idols* – proceeds in a distilled version of Nietzsche's established aphoristic manner. Two – *The Anti-Christ* and *The Case of Wagner* – are sustained polemics, directed, respectively, against institutionalized Christianity and Richard Wagner's music dramas. One – *Ecce Homo* – is a strange sort of autobiography. And the remaining work – *Nietzsche Contra Wagner* – is an anthology of aphorisms culled, sometimes with minor alterations, from Nietzsche's other books.[8] But variety is hardly a sign of madness.

It used to be common to say that 1888 marked a falling-off of Nietzsche's creativity as a thinker, and to link this to a decline in his mental capacities. So, for example, *Twilight of the Idols* was often said to be little more than a noisy résumé of some of his more strongly held opinions. And there is a measure of truth in this. It is true that comparatively few of the ideas that Nietzsche committed to paper in that book had not been expressed by him before. But this is entirely to overlook the kind of expression that they receive there. *Twilight* represents a pinnacle of aphoristic economy and wit, an example of Nietzsche's mature style at its very best. And this is hard to square with the suspicion of mental decline.

I think that this conclusion is now generally accepted, certainly as far as *Twilight* is concerned. Elsewhere matters may be less clear-cut. *The Case of Wagner*, for instance, has been very widely ignored, presumably for two main reasons. First, not many Nietzsche scholars regard Nietzsche's attitude towards Wagner as the most interesting thing about him; and second, he'd been going on about Wagner in broadly similar terms for years, as the passages assembled in *Nietzsche Contra Wagner* attest.[9] But – again – this latter fact is no mark of mental decline. *The Case of Wagner* is an exhilarating read, fully the equal of *Twilight* in the pithiness of its delivery, and if anything even funnier. And although it is true that much of what he says there he had said before, it would be a mistake to imagine that he says nothing new. *The Case of Wagner* would repay more attention than it has received.

The question mark looms largest over the remaining two works, *The Anti-Christ* and *Ecce Homo*. *The Anti-Christ* is Nietzsche's longest sustained

---

[8] There is in fact a sixth work from 1888, *Dionysian Dithyrambs*, not included here. This is a collection of poems whose absence is not to be regretted.

[9] Indeed, this was probably the point of *Nietzsche contra Wagner*. *The Case of Wagner*, when it was published, went down badly. Wagner had died in 1883, and the book was taken as a rather graceless posthumous attack on him by an erstwhile devotee. *Nietzsche contra Wagner* demonstrated that Nietzsche had been being nasty about Wagner since at least 1878.

discussion of a single topic since the mid 1870s, when he wrote the four *Untimely Meditations*. In tone it is quite unlike *Twilight* (with which it is often compared). Where *Twilight* is graceful, light, and even effervescent in its intensity, *The Anti-Christ* strikes one as over-emphatic and rather tiring. Nietzsche really *hates* Christianity, and he makes the reader feel it. He hectors; he insists. But it is surely the degree of his antipathy that has got the better of him here, rather than any diminution of his powers. He is sharp and incisive throughout; and much of his material – which is like a concrete, historically more rooted version of themes treated in *On the Genealogy of Morality* – is distinctive and new. *The Anti-Christ* should be read, I think, as the work of someone who finds Christianity genuinely maddening, not as the work of someone who is already mad.

Ecce Homo, Nietzsche's autobiography, is the hardest case of all. Even R. J. Hollingdale, Nietzsche's excellent and sympathetic biographer, has problems with this book. While he praises it as 'undoubtedly one of the most beautiful in German', and remarks that many 'passages are a *non plus ultra* of richness combined with economy',[10] he also picks out a current in the book that strikes him as insane. 'Where Nietzsche leaves philosophy and writes about himself', says Hollingdale, 'his sense of his own quality passes the bounds of reasonableness and lands in absurdity... Nietzsche quietly attributes to himself impossible abilities.'[11] What Hollingdale hears in the passages that bother him he takes to be symptomatic of Nietzsche's impending mental collapse: euphoria, megalomania.

He may be right about this: I don't know. Nor does it seem tremendously important to know. Incipient insanity may take the form of hyperbole, and what is exaggerated may be true, or interesting, even when pitched at a level that can seem deranged. And I think that there are good reasons to conclude that this is so with *Ecce Homo*. Precisely the kinds of passage that Hollingdale singles out as early signs of madness strike me as helpful dramatizations of a distinctive strand in Nietzsche's later philosophy, a strand having to do with freedom and self-realization – with what, in the subtitle to *Ecce Homo*, he calls becoming 'what you are'. Indeed, I propose to build the bulk of this introduction around just this aspect of Nietzsche's thought.

Overall, then, there would seem to be little reason to worry about the sanity of these final writings. It is true that Nietzsche's letters at this period reveal a state of mind that is almost certainly to be explained by the progress of his illness. But it appears that in his work he retained a

---

[10] Hollingdale, *Nietzsche*, p. 216.   [11] *Ibid.*, pp. 199–200.

focus and a kind of mastery over his material that insulated it from the effects of his condition. As Hollingdale puts it, 'The philosopher has not lost his grip on his material, he has tightened it . . . There is no intellectual degeneration: the mind is as sharp as ever.'[12] And, unlike Hollingdale, I am inclined to think that this verdict is as good as safe for the last works in their entirety – not just for those parts of them that Hollingdale identifies as 'philosophy'.

BECOMING WHO YOU ARE

Nietzsche had first begun to take the idea of becoming 'who you are' seriously some years earlier. An aphorism in the 1882 edition of *The Gay Science* reads: '*What does your conscience say?* – "You shall become who you are"' (*GS* 270); and Nietzsche expands on the thought in a later section called '*Long live physics!*' It is important, he says, not to take the deliverances of conscience at face value, as if their source somehow guaranteed their truth: 'Your judgement "this is right" has a pre-history in your instincts, likes, dislikes, experiences and lack of experiences'; indeed, 'that you take this or that judgement for the voice of conscience . . . may be due to the fact that you have never thought much about yourself and have simply accepted blindly that what you had been *told* ever since your childhood was right' (*GS* 335).

What is needed to rectify this '*faith*', he claims, is 'an intellectual con-science', a 'conscience behind your "conscience"' (*GS* 335) – a determina-tion, precisely, to think about yourself, 'to scrutinize [your] experiences as severely as a scientific experiment – hour after hour, day after day' (*GS* 319). By these means we can

become who we are – human beings who are new, unique . . . who give themselves laws, who create themselves! To that end we must become the best students and discoverers of everything lawful and necessary in the world: we must become *physicists* in order become creators in this sense . . . So, long live physics! And even more so that which *compels* us to turn to physics – our honesty! (*GS* 335)

Thus, it is our 'intellectual conscience', our 'honesty', that both says 'You shall become who you are' and also makes becoming who you are possible.

At one level, Nietzsche's thought here is straightforward. One becomes who one is by getting to know oneself, and by getting to know the con-ditions under which one operates ('everything lawful and necessary in the

---

[12] *Ibid.*, pp. 199, 216.

world'). One ceases, on the one hand, idly to accept falsehoods about oneself – for instance, that one has an infallible organ of judgment, one's 'conscience', whose deliverances are somehow independent of one's 'instincts, likes, dislikes, experiences' etc. – and one ceases, on the other hand, to accept falsehoods about the world – for instance, that it is governed by 'providential reason and goodness' (GS 277), or that it is somehow organized with human purposes in mind, or indeed with any purpose at all.[13] At this level, then, one becomes who one is by honestly acknowledging, first, that one is essentially just an animal, rather than a creature with supernatural capacities, and second, that the world in which one has one's being, in which one must act and try to make sense of oneself, is a world without God. We necessarily misunderstand ourselves, Nietzsche holds, if we fail to acknowledge either kind of truth.

But we are more than *merely* animals. Unlike the other animals, we also have a 'second nature',[14] a nature produced by culture. And it is this that is expressed through our practices, including those practices in which various misunderstandings of ourselves are encoded. An animal without a 'second nature' could no more mistake itself for a transmitter of the 'voice of conscience', or for an inhabitant of a divinely ordered world, than it could enter into a contract, form a friendship, or go to war. Our 'second nature' is what makes us 'interesting', as Nietzsche later has it,[15] and the 'experiences' that are rooted there are pre-eminently among those to be subjected to the 'intellectual conscience'. In order to 'become who we are', then, we must be honest with ourselves not merely as pieces of nature, as animals in an undesigned world, but as pieces of 'second nature', as animals whose character and circumstances are significantly constituted by culture.

There are many ways in which we can misunderstand ourselves. We can, as it were, be factually wrong about some matter concerning nature or second nature. Or we can adopt, perhaps unconsciously, a perspective on such matters that systematically occludes or distorts them. Nietzsche is particularly interested in misunderstandings of this latter kind – in habits of thought that have the effect of making whole dimensions of ourselves and of our worldly circumstances obscure to us. The most famous example, of course, is the perspective that Nietzsche diagnoses under the label 'morality'. But that is a diagnosis that advances along several fronts: here, I will focus on just one of these, and attempt to indicate how Nietzsche understands the relation – obscured, he holds, by 'morality' – between our

---

[13] See, e.g., GS 109.   [14] See, e.g., *Daybreak* (D) 38.
[15] See, e.g., *On the Genealogy of Morality* (GM) 1.6.

becoming our own 'creators' and our being the 'discoverers of everything lawful and necessary in the world'.

Two well-known passages from *The Gay Science* are helpful here. In one, Nietzsche speaks of the 'great and rare art' of giving '"style" to one's character':

It is practised by those who survey all the strengths and weaknesses of their nature and then fit them into an artistic plan . . . Here a large mass of second nature has been added; there a piece of original nature has been removed – both times through long practice and daily work at it. Here the ugly that could not be removed is concealed; there it has been reinterpreted and made sublime. (*GS* 290)

Four points are worth making about this passage. First, what Nietzsche is here describing is a form of self-creation, that is, a version of becoming who you are; second, this form of self-creation depends upon self-understanding, upon surveying one's nature and identifying the strengths and weaknesses in it; third, weaknesses or uglinesses are sometimes removable; and fourth, irremovable uglinesses are to be concealed if they cannot be 'reinterpreted' and transformed. The first two points connect this passage directly to our discussion so far: becoming who you are depends upon the exercise of the intellectual conscience. And the remaining two points provide the connection to the second passage:

I want to learn more and more to see as beautiful what is necessary in things; then I shall be one of those who make things beautiful. *Amor fati*: let that be my love henceforth! (*GS* 276)

The connection comes to this: becoming who you are requires that you distinguish between what is and what is not necessary in things, including yourself (a job for the intellectual conscience). What is not necessary, and is weak or ugly, should be removed. What *is* necessary should, if weak or ugly, either be concealed ('*Looking away* shall be my only negation' (*GS* 276)) or else 'reinterpreted', so that one learns to see it as beautiful, as a strength.

A distinctive conception of the relation between self-creation and necessity – whether in nature, second nature, or circumstance – is implicit in these passages, and it is this that Nietzsche regards as obscured by the perspective of 'morality'. He develops the point explicitly in *Beyond Good and Evil* (1886). 'Morality', he claims, trades on an impossible notion of freedom. It encourages 'the desire to bear the entire and ultimate responsibility for one's actions oneself, and to absolve God, the world, ancestors, chance and society'. It encourages, that is, a quite peculiar conception of autonomy, according to which we are properly self-governing and properly responsible for our actions only to the extent that what we do is the product of '"freedom of the will" in the superlative metaphysical sense', a freedom that is supposedly operative independently of our nature, our second nature, or our circumstances. But this, observes Nietzsche, 'is the best self-contradiction that has been conceived so far'; it involves the desire 'to pull oneself up into existence by the hair, out of the swamps of nothingness'. And – crucially – it encourages us to perceive in every necessity 'something of constraint, need, compulsion to obey, pressure and unfreedom' (*BGE* 21).

The truth, Nietzsche holds, is quite otherwise. As the self-stylization and the *amor fati* passages make clear, he treats necessities of various kinds as material to be exploited and, where possible, affirmed. Indeed, he treats them as *conditions* of effective action, rather than as impediments to it, and hence as integral to the possibility of freedom, rather than as limits upon it:

one should recall the compulsion under which every language so far has achieved strength and freedom – the metrical compulsion of rhyme and rhythm. How much trouble the poets and orators . . . have taken . . . 'submitting abjectly to capricious laws', as anarchists say, feeling 'free' . . . But the curious fact is that all there is or has been on earth of freedom, subtlety . . . and masterly sureness . . . in thought itself . . . in the arts just as in ethics, has developed only owing to the 'tyranny of such capricious laws'; and in all seriousness, the probability is . . . that this is 'nature' and 'natural' – and *not* that *laisser aller*. (*BGE* 188)

So Nietzsche offers a picture of freedom that roots it explicitly in the 'tyranny' of 'capricious laws', which is to say, in the necessities that constitute our second nature.

Only someone who acknowledges the rules of language has the capacity – the freedom – to communicate in it. Only someone who acknowledges the laws of chess has the freedom to castle his king, say. Only someone who acknowledges the norms and courtesies of conversation has the freedom to engage in one. And so on, for any human practice at all. To resent such 'necessities' as a threat to one's '"responsibility"', to one's 'belief in' *oneself*, to one's 'personal right to [one's *own*] merits at any price' would be, quite simply, to render oneself impotent (*BGE* 21). Yet it is precisely such a resentment that 'morality', with its fantasy of freedom in the 'superlative metaphysical sense', expresses. Nietzsche's point, then, is that if we are to understand ourselves as actors in the world as it is, we have to acknowledge that certain necessities are integral to our agency, to our 'freedom' and 'responsibility'.[16] And this is a form of self-understanding – a finding of the intellectual conscience – that the peculiar perspective of 'morality' necessarily occludes; which is one of the reasons why it stands in the way of our becoming who we are.

When Nietzsche says, therefore, that we must become 'discoverers of everything lawful and necessary in the world' if we are to become 'creators' of ourselves, part of what he means is that we must determine *which* of the circumstances of our existence really are necessities. Some of these circumstances, for instance, 'morality', may appear to be or may present themselves as being necessities,[17] when in fact they are only contingent sources of self-misunderstanding: such circumstances are uglinesses or weaknesses, and they should be removed. Other of our circumstances really are necessities. And, of these, some will be ineluctably ugly, and will have to be concealed or looked away from.[18] The remainder, however, are to be understood – perhaps *via* 'reinterpretation' – as conditions of the possibility of agency, of freedom. And it is through the acknowledgement and affirmation of these that the discovery, development, and – perhaps –the perfection of one's capacities is to be realized. To the extent that those capacities *are* realized, one has succeeded in becoming who one is.

It is not surprising that Nietzsche should link this process to art and creativity. Artistry is law-like, in the sense that it is possible to go wrong, to make mistakes. Yet the laws against which these mistakes offend often declare themselves only in the moment at which they are breached, indeed *in* the breaching of them. And this is why getting something *right* feels like – is – getting what one was after all along, even when one could not have said in advance precisely what that was. In this way, successful artistry is also a form of self-discovery – it is the discovery, in the lawfulness of one's actions, of the innermost character of one's intentions:

Every artist knows how far from any feeling of letting himself go his most 'natural' state is – the free ordering, placing . . . giving form in the moment of 'inspiration' – and how strictly and subtly he obeys thousandfold laws precisely then, laws that precisely on account of their hardness and determination defy all formulation through concepts . . . (*BGE* 188)

– and this, in turn, is a large part of the reason why Nietzsche so consistently connects self-creation to having one's *own* laws. In becoming who we are,

---

[16] Cf. *TI*, 'Skirmishes', 38.
[17] Morality 'says stubbornly and inexorably: "I am morality itself, and nothing besides is morality"' (*BGE* 202).
[18] Cf. *BGE* 39.

he says, we become 'human beings who are new, unique, incomparable, who give themselves laws, who create themselves!' (*GS* 335); self-stylists 'enjoy their finest gaiety . . . in being bound by but also perfected under a law of their own' (*GS* 290); 'the "individual" appears, obliged to give himself laws and to develop his own arts and wiles for self-preservation, self-enhancement, self-redemption' (*BGE* 262).

So artistry represents a limit case of Nietzsche's understanding of agency. Like every kind of agency, artistry is possible only for those who acknowledge necessity as a condition of, rather than as a limit upon, their freedom to act. We misunderstand ourselves if we misunderstand this. But in artistry we also perpetually discover ourselves, as our actions express those 'thousandfold' unformulable laws which are, Nietzsche suggests, most truly our own. We become most fully who we are, as he puts it at one point, when we become the 'poets of our lives' (*GS* 299).

NIETZSCHE ON NIETZSCHE

This gives some of the background required to understand *Ecce Homo*, much of which is devoted to explaining – or perhaps to dramatizing – how Nietzsche has become who he is. But Nietzsche does not merely present his life as a work of art; he presents it as a fully achieved work of art, one that exhibits 'masterly sureness' throughout – that shows at every point his '*sureness of instinct* in practice' (*EH*, 'Wise', 6).

It is important to bear this latter point in mind, if the text is to stay in its proper focus. It can appear, for instance, that Nietzsche's conception of *amor fati* must have changed since 1882. In *The Gay Science*, as we have seen, *amor fati* involves learning 'to see as beautiful what is necessary in things' (*GS* 276), which leaves it open just how much *is* necessary in things (an indeterminacy that is vital if self-stylization, for instance, is to remain intelligible). In *Ecce Homo*, by apparent contrast, we read this: 'My formula for human greatness is *amor fati*: that you do not want anything to be different, not forwards, not backwards, not for all eternity. Not just to tolerate necessity . . . but to *love* it' (*EH*, 'Clever', 10), which may suggest that Nietzsche now regards *everything* as necessary.

But this is misleading. His claim, rather, is that a great human being is one who has learned to see as beautiful every circumstance of his life, has learned to treat every fact about himself and his world as necessary conditions of his freedom to act and to create himself under laws of his own. And *this* achievement may well require that quite a lot that is true of him now has only become true of him because of (unnecessary) things in his life that he has changed – for instance, that he has cast off certain weaknesses or uglinesses that masqueraded as necessities: examples that Nietzsche gives in his own case include ridding himself of the conviction that he is just 'like everyone else', of 'a forgetting of distance' between himself and others, an '"idealism"' (*EH*, 'Clever', 2). Or perhaps the great human being has altered one set of circumstances in his life so as to accommodate another, as Nietzsche reports himself as having altered his diet and his environs in order to accommodate his physiology (*EH*, 'Clever', 1, 2). Nor does this mean that he must necessarily have cause to regret the *status quo ante*, to want things 'to be different... backwards'. For he may well understand it as a condition of his having arrived where he is now that he had to overcome things as they were before: 'he uses mishaps to his advantage', Nietzsche says; 'what does not kill him makes him stronger' (*EH*, 'Wise', 2).

The best way to construe *amor fati* throughout Nietzsche's work, then, is as an ethical injunction concerning one's attitude towards the world, rather than as a (disguised) metaphysical thesis about how much of the world is necessary. Indeed, the only difference between 1882 and 1888 is that whereas in *The Gay Science* the presentation had been aspirational ('I want to learn more and more...'), in *Ecce Homo* the learning-process is presented as complete. He now (he claims) affirms *all* of his worldly circumstances: '*How could I not be grateful to my whole life?*' (*EH*, 'On this perfect day'[19]); and, in this limiting case, he achieves 'masterly sureness' in every aspect of his existence – he has '*learned*', as Nietzsche elsewhere puts it, '*to love*' himself (*GS* 334).[20]

These points bring out another strong continuity between the work of the earlier and the later 1880s, a kind of naturalized theodicy that Nietzsche first airs in the section of *The Gay Science* that immediately follows the *amor fati* passage:

Personal providence – There is a certain high point in life: once we have reached that, we are, for all our freedom, once more in the greatest danger of spiritual unfreedom... For it is only now that the idea of a personal providence confronts us... now that we can see how palpably always everything that happens to us turns out for the best... Whatever it is, bad weather or good, the loss of a friend, sickness... it proves to be something that 'must not be missing'; it has a profound significance and use precisely for *us*. (*GS* 277)

---

[19] Inscription placed between the Preface and the first chapter.
[20] *GS* 334 provides an essential hinge between the notions of *amor fati* and of becoming who one is.

The 'high point', clearly enough, is attained when one has learned to affirm all of one's worldly circumstances, when one's *amor fati* is complete; and the 'danger of spiritual unfreedom' is posed by the temptation to believe that there must, as an explanation for this, be 'some petty deity who is full of care and personally knows every little hair on our head', a supernatural source of 'providential reason and goodness' in our lives (*GS* 277). The danger, in other words, is that one will start to misunderstand oneself (to become who one isn't) by believing that it is a condition of one's freedom that there be a God who ensures that all is for the best in this, the best of all possible worlds.

The truth, of course, in Nietzsche's view, is that the condition of our freedom is not a benevolent God, but nature, second nature, and our attitude to these. If we are 'strong enough', he says, then 'everything *has to* turn out best' for us (*EH*, 'Wise', 2), for which the credit should be given, not to anything supernatural, but to 'our own practical and theoretical skill in interpreting and arranging events' (*GS* 277). As an example, Nietzsche describes how his illness has had 'a profound significance and use precisely for' *him*: sickness can

be an energetic *stimulus* to life . . . This is, in fact, how that long period of illness looks to me *now*: I discovered life anew . . . myself included, I tasted all good and even small things in ways that other people cannot easily do . . . [Indeed,] the years of my lowest vitality were the ones when I *stopped* being a pessimist. (*EH*, 'Wise', 2)

Nietzsche's illness has turned out to be for the best, to be one of those things that "'must not be missing'".

So if a traditional, more or less Leibnizian, theodicy seeks to show that every apparent evil is a necessary part of God's benevolent grand plan, Nietzsche's naturalized version of it urges us to find a perspective on our circumstances from which even the most grim-seeming of them can be regarded as indispensable *to us*. In place of Leibniz's ambition to redeem the whole world from a God's-eye point of view, that is, Nietzsche's hope is that individual lives might be redeemed from the point of view of those who live them, from a first-person perspective.[21]

This dimension of Nietzsche's thought is largely backward-looking. One is to look back and interpret one's past as having been for the best; but one is to do so from a present whose character – whose rightness – is partly to

---

[21] Nietzsche does occasionally seem tempted by supra-mundane world-redemption, especially when he starts talking about 'eternal recurrence'. But eternal recurrence is different from *amor fati*, and it is the strand of his thought that stems from the latter that concerns us here.

be constituted by one's success in this very enterprise. Of course, one's past might need a good deal of interpretation in order to bring this off. It is not as if one had been all along the deliberate architect of one's life – indeed, one must *not* be such an architect:

> you [must] not have the slightest idea *what* you are. If you look at it this way, even life's *mistakes* have their own meaning and value . . . [Here, *know thyself*] is the recipe for decline . . . *misunderstanding* yourself, belittling, narrowing yourself, making yourself mediocre . . . the threat that instinct will 'understand itself' too early. – In the mean time, the organizing, governing 'idea' keeps growing deep inside . . . it slowly leads *back* from out of the side roads and wrong turns, it gets the *individual* qualities and virtues ready [which] will prove indispensable as means to the whole . . . Viewed in this light, my life is just fantastic [– the product of] the lengthy, secret work and artistry of my instinct. (*EH*, 'Clever', 9)

To have turned out well, from this point of view, is to be able to interpret one's development as the unconscious unfolding of one's latent potential, as the gradual, invisible piecing-together of a coherent self. And the 'happiness' of such a development lies, as Nietzsche puts it, 'in its fatefulness' (*EH*, 'Wise', 1).

In *Ecce Homo*, then, Nietzsche presents his life as a species of artistry, in several senses. First, his life as it is now is one that he can affirm in all of its circumstances; he has learned to treat everything about himself and his world as necessary to his freedom to act and to create himself under his own laws. Second, he has interpreted his history in such a way that everything in it is 'for the best', so that his past unfolds like a work of art. And third, he attributes that unfolding to the 'artistry' of his 'instinct', since much that contributed to its course was not (and perhaps could not have been) consciously chosen. In each of these senses, Nietzsche portrays himself as the poet of his life, and hence as one who has become who he is.

NIETZSCHE'S INTEGRITY

In the final sections of this introduction I turn to two of the circumstances of Nietzsche's life that make it most distinctively *his* – namely Christianity and Wagner. But before that, it might be worth asking what – in the light of the foregoing – we should make of *Ecce Homo*. I suggested at the outset that the book is not in any interesting or important way the product of insanity. But it may now seem as if the truth is if anything worse than that – that *Ecce Homo* is actually no more than a self-help manual, of a sort that endorses a peculiarly self-serving variety of positive thinking. It may seem, too, as if the demands of the 'intellectual conscience', upon which I have laid a good deal of weight, have disappeared without trace. One is, it appears, opportunistically to reinterpret one's past in a way that makes it seem providential. And one is to take seriously the thought – the fantasy, surely – that one might regard one's life as a work of art, and oneself as its moment-by-moment creator.

The first thing to say is that Nietzsche remains fully committed at this period to the value of honesty and the intellectual conscience. Sections 50–6 of *The Anti-Christ* contain one of the longest discussions of 'the service of truth' (*AC* 50) in any of Nietzsche's works, and he summarizes that discussion in *Ecce Homo*: 'How much truth can a spirit *tolerate*, how much truth is it willing to *risk*? This increasingly became the real measure of value for me . . . [E]very step forward in knowledge comes from *courage*, from harshness towards yourself' (*EH*, Preface, 3). These are not the words of a witting fantasist, or of one bent on falsifying his past. Moreover, the positions – such as 'morality' – against which Nietzsche most consistently ranges himself in *Ecce Homo*, and which he labels 'idealism', he regards as 'errors' and as the products of 'cowardice' (*EH*, Preface, 3).

But Nietzsche's objection to 'idealism' is not merely that it falsifies the world – by pretending that there is a God, for example, or by pretending that freedom in 'the superlative metaphysical sense' is possible. It is also that 'idealism' devalues the world, by according the highest value to its own inventions, at the world's expense and out of resentment against it – out of a 'deadly hostility to life' (*EH*, 'Destiny', 8). And this means that Nietzsche's own project also has two dimensions. One is to diagnose the errors of 'idealism'; the other is to suggest how life and the world might still have value for us once we have refused to resort to supernatural or metaphysical remedies. The thoughts canvassed in the previous section are an important part of Nietzsche's attempt to engage with the second of these issues. They are, in effect, an exploration of the intuition, first expressed in 1882, that 'As an aesthetic phenomenon existence is still *bearable* for us' (*GS* 107).

It is true that nothing could correspond to living one's life, from moment to moment, as if it were a work of art. So in this sense, Nietzsche's self-presentation does have an air of fantasy about it. But two points are worth making. The first is that, as I have argued, Nietzsche understands artistry as a limit case of agency in general, a limit at which one is, as it were, perfectly intelligible to oneself. And while it is surely true that that limit is not occupiable indefinitely, it is at least visitable from time to time; and it seems plausible to say that one is better off, by and large, for being closer to it than otherwise. And if this is right, it is hard to see why one might not try to imagine, as Nietzsche does, what it would be like if, *per impossibile*, one could occupy that limit for the whole of the time – if only as a way of dramatizing a regulative ideal. The other point is that the expression of *Ecce Homo* is, as I said earlier, often hyperbolic. In part, of course, this is just to say that it is exaggerated, and to that extent the present point is the same as the first. But hyperbole is also a means of self-deflation, a form of deliberate over-statement that is meant to be seen through, if not at once, then at least pretty quickly. And from this point of view, it is not implausible to read Nietzsche as debunking his aesthetic ideal, as admitting that it is not fully realizable, at the same time as he dramatizes its realization.

So one shouldn't worry about the essential honesty of *Ecce Homo*, I think. Nor is it very troubling to think that it might be taken as a self-help manual, as a promoter of positive thinking. Positive thinking is surely better than the reverse; and, if Nietzsche is right that supernatural or metaphysical remedies are hard to do without, it seems entirely reasonable to suppose that, in their absence, some self-help might be needed. Nor, finally, do the charges of self-servingness and opportunism seem well directed. Nietzsche is explicitly out to serve the self; he says so repeatedly. And we can pointfully be charged with opportunism only when there are alternatives available to us. Confronted with some grim fact about our past, we can of course try to forget it; indeed, Nietzsche speaks warmly and often about the value of forgetting.[22] But if that is not possible, it is scarcely opportunistic to try to see it instead as something that '"must not be missing"', that has 'a profound significance and use precisely for *us*'. To refuse to recuperate what we can out of life is to turn our backs on it. And that, according to Nietzsche, is exactly what 'idealists' do.

NIETZSCHE ON CHRISTIANITY

Nietzsche does tell at least one clear lie in *Ecce Homo*, and it is this: 'I only attack things where there is no question of personal differences, where there has not been a history of bad experiences . . . I have the right to wage war on Christianity because I have never been put out or harmed by it' (*EH*, 'Wise', 7). Most of Nietzsche's readers will find this assertion hard to square with the temperature of his rhetoric whenever Christianity is in his sights; and readers of the *Genealogy*, in particular, will find the following claim equally unbelievable: '"God", "immortality of the soul", "redemption",

---

[22] See, e.g., *EH*, 'Wise', 2.

"beyond", are simply ideas that I have not paid any attention to or devoted any time to' (*EH*, 'Clever', 1).

The truth is that Nietzsche's relation to Christianity and to Christian concepts is both personal and intense. On the one hand, he regards Christianity as a calamity, as the worst sort of life-slandering 'idealism', existing only 'to *devalue* nature' (*AC* 38). On the other hand, faith in God had given life meaning, and once 'God is dead' (*GS* 125) we are cast adrift in a world whose emptiness Nietzsche feels acutely. So if Nietzsche attacks Christianity, frequently and vehemently, he is also keenly aware that victory must come at a price: the 'uncovering' of Christianity, he says, is 'an event without equal, a real catastrophe. Anyone who knows about this . . . splits the history of humanity into two parts. Some live *before* him, some live *after* him' (*EH*, 'Destiny', 8).

If *Ecce Homo* is, at least in part, an effort to see how one might live 'after him', *The Anti-Christ* is Nietzsche's most sustained attempt to ensure that the history of mankind is, indeed, split in two. At the heart of the book lies a contrast between the figure of Christ and institutionalized Christianity, a contrast that Nietzsche pursues energetically, and across several different dimensions, but always to the detriment of Christianity. His crispest *précis* of the contrast is this: 'A new way of life, *not* a new faith' (*AC* 33). And his claim, in a nutshell, is that the church (pre-eminently St Paul) has systematically perverted and distorted Christ's real significance – which lay in *how* he lived his life – by turning his example into the set of beliefs, doctrines, and dogmas that we know as 'Christianity'.

It is worth distinguishing between two aspects of Nietzsche's critique. One is concerned with the form of Christianity (i.e. with the fact that it consists of doctrines and dogmas), and the other is concerned with its content (i.e. with what those doctrines and dogmas actually are). I will treat these aspects in turn, and try to indicate how each connects to issues touched on earlier.

Nietzsche's objection under the first head is essentially Aristotelian. We might hope to do what an exemplary figure does by learning some rules, by acquiring a set of beliefs about what is required and what is prohibited. But no such rules or beliefs can, by themselves, enable us to do what the exemplary figure does *as* he does it.[23] We cannot move, that is, from a 'way of life' to a set of requirements or prohibitions that is equivalent to it: something goes missing. And what goes missing, in effect, is the relation

---

[23] See Aristotle, *Nicomachean Ethics*, Book II, chapter 4.

between who we are and what we do.[24] Christianity, as Nietzsche construes it, takes that relation to be externally mediated – by a learnable rule or prescription that is specifiable independently of the relevant 'way of life'. In the exemplary figure, by contrast, that relation is altogether internal: he does as he does because it is his nature to do so (whether that nature be original or second). The exemplar expresses and discloses himself in his actions. He is, in short, one of those whose 'most "natural" state' is to obey a 'thousandfold laws... that precisely on account of their hardness and determination defy all formulation through concepts' (*BGE* 188).

In seeking to extract a set of beliefs or rules from the life of Christ, then, Christianity has failed to treat Christ as an exemplar, and so has falsified the significance that his 'way of life' has. As Nietzsche puts it, Christ's faith 'does not prove itself with miracles, rewards, or promises... at every moment it is its own miracle, its own reward, its own proof... This faith does not formulate itself either – it *lives*, it resists formulas' (*AC* 32); indeed, it

projects itself into a new *practice*, the genuinely evangelical practice. Christians are not characterized by their 'faith': Christians... are characterized by a *different* way of acting... The life of the redeemer was nothing other than *this* practice, – even his death was nothing else... He no longer needed formulas... or even prayer. He... knew how the *practice* of life is the only thing that can make you feel 'divine', 'blessed'... 'Atonement' and 'praying for forgiveness' are *not* the way to God: *only the evangelical practice* leads to God, in fact it *is* 'God'. (*AC* 33)

'The "kingdom of God" is not', therefore, 'something that you wait for; it does not have a yesterday or a day after tomorrow... it is an experience of the heart; it is everywhere and it is nowhere' (*AC* 34). And it is this that is shown in the life of Christ.

Yet it is also this, precisely this, that goes missing when Christianity, as Nietzsche construes it, translates Christ's practice into a set of 'formulas'. Indeed, 'the history of Christianity... is the story of [a] progressively cruder misunderstanding', as a new way of life is obscured more and more by 'doctrines and rites' (*AC* 37). And the effect of this is that Christ's '*glad tidings*', that 'any distance between God and man', is 'abolished' (*AC* 33), is turned upside down. In place of a practice, which '*is* God', the church erects 'formulas' which mediate between man and God, and so hold them apart. '[Y]ou will not find a greater example of *world-historical irony*' than 'that humanity knelt down before the opposite of the origin, the meaning... of

---

[24] Nietzsche had long been interested in the ethical role of exemplars, as the third of the *Untimely Meditations*, *Schopenhauer as Educator* (1874), attests.

the evangel, the fact that in the concept of "church", humanity canonized the very thing the "bearer of glad tidings" felt to be *beneath* him, *behind* him' (*AC* 36).

For present purposes it doesn't greatly matter whether Nietzsche is right about Christ or the church. What matters is the point about the *form* of Christianity (or at any rate of Nietzsche's version of it), the fact that it replaces practices with 'formulas'. For this, in Nietzsche's view, is to promote a distorted picture of a person's relation to his own actions. It is to privilege those cases in which one puts a statable policy into effect over those in which one's policy is disclosed in getting one's actions right. It is to privilege conformity *in abstracto* over self-discovery *in concreto*. And that is why Nietzsche claims that 'for two thousand years' Christianity has been 'just a psychological self-misunderstanding' (*AC* 39); and why he claims elsewhere that to root one's entire ethics in impersonal, codified prescriptions is 'not yet [to have] taken five steps toward self-knowledge' (*GS* 335). His point, in other words, is that the form of Christianity impedes the kind of understanding of oneself that is integral to 'becoming who one is' – indeed, that it renders the very possibility of doing that invisible.

The second aspect of Nietzsche's critique concerns the content of Christianity, what its 'formulas' actually are. These are derived, obviously enough, from Christ's 'way of life'; and this way of life Nietzsche regards as 'necessary' (*AC* 39) for the 'psychological type of the redeemer' (*AC* 29). This type has two defining traits, of which the second is essentially an elaboration of the first:

The instinct of hatred for reality: the consequence of an extreme over-sensitivity and capacity for suffering that does not want to be 'touched' at all because it feels every contact too acutely.
The instinctive exclusion of all aversion, all hostility . . . the consequence of an extreme over-sensitivity and capacity for suffering that perceives every reluctance . . . as . . . an unbearable *pain* . . . and only experiences bliss . . . when it stops resisting everyone and anything, including evil, – love as the only, the *final* possibility for life. (*AC* 30)

And so in Christ's life, according to Nietzsche, these traits are exemplified: 'The polar opposite of struggle . . . has become instinct here . . . blessedness in peace . . . in an *inability* to be an enemy.' His nature is expressed 'as a flight into the "unimaginable", into the "inconceivable" . . . as a being-at-home in a world that has broken off contact with every type of reality, a world that has become completely "internal", a "true" world, an "eternal" world . . . "The kingdom of God is *in each of you*"' (*AC* 29).

The practice of Christ's life is entirely proper to him. He becomes who he is through his way of life, freely creating himself under a law of his own.[25] But such a life is not for everyone. And when Christianity lays hold of it, with its determination to '*vulgarize*' it into a set of formulas (*AC* 37), the result is calamitous.

> From now on, a number of different things started seeping into the type of the redeemer: the doctrines of judgment and return . . . the doctrine of the *resurrection*; and at this point the whole idea of 'blessedness', the solitary reality of the evangel, vanishes with a wave of the hand – and all for the sake of a state *after* death! . . . And in one fell swoop, the evangel becomes the most contemptible of all unfulfillable promises, the *outrageous* doctrine of personal immortality. (*AC* 41)

And when, by these means, 'the emphasis of life is put on the "beyond" rather than on life itself – when it is put *on nothingness* . . . the emphasis has been completely removed from life' as such (*AC* 43).

An important dimension, then, of Nietzsche's critique is that Christianity, as an integral part of its '*disvaluing*' of life, encourages precisely the sorts of views about the self (as immortal) and the world (as a divinely ordered prelude to the 'Beyond') that guarantee self-obscurity. So the content of Christianity, he claims, no less than its form, stands squarely in the way of becoming 'who you are'.

'Have I been understood? – *Dionysus versus the crucified*': that is the famous final slogan of *Ecce Homo* (*EH*, 'Destiny', 9). And a rich slogan it is, too. Nietzsche is insistent that one's opponents should be worthy of one – 'an attack is proof of good will . . . I do something or someone honour, I confer distinction on it when I associate my name with it: for or against' (*EH*, 'Wise', 7). And '*the crucified*' passes muster. As one who has become who he is, Christ earns Nietzsche's respect, even if the psychological type that he represents is not remotely to Nietzsche's taste. And as the saviour concocted by Christianity, he is the most momentous foe imaginable: in *his* name, the world has been stripped of all value, and the possibility of human freedom has been removed from view.

NIETZSCHE ON DECADENCE

Christ is a 'decadent', Nietzsche claims (*AC* 31); and he says the same of himself. Indeed, he attributes the fact that 'I have a subtler sense of smell for the signs of ascent and decline than anyone has ever had' to a 'double birth,

---

[25] I return to this claim in the following section.

from the highest and lowest rungs on the ladder of life . . . simultaneously decadent and *beginning*'. It is this, he claims, that allows him to look 'from the optic of sickness towards *healthier* concepts' and, conversely, 'to look down from the fullness and self-assurance of the *rich* life into the secret work of the instinct of decadence . . . if I became the master of anything, it was this' (*EH*, 'Wise', 1).

'Decadence' is a tricky concept to handle, however. We should begin by noting that Nietzsche, as his own case attests, does not regard decadence as incompatible with becoming who one is: decadence can be an ingredient in self-creation. Decadence is not, therefore, equivalent to the kinds of 'idealism' that he attacks in *Ecce Homo*, even if, in the event, 'idealism' may be one of its most frequent effects. The fact that Nietzsche uses the term 'decadence' indiscriminately to refer to both cause *and* effect often tends to obscure this. But we must keep them apart, and understand decadence as a necessary, but not as a sufficient, condition of 'idealism'. Construed thus, decadence is a form of suffering from life, of suffering from being oneself. As one component of a psyche, it can be something which, if it 'does not kill' one, makes one 'stronger'; it can be one of those 'qualities' which 'will prove indispensable as means to the whole', an element subordinated to an 'organizing . . . "idea"' which produces a totality whose 'incredible multiplicity . . . is nonetheless the converse of chaos'. And this, according to Nietzsche, is how his own decadence is to be understood, as having been woven by the 'secret work and artistry' of his 'instinct' into that greater whole which is 'what he is' (*EH*, 'Clever', 9). Where no such 'secret work and artistry' is present, on the other hand, one is apt to be driven to 'idealism' – to be driven by one's suffering to falsify and devalue the world.

Twilight of the Idols is devoted to the uncovering and diagnosis of decadence, both as cause (suffering) and as effect ('idealism'). It also, via the person of Socrates, offers a case study in how one *ceases* to be who one is. Nietzsche portrays Socrates as the product of decay. Standing behind him is an idealized Greek noble – vibrant, healthy, in tune with himself and his instincts, an artist of his life to his finger-tips – and it is this figure whose decay Socrates represents. '[D]egeneration was quietly gaining ground everywhere', Nietzsche says: 'old Athens was coming to an end . . . Everywhere, instincts were in anarchy' (*TI*, 'Socrates', 9). In place of a more or less unconscious regulation of the instincts, chaos threatened; the 'organizing "idea"' of the Athenian soul was loosening its grip; and people began to suffer from themselves and from life as if it were a sickness (*TI*, 'Socrates', 1). The Athenians became decadent.

But in Socrates there appeared to be a cure at hand. He became 'master of *himself*'. Although he was only 'an extreme case' of the general crisis, he nevertheless held out the prospect that 'a stronger *counter-tyrant*' might be opposed to the tyranny of the instincts (*TI*, 'Socrates', 9). And this tyrant was to be dialectic – '*reason*':

> Rationality was seen as the *saviour*, neither Socrates nor his 'patients' had any choice about being rational . . . it was their *last* resort. [T]hey had only one option: be destroyed or – be *absurdly rational* . . . [Socrates established] a permanent state of *daylight* against all dark desires – the daylight of reason. You have to be clever, clear, and bright at any cost: any concession to the instincts . . . leads *downwards*. (*TI*, 'Socrates', 10)

So Socrates became an 'idealist'. He accorded absolute value to a hypertrophied version of one human capacity, rationality, invented a realm of the Forms that would answer to it, and then used it as a rod with which to beat and denigrate the rest of human nature and the world. And this, although it may well have addressed the 'anarchy' of the instincts, also confirmed him in the view that life is to be suffered as a sickness. What appeared as 'salvation', that is, turned out to be 'only another expression [i.e. effect] of decadence' (*TI*, 'Socrates', 11).

Three things are worth highlighting here. First, 'anarchy' of the instincts is already sufficient for someone to cease to be (or not yet to have become) who he is; no 'organizing "idea"' is present; and this explains Nietzsche's remark that 'our modern concept of "freedom"' – that is, '*laisser aller*', letting go – is 'a symptom of *decadence*', is another 'proof of the degeneration of the instincts' (*TI*, 'Skirmishes', 41). Second, the counter-tyranny – the 'idealism' – that Socrates proposes as a cure for 'anarchy' serves further to obscure oneself to oneself: 'instinctively to choose what is harmful to *yourself*' [that is, for the self who one is to become], 'to be *tempted* by "disinterested" motives, this is practically the formula for decadence [as effect, as "idealism"]' (*TI*, 'Skirmishes', 35). And third, and the foregoing notwithstanding, 'anarchy' of the instincts is not a necessary feature of decadence. Such 'anarchy' was present in the Greeks' case, perhaps – was what *they* suffered from; and for them it might have been true that 'To *have* to fight the instincts' was 'the formula for decadence [as cause]' (*TI*, 'Socrates', 11). But decadence can be rooted in other sources than this.

In Nietzsche's own case, he tells us, it was rooted largely in his illness. 'Anarchy' threatened, no doubt, and he suffered from himself; but thanks to the 'organizing "idea"' that was secretly germinating within him, he succeeded in becoming who he was anyway. And the case of Christ makes the point still more clearly. Christ is a decadent. Yet in his case there simply aren't enough instincts in play to allow for an anarchic free-for-all between them; there is no multiplicity in him (*AC* 31). Rather, Christ's decadence, as Nietzsche diagnoses it, is expressed directly in a single instinct, in a no-holds-barred '*hatred of reality*'. He is, in this sense, decadence incarnate; his life just *is* a suffering from life. And this is why he is no 'idealist'. He has no other resources to draw upon: he stands

outside... all natural science, all experience of the world, all knowledge... he never had any reason to negate 'the world', the... concept of 'world' never occurred to him... *Negation* is out of the question for him. – Dialectic is missing as well, there is no conception that... a 'truth' could be grounded in reasons (– *his* proofs are inner 'lights'.). (*AC* 32)

And so he inhabits 'a merely "inner" world, a "real" world, an "eternal" world'; and he becomes who he is there by becoming, in effect, no one at all, by sublimating himself into a pure symbol of love.

NIETZSCHE ON WAGNER

Decadence is not a univocal phenomenon, then. One can suffer from being oneself in many different ways and to many different effects. And this should arm one against thinking that Nietzsche's late writings about Wagner, in which he presents Wagner as the modern decadent *par excellence*, are likely to be especially one-dimensional. Indeed, it should alert one to the strong possibility that in this case, where Nietzsche's claim to be personally unembroiled is even less plausible than in the case of Christianity, his judgment may go awry.

Nietzsche is not unaware of this potential worry, and in *Ecce Homo* he seeks to disarm it directly: 'I need to express my gratitude', he says, 'for what was by far the friendliest and most profound' relationship of my life, that with Richard Wagner (*EH*, 'Clever', 5). 'I know better than anyone what tremendous things Wagner could do... and being what I am, strong enough to take advantage of the most questionable and dangerous things and become even stronger in the process, I name Wagner as the greatest benefactor of my life' (*EH*, 'Clever', 6). So Wagner is one of those things in Nietzsche's biography that 'must not be missing': he is one of the conditions of Nietzsche's having become who he is.

Indeed, Nietzsche makes a stronger claim than this. He suggests in *The Case of Wagner* that, as a decadent, Wagner is indispensable, not merely for Nietzsche, but for every philosopher. 'Modernity speaks its most *intimate*

language in Wagner: it does not hide its good or its evil... And vice versa: if
you are clear about... Wagner, you have just about summed up the *value* of
modernity' (*CW*, Preface). So for a philosopher interested in modernity –
and hence, Nietzsche insists, in decadence – Wagner is a '*lucky case*' (*CW*,
Epilogue). But he is also complex, multifaceted, and wide-ranging; and
Nietzsche's treatment of him reflects that. His objections are legion, but
are also closely interconnected. And this makes it more or less impossible
to give a convincing *précis*. So instead, I focus here on three aspects of
Nietzsche's critique that link directly to the discussion so far, and hope that
something of the general flavour will emerge through that. The issues that
I focus on are style, 'idealism', and who Wagner *is*.

We have already seen that 'style' matters to Nietzsche. It is, after all, what
one has to give to one's character if one is to create oneself under a law
of one's own. And Nietzsche's model of style – which is drawn, obviously,
from art – is a conventional one: style is a higher 'lawfulness' (*CW* 8), he
says, marked by the fact that 'life' dwells 'in the totality', with the parts
being related to one another in an 'organic' way (*CW* 7); it is marked by
'*necessity*' but gives 'the impression of freedom' (*CW* 9); it has its own sort
of 'logic' (*CW* 2). It is, in short, precisely what one gets when an 'organizing
"idea"' is at work. And style, according to Nietzsche, is what Wagner lacks:
indeed, Wagner has 'no stylistic facility whatsoever' (*CW* 7).

In part, Nietzsche's objection arises from his dislike of so-called 'endless
melody', which '*wants* to break up all evenness of tempo', with the result
that the listener finds himself 'Swimming, floating – no longer walking,
dancing': there is a 'complete degeneration of the feeling for rhythm, *chaos
in place of rhythm*...' (*Nietzsche Contra Wagner* (*NCW*)), 'Wagner as a
Danger', 1). But chaos, to Nietzsche's ear, is endemic to Wagner's music:
there is 'an anarchy of the atom, disintegration of the will'; '[p]aralysis
everywhere, exhaustion... *or* hostility and chaos: both becoming increasingly obvious the higher you climb in the forms of organization. The
whole does not live at all any more.' Wagner 'forges little unities', 'animates
them', and 'makes them visible. But this drains him of strength: the rest is
no good.' 'Wagner is admirable... only in his inventiveness with the very
small'; he is 'our greatest *miniaturist* in music' (*CW* 7).

In the light of the huge scale of Wagner's works, it is perhaps unsurprising
that Nietzsche should enjoy the charge of 'miniaturism'; he returns to it
repeatedly. Wagner specializes, he says, in

some very small and microscopic features of the soul, the scales of its amphibious
nature, as it were –, yes, he is *master* at the very small. But he doesn't *want* to

be! His *character* likes great walls and bold frescos much better!... It escapes him that his *spirit* has a different taste and disposition... [H]idden from himself, he paints his real masterpieces, which are all very short, often only a bar long. (*NCW*, 'Where I Admire')

But it is not just the (alleged) 'decline in organizing energy', 'the abuse of traditional methods without any ability to *justify* this abuse', the 'counterfeit in duplicating great forms' (*CW*, Second Postscript), or the 'miniaturism' that attracts Nietzsche's fire. It is the *content* of Wagner's 'small units', the fact that each one of them has been drawn from the 'drained cup' of 'human happiness', where 'the most bitter and repulsive drops have merged... with the sweetest ones' (*NCW*, 'Where I Admire'). Wagner's states are uniformly pathological; and strung together in a way that is at once '*brutal*', '*artificial*', and '*innocent*', they result, not in a style, but in something closer to a nervous condition: Wagner, says Nietzsche, '*est une névrose* [neurosis]' (*CW* 5).

What Nietzsche construes as Wagner's incapacity for style, then, is the absence of an 'organizing "idea"' in his works, which is, in turn, symptomatic of a nervous and 'physiological degeneration (a form of hysteria, to be precise)' (*CW* 7). 'Wagner's art is sick', Nietzsche says (*CW* 5). It is a sign of 'declining life' (*CW*, Epilogue), of life that lacks the energy for itself – indeed, that suffers of itself. It is, in a word, decadent.

This connects directly to the second aspect of Nietzsche's critique, the one concerning 'idealism'. Wagner's audience, like him, are decadents, and so hunger for something that will call them 'back to life' (*CW* 5), for something 'sublime', 'profound', 'overwhelming' (*CW* 6). They 'do not even *want* to be clear about themselves' (*EH*, 'Wagner', 3); instead, they want 'presentiments'. And Wagner obliges – 'Chaos' induces 'presentiments' (*CW* 6) – and turns his listeners into 'moon-cal[ves]' – into '"idealist[s]"' (*CW*, Postscript). But 'It was not *music* that Wagner conquered them with, it was the "Idea": – the fact that his art... plays hide-and-seek under a hundred symbols' (*CW* 10). Indeed, claims Nietzsche, Wagner's elusiveness is a major source of his power to corrupt:

He has an affinity for everything equivocal... everything that in general persuades the uncertain without letting them know *what* they are being persuaded of. Wagner is a seducer in the grand style. There is nothing tired... life-threatening, or world-denying in matters of spirit that his art fails secretly to defend... He flatters every nihilistic... instinct and disguises it in music, he flatters every aspect of Christianity... Just open your ears: everything that has ever grown on the soil of *impoverished* life, the whole counterfeit of transcendence and the beyond, has its most sublime advocate in Wagner's art. (*CW*, Postscript)

And – to Nietzsche's ears, at least – Wagner's relation to 'idealism' reaches its most intimate pitch in his final work, *Parsifal*. 'Did *hatred of life* gain control over him?' Nietzsche asks: 'Because Parsifal is a work of malice, of vindictiveness, a secret poisoning of the presuppositions of life, a *bad* work. – The preaching of chastity remains an incitement to perversion: I despise anyone who does not regard Parsifal as an attempt to assassinate ethics' (*NCW*, 'Wagner as Apostle of Chastity', 3).

So Wagner is a decadent; he lacks style, an 'organizing "idea"'; his art stands in perilously close relations to 'idealism'. But who *is* he? *What* is he? Nietzsche canvasses several possibilities: 'Is Wagner even a person?' he asks; 'Isn't he really just a sickness?' (*CW* 5). Is he 'a dramatist'? No: 'He loved the word "drama": that is all' (*CW* 9). Is he even 'a musician'? Perhaps; but 'he [is] something *more*: an incomparable histrion', an 'excellent actor' – that is 'who this Wagner is' (*CW* 8).

To be an 'actor', in Nietzsche's sense, is to want 'effects, nothing but effects' (*CW* 8).[26] And his claim in Wagner's case can be taken at two levels. First, Wagner is an actor with respect to his art: he produces the effect of art, but not its substance. He counterfeits style; he mimics drama; his characters are forgeries. 'Wagner's music is never true', Nietzsche says (*CW* 8). But second, and perhaps more importantly, Wagner is an actor with respect to life. He is made for the modern age: 'in declining cultures . . . genuineness becomes superfluous . . . a liability. Only actors arouse *large* amounts of enthusiasm. – This ushers in the *golden age* for actors' (*CW* 11). In a robust culture, the instincts are in good shape; people can be seen to have 'turned out well' (*CW*, Epilogue), to have become masters and creators of themselves. In a declining culture, by contrast, where the 'instinct is weakened' (*CW* 5), the resources required for self-creation are largely absent. And hence the importance, the timeliness, of the actor. With him, one gets the *effect* of personality, at least – even if the substance is entirely lacking.

'Is it any wonder', Nietzsche asks, 'that falseness has become flesh and even genius in precisely our age? That *Wagner* "dwelled among us"?' (*CW*, Epilogue). And he pursues the issue of Wagner's falseness into his 'idealism'. He imagines Wagner addressing his fellow composers:

Let us be idealists! – This is . . . certainly the wisest thing we can do. In order to raise people up, we need to be elevated ourselves. Let us wander over the clouds, haranguing the infinite, surrounding ourselves with great symbols! . . . 'How could anyone who improves us not be good himself?' This is how humanity has always reasoned. So let us improve humanity! – that will make us good. (*CW* 6)

[26] Cf. *GS* 361.

Wagner's 'idealism' is thus presented as a policy – as a policy that he adopts, like an actor, exclusively for the sake of 'effects'. And in the face of this, Nietzsche suddenly becomes rather warm about Christianity:

The need for *redemption*, the embodiment of all Christian needs ... is the most honest expression of decadence, it affirms decadence in the most convinced, most painful way ... The Christian wants to *escape* from himself. *Le moi est toujours haïssable* [The 'I' is always hateful]. (*CW*, Epilogue)

So there is at least some honesty in the Christian's 'idealism'. In Wagner's, by contrast, Nietzsche sees nothing but mendaciousness – the absence of an intellectual conscience – all the way down.

One might summarize the aspects of Nietzsche's critique that I have discussed in the following way: Wagner lacked style, an 'organizing "idea"'; he was a decadent, he suffered from himself; therefore he was drawn to 'ideals' that slander the world; but, since there was, strictly speaking, no one who he *was* (no 'organizing "idea"'), he became an actor; and he became an actor *even* in his 'idealism'. And this, in Nietzsche's view, is decadence taken to the limit – the polar opposite of the conditions required for self-creation, for becoming who one is.

Nietzsche is quite wrong about Wagner, it seems to me – as perhaps he is too about Christ and Socrates, although that is a different matter. Certainly there is a temptation to read his writings on Wagner as a (mostly) unwitting self-portrait – and to wonder why Wagner mightn't have redeemed himself, *à la* Nietzsche, through his own version of *Ecce Homo*.[27] But these are questions for another occasion. Here, I have tried only to show how the idea of becoming 'who one is' runs through all of Nietzsche's final works, and to show how it rounds off a line of thought that characterizes his maturity as a whole. And if the effect of that, at certain levels, is to make it quite hard to regret that Nietzsche had to stop writing when he did, then perhaps that is no more than another – indeed, the ultimate – sign of his *'sureness of instinct* in practice'.[28]

---

[27] Wagner's *Mein Leben* doesn't quite count as that.

[28] For comments on earlier versions of this introduction, I am grateful to Chris Janaway and Alex Neill. My principal debt, however, is to David Owen. The main ideas expressed here are uniformly the product of our conversations over the years, as is the general conception of Nietzsche's philosophy which underlies those ideas.

CHAPTER II

Nietzsche: Writings from the late notebooks

Rüdiger Bittner

Nietzsche is a writer whose work stands visibly unfinished. Others by and large completed what they had to say, but in Nietzsche's case the gap between the task he envisaged and the writing he carried out grew wider, not smaller, during his active life – and dramatically so in its last few years. Thus, the texts collected in the present volume may be taken to mark Nietzsche's frontier: this is how far he came. In what follows I will look at the history of these texts, their origin and the way they were handed down to us, as well as the way the present selection has been made. Secondly, I will indicate some of the basic lines of argumentation and some of the philosophical import of these texts.

THE TEXTS

All through his life as a writer, Nietzsche recorded his thoughts in notebooks or on sheets of paper he carried with him. In this way he could keep writing virtually anywhere, and indeed he made a point of this habit (see TI Maxims 34). While the notebooks and papers contain some material of a merely occasional nature, such as travelling plans or recipes, by far the largest part deals with substantive issues. Nietzsche normally saved these notes, using them as a basis for the manuscripts of his published works, and so a large number of them were preserved. How many are missing is hard to gauge from what we have, but it would seem that a representative portion of Nietzsche's total production has survived. With a few exceptions, all these papers are now kept in the Goethe-Schiller Archive in Weimar.

The relation between Nietzsche's handwritten notes and his publications changed over his lifetime. While the published works never exhausted the content of the notes, it was only from 1885, after the completion of *Thus Spoke Zarathustra*, that the disparity between what Nietzsche wrote down in his notebooks and what he brought to a definitive form for publication grew radical. In fact, Nietzsche sensed he was becoming alienated from the medium he had hitherto relied on. 'My philosophy, if that is what I am entitled to call what torments me down to the roots of my nature, is no longer communicable, at least not in print', he wrote to Franz Overbeck on 2 July 1885. Writing down ideas in his notebooks, in contrast, seemed 'less impossible'. The notebooks became the field where Nietzsche was still able if not to communicate, then at least to express, his ideas. This is why Nietzsche's unpublished manuscript material from the last years of his productive life has been deemed worth publishing by all his editors, from the very first down to the present one.

For all his doubts about communicating his thoughts in print, Nietzsche pursued publication plans in these late years rather more vigorously than he had before. *Beyond Good and Evil* was completed in the spring of 1886 and published in the summer of that year, and *On the Genealogy of Morality* followed a year later. However, *Beyond Good and Evil* was called in the subtitle 'Prelude to a Philosophy of the Future', and Nietzsche saw *On the Genealogy of Morality* as an accompaniment to the earlier book, complementing and clarifying it, as he indicated in a note following the title page in the original edition of GM. Thus *On the Genealogy of Morality* was a supplement to *Beyond Good and Evil*, which itself was a prelude – and the philosophy of the future that these writings aimed to prepare was to be presented in a major new work. As he told his readers in GM III § 27, Nietzsche at this time intended to call it 'The Will to Power. Attempt at a Re-valuation of all Values'.

'The Will to Power' is the largest and most ambitious literary project of Nietzsche's last years, indeed of his whole life; and while it is by no means the only project he considered pursuing during those years, it is the one he worked on most consistently. Thus, he did bring it to an advanced stage of preparation. In note number 12[1], dating from early 1888 (not reprinted here), he put together a list of 374 texts, in most cases deciding which of the planned work's four books they were to go into and dividing the four books into twelve chapters. Completion of the project must have seemed within his reach at this point. Nietzsche was not really satisfied, though, with the emerging book. On 13 February 1888, telling Peter Gast that the first draft of his 'Attempt at a Re-valuation' was finished, he added: 'All in all, it was a torment. Also, I do not yet in any way have the courage for it. Ten years from now I will do it better.' He kept considering alternative ways of organising the material, until early September 1888 brought a change of plans. As shown by fragments 9[3–6], again not reprinted here, he decided to publish an extract of his philosophy that would consist of a number of finished texts previously intended for 'The Will to Power'. A major work remained on his agenda, but from now on it was always called 'Re-valuation of all Values' rather than 'The Will to Power', and was organised in a notably different way from the arrangements previously considered for 'The Will to Power'. Only a short time later, however, he divided the material into two books, one the extract proper, which eventually became *Twilight of the Idols*, and the other *The Antichrist*, which Nietzsche at the time regarded as the first book of the planned 'Re-valuation'. In other words, Nietzsche gave up his plans for a book called *The Will to Power* in the autumn of 1888.[1]

Even so, the history of the project 'The Will to Power' is important for the present purposes. For one thing, many of Nietzsche's notes from the years 1885–89 were at some time intended to form part of the book of that name. A further reason is that in 1901 Nietzsche's first editors, his sister Elizabeth Förster-Nietzsche and his friend Peter Gast, published a selection of notes from his notebooks under the title *Der Wille zur Macht* ('The Will to Power'), suggesting that this book was the execution of a plan which Nietzsche had only been prevented from completing by his illness. A much larger selection followed in 1906, and especially in this version the collection was extremely successful: it became the standard source on the late Nietzsche's thought, in spite of the fact that doubts about its philological reliability had been raised quite early on. In English, Walter Kaufmann and R. J. Hollingdale's 1967 translation of *Der Wille zur Macht* as *The Will to Power* acquired a similarly dominant position.

The Will to Power is a dubious text for several reasons. Firstly and most importantly, the evidence shows that Nietzsche abandoned the project 'The Will to Power' early in September 1888, so that publishing a book of this title under his name falsifies his intentions. Secondly, if we waive this objection and suppose that 'The Will to Power' remained Nietzsche's dominant concern right to the end of his writing life, it is in any case arbitrary to arrange the material, as the editors of *The Will to Power* did, in the order Nietzsche sketched in the fragment 7[64] of 1886/1887 (not reprinted here). A number of such projected tables of contents can be found in the notebooks of these years, so why choose this one in particular? It may be replied that the order sketched in 7[64] is also the basis for the list of 374 texts in fragment 12[1], mentioned above. Yet if that is the reason for using the order of 7[64], it would seem natural also to follow the detailed plan

---

[1] The preceding is an abbreviated version of Mazzino Montinari's account, to be found in the German paperback edition of Nietzsche's collected works, an edition closely based on the KGW: *Friedrich Nietzsche, Sämtliche Werke, Kritische Studienausgabe*, ed. G. Colli and M. Montinari (Munich: Deutscher Taschenbuch Verlag / Berlin: de Gruyter, 1988), vol. 14, pp. 383–400.

set out in 12[1], and that is not what Förster-Nietzsche and Gast did. They excluded roughly a quarter of the texts Nietzsche at that time intended to include in 'The Will to Power', some of these going instead into volumes 13 or 14 of the *Grossoktav* edition produced by the Nietzsche Archive under the direction of Elizabeth Förster-Nietzsche, but most being suppressed entirely; and a good proportion of the texts that were included suffered various changes at the hands of the editors, such as division into separate fragments or the omission of parts of the text.

An attempt was made in the 1930s to remedy this situation by publishing a critical edition, but the enterprise came to a halt after the first five volumes, which covered only the years from 1854 to 1869. It is only now, thanks to the new critical edition by Giorgio Colli and Mazzino Montinari (the 'KGW'), that we have complete and reliable German texts of all of Nietzsche's philosophical writings. The present selection of texts is based on this new edition. It invites English-speaking readers to benefit as well from the massive improvement in the availability of the texts from Nietzsche's literary estate, or *Nachlass*, an improvement owed above all to the efforts of Mazzino Montinari.

Given that the KGW is the sole source of the texts I have included here, it may be useful to indicate how it arranges the material. The whole edition is divided into eight parts, the seventh containing the *Nachlass* material from July 1882 to autumn 1885 and the eighth that from autumn 1885 to January 1889. For the sake of convenience, let us call any notebook, single sheet of paper or collection of sheets that Nietzsche used for his notes a 'manuscript'; the KGW presents the texts from the late *Nachlass* in chronological order throughout, both as regards the sequence of entire manuscripts and the sequence of texts within each manuscript. While manuscripts are normally easy to tell apart, fragments within a manuscript may not be. Sometimes Nietzsche numbered fragments or indicated in other ways where one fragment ends and another begins. Sometimes this emerges from such evidence as the position of text on the page, the style of the handwriting, or similar clues, but sometimes the matter really is not clear. The division of the text into fragments was made by the KGW editors, taking such evidence into account wherever it existed.

The KGW numbers manuscripts chronologically within each part and, in turn, numbers the texts within each manuscript chronologically. The present volume offers a selection of texts dating from between April 1885 and January 1889, which are taken from the latter part of the seventh and the whole of the eighth part of the KGW. Manuscripts numbered 34 and higher are taken from the seventh part, those numbered 1–18 from the eighth. The manuscript number is followed in each case by the chronological fragment number in square brackets. The reason for drawing the starting line at the seventh part, manuscript 34 is the fact that this manuscript marks the beginning of the post-*Zarathustra* phase, which differs markedly, both in substance and in style, from Nietzsche's previous writing; and as I have mentioned, it is the post-*Zarathustra* Nietzsche whose philosophical projects, no longer finding adequate expression in his published writing, have to be gathered from the notebooks.

Let me repeat that this volume offers a *selection* of texts dating from 1885 to 1889. In contrast to Förster-Nietzsche and Gast, I do not pretend that the collection presented here forms a whole, let alone a whole fulfilling Nietzsche's true intentions at any point in his life. As far as we can tell, Nietzsche had no clear, settled and detailed intentions that might be followed in forming a book out of this material. What we have are fragments, and it is of fragments that the present selection consists. It should also be noted that this is a small selection: speaking very approximately, this volume may contain something in the order of a third of Nietzsche's handwritten material from the period.

Individual fragments, in contrast, have not been used selectively. They always appear here in their entirety, with two kinds of exception. The first is that Nietzsche's own occasional numbering of his texts has been deleted throughout, to avoid confusion with the editors' numbering. The second kind of exception concerns notebook 7, of 1886–87. In this manuscript Nietzsche later, in the autumn of 1888, assembled several of his texts under chapter headings derived from the plan for 'The Will to Power' set out in 18[17], and the editors of the KGW decided to treat as one fragment all the texts that Nietzsche placed in one chapter. Given how disparate some of those texts are, this does not seem convincing. I thus felt free to take apart these overly large 'fragments' and include separately some of the texts they contained.

The texts are given here, as in the KGW, in chronological order. The KGW's numbering of the fragments has been retained, since the literature now always refers to Nietzsche's *Nachlass* texts by these numbers. Of course, the selectivity of the present collection means that here the numbers do not form a continuous sequence, only an ordered one.

Turning now to the material considerations guiding the present selection, the chief criterion for including a text here was its philosophical import – and not its historical or, more particularly, biographical interest. My aim was not to offer information about the development of Nietzsche's thought in this period or about the changes in his plans for a major work. Instead, the present collection is intended to serve those readers wishing to know what Nietzsche has to say on a number of topics and also whether what he says is true. Their interest may focus not really on Nietzsche himself but rather on his thoughts.

Hence, none of the many title pages that Nietzsche envisaged for future books has been included. Neither have projected tables of contents, lists of aphorisms and the like. For the same reason, earlier versions of texts eventually published in Nietzsche's books of these years have not been admitted, except where it seemed that the differences between the earlier and final versions could be illuminating. Nietzsche's excerpts from other authors, filling much of manuscript II, for example, were excluded – again, except where Nietzsche's noting a passage from another author would appear to shed special light on his own thought. To be sure, I may have violated this rule unwittingly: probably not all of Nietzsche's quotes have been identified as such (and those identified have not all been traced to their sources).

For similar reasons, Nietzsche's reflections on himself and his life, not very numerous anyway, have been left aside. Exceptions to this rule are a number of notes which, on the face of it, seem merely to deal with particulars of Nietzsche's life, but in fact also provide a glimpse of some Nietzschean concern or assumption that is philosophically revealing (the very first note in the present selection, 34[3], is a case in point).

Following the criterion of philosophical import also meant entirely neglecting a number of themes to which Nietzsche devoted some attention in his writing, like that of men and women, or of 'peoples and fatherlands', as *Beyond Good and Evil* phrases it. To the best of my understanding, Nietzsche had nothing of interest to say on either of these matters – nothing of philosophical interest, that is. His views on women and on Germans, say, suffer from reckless generalising; to be more precise they are chauvinist. As such they may yield some interest for the historian of ideas, showing how deep these prejudices go in the late nineteenth century, even in an individual of so critical a cast of mind as Nietzsche. For someone interested in the topics themselves, Nietzsche's writings offer no enlightenment.

This raises the question of which topics the late Nietzsche does have enlightening things to say about. I shall try to answer that question in the remainder of the Introduction, in broad strokes of course, indicating a number of threads running through the material collected here and showing their philosophical importance. I shall suggest, moreover, that these threads have a common starting-point and that there is a central task Nietzsche is pursuing in his late writings.

THE TASK

The task Nietzsche sets himself is to work out a comprehensive and credible naturalism. In BGE § 230 Nietzsche declares that we, 'free, *very* free spirits', have chosen the task of 'translating man back into nature'. The metaphor bears closer attention. Translating back is what you might do if the text you have is a translation, but a bad one: you might try to retrieve the original from the distorted version in your hands. Translating back is not a kind of translating. It does not aim to preserve as much as possible of the text we have before us, as translations do, but instead to recover what that text has failed to preserve. It is an 'untranslating', by analogy, say, to 'untying'. Without the metaphor, then, Nietzsche is saying that traditional conceptions give a distorted picture of what man is, indeed a rosy and flattering one, as he goes on to suggest; and the free spirits' chosen undertaking is to bring to light what was misrepresented in those conceptions. As an Enlightenment writer, Nietzsche both intends and hopes to cast off the misconceptions we have inherited. As a critical writer, he does not presume to do this simply on the strength of deciding to; he does not pretend to say immediately what, viewed without distortions, man is. Bringing that to light means having to take the detour through traditional misconceptions. It means untranslating them.

Looked at this way, the polemical attitude implicit in many of the texts collected here becomes intelligible. It is not that Nietzsche frequently attacks particular figures. Rather, he seems to be constantly up in arms against enemies none the less enraging for remaining unnamed. Nowhere in these pages do we find a writer at peace, which Nietzsche often pretended to be and sometimes, perhaps unwittingly, actually was. This is not because Nietzsche had a warrior nature, as he claimed in *Ecce Homo* (Why I am so wise § 7). What we know suggests that he did not, and the passage from *Ecce Homo* is embarrassing to read not because of its arrogance, but because of its blindness. The polemical character of the writings presented in this collection has less to do with Nietzsche in particular than with the situation he faces: error can no longer be traced to a specific source, for instance the fraudulent despots and hypocritical priests of the classic Enlightenment scenario, and thus can no longer be rebutted in a polemical *hors d'oeuvre* which then gives way to an unperturbed statement of the truth. Instead, error is now in the air, and any conception of ourselves we are offered is likely to be one of the high-flown interpretations that, according to BGE § 230, tradition scribbled and painted over the original text of man as nature. What we are can only be recovered by fighting those interpretations.

However, the objective of our fight can be gathered, negatively, from the promises of the seductive voices in BGE § 230 to which Nietzsche asks us to turn a deaf ear: 'You are more! You are higher! You are of a different origin!' Accordingly, the naturalisers must be telling us: you are nothing more, nothing higher, not of a different origin – which, in turn, leaves us wondering: nothing more and higher than what, of an origin no different from what? This is precisely what the naturalisation project will have to determine: the contours of natural man which, once found, will permit us to dismiss as a mere product of human vanity any richer conception of ourselves. Nietzsche's project, then, is reductive. What he envisages is a human self-understanding in radically more modest terms than those traditionally employed. 'Reduction' is to be taken here not in one of the technical meanings current in chemistry and in philosophy of science, but in the ordinary sense where people are told to reduce their weight: naturalisers invite us to cut back to the lowest level the conceptual expenses incurred in understanding ourselves.

Nietzsche is convinced that this basic conceptual level – poor but adequate, indeed singularly illuminating, for understanding ourselves – is that of the concepts we use to describe living things. To naturalise something is to understand it in terms of life. This is one reason why his reductive stance differs from that of contemporary reductionists – differs so much, indeed, that many will baulk at hearing him called a reductionist at all. Actually, there should be no quarrel here. Reduction in the general sense was certainly his enterprise. When, in that passage from BGE § 230, he describes the task at hand as that of mastering 'the many conceited and high-flown interpretations and secondary meanings scribbled and painted to this day over the eternal basic text of man as nature', the word 'high-flown' (*schwärmerisch*) leaves no doubt that philosophers are going to see their conceptual wings clipped. Nietzsche's aim was not reduction in the stronger and more specific sense current today, reduction of the kind that eliminates mental terms in favour of physical ones or, more relevantly, concepts of life processes in favour of those of mechanical or electrical processes. He saw no reason to think that mechanical processes could account for life.

Quite the contrary, he saw reason to think that there is no such thing as a merely mechanical process. Pursuing 'the human analogy consistently to the end', he held that the concept of force needs supplementing with an inner side, and that motion is a mere symptom of inner events.[2] A mechanistic reduction was thus a case of putting the cart before the horse. There is nothing deeper for our understanding to turn to than processes of life. It would be misleading to express this by saying that Nietzsche's naturalism is biologistic. After all, he found plenty to disagree with in the biology of his day, even if the notes from his last years, especially, show him deeply indebted to the ideas of biologists. It would be better to say that Nietzsche's naturalism is the commitment to a philosophy that is, from beginning to end, a philosophy of life. ' "Being" –', he notes in 2[172], 'we have no other idea of this than "*living*".'

In this way, Nietzsche's chosen task of translating man back into nature becomes more specific, as the task of understanding some of the basic phenomena of human existence in terms of life. This task can only be completed in a responsible way on the basis of a viable understanding of life. Hence Nietzsche writes: 'here a new, more definite version of the concept "life" is needed' (2[190]).

That passage continues: 'My formula for it is: life is will to power.'[3] While in the late notes other famous notions from Nietzsche's earlier writings loom much less large than before, the will to power is their central theme. The book that Nietzsche intended to write in this period would certainly have borne the right title.

WILL TO POWER

The first difficulty that might strike readers here is the phrasing: why 'will *to* power' and not 'of' or 'for'? In fact, 'will to power' does mean 'will for power': a will to power is a will such that the thing willed is power.[4] The expression 'will to power' was presumably modelled on Schopenhauer's 'will to life', to which Nietzsche's concept was meant to be the counterpart.[5]

The term 'will to power' may have recommended itself for a less respectable reason as well. As GM III § 28, for example, shows, Nietzsche had a tendency to regard the meaning of something, in the sense

---

[2] See 36[31]; also 34[247], 1[28], 2[69].

[3] Similarly, BGE § 13. The connection between the idea of translating man back into nature (BGE § 230) and the doctrine of will to power is confirmed, if somewhat laconically, by 2[131]: 'Homo natura. The "will to power".'

[4] For evidence see GM II § 12 and, in the present collection, fragments 14[79], 14[121], 14[174]. Also revealing is the earlier note IV 23[63], dating from 1876/77 and thus not included here, where Nietzsche uses 'will to power' without terminological weight. There it clearly means a person's state of willing power.

[5] Z II, Of Self-Overcoming, makes this evident. For Schopenhauer, see Arthur Schopenhauer, *Die Welt als Wille und Vorstellung*, 3rd edn (Leipzig: Brockhaus, 1859), § 54.

used in phrases like 'the meaning of human existence', as something one would refer to in answering the question 'To what end such and such?', in this case 'To what end human existence?' The expression 'will to power', then, unlike the other expressions that would have been possible, had the advantage of seeming to banish the threat of meaninglessness: this will is not in vain, because it is a will to something, namely to power. The reasoning is doubly fallacious: meaning and purpose may or may not coincide and, above all, purpose and content are two different things. Still, it may have been this reasoning which made the phrasing attractive.

A further question is what precisely is asserted in the doctrine of will to power, for Nietzsche puts forward different claims in different passages. One is the claim in GM II § 12:

that all that happens in the organic world is an *overpowering*, a *becoming master*.

The natural way to read this would be as saying that however different the things happening in the organic world otherwise are, they share this character of being overpowerings. The cat's purring, my making breakfast, Michael's falling asleep, they all are overpowerings. This, however, can hardly be what Nietzsche has in mind, for two reasons. For one thing, he would in effect be applying a distinction between how things appear and how they are – precisely the distinction he attacks so forcefully in other passages. He must be applying that distinction, for there seems to be no other way to make sense of the statement that this event is a cat's purring together with the statement that this event is an overpowering, unless we add such riders as 'on the face of it', 'appears to be' on the one hand, and 'really', 'essentially' on the other.

The second reason not to follow GM II § 12's exposition here is that in this reading, the doctrine of will to power would not satisfy Nietzsche's intention in turning from a mechanistic understanding of events to one put in terms of life; and, remember, will to power was to be 'the new, more definite version of the concept "life"'. As he says in 36[31], Nietzsche turned to life, and thus to will to power, as a way of supplementing with an inner side, even 'an inner world', the 'force' spoken of by the physicists. However, what happens in the organic world does not acquire an inner side simply by virtue of being an overpowering. An overpowering is as much an outer event as the cat's purring is.

Zarathustra, in the speech on self-overcoming, propounded a different version of the doctrine of will to power:

Where I found a living thing, there I found will to power.

However, he evidently puts it this way in order to give himself a smoother argument for his claim that even those who serve and obey are inspired by a will to power. For the larger theoretical purposes that Nietzsche pursues in other passages, this version is certainly too weak. If the will to power is only something to be found, possibly alongside other things, in everything living, we cannot reach anything like the famous line in 38[12]:

This world is the will to power – and nothing besides!

A more promising thought comes from 14[121]:

That there is considerable enlightenment to be gained by positing power in place of the individual 'happiness' each living thing is supposed to be striving for: 'It strives for power, for an augmentation of power'.[6]

The interesting suggestion here is that will to power should be understood not, as in GM II § 12, as a uniform *character*, but as a uniform kind of *source* of whatever happens in the organic world. Aristotle taught that in all their actions, humans strive for one highest goal, which is happiness; and while he denied that non-human animals are capable of happiness, both Schopenhauer and the Utilitarians suggested that they pursue happiness as we do, though they find it in different things. Substituting in this statement 'power' or 'increase of power' for 'happiness', and extending the range of creatures who share the striving from all animals to everything that lives, we arrive at Nietzsche's doctrine of the will to power. In this reading, then, the doctrine maintains that any living thing does whatever it does for the sake of gaining power or of augmenting the power it already has.

This reading does supplement the physicists' notion of force with an inner world, as required in 36[31]. It is not that the living only do things of a certain sort. Rather, they do things – a great variety of things – with an intention of a certain sort; and if anything can be called inner, it is an intention like this. Moreover, at least some of Nietzsche's sweeping statements on the will to power become, if not derivable, at least intelligible with this reading. 'Life is will to power', we read earlier (2[190]), but this statement is certainly not true: something's being alive and its striving for more power remain two different things, and would do even if they were always found together. Still, 'life is will to power' is an understandable overstatement of the claim that, in everything they do, living things strive for more power. Finally, this reading is strongly supported by one of Nietzsche's published

---

[6] See also 11[111].

statements of his doctrine, BGE § 36. This passage considers the possibility that 'all organic functions can be derived from this will to power'; if they could, it continues, we would be entitled to hold that 'all effective force is nothing other than: will to power'. Like the present reading, then, BGE § 36 takes will to power to be not a shared character, but a shared kind of source, of what happens in the organic world.

It might now be asked what grounds Nietzsche believed he had for moving, within BGE § 36, from the statement that 'all organic functions' spring from the will to power to the statement that 'all effective force' does so. Similarly, in 14[121], having said that living things strive for power or for more power, he goes on to claim

That all driving force is will to power, that there is no physical, dynamic or psychological force apart from this.

Again, in GM II § 12 the domain of the will to power is abruptly extended from 'all that happens in the organic world' to 'all that happens'. What could seem to justify these swift transitions? Nietzsche had no qualms here because, as mentioned earlier, he rejected the very idea of a merely mechanical event:

one must understand all motion . . . as mere symptoms of inner events . . . (36[31])

Thus all motion, organic or not, has an inner side; and once it is established that in the organic world this inner side is will to power, it may seem a small step to claim that it is will to power in all that happens. The difference between the organic and the inorganic world is superficial, since it does not touch on the inner sources of things happening. The somewhat cavalier fashion in which Nietzsche proceeds here may be explained by the fact that in this point he is following his 'great teacher Schopenhauer' (GM Preface 5), who was quite as swift to claim that 'it is one and the same will that manifests itself both in the forces of inorganic and the forms of organic nature'.[7] As far as its scope is concerned, Nietzsche's 'will to power' simply takes over the place of Schopenhauer's 'will'.

The great defect of the present reading is that, understood this way, the doctrine of will to power has no chance of being true. Take the animals we know best, humans: there seem to be no good grounds whatsoever for saying that power is what they strive for in everything they do, even if it should be true to say that whenever they succeed in what they do they feel better or indeed more powerful. True, neither is it happiness they are

---

[7] Schopenhauer, *Die Welt*, vol. 1, § 27, p. 170; see also § 23, pp. 140–41.

striving for in whatever they do. Nietzsche is certainly right to say that 'Man does *not* strive for happiness' (TI Maxims 12). Our experience shows that humans do not strive for any one thing at all; instead, different people, and the same people at different times, and indeed the same people at the same time, strive for different things. To say that these different things only represent various amounts of power seems arbitrary, for why should ice-cream be, or represent, power? The reply is sometimes made that it is never the ice-cream, but one's showing oneself to be master over the ice-cream, that is sought for.[8] In fact, though, this is not our experience. What we find ourselves pursuing is the thing, not the fact of having subdued it. Nor would it be easy to explain along these lines why the demand for ice-cream tends to go up on hot days: after all, the pleasures of mastery should be independent of the temperature. Indeed, in the case of some things we strive for, it makes little sense to speak of 'mastering' them at all. If, say, relief from the constant stress in your office is what you are after, then even when you have achieved it this will not count as having subdued it; and thus neither did you strive to subdue it before you had achieved it.

While it is a defect that the present reading makes the doctrine of will to power come out false, it is not a decisive one: I see no reading intelligible in itself and reasonably true to the texts that does better. The will to power as a theory is really sunk, just as the book of that title is – and perhaps the book sank because the theory did. The theory is Nietzsche's belated attempt to be a 'philosopher' of the sort he simultaneously denounces. It is a piece of mummification, of Egyptticism, to use his own terms in TI Reason 1. It is no less 'mummifying' to cut down the variety of things striven for by humans – and by living things in general – to that one thing, power, than to arrest the diversity of shapes a thing may exhibit over time, as the philosophers do. To be sure, Nietzsche's will to power is not a single thing, and is present only in the manifold willings to power; to indicate this, Nietzsche often uses phrases like 'points of will' (11[73]), 'dynamic quanta' (14[79]) or 'quanta of will' (14[82]). Still, the claim that all the willings originating change are willings for *power* displays a generalisation, a simplification, a making uniform as ruthless as any that Nietzsche criticised.

This may explain why Nietzsche, at times proclaiming the thesis that life is will to power as an established truth,[9] is curiously coy about it at other times, as in BGE § 36, where the doctrine is insistently presented as a mere hypothesis. It is quite likely that Nietzsche actually was divided about his

---

[8] In 9[151] Nietzsche may be read as taking this line himself.
[9] Notably in Z II, Of Self-Overcoming, but also in, for instance, 14[82] and 14[121].

idea, on the one hand too eagerly hoping to have found the philosophical solution to all the riddles of the world (38[12]) not to persuade himself again and again that he had indeed done so; on the other hand too critical to believe that things are really as simple as that idea makes them.

The reason Nietzsche's idea of the will to power is so philosophically significant, then, is not that it describes the world's 'intelligible character' (BGE § 36) or 'the innermost essence of being' (14[80]) – in fact it does no such thing. It is significant because it served Nietzsche as the conceptual basis, albeit a much too narrow conceptual basis, for his attempt to reinterpret human existence in terms of life. It served him as the grammar of the target language when he tried to 'translate man back into nature' (BGE § 230). That Nietzschean attempt, in turn, is philosophically significant not because it was the first or even the only one of its kind at the time, for in fact it belongs to the broad movement towards a 'philosophy of life' dominant in Continental Europe in the late nineteenth and early twentieth centuries. It is significant because of its radicality. And while 'will to power' was too narrow a translation manual, what he did in using it is not only a remarkable feat, but also philosophically illuminating. For while not 'all driving force is will to power' (14[121]), some certainly is; and more importantly, the translating back that Nietzsche did on the basis of the concept of will to power provides a model for similar attempts to be undertaken today, on a less restricted conceptual basis. This implies that the task is not yet completed, and that it remains a task for philosophy.

COMING TO KNOW

Turning now to Nietzsche's reinterpretation of basic phenomena of human existence in terms of life, I shall limit myself to two topics. One is cognition, the other religion and morality; I will leave aside such themes as art and history for reasons of space. In fact, even if Nietzsche considered 'will to power' the central concept in understanding living things, he did not cast all his reinterpretations of cognition, or of morality and religion, in terms of this doctrine. 'Will to power' was to be his 'philosophy', in the dubious sense of the word touched upon earlier; but he did not allow his philosophy to regiment all of his thought. In this respect he was right about himself when he claimed to mistrust and avoid system-builders (TI Maxims 26).

However, cognition is based on will to power in 2[90]:

On the understanding of *logic::: the will to sameness is the will to power.*
– the belief that something is thus and thus, the essence of *judgement*, is the consequence of a will that as far as possible it *shall* be the same.[10]

Knowledge involves judgement, for Nietzsche as for the philosophical tradition; and judgement, he tells us here, involves believing that something is thus and thus. But according to this passage, such believing is based on willing things to be such and such. Since this willing is a kind of will to power, knowledge is based on will to power.

Why, though, does Nietzsche speak of sameness here, as in fact he does quite often in this context, if what he means is inherence, that is, the relation between a property and a thing having that property? It is inherence that he means, for otherwise the inserted phrase 'the essence of judgement' would make no sense.[11] As we can use 'is' both to indicate identity and to indicate inherence, Nietzsche probably confused the two. The claim he is putting forward here is actually that *believing* things to be thus and thus rests on *willing* things as far as possible to be thus and thus. The material question now is why this should be so. Why should it not be possible simply to consider things to be such and such, with no willing involved?

Nietzsche notes in 7[54]:

Knowledge as such impossible within becoming; so how is knowledge possible? As error about itself, as will to power, as will to deception.[12]

The verdict here 'knowledge as such impossible' is not based on the traditional epistemological scruple that we can never justify our beliefs against all reasonable doubts, but on metaphysical worries. In a world of becoming, Nietzsche says, knowledge does not find a foothold. It is not that everything changes so fast that knowledge cannot keep pace with what happens. It can: we do describe things moving, despite Zeno's paradoxes. The idea is that in a world of becoming, there are no knowables.[13] For in a world of becoming there is no being.[14] The sense in which there is no being is not that there is no reality underlying or encompassing things, but simply that things fail to be *thus and thus*. The very idea of something being thus and thus, of being some way, is inadmissible.

Given that being, in the humble predicative sense of the word, is not to be found in the world, how do we come to speak of it all the time? Nietzsche's

---

[10] See also 1[125].   [11] This reading is also supported by 4[8].
[12] 36[23] presents a similar line of thought.
[13] This, I take it, is the point Nietzsche is expressing, not very happily, when he says that 'the world is false', for example in 9[91].
[14] See 14[93] on this point.

answer is that we put it in. We 'made' the world 'to be' (9[91]); not in the sense of calling it into existence, certainly (although Nietzsche occasionally does use the vocabulary of creating), but in the sense of imprinting upon it the schema of things being some way (9[97]).

We put being into the world, and we did it 'for practical, useful, perspectival reasons' (11[73]). We need a world of this kind. We could not live in a world of sheer becoming, so we posit being, to preserve ourselves.[15] The being of things, posited rather than found, is only '*a perspectival illusion*' (9[41]), however – it is prompted only by our needs. Still, it is the illusion that provides the basis for any truth. Hence Nietzsche's intentionally shocking claim:

> *Truth is the kind of error* without which a particular kind of living creature could not live. The value for life is what ultimately decides.[16]

In accordance with the programmatic statement in BGE § 230, then, Nietzsche does understand cognition in terms of life. His argument runs as follows. Knowledge involves believing that something is thus and thus. Such believing is always false, since this is a world of becoming, and in such a world there is no being thus and thus. Hence we do not find such being, but posit it; and we do this because we could not live without it. We thus know only because we live and try to keep on living – without that, cognition would not encounter anything knowable.

Several things call for comment here, of which I shall take up three. First, this understanding of cognition in terms of life does not amount to a pragmatic theory of truth, as various writers have suggested. A pragmatic theory of truth holds that a statement is true just in case it fulfils certain needs or desires; for example, just in case it enhances one's feeling of power. While there are passages that support the ascription of such a view to Nietzsche,[17] it does seem to be incompatible with other passages, for example his insistence, in 11[108], that 'the truth is ugly'. Materially speaking, Nietzsche would seem to be on the right track with the latter statement, and not with the former: perhaps *the* truth is not ugly, but certainly some truths are. The argument I outlined in the previous paragraph shows where the pragmatic interpretation goes wrong. The pragmatic line of interpretation requires any putative piece of knowledge to furnish proof of some service rendered. But in the present line of argument, it is not

---

[15] This line of reasoning also appears in 34[49], 34[247], 36[23] and 14[93].

[16] 34[253]. A similar line of thought appears in BGE § 4 and, much earlier, in the eighth paragraph of the essay 'On Truth and Lying in a Non-Moral Sense' (1873).

[17] For example 34[264] and 9[91].

individual statements which earn their status by being useful. Instead, it is the form of knowability, that is, things being some way, which, once projected onto the world, satisfies a basic need we have.

For all his polemic against Kant, in this respect Nietzsche continues the tradition of transcendental philosophy. Kant's concern was to understand the objectivity of judgements in general, not to establish standards of justification for particular judgements. Similarly, when Nietzsche writes

We are 'knowers' to the extent that we are able to satisfy our needs... (34[46])

he is not suggesting that we satisfy our needs statement by statement. His point is that in general we hold the position of knowers who confront knowables because we need to do so. Just as in Kant the objectivity of judgements is partly our own doing, so in Nietzsche we ourselves posit the needed being of things. Kant and Nietzsche differ in the kind of danger that is being warded off: in Kant's view a world without the form of objectivity would be unintelligible for us, while in Nietzsche's a world without being would be unliveable for us. Nietzsche has thus granted life the position that understanding used to hold, but on the new basis transcendental conditions of knowledge are provided, just as before.

Secondly, this understanding of cognition in terms of life does not feature the will to power, even though, as we saw above, life was supposed to be essentially will to power. Instead, Nietzsche's argument turns on our seeking to preserve ourselves, which is a different thing.[18] He does not, then, abide by the strategy of parsimony of principles that led him (or so he claims in BGE §§ 13 and 36) to make will to power the sole moving force among living things. And there are good reasons for him to abandon it. It is not credible that by sheer exuberance of force we should have turned a world of becoming into a world of things being some way, that the 'narrower, abridged and simplified world' (9[41]) we have set up should have been born from an urge to show our strength – the urge characteristic of will to power, according to BGE § 13. The origin of a world made to be is not ecstatic overflowing (14[89]) but need.

Yet this need is life's need, just as it is life which expresses itself in ecstatic overflowing. This is to say that Nietzsche's concept of life is ambivalent, and so is the attempted interpretation of basic phenomena of human existence in terms of life. The fullness of life manifests itself in boundless unbelief and 'freedom of the mind' (9[39]), in denying anything to be this way rather than another (9[41]). On the other hand, in 9[91] 'life is founded

---

[18] See BGE § 13, also 14[82].

on the presupposition of a belief in things lasting and regularly recurring', and 'logicising, rationalising, systematising' are taken 'as life's resources'.[19] Nietzsche failed to make up his mind as to which kind of life he meant,[20] thus leaving his project of reinterpretation indeterminate.

Thirdly, the central premise of Nietzsche's argument is not justified, and neither is it self-evident. This premise has it that ours is a world of becoming which 'could not, in the strict sense, be "grasped", be "known"' (36[23]) and into which things' being some way could only be 'inserted' (11 [73]). People generally assume the opposite. They suppose that snow comes as white, and that we have not had to trim things into such shapes for the sake of preserving ourselves. Now, Nietzsche knows that people think this way, and indeed his argument explains why they do so. Yet why could they not just be right, which would also explain it, and more simply?

Nietzsche never said why not. He did, though, indicate what kind of suspicion such a line of thought would prompt – that of wishful think-ing. It is just too good to be true that what we encounter should be things with properties.[21] Nietzsche, in contrast, often saw himself as a sceptic, wary above all of falling for 'fat and good-natured desirabilities' (BGE § 39), and things' being some way seemed to be one of those. In this passage of *Beyond Good and Evil*, he goes on to remind us that the same holds for the negative case. Just as the desirable need not obtain, neither is the harmful and dangerous precluded from obtaining. He does not, however, go on to remind himself that the opposite statement is also true. No, the desirable is not bound to hold nor the undesirable to be absent; but neither is the undesirable bound to hold and the desirable to be absent. Desirabilities are, literally, neither here nor there. In never even entertaining the thought that this might be a world of things being some way, and thus a world ready for cognition, Nietzsche was bracing himself for an epistemological worst case scenario. Now, however, with-out the need for such a heroic stance, we no longer need to imagine that beyond our garden of things being some way there are tigers roam-ing, chaos reigning or, more philosophically, a world of sheer becoming.[22] In fact, it would seem to be in the spirit of naturalism, in the sense

---

[19] A similar line of thought already appears in GS § 111 and in BGE § 24.
[20] This duality of conceptions of life is related to the opposition of Dionysus and Apollo in Nietzsche's early *The Birth of Tragedy*, which is taken up in the late notes, e.g., 2[106]. In a curious way it returns in Nietzsche's self-characterisation in 7[23].
[21] That this is Nietzsche's view is suggested by passages like GS § 109; BGE §§ 2, 5, 25, 34, 39; 7[54].
[22] For the tiger see 'On Truth and Lying in a Non-Moral Sense', third paragraph; for chaos GS § 109.

explained above, to reject such notions. If man as nature is the basic text we are trying to restore, it is more likely that the world is already humanly intelligible, and is not only made to be so by us. Where else but at the world's knee should we have acquired our understanding of what we encounter?

LIVING WELL

Nietzsche's project of 'translating man back into nature' required a reinterpretation of the phenomena of religion and morality. Indeed, perhaps there was nothing it required more urgently. The supernatural stands at the centre of the dominant religious tradition of the West, Christianity, and ever since Christianity acquired its dominant position, morality too has been understood as independent from, if not opposed to, the course of nature. In religion and morality Nietzsche very properly saw the chief fortress to attack under the banner of 'man as nature'. And that is what he did: to no topic, probably, did he devote more attention in his late notes than this one. Likewise, most of his published writings of the period deal, largely or exclusively, with religion and morality, as their titles show: 'Beyond Good and Evil', 'On the Genealogy of Morality', 'Twilight of the Idols', 'The Antichrist'.

In fact, given this series of works published or, in the case of *The Antichrist*, intended for publication by Nietzsche himself, one might wonder why the unpublished notes on these topics still deserve consideration: did he not exploit them to the full in the published books? The fact is that he did not. The published writings, probably for purposes of exposition, draw their lines starkly, while the notes admit of contingencies and alternatives, thereby producing a subtler and indeed more credible picture. An instance of this is relevant at this point. I have been speaking of 'religion and morality' as if these formed one topic, and the published Nietzsche often writes this way, for instance passing smoothly, in the arguments of *Genealogy* II and III, over the difference between them. It is the unpublished Nietzsche who reminds us that 'in itself, a religion has nothing to do with morality' (2[197]). Thus, the link between religion and morality, taken for granted in the published writings, is really accidental, something resulting from the peculiarity of Christianity (and Islam) in being

essentially moral religions, ones that prescribe how we *ought* to live and gain a hearing for their demands with rewards and punishments ... (2[197])

It would therefore be a mistake to read *Genealogy* and *The Antichrist* as presenting a philosophy of religion. In joining morality and religion as intimately as they do, they show themselves to be concerned above all with Christianity. True, the notes do not cast their net substantially wider: reflections on religion in general are rare, and Christianity is the focus throughout. Yet by distinguishing between the special case of Christianity as a moral religion and religion as such, the notes, despite their critique of Christianity, open the space for a positive conception of religion – positive, that is, with respect to life. Nietzsche never filled that space. He did, though, frequently use terms like 'God' and, especially, 'divine' without the dismissive tone one would expect in a critic of religion, often even with glowing enthusiasm.[23] Indeed, he can occasionally be found defending the truly divine against its Christian detractors.[24]

A distinction similar to that between Christianity and religion also needs to be drawn in the case of Nietzsche's critique of morality, a point that does appear in the published writings, but becomes especially clear in the notes. Contrary to what many passages, published and unpublished, suggest,[25] the target of Nietzsche's critique is actually not morality, it is *a* morality. Consider 10[86]: here we have, on the one hand, 'the modest virtues' of 'little people' exalted by Jesus and Paul, and on the other 'the more valuable qualities of virtue and of man' which became discredited in the process. What Nietzsche is calling into question here is one morality, that of the little people, in contrast to another, the one with the more valuable qualities. He is evidently not calling into question morality *tout court* or 'all morality' (GM Preface 6).

On the contrary, he insists that we do need some morality.[26] His argument runs like this. A morality is an ordering of human traits and actions by the relation 'better than'. Such orderings tell people what is likely to preserve them, to make them grow or make them decline. Knowing that, however, is itself a part of your strength, less by saving you from mistakes than by giving an interpretation of yourself and the world that answers to your needs and aspirations. A morality allows you to make practical sense of the world: you know where *your* hopes and *your* dangers lie, and that consciousness makes your life a better one. Thus you need a

---

[23] See, for instance, 2[107], 14[11], 14[89]; see also GM II § 23.   [24] See 10[90], 11[95], 11[122].
[25] This applies notably to the title of GM, which should read *On the Genealogy of a Morality*. The title of BGE may also mislead, as Nietzsche admits by expressly insisting that 'Beyond Good and Evil' does not mean 'Beyond Good and Bad' (GM I § 17). See also passages in 5[98], 10[45], 10[192].
[26] 35[17], 10[68]; also 10[194]; perhaps 7[42] can be read this way as well.

morality, since you grow by knowing what you are and where you are heading.[27]

Actually, the need for morality is normally a social rather than an individual need:

Up to now a morality has been, above all, the expression of a conservative will to breed the same species. (35[20])

As the context indicates, 'species' does not here mean a kind of animal, but a community of humans. So in the human case, breeding works with social rather than biological units; and a morality is, or at any rate has been, a human community's self-interpretation and self-justification for the sake of its own preservation and growth.[28]

In this way Nietzsche completes the programme 'man as nature' for the case of morality. A morality is not a voice from on high, nor do its demands hold an authority independent of what is happening in the lives of the individuals addressed. Instead, it grows from the way they live[29] and in turn supports and enhances their lives. A morality is therefore a good thing for people to have – and why else should they have troubled to set one up in the first place?

Taking 'morality' in this sense, then, Nietzsche is no immoralist, contrary to his own declaration in *Ecce Homo* (EH Untimely 2). Not only does he recognise the existence and effectiveness of moralities (D § 103), he also justifies them by showing how they serve life. He is an immoralist only in the sense of rejecting the morality that he sees as dominant in his time and cultural area. He often calls this morality simply 'morality', thus falling prey to a short-sightedness similar to the one he deplores in 'most moral philosophers', who 'only present the order of rank that rules *now*' (35[5]). Still, the target of his critique cannot be misunderstood. Anyone who asks 'whether "good" is really "good"' (1[53]) is evidently not discarding the vocabulary of 'good' and 'bad', but inquiring whether it is properly used in current judgements.

If Nietzsche's enterprise is the critique of a dominant morality, one wonders what that morality exactly is. Which valuations belong to it,

---

[27] Ascribing this argument to Nietzsche is based on 35[5], 35[17], 40[69], 9[66], 9[77], 11[73]; GS §§ 268, 271, and also the splendid GS § 289.

[28] This accords with Zarathustra's teaching in the speech 'Of the Thousand and One Goals', Z I. The idea already appears, in a rudimentary version, in D § 165.

[29] See 14[76]. Hence, in his reflections in 10[135] and [181] on the social conditions of Christianity, surprising as they may first appear, Nietzsche is staying true to his basic line of argument: a morality is a natural thing, so it can be understood by tracing it back to 'the *soil* from which it grew' (14[76]), which is largely a social soil.

and which belong to a neighbouring one in time or in space? The late Nietzsche nowhere gives a satisfying answer to this question. At times he describes the object of his critique as 'the morality of compassion' (GM Preface § 5–6), but this is simply to suppose that Schopenhauer is right in basing the current morality on compassion, whereas this is in fact a matter of dispute, as Nietzsche himself points out (GM Preface § 5). At other points he speaks of 'a *critique of Christian morality*' (2[127]), but that will not do, either. Christianity has been too many different things in different times and places for us to know what is part of Christian morality and what is not. In the end, Nietzsche does not give us a criterion, and we have to content ourselves with the vague concept of 'the morality dominant in his time and culture' – which presumably is also the morality dominant in our time and culture.

One wonders, secondly, what Nietzsche's objection is. He tried different lines, of which the following might be called the 'official' one in view of its prominence in both published and unpublished writings. Our morality is hostile to life,[30] as is evident especially in how it treats noble and powerful human beings: it discourages and eventually destroys them or, worse still, leads them to destroy themselves.[31] As the naturalist reminds us, we are primarily living creatures; because it is hostile to life, our morality is thus the negation of our very being. Hence we should try to liberate ourselves from it.

Yet it is difficult to understand how there can be such a thing as a morality hostile to life. If we had received our morality from above, it might easily clash with how we live. In Nietzsche's view, however, our morality arises from the way we live – so how can it turn against it? Nietzsche is certainly aware of the problem.[32] The solution he proposes in GM III § 13 is this: our morality has its origin in the protective and healing instinct of a degenerating life. The idea seems to be that the reason we have a morality which denies us great and noble humanity is either to prevent us from getting too excited or to shake us out of being too lethargic, both dangers stemming from our degeneration. This will hardly solve the problem of the clash. For one thing, the question arises of what it is we actually need in our state of degeneration: protection or self-inflicted wounds. But the main difficulty is that in the case Nietzsche sketches, our morality would

---

[30] See GM III § 11, also I § 11; and fragments 5[98], 9[86].
[31] A memorable accusation of this kind is put forward in 11[55]. True, it is directed at Christianity, not at morality, but that matters little given that similar, if less impressive, language is used for current morality as well, as in 10[192], 14[5].
[32] GM III § 13, and perhaps 10[192] as well. 7[15] and 11[227] make a similar point.

not be hostile to life after all. It would help life, if by painful means, and so there would be no reason to get rid of it – on the contrary. True, people might complain about our morality, but this would only show they did not understand: in fact our morality is good for us.

Another line of thought that comes to the fore in some of the notes appears more promising. Its key feature is the introduction of a historical dimension. Our morality did grow from the way we live, but now it no longer fits; we have outgrown it. Hence, our morality is not our enemy. The shoes a child wore last year are not hostile to her feet now, though they would harm her if she kept wearing them. Our morality is not something we should fight but something we should discard, for life has moved beyond it. Nietzsche writes:

Deepest gratitude for what morality has achieved so far: but *now* it's *only a pressure* that would prove disastrous![33]

What we need to do now is

extricate ourselves from the lazy routine of old valuations which degrade us in the best and strongest things we have achieved . . . (9[66])

In Nietzsche's view, the best and strongest thing we have achieved is the fact that we no longer need a communal morality. Not only has the morality we now call 'ours' had its day, but we no longer need any other morality to become 'ours'. We can now go it alone, as individuals – we will not be without morality, but the morality we have will be a matter of '*individual legislation*' (35[20]). In this way, Nietzsche rejoins the autonomy tradition of modern moral philosophy, as witness also the 'autonomous individual' of GM II § 2. To be sure, his is not a Kantian autonomy: Nietzsche's individuals do not undertake to legislate for all rational beings. Yet they do legislate, for themselves, and thus do not act erratically but according to their own self-given form.[34]

Perhaps life has moved even beyond what Nietzsche envisaged, and the moralist was not radical enough. After the demise of what we now call *our* morality, will we each still need a morality of our own? Will we still need to justify and glorify ourselves, as is claimed in 35[17], if only in terms of our individual valuations? In the end, it might appear childish to insist on being in the right and on being a glorious individual. To do so might appear especially strange in human beings 'translated back into nature'.

[33] 5[58]. See also GM II § 2 and 5[61], 10[23], 15[74]. The past tense in 35[20], quoted above, is relevant too.
[34] A precursor of this idea is GS § 290.

One might expect such human beings just to do their human things, rather than subject themselves to any form, self-given or not. Nietzsche at times seems to support this idea himself, for example when he envisions humans who do not even want praise (9[27]); or when he writes in 6[18]:

We no longer eat a particular dish for moral reasons; one day we will no longer 'do good' for moral reasons either.

Select bibliography

WORKS BY NIETZSCHE FROM CAMBRIDGE UNIVERSITY PRESS

Ansell-Pearson, Keith, ed. *On the Genealogy of Morality*, trans. Carol Diethe. Cambridge University Press, 2006.

Bittner, Rüdiger, ed. *Writings from the Late Notebooks*, trans. Kate Sturge. Cambridge University Press, 2003.

Breazeale, Daniel, ed. *Untimely Meditations*, trans. R. J. Hollingdale. Cambridge University Press, 1997.

Clark, Maudemarie, and Brian Leiter, eds. *Daybreak: Thoughts on the Prejudices of Morality*, trans. R. J. Hollingdale. Cambridge University Press, 1997.

Geuss, Raymond, and Alexander Nehamas, eds. *Friedrich Nietzsche: Writings from the Early Notebooks*, trans. Ladislaus Löb. Cambridge University Press, 2009.

Geuss, Raymond, and Ronald Speirs, eds. *The Birth of Tragedy and Other Writings*, trans. Ronald Speirs. Cambridge University Press, 1999.

Hollingdale, R. J., ed. and trans. *Human, All Too Human*. Cambridge University Press, 1996.

Horstmann, Rolf-Peter, and Judith Norman, eds. *Beyond Good and Evil: Prelude to a Philosophy of the Future*, trans. Judith Norman. Cambridge University Press, 2002.

Pippin, Robert, ed. *Thus Spoke Zarathustra: A Book for all and None*, trans. Adrian del Caro. Cambridge University Press, 2006.

Ridley, Aaron, and Judith Norman, eds. *The Anti-Christ, Ecce Homo, Twilight of the Idols, and Other Writings*, trans. Judith Norman. Cambridge University Press, 2005.

Williams, Bernard, ed. *The Gay Science: With a Prelude in German Rhymes and an Appendix of Songs*, trans. Josefine Nauckhoff and Adrian del Caro. New York: Cambridge University Press, 2001.

BROAD TREATMENTS OF NIETZSCHE'S PHILOSOPHY

Ackermann, Robert John. *Nietzsche: A Frenzied Look*. Amherst: University of Massachusetts Press, 1990.

Alderman, Harold. *Nietzsche's Gift*. Athens: Ohio University Press, 1977.

Allison, David B. *The New Nietzsche: Contemporary Styles of Interpretation.* Cambridge, Mass.: MIT Press, 1977.
Reading the New Nietzsche: The Birth of Tragedy, the Gay Science, Thus Spoke Zarathustra, and on the Genealogy of Morals. Lanham, Md.: Rowman & Littlefield, 2001.
Ansell-Pearson, Keith. *A Companion to Nietzsche.* Malden, Mass.: Blackwell Publishing, 2006.
Ansell-Pearson, Keith, and Howard Caygill, eds. *The Fate of the New Nietzsche.* Aldershot: Avebury, 1993.
Bataille, Georges. *On Nietzsche.* New York: Paragon House, 1992.
Clark, Maudemarie. "Nietzsche," in Edward Craig, ed. *Routledge Encyclopedia of Philosophy.* New York: Routledge, 1998.
Darby, W. T., Béla Egyed, and Ben Jones. *Nietzsche and the Rhetoric of Nihilism: Essays on Interpretation, Language and Politics.* Ottawa: Carleton University Press, 1989.
Deleuze, Gilles. *Nietzsche and Philosophy,* trans. Hugh Tomlinson. New York: Columbia University Press, 1983.
Fink, Eugen. *Nietzsche's Philosophy.* London: Continuum, 2003.
Gillespie, Michael Allen, and Tracy B. Strong, eds. *Nietzsche's New Seas: Explorations in Philosophy, Aesthetics, and Politics.* University of Chicago Press, 1988.
Heidegger, Martin. *Nietzsche,* ed. David Farrell Krell (4 vols.). San Francisco: Harper & Row, 1982.
Hollingdale, R. J. *Nietzsche.* London: Routledge & Kegan Paul, 1965.
Jaspers, Karl. *Nietzsche: An Introduction to the Understanding of His Philosophical Activity.* Baltimore: Johns Hopkins University Press, 1997.
Kaufmann, Walter Arnold. *Nietzsche: Philosopher, Psychologist, Antichrist.* Princeton University Press, 1975.
Magnus, Bernd, and Kathleen Marie Higgins, eds. *The Cambridge Companion to Nietzsche.* Cambridge University Press, 1996.
Montinari, Mazzino. *Reading Nietzsche.* Urbana: University of Illinois Press, 2003.
Müller-Lauter, Wolfgang. *Nietzsche: His Philosophy of Contradictions and the Contradictions of His Philosophy.* Urbana: University of Illinois Press, 1999.
Nehamas, Alexander. *Nietzsche, Life as Literature.* Cambridge, Mass.: Harvard University Press, 1985.
Pasley, Malcolm. *Nietzsche, Imagery and Thought: A Collection of Essays.* London: Methuen, 1978.
Richardson, John. *Nietzsche's New Darwinism.* Oxford University Press, 2004.
Richardson, John, and Brian Leiter. *Nietzsche.* Oxford University Press, 2001.
Schacht, Richard. *Nietzsche.* London: Routledge & Kegan Paul, 1983.
Making Sense of Nietzsche: Reflections Timely and Untimely. Urbana: University of Illinois Press, 1995.
Schutte, Ofelia. *Beyond Nihilism: Nietzsche without Masks.* University of Chicago Press, 1984.

Sedgwick, Peter R. *Nietzsche: A Critical Reader.* Oxford: Blackwell, 1995.
Solomon, Robert C., ed. *Nietzsche: A Collection of Critical Essays.* University of Notre Dame Press, 1980.
Solomon, Robert C., and Kathleen Marie Higgins. *What Nietzsche Really Said.* New York: Schocken Books, 2000.
Reading Nietzsche. New York: Oxford University Press, 1988.
Stambaugh, Joan. *The Other Nietzsche.* Albany: State University of New York Press, 1994.
Staten, Henry. *Nietzsche's Voice.* Ithaca, N.Y.: Cornell University Press, 1990.
Stern, J. P. *Nietzsche.* Glasgow: Fontana/Collins, 1978.
Tanner, Michael. *Nietzsche: A Very Short Introduction.* Oxford University Press, 1994.
White, Alan. *Within Nietzsche's Labyrinth.* New York: Routledge, 1990.
Yovel, Yirmiyahu, ed. *Nietzsche as Affirmative Thinker: Papers Presented at the Fifth Jerusalem Philosophical Encounter, April 1983.* Dordrecht: Kluwer Academic Publishers, 1986.
Zupančič, Alenka. *The Shortest Shadow. Nietzsche's Philosophy of the Two.* Cambridge, Mass.: MIT Press, 2003.

TREATMENTS OF SPECIFIC WRITINGS

BIRTH OF TRAGEDY AND OTHER EARLY WRITINGS

Andresen, Joshua. "Truth and Illusion Beyond Falsification: Re-Reading *On Truth and Lie in the Extra-Moral Sense.*" *Nietzsche-Studien* 39 (2010): 225–281.
Brobjer, Thomas H. "Sources of and Influences on Nietzsche's *The Birth of Tragedy.*" *Nietzsche-Studien* 34 (2005): 278–299.
Came, Daniel. "Nietzsche's Attempt at a Self-Criticism: Art and Morality in *The Birth of Tragedy.*" *Nietzsche-Studien* 33 (2004): 37–67.
Clark, Maudemarie. "Deconstructing the *Birth of Tragedy.*" *International Studies in Philosophy* 19.2 (1987): 67–75.
Harloe, Katherine. "Metaphysical and Historical Claims in the *Birth of Tragedy,*" in Manuel Dries, ed. *Nietzsche on Time and History.* Berlin: Walter de Gruyter, 2008, 275–290.
Pippin, Robert B. "Truth and Lies in the Early Nietzsche," in *Idealism as Modernism: Hegelian Variations.* Cambridge University Press, 1997, 311–329.
Porter, James I. *The Invention of Dionysus: An Essay on the "Birth of Tragedy".* Stanford University Press, 2000.
Rethy, Robert. "The Tragic Affirmation of the *Birth of Tragedy.*" *Nietzsche-Studien* 17 (1988): 1–44.
Sallis, John. *Crossings: Nietzsche and the Space of Tragedy.* University of Chicago Press, 1991.
Schacht, Richard. "Nietzsche on Art in the *Birth of Tragedy,*" in George Dickie and Richard Sclafani, eds. *Aesthetics: A Critical Anthology.* New York: St. Martin's Press, 1977, 268–312.

Silk, M. S. and J. P. Stern. *Nietzsche on Tragedy*. Cambridge University Press, 1983.

Sloterdijk, Peter. *Thinker on Stage: Nietzsche's Materialism*. Minneapolis: University of Minnesota Press, 1989.

Winfree, Jason Kemp. "Before the Subject: Rereading the *Birth of Tragedy*." *Journal of Nietzsche Studies* 25 (2003): 58–77.

NIETZSCHE'S "MIDDLE PERIOD": *UNTIMELY MEDITATIONS, HUMAN,
ALL TOO HUMAN, DAYBREAK,* AND *THE GAY SCIENCE*

Abbey, Ruth. *Nietzsche's Middle Period*. Oxford University Press, 2000.

Ansell-Pearson, Keith. "Nietzsche, the Sublime, and the Sublimities of Philosophy: An Interpretation of *Dawn*." *Nietzsche-Studien* 39 (2010): 201–232.

Arrowsmith, William. "Introduction," in *Unmodern Observations*. New Haven: Yale University Press, 1990.

Cavell, Stanley. "Aversive Thinking: Emersonian Representations in Heidegger and Nietzsche," in *Conditions Handsome and Unhandsome: The Constitution of Emersonian Perfectionism*. University of Chicago Press, 1990, 33–63.

Conant, James. "Nietzsche's Perfectionism: A Reading of *Schopenhauer as Educator*," in Richard Schacht, ed. *Nietzsche's Postmoralism*. New York: Cambridge University Press, 2001, 181–257.

Gray, Richard T. "Afterword," in *Unfashionable Observations*. Stanford University Press, 1995, 463–495.

Helsloot, Niels. "Gaya Scienza: Nietzsche as a Friend." *New Nietzsche Studies* 5/6 (2003): 89.

Higgins, Kathleen. *Comic Relief: Nietzsche's Gay Science*. New York: Oxford University Press, 2000.

Jensen, Anthony K. "*Geschichte* or *Historie*? Nietzsche's Second Untimely Meditation in the Context of Nineteenth-Century Philological Studies," in Manuel Dries, ed. *Nietzsche on Time and History*. Berlin: Walter de Gruyter, 2008, 213–230.

Johnson, Dirk Robert. "Nietzsche's Early Darwinism: The 'David Strauss' Essay of 1873." *Nietzsche-Studien* 30 (2001): 62–79.

Kofman, Sara. "Accessories (*Ecce Homo*, 'Why I Write Such Good Books,' 'The Untimelies', 3)," trans. Duncan Large, in Peter R. Sedgwick, ed. *Nietzsche: A Critical Reader*. Oxford: Blackwell, 1995, 144–157.

Lemm, Vanessa. "Animality, Creativity, and Historicity: A Reading of Friedrich Nietzsche's *Vom Nutzen Und Nachtheil Der Historie Für Das Leben*." *Nietzsche-Studien* 36 (2007): 182–213.

Pippin, Robert B. "Gay Science and Corporeal Knowledge." *Nietzsche-Studien* 29 (2000): 136–152.

Ure, Michael. *Nietzsche's Therapy: Self-Cultivation in the Middle Works*. Lanham, Md.: Lexington Books, 2008.

"Nietzsche's Free Spirit Trilogy and Stoic Therapy." *Journal of Nietzsche Studies* 38 (2009): 60–84.

Zuckert, Catherine. "Nature, History and the Self: Friedrich Nietzsche's 'Untimely Considerations.'" *Nietzsche-Studien* 5 (1976): 55–82.

THUS SPOKE ZARATHUSTRA

Aiken, David W. "Nietzsche's Zarathustra: the Misreading of a Hero." *Nietzsche-Studien* 35 (2006): 70–103.

Conway, Daniel W. "Solving the Problem of Socrates: Nietzsche's *Zarathustra* as Political Irony." *Political Theory* 16:2 (1998): 257–280.

Frazer, Michael L. "The Compassion of Zarathustra: Nietzsche on Sympathy and Strength." *Review of Politics* 68 (2006): 49–78.

Goicoechea, David, ed. *The Great Year of Zarathustra (1881–1981)*. Lanham, Md.: University Press of America, 1983.

Gooding-Williams, Robert. *Zarathustra's Dionysian Modernism*. Stanford University Press, 2001.

Heidegger, Martin. "Who is Nietzsche's Zarathustra?" in *Nietzsche*, Vol. 2, trans. David Farrell Krell. San Francisco: Harper & Row, 1984, 101–126.

Higgins, Kathleen. "*Zarathustra* IV and Apuleius: Who is Zarathustra's Ass?" *International Studies in Philosophy* 20 (1988): 29–53.

Nietzsche's Zarathustra. Lanham, Md.: Lexington Books, 2010.

Jung, C. G. *Nietzsche's Zarathustra: Notes of the Seminar Given in 1934–1939*, trans. James L. Jarrett. Princeton University Press, 1988.

Lampert, Laurence. *Nietzsche's Teaching: An Interpretation of "Thus Spoke Zarathustra."* New Haven: Yale University Press, 1986.

Loeb, Paul S. "The Conclusion of Nietzsche's *Zarathustra*." *International Studies in Philosophy* 32.3 (2000): 137–152.

"The Dwarf, the Dragon, and the Ring of Eternal Recurrence: A Wagnerian Key to the Riddle of Nietzsche's *Zarathustra*." *Nietzsche-Studien* 31 (2002): 91–113.

The Death of Nietzsche's Zarathustra. Cambridge University Press, 2010.

Luchte, James. *Nietzsche's "Thus Spoke Zarathustra": Before Sunrise*. London: Continuum, 2008.

Pangle, Thomas. "The 'Warrior Spirit' as an Inlet to the Political Philosophy of Nietzsche's *Zarathustra*." *Nietzsche-Studien* 15 (1986): 140–179.

Pippin, Robert B. "Irony and Affirmation in Nietzsche's *Thus Spoke Zarathustra*," in Michael Allen Gillespie and Tracy B. Strong, eds. *Nietzsche's New Seas*. University of Chicago Press, 1988, 45–74.

Rosen, Stanley. *The Mask of Enlightenment: Nietzsche's Zarathustra*. Cambridge University Press, 1995.

Santaniello, Weaver. *Zarathustra's Last Supper: Nietzsche's Eight Higher Men*. Aldershot: Ashgate, 2005.

Seung, T. K. *Nietzsche's Epic of the Soul: "Thus Spoke Zarathustra"*. Lanham, Md.: Lexington Books, 2005.

Shapiro, Gary. "Rhetoric of Nietzsche's *Zarathustra*," in Berel Lang, ed. *Philosophical Style*. Chicago: Nelson-Hall, 1980, 192–217.

Weiss, Allen. "The Symbolism and Celebration of the Earth in Nietzsche's *Zarathustra*." *Sub-Stance* 22 (1979): 39–47.

Westall, Joseph. "Zarathustra's Germany: Luther, Goethe, Nietzsche." *Journal of Nietzsche Studies* 27 (2004): 42–63.

Westerdale, Joel. "Zarathustra's Preposterous History." *Nietzsche-Studien* 35 (2006): 47–69.

Whitlock, Greg. *Returning to Sils-Maria: A Commentary to Nietzsche's "Also Sprach Zarathustra."* New York: P. Lang, 1990.

Williams, Robert. "Literary Fiction as Philosophy: The Case of Nietzsche's *Zarathustra*." *Journal of Philosophy* 83 (1986): 667–675.

BEYOND GOOD AND EVIL

Allison, David B. "A Diet of Worms: Aposiopetic Rhetoric in *Beyond Good and Evil*." *Nietzsche-Studien* 19 (1990): 43–58.

Burnham, Douglas. *Reading Nietzsche: An Analysis of "Beyond Good and Evil*." Montréal: McGill-Queen's University Press, 2007.

Lampert, Laurence. *Nietzsche's Task: An Interpretation of "Beyond Good and Evil*." New Haven: Yale University Press, 2001.

Lomax, John Harvey. *Nietzsche's New Nobility and the Eternal Return in "Beyond Good and Evil": A Proemium*. Lanham, Md.: Lexington Books, 2003.

Nehamas, Alexander. "Will to Knowledge, Will to Ignorance, and Will to Power in *Beyond Good and Evil*," in Yirmiyahu Yovel, ed. *Nietzsche as Affirmative Thinker*. Dordrecht: Martinus Nijhoff, 1986, 90–108.

"Who are 'the Philosophers of the Future'?: A Reading of *Beyond Good and Evil*," in Robert C. Solomon and Kathleen Higgins, eds. *Reading Nietzsche*. New York: Oxford University Press, 1988, 46–67.

Strauss, Leo. "Notes on the Plan of Nietzsche's *Beyond Good and Evil*." *Interpretation* 3.2 (1973): 97–113.

ON THE GENEALOGY OF MORALITY

Acampora, Christa Davis. *Nietzsche's "On the Genealogy of Morals": Critical Essays*. Lanham, Md.: Rowman & Littlefield Publishers, 2006.

Bergoffen, Debra B. "Why a Genealogy of Morals?" *Man and World* 16 (1983): 129–138.

Blondel, E. "Nietzsche's Style of Affirmation: The Metaphors of Genealogy," in Y. Yovel, ed. *Nietzsche as Affirmative Thinker*. Dordrecht: Martinus Nijhoff, 1986, 132–146.

Foucault, Michel. "Nietzsche, Genealogy, History," in Paul Rabinow, ed. *The Foucault Reader*. New York: Vintage, 1984, 76–100.

Geuss, Raymond. "Nietzsche and Genealogy," in *Morality, Culture and History*. Cambridge University Press, 1999, 1–28.

"Genealogy as Critique," in *Outside Ethics*. Princeton University Press, 2005, 153–160.

Hatab, Lawrence J. "How does the Ascetic Ideal Function in Nietzsche's *Genealogy?*" *Journal of Nietzsche Studies* 35 (2008): 106–140.

Havas, Randall. *Nietzsche's Genealogy: Nihilism and the Will to Knowledge.* Ithaca, N.Y.: Cornell University Press, 1995.

Hoy, David C. "Nietzsche, Hume, and the Genealogical Method," in Y. Yovel, ed. *Nietzsche as Affirmative Thinker.* Dordrecht: Martinus Rijhoff, 1986, 20–38.

Kemal, S. "Some Problems of Genealogy." *Nietzsche-Studien* 19 (1990): 30–43.

Loeb, Paul S. "Finding the *Übermensch* in Nietzsche's *Genealogy of Morality.*" *Journal of Nietzsche Studies* 30 (2005): 70–101.

Morrisson, Iain. "Slave Morality, Will to Power, and Nihilism in the *Genealogy of Morals.*" *International Studies in Philosophy* 33 (2001): 127–144.

Newman, Michael. "Reading the Future of Genealogy: Kant, Nietzsche, and Plato," in K. Ansell-Pearson, ed. *Nietzsche and Modern German Thought.* London: Routledge, 1991, 257–282.

Ridley, Aaron. *Nietzsche's Conscience: Six Character Studies from the "Genealogy."* Ithaca, N.Y.: Cornell University Press, 1998.

"Guilt before God, Or God before Guilt? The Second Essay of Nietzsche's *Genealogy.*" *Journal of Nietzsche Studies* 29 (2005): 35–45.

Risse, Mathias. "Origins of *Ressentiment* and Sources of Normativity." *Nietzsche-Studien* 32 (2003): 142–170.

Schacht, Richard. *Nietzsche, Genealogy, Morality: Essays on Nietzsche's "Genealogy of Morals."* Berkeley: University of California Press, 1994.

Schrift, Alan D. "Between Perspectivism and Philology: Genealogy as Hermeneutic." *Nietzsche-Studien* 16 (1987): 91–112.

"Genealogy and/as Deconstruction: Nietzsche, Derrida and Foucault on Philosophy as Critique," in Hugh J. Silverman, ed. *Postmodernism and Continental Philosophy.* New York: SUNY Press, 1988, 193–214.

Sedgwick, Peter R. "Violence, Economy and Temporality: Plotting the Political Terrain of *On the Genealogy of Morality.*" *Nietzsche-Studien* 34 (2005): 163–185.

Thatcher, David S. "*Zur Genealogie der Moral*: Some Textual Annotations." *Nietzsche-Studien* 18 (1989): 587–600.

White, Richard. "The Return of the Master: An Interpretation of Nietzsche's *Genealogy of Morals.*" *Philosophy and Phenomenological Research* 48 (June 1988): 683–696.

Zuckert, Catherine. "Nietzsche on the Origins and Development of the Distinctively Human." *Polity* (Fall 1983): 48–71.

LATE WRITINGS: *TWILIGHT OF THE IDOLS, ANTICHRIST, CASE OF WAGNER, ECCE HOMO, NIETZSCHE CONTRA WAGNER*

Conway, Daniel W. "Nietzsche's Doppelganger: Affirmation and Resentment in *Ecce Homo,*" in Keith Ansell-Pearson, ed. *The Fate of the New Nietzsche.* Avebury: Brookfield, 1993, 55–78.

Nietzsche's Dangerous Game: Philosophy in the Twilight of the Idols. Cambridge University Press, 1997.

Magnus, Bernd. "Nietzsche's Philosophy in 1888: The *Will to Power* and the *Übermensch.*" *Journal of the History of Philosophy* 36 (1983): 79–98.

Schütz, Anton. "A Sad Science? Europe, Law, Anti-Legalism and the Roots of Nietzsche's *Antichrist.*" *New Nietzsche Studies* 7.3/4 (2007): 107.

Shapiro, Gary. "The Writing on the Wall: *The Antichrist* and the Semiotics of History," in Robert C. Solomon and Kathleen Higgins, eds. *Reading Nietzsche.* New York: Oxford University Press, 1988, 192–217.

Siemens, Herman. "*Umwertung*: Nietzsche's 'War-Praxis' and the Problem of Yes-Saying and No-Saying in *Ecce Homo.*" *Nietzsche-Studien* 38 (2009): 182–206.

Steinbuch, Thomas. *A Commentary on Nietzsche's Ecce Homo.* Lanham, Md.: University Press of America, 1994.

Strong, Tracy. "Introduction," in *Twilight of the Idols*, trans. Richard Polt. Indianapolis: Hackett, 1997.

NIETZSCHE'S POETRY

Del Caro, Adrian. "Anti-Romantic Irony in the Poetry of Nietzsche." *Nietzsche-Studien* 12 (1983): 372–378.

Gilman, Sander L. "*Incipit Parodia*: The Function of Parody in the Lyrical Poetry of Friedrich Nietzsche." *Nietzsche-Studien* 4 (1975): 52–74.

Grundlehner, Philip. *The Poetry of Friedrich Nietzsche.* New York: Oxford University Press, 1986.

Rohit, Sharma. *On the Seventh Solitude: Endless Becoming and Eternal Return in the Poetry of Friedrich Nietzsche.* New York: Peter Lang, 2006.

MAJOR THEMES IN NIETZSCHE SCHOLARSHIP
ART, MUSIC, AND AESTHETICS

Abraham, Gerald. "Nietzsche's Attitude toward Wagner: A Fresh View." *Music and Letters* 13.1 (January 1932): 67–74.

Berrios, Ruben. "Nietzsche's Vitalistic Aestheticism." *Nietzsche-Studien* 32 (2003): 78–102.

Borchmeyer, Dieter. "Wagner and Nietzsche," in *The Wagner Handbook*, trans. John Deathridge. Cambridge, Mass.: Harvard University Press, 1992.

Del Caro, Adrian. *Dionysian Aesthetics: The Role of Destruction in Creation as Reflected in the Life and Works of Friedrich Nietzsche.* Frankfurt am Main: Lang, 1981.

Eilon, Eli. "Nietzsche's Principle of Abundance as Guiding Aesthetic Value." *Nietzsche-Studien* 30 (2001): 200–221.

Fischer-Dieskau, Dietrich. *Wagner and Nietzsche*, trans. Joachim Neugroschel. New York: Seabury, 1976.

Heller, Erich. *The Importance of Nietzsche: Ten Essays.* University of Chicago Press, 1988.

Higgins, Kathleen. "Nietzsche on Music." *Journal of the History of Ideas* 47.4 (1986): 663–672.

Hinman, Lawrence. "Nietzsche, Metaphor and Truth." *Philosophy and Phenomenological Research* 43.2 (December 1982): 179–199.

Hollinrake, Roger. *Nietzsche, Wagner, and the Philosophy of Pessimism.* London/ Boston: Allen and Unwin, 1982.

Kemal, Salim, Ivan Gaskell, and Daniel W. Conway. *Nietzsche, Philosophy and the Arts.* Cambridge University Press, 1998.

Leiter, Brian. "Nietzsche and Aestheticism." *Journal of the History of Philosophy* 30 (1992): 275–280.

Levine, Peter. *Nietzsche and the Modern Crisis of the Humanities.* Albany: State University of New York Press, 1995.

Liébert, Georges. *Nietzsche and Music.* University of Chicago Press, 2004.

Love, Frederic C. *The Young Nietzsche and the Wagnerian Experience.* Chapel Hill: University of North Carolina Press, 1963.

Martin, Nicholas. *Nietzsche and Schiller: Untimely Aesthetics.* Oxford University Press, 1996.

Moore, Gregory. "Hysteria and Histrionics: Nietzsche, Wagner and the Pathology of Genius." *Nietzsche-Studien* 30 (2001): 246–266.

Nabais, Nuno. *Nietzsche and the Metaphysics of the Tragic,* trans. Martin Earl. London: Continuum, 2006.

Rampley, Matthew. *Nietzsche, Aesthetics, and Modernity.* Cambridge University Press, 2000.

Rolleston, James. "Nietzsche, Expressionism, and Modern Poetics." *Nietzsche-Studien* 9 (1980): 285–301.

Schacht, Richard. "Nietzsche's Second Thoughts about Art." *Monist* 64.2 (1982): 231–246.

Schrift, Alan D. *Why Nietzsche Still? Reflections on Drama, Culture, and Politics.* Berkeley: University of California Press, 2000.

Taylor, Charles S. "Some Thoughts on Nietzsche, Kazantzakis and the Meaning of Art." *Nietzsche-Studien* 12 (1983): 379–386.

Young, Julian. *Nietzsche's Philosophy of Art.* Cambridge University Press, 1992.

Zuckerman, Elliott. "Nietzsche and Music: *Birth of Tragedy* and *Nietzsche Contra Wagner.*" *Symposium* 28 (1984): 17–32.

BIOGRAPHICAL STUDIES

Brobjer, Thomas H. *Nietzsche's Philosophical Context: An Intellectual Biography.* Urbana: University of Illinois Press, 2008.

Cate, Curtis. *Friedrich Nietzsche.* New York: Overlook Press, 2005.

Chamberlain, Lesley. *Nietzsche in Turin: An Intimate Biography.* New York: Picador, 1996.

Gilman, Sander L. *Conversations with Nietzsche: A Life in the Words of His Contemporaries.* New York: Oxford University Press, 1987.

Hayman, Ronald. *Nietzsche: A Critical Life.* London: Weidenfeld and Nicolson, 1980.

Hollingdale, R. J. *Nietzsche: The Man and his Philosophy.* Cambridge University Press, 2001.

Krell, David Farrell, and Donald L. Bates. *The Good European: Nietzsche's Work Sites in Word and Image.* University of Chicago Press, 1997.

Pletsch, Carl. *Young Nietzsche: Becoming a Genius.* New York: Free Press, 1991.

Safranski, Rüdiger. *Nietzsche: A Philosophical Biography.* New York: W. W. Norton, 2002.

Schaberg, William H. *The Nietzsche Canon: A Publication History and Bibliography.* University of Chicago Press, 1995.

Small, Robin. *Nietzsche and Rée: A Star Friendship.* New York: Oxford University Press, 2005.

Young, Julian. *Friedrich Nietzsche: A Philosophical Biography.* Cambridge University Press, 2010.

CLASSICS AND PHILOLOGY

Acampora, Christa Davis. "Nietzsche Contra Homer, Socrates, and Paul." *Journal of Nietzsche Studies* 24 (2002): 25–53.

Barnes, Jonathan. "Nietzsche and Diogenes Laertius." *Nietzsche-Studien* 15 (1986): 16–40.

Bishop, Paul. *Nietzsche and Antiquity: His Reaction and Response to the Classical Tradition.* Rochester, N.Y.: Camden House, 2004.

Brobjer, Thomas H. "Nietzsche's Relation to the Greek Sophists." *Nietzsche-Studien* 34 (2005): 256–277.

Geuss, Raymond. "Thucydides, Nietzsche, and Williams," in Manuel Dries, ed. *Nietzsche on Time and History.* Berlin: Walter de Gruyter, 2008, 35–50.

Grant, George. "Nietzsche and the Ancients: Philosophy and Scholarship." *Dionysius* 3 (1979): 5–16.

Most, Glenn. "Friedrich Nietzsche: Between Philosophy and Philology." *New Nietzsche Studies* 4.1 (2000): 163–170.

"On the Use and Abuse of Ancient Greece for Life." *Cultura Tedesca* 20 (2002): 31–53.

O'Flaherty, James, Timothy Sellner, and Robert Helm, eds. *Studies in Nietzsche and the Classical Tradition.* Chapel Hill: University of North Carolina Press, 1976.

Porter, James I. "After Philology: Nietzsche and the Reinvention of Antiquity." *New Nietzsche Studies* 4.1/2 (2000): 33.

Nietzsche and the Philology of the Future. Stanford University Press, 2000.

Przybyslawski, Artur. "Nietzsche Contra Heraclitus." *Journal of Nietzsche Studies* 23 (2002): 88–95.

Riedel, Manfred. "The Origin of Europe: Nietzsche and the Greeks." *New Nietzsche Studies* 4.1/2 (2000): 141.

Small, Robin. "Nietzsche and the Platonist Tradition of the Cosmos: Center Everywhere and Circumference Nowhere." *Journal of the History of Ideas* 44 (1983): 89–103.

Tejera, V. *Nietzsche and Greek Thought.* Dordrecht: Kluwer Academic Publishers, 1987.

Tongeren, Paul van. "Nietzsche's Greek Measure." *Journal of Nietzsche Studies* 24 (2002): 5–24.

Zuckert, Catherine. "Nietzsche's Rereading of Plato." *Political Theory* 13 (1985): 213–238.

EPISTEMOLOGY, LANGUAGE, AND TRUTH

Anderson, R. Lanier. "Truth and Objectivity in Perspectivism." *Synthèse* 115 (1988): 1–32.

Atwell, John E. "Nietzsche's Perspectivism." *Southern Journal of Philosophy* 19 (1981): 157–170.

Conant, James. "The Dialectic of Perspectivism, I." *Sats – Nordic Journal of Philosophy* 7:1 (2006): 5–50.

"The Dialectic of Perspectivism, II." *Sats – Nordic Journal of Philosophy* 7:2 (2006): 6–57.

Crawford, Claudia. *The Beginnings of Nietzsche's Theory of Language.* Berlin: Walter de Gruyter, 1988.

Emden, Christian. *Nietzsche on Language, Consciousness, and the Body.* Urbana: University of Illinois Press, 2005.

Gemes, Ken. "Nietzsche's Critique of Truth." *Philosophy and Phenomenological Research* 52 (1992): 47–65.

Grimm, Rüdiger Hermann. *Nietzsche's Theory of Knowledge.* Berlin: Walter de Gruyter, 1977.

Hales, Steven D., and Rex Welshon. *Nietzsche's Perspectivism.* Urbana: University of Illinois Press, 2000.

Magnus, Bernd. "Nietzsche's Mitigated Skepticism." *Nietzsche Studien* 9 (1980): 260–267.

Nehamas, Alexander. "Immanent and Transcendent Perspectivism in Nietzsche." *Nietzsche-Studien* 12 (1983): 473–490.

Nola, Robert. "Nietzsche's Theory of Truth and Belief." *Philosophy and Phenomenological Research* 47 (1987): 525–562.

Rayman, Joshua. "Nietzsche, Truth, and Reference." *Nietzsche-Studien* 36 (2007): 168–181.

Reginster, Bernard. "Perspectivism, Criticism, and Freedom of Spirit." *Philosophy and Phenomenological Research* 57 (1997): 281–305.

"The Paradox of Perspectivism." *Philosophy and Phenomenological Research* 62.1 (2001): 217–233.

Rosen, Stanley. "Poetic Reason in Nietzsche: *Die Dichtende Vernunft*," in *The Ancients and the Moderns: Rethinking Modernity*. New Haven: Yale University Press, 1989, 209–234.

Schacht, Richard. "Nietzschean Cognitivism." *Nietzsche-Studien* 29 (2000): 12–40.

Schrift, Alan D. "Language, Metaphor, Rhetoric: Nietzsche's Deconstruction of Epistemology." *Journal of the History of Philosophy* 23.3 (1985): 371–395.

Strong, Tracy B. "Texts and Pretexts: Reflections on Perspectivism in Nietzsche." *Political Theory* 13.2 (1985): 164–182.

Welshon, Rex. "Saying Yes to Reality: Skepticism, Antirealism, and Perspectivism in Nietzsche's Epistemology." *Journal of Nietzsche Studies* 37 (2009): 23–43.

Wilcox, John T. *Truth and Value in Nietzsche: A Study of His Metaethics and Epistemology*. Washington, DC: University Press of America, 1982.

ETERNAL RECURRENCE, TIME, AND HISTORY

Aydin, Ciano. "Nietzsche, Eternal Recurrence, and the Horror of Existence." *Journal of Nietzsche Studies* 33 (2007): 49–63.

Bergoffen, Debra B. "The Eternal Recurrence Again." *International Studies in Philosophy* 15.2 (1983): 35–46.

Bornedal, Peter. "Eternal Recurrence in Inner-Mental-Life." *Nietzsche-Studien* 35 (2006): 104–165.

Cohen, Jonathan. "Nietzsche's Musical Conception of Time," in Manuel Dries, ed. *Nietzsche on Time and History*. Berlin: Walter de Gruyter, 2008, 291–308.

Dries, Manuel. "Towards a Dualism: Becoming and Nihilism in Nietzsche's Philosophy," in Manuel Dries, ed. *Nietzsche on Time and History*. Berlin: Walter de Gruyter, 2008, 113–148.

Grant, George, and William Christian. *Time as History*. University of Toronto Press, 1995.

Hatab, Lawrence J. *Nietzsche's Life Sentence: Coming to Terms with Eternal Recurrence*. New York: Routledge, 2005.

"Shocking Time: Reading Eternal Recurrence Literally," in Manuel Dries, ed. *Nietzsche on Time and History*. Berlin: Walter de Gruyter, 2008, 149–162.

Hillard, Derek. "History as a Dual Process." *Nietzsche-Studien* 31 (2002): 40–56.

Klossowski, Pierre. *Nietzsche and the Vicious Circle*, trans. Daniel W. Smith. London: Athlone, 1997.

Löwith, Karl. *Nietzsche's Philosophy of the Eternal Recurrence of the Same*, trans. J. Harvey Lomax. Berkeley: University of California Press, 1997.

Magnus, Bernd. "Eternal Recurrence." *Nietzsche-Studien* 8 (1979): 362–377.

Nietzsche's Existential Imperative. Bloomington: Indiana University Press, 1978.

Pearson, Keith Ansell. "The Eternal Return of the Overhuman: The Weightiest Knowledge and the Abyss of Light." *Journal of Nietzsche Studies* 30 (2005): 1–21.

Pfeffer, Rose. *Nietzsche: Disciple of Dionysus*. Lewisburg Pa.: Bucknell University Press, 1972.

Richardson, John. "Nietzsche's Problem of the Past," in Manuel Dries, ed. *Nietzsche on Time and History*. Berlin: Walter de Gruyter, 2008, 87–112.
Siemens, Herman. "Nietzsche and the Temporality of (Self-)Legislation," in Manuel Dries, ed. *Nietzsche on Time and History*. Berlin: Walter de Gruyter, 2008, 191–212.
Small, Robin. "Three Interpretations of Eternal Recurrence." *Dialogue, Canadian Philosophical Review* 22 (1983): 21–112.
Stambaugh, Joan. *Nietzsche's Thought of Eternal Return*. Baltimore: Johns Hopkins University Press, 1972.
  The Problem of Time in Nietzsche. Lewisburg, Pa.: Bucknell University Press, 1987.
Sterling, M. C. "Recent Discussions of Eternal Recurrence: Some Critical Comments." *Nietzsche-Studien* 6 (1977): 261–291.

FREEDOM AND FREE WILL

Dudley, Will. *Hegel, Nietzsche, and Philosophy: Thinking Freedom*. Cambridge University Press, 2002.
Gemes, Ken. "Nietzsche on Free Will, Autonomy and the Sovereign Individual." *Proceedings of Aristotelian Society* 80 (2006): 339–357.
Gemes, Ken, and Simon May, eds. *Nietzsche on Freedom and Autonomy*. Oxford University Press, 2009.
Grillaert, Nel. "Determining One's Fate: A Delineation of Nietzsche's Conception of Free Will." *Journal of Nietzsche Studies* 31 (2006): 42–60.
Leiter, Brian. "The Paradox of Fatalism and Self-Creation in Nietzsche," in C. Janaway, ed. *Willing and Nothingness*. Oxford University Press, 1998, 217–257.
Mandalios, John. "Nietzsche, Freedom, and Power." *European Journal of Social Theory* 6.2 (2003): 191–208.
Poellner, Peter. "Nietzschean Freedom," in K. Gemes and S. May, eds. *Nietzsche on Freedom and Autonomy*. Oxford University Press, 2009, 151–180.
Siemens, H. W. "Nietzsche Contra Liberalism on Freedom," in Keith Ansell-Pearson, ed. *A Companion to Nietzsche*. Malden, Mass.: Blackwell Publishing, 2006, 437–454.
Solomon, Robert C. "Nietzsche on Fatalism and 'Free Will.'" *Journal of Nietzsche Studies* 23 (2002): 63–87.
White, Richard J. *Nietzsche and the Problem of Sovereignty*. Urbana: University of Illinois Press, 1997.

INFLUENCES AND PRECURSORS

Ansell-Pearson, Keith. *Nietzsche contra Rousseau: A Study of Nietzsche's Moral and Political Thought*. Cambridge University Press, 1991.
Berry, Jessica. *Nietzsche and the Ancient Skeptical Tradition*. Oxford University Press, 2010.

Binion, Rudolf. *Frau Lou: Nietzsche's Wayward Disciple.* Princeton University Press, 1968.
Brobjer, Thomas H. "Nietzsche's Knowledge of Marx and Marxism." *Nietzsche-Studien* 31 (2002): 298–320.
Nietzsche and the English: The Influence of British and American Thinking on His Philosophy. Amherst, NY: Humanity Books, 2008.
"Nietzsche, Voltaire and French Philosophy," in Clemens Pornschlegel and Martin Stingelin, eds. *Nietzsche und Frankreich.* Berlin: Walter de Gruyter, 2009, 13–32.
Conant, James. "Nietzsche, Kierkegaard and Anscombe on Moral Unintelligibility," in D. Z. Phillips, ed. *Religion and Morality.* New York: St. Martins Press, 1996, 250–301.
Del Caro, Adrian. *Nietzsche Contra Nietzsche: Creativity and the Anti-Romantic.* Baton Rouge: Louisiana State University Press, 1989.
Donnellan, Brendan. *Nietzsche and the French Moralists.* Bonn: Bouvier, 1982.
Doyle, Tsarina. "Nietzsche's Appropriation of Kant." *Nietzsche-Studien* 33 (2004): 180–204.
Geuss, Raymond. "Thucydides, Nietzsche, and Williams," in *Outside Ethics.* Princeton University Press, 2005, 219–30.
Gillespie, Michael Allen. *Nihilism Before Nietzsche.* University of Chicago Press, 1995.
Hill, R. K. *Nietzsche's Critiques: The Kantian Foundations of His Thought.* Oxford: Clarendon Press, 2003.
"From Kantian Temporality to Nietzschean Naturalism," in Manuel Dries, ed. *Nietzsche on Time and History.* Berlin: Walter de Gruyter, 2008, 75–86.
Janaway, Christopher, ed. *Willing and Nothingness: Schopenhauer as Nietzsche's Educator.* Oxford University Press, 1998.
Lampert, Lawrence. *Leo Strauss and Nietzsche.* University of Chicago Press, 1996.
Löwith, Karl. *From Hegel to Nietzsche: The Revolution in Nineteenth Century Thought.* New York: Columbia University Press, 1991.
Martin, Nicholas, ed. *Nietzsche and the German Tradition.* Oxford: Peter Lang, 2003.
Molner, David. "The Influence of Montaigne on Nietzsche." *Nietzsche-Studien* 22 (1993): 80–93.
Riccardi, Mattia. "Nietzsche's Critique of Kant's Thing in Itself." *Nietzsche-Studien* 39 (2010): 333–351.
Simmel, Georg. *Schopenhauer and Nietzsche.* Amherst: University of Massachusetts Press, 1986.
Small, Robin. *Nietzsche in Context.* Aldershot and Burlington, Vermont: Ashgate, 2001.
Stack, George J. *Lange and Nietzsche.* Berlin: Walter de Gruyter, 1983.
Nietzsche and Emerson: An Elective Affinity. Athens: Ohio University Press, 1992.
Wilcox, John. "The Birth of Nietzsche Out of the Spirit of Lange." *International Studies in Philosophy* 21.2 (1989): 81–89.

Williams, William David. *Nietzsche and the French: A Study of the Influence of Nietzsche's French Reading on His Thought and Writing.* Oxford: Blackwell, 1952.

JEWS, ANTI-SEMITISM, AND THE NAZI MISAPPROPRIATION

Fischer, Kurt Rudolf. "Nazism as a Nietzschean 'Experiment.'" *Nietzsche-Studien* 6 (1977): 116–122.
Golomb, Jacob. *Nietzsche and Jewish Culture.* New York: Routledge, 1996.
Golomb, Jacob, and Robert S. Wistrich. *Nietzsche, Godfather of Fascism?: On the Uses and Abuses of a Philosophy.* Princeton University Press, 2002.
Holub, Robert. "Nietzsche and the Jewish Question." *New German Critique* 66 (1995): 94–121.
Kofman, Sarah. "Contempt of / for the Jews: Nietzsche, the Jews, Anti-Semitism." *New Nietzsche Studies* 7.3/4 (2007): 7.
Kuenzli, Rudolph. "The Nazi Appropriation of Nietzsche." *Nietzsche-Studien* 4 (1983): 36–51.
Santaniello, Weaver. *Nietzsche, God, and the Jews: His Critique of Judeo-Christianity in Relation to the Nazi Myth.* Albany: State University of New York Press, 1994.

LEGACY AND RECEPTION

Ansell-Pearson, Keith. *Nietzsche and Modern German Thought.* London: Routledge, 1991.
Aschheim, Steven E. *The Nietzsche Legacy in Germany, 1890–1990.* Berkeley: University of California Press, 1992.
Behler, Ernst. "Nietzsche in the Twentieth Century," in Bernd Magnus and Kathleen Higgins, eds. *The Cambridge Companion to Nietzsche.* Cambridge University Press, 1996, 281–322.
Forth, Christopher E. *Zarathustra in Paris: The Nietzsche Vogue in France, 1891–1918.* Dekalb: Northern Illinois University Press, 2001.
Mann, Thomas. *Nietzsche's Philosophy in the Light of Contemporary Events.* Washington, DC: Library of Congress, 1947.
Reichert, Herbert William. *Friedrich Nietzsche's Impact on Modern German Literature: Five Essays.* Chapel Hill: University of North Carolina Press, 1975.
Rosen, Stanley. "Nietzsche's Revolution," in *The Ancients and the Moderns: Rethinking Modernity.* New Haven: Yale University Press, 1989, 189–208.
Schrift, Alan D. *Nietzsche's French Legacy: A Genealogy of Poststructuralism.* New York: Routledge, 1995.
Thatcher, David S. *Nietzsche in England, 1890–1914: The Growth of a Reputation.* University of Toronto Press, 1970.
Thomas, R. H. *Nietzsche in German Politics and Society, 1890–1918.* Manchester University Press, 1983.

METAPHYSICS

Ansell-Pearson, Keith. "Nietzsche's Overcoming of Kant and Metaphysics: From Tragedy to Nihilism." *Nietzsche-Studien* 16 (1987): 310–339.
Gelven, Michael. "Nietzsche and the Question of Being." *Nietzsche-Studien* 9 (1980): 209–223.
Haar, Michel, and Michael Gendre. *Nietzsche and Metaphysics.* Albany: State University of New York Press, 1996.
Heidegger, Martin. "The Word of Nietzsche: 'God is Dead,'" in *The Question Concerning Technology & Other Essays,* trans. William Lovitt. New York: Harper & Row, 1977, 53–112.
Poellner, Peter. *Nietzsche and Metaphysics.* Oxford University Press, 1995.
Richardson, John. *Nietzsche's System.* New York: Oxford University Press, 1996.
Rosen, Stanley. "Nietzsche's Image of Chaos." *International Philosophical Quarterly* 20 (1980): 3–23.

MODERN CULTURE, MODERNITY, AND POSTMODERNITY

Ahern, Daniel R. *Nietzsche as Cultural Physician.* University Park: Pennsylvania State University Press, 1995.
Ansell-Pearson, Keith. "Nietzsche and the Problem of the Will in Modernity," in Keith Ansell-Pearson, ed. *Nietzsche and Modern German Thought.* London: Routledge, 1991, 165–191.
Koelb, Clayton. *Nietzsche as Postmodernist: Essays Pro and Contra.* Albany: State University of New York Press, 1990.
Lampert, Laurence. *Nietzsche and Modern Times: A Study of Bacon, Descartes, and Nietzsche.* New Haven: Yale University Press, 1993.
Love, Nancy S. *Marx, Nietzsche, and Modernity.* New York: Columbia University Press, 1986.
Magnus, Bernd. "Nietzsche and Postmodern Criticism." *Nietzsche-Studien* 18 (1989): 301–316.
Owen, David. *Maturity and Modernity: Nietzsche, Weber, and Foucault.* London: Routledge, 1994.
Pippin, Robert B. "Nietzsche and the Origin of the Idea of Modernism." *Inquiry* 26.2 (1983): 151–180.
"Nietzsche's Alleged Farewell: The Premodern, Modern, and Postmodern Nietzsche," in Bernd Magnus and Kathleen Higgins, eds. *The Cambridge Companion to Nietzsche.* Cambridge University Press, 1996, 252–280.
"Nietzsche and the Melancholy of Modernity." *Social Research* 66.2 (1999): 495–519.

MORALS, ETHICS, VALUES

Andresen, Joshua. "Nietzsche's Conception of Value: A Story of Three Errors." *Nietzsche-Studien* 38 (2009): 207–228.

Ansell-Pearson, Keith. "Nietzsche on Autonomy and Morality: the Challenge to Political Theory." *Political Studies* 34:2 (1991): 270–286.

Berkowitz, Peter. *Nietzsche: The Ethics of an Immoralist.* Cambridge, Mass.: Harvard University Press, 1995.

Bernstein, John Andrew. *Nietzsche's Moral Philosophy.* New Jersey: Associated University Presses, 1987.

Brobjer, Thomas H. *Nietzsche's Ethics of Character: A Study of Nietzsche's Ethics and its Place in the History of Moral Thinking.* Uppsala University Press, 1995.

"Nietzsche's Affirmative Morality: An Ethics of Virtue." *Journal of Nietzsche Studies* 26 (2003): 64–78.

"The Origin and Early Context of the Revaluation Theme in Nietzsche's Thinking." *Journal of Nietzsche Studies* 39 (2010): 12–29.

Clark, Maudmarie. "Nietzsche's Immoralism and the Concept of Morality," in Richard Schacht, ed. *Nietzsche, Genealogy, and Morality.* Berkeley: University of California Press, 1994, 15–34.

Conway, Daniel W. "A Moral Ideal for Everyone and No One." *International Studies in Philosophy* 22.2 (1990): 17–29.

Foot, Philippa, "Nietzsche: The Revaluation of Values," in *Nietzsche: A Collection of Critical Essays.* South Bend: University of Notre Dame Press, 1973.

Geuss, Raymond. "Nietzsche and Morality," in *Morality, Culture, and History: Essays on German Philosophy.* Cambridge University Press, 1999, 167–198.

Hunt, Lester H. *Nietzsche and the Origin of Virtue.* London and New York: Routledge, 1991.

Leiter, Brian. "Beyond Good and Evil." *History of Philosophy Quarterly* 10 (1993): 261–270.

"Morality in the Pejorative Sense: On the Logic of Nietzsche's Critique of Morality." *British Journal for the History of Philosophy* 3.1 (1995): 113–145.

"Nietzsche and the Morality Critics." *Ethics* 107 (1997): 250–285.

Nietzsche on Morality. London: Routledge, 2002.

Leiter, Brian, and Neil Sinhababu, eds. *Nietzsche and Morality.* Oxford University Press, 2007.

May, Simon. *Nietzsche's Ethics and His War on "Morality."* Oxford University Press, 1999.

Metzger, Jeffrey A. *Nietzsche, Nihilism and the Philosophy of the Future.* London: Continuum, 2009.

Pippin, Robert B. "Nietzsche's Moral Psychology and the French Moralist Tradition." *Nietzsche-Forschung* 12 (2006): 313–334.

Reginster, Bernard. "Nietzsche's 'Revaluation' of Altruism." *Nietzsche-Studien* 29 (2000): 199–219.

The Affirmation of Life: Nietzsche on Overcoming Nihilism. Cambridge, Mass.: Harvard University Press, 2006.

Robertson, Simon. "Nietzsche's Ethical Revaluation." *Journal of Nietzsche Studies* 37 (2009): 66–90.

Schacht, Richard. *Nietzsche's Postmoralism: Essays on Nietzsche's Prelude to Philosophy's Future.* Cambridge University Press, 2001.

Siegfried, Hans. "Nietzsche's Natural Morality." *Journal of Value Inquiry* 26 (1992): 423–431.

Sleinis, E. E. *Nietzsche's Revaluation of Values: A Study in Strategies.* Urbana: University of Illinois Press, 1994.

Thiele, Leslie Paul. *Friedrich Nietzsche and the Politics of the Soul: A Study of Heroic Individualism.* Princeton University Press, 1990.

Zuckert, Catherine. *Postmodern Platos: Nietzsche, Heidegger, Gadamer, Strauss, Derrida.* University of Chicago Press, 1996.

PHILOSOPHY AND PHILOSOPHERS

Blondel, Eric. *Nietzsche, the Body and Culture: Philosophy as a Philological Genealogy,* trans. Sean Hand. London: Athlone Press, 1991.

Bowles, M. J. "The Practice of Meaning in Nietzsche and Wittgenstein." *Journal of Nietzsche Studies* 26 (2003): 12–24.

Campbell, David. "Nietzsche, Heidegger, and Meaning." *Journal of Nietzsche Studies* 26 (2003): 25–54.

Clark, Maudemarie. *Nietzsche on Truth and Philosophy.* Cambridge University Press, 1990.

Cooper, David Edward. "Nietzsche and the Analytical Ambition." *Journal of Nietzsche Studies* 26 (2003): 1–11.

Dannhauser, Werner J. *Nietzsche's View of Socrates.* Ithaca, N.Y.: Cornell University Press, 1974.

Danto, Arthur Coleman. *Nietzsche as Philosopher.* New York: Columbia University Press, 1965.

Hicks, Steven V., and Alan Rosenberg. "Nietzsche and Untimeliness: The 'Philosopher of the Future' as the Figure of Disruptive Wisdom." *Journal of Nietzsche Studies* 25 (2003): 1–34.

Klein, Wayne. *Nietzsche and the Promise of Philosophy.* Albany: State University of New York Press, 1997.

Krell, David Farrell. "Heidegger's Reading of Nietzsche: Confrontation and Encounter." *Journal of the British Society for Phenomenology* 14.3 (1983): 271–282.

Magnus, Bernd, Stanley Stewart, and Jean-Pierre Mileur. *Nietzsche's Case: Philosophy as/and Literature.* New York: Routledge, 1993.

Neumann, Harry. "Socrates and History: A Nietzschean Interpretation of Philosophy." *Nietzsche-Studien* 6 (1977): 64–74.

Pippin, Robert B. "The Erotic Nietzsche: Philosophers without Philosophy," in Shadi Bartsch and Thomas Bartscherer, eds. *Erotikon.* University of Chicago Press, 2005, 172–191.

Wininger, Kathleen J. *Nietzsche's Reclamation of Philosophy.* Amsterdam: Rodopi, 1997.

POLITICS AND DEMOCRACY

Ansell-Pearson, Keith. "The Significance of Michel Foucoualt's Reading of Nietzsche: Power, the Subject, and Political Theory." *Nietzsche-Studien* 20 (1991): 267–284.
  An Introduction to Nietzsche as Political Thinker: The Perfect Nihilist. Cambridge University Press, 1994.
Appel, Fredrick. *Nietzsche Contra Democracy.* Ithaca, N.Y.: Cornell University Press, 1999.
Bergmann, Peter. *Nietzsche, "the Last Antipolitical German."* Bloomington: Indiana University Press, 1987.
Brobjer, Thomas H. "The Absence of Political Ideals in Nietzsche's Writings: The Case of the Laws of Manu and the Associated Caste-Society." *Nietzsche-Studien* 27 (1998): 300–318.
Connolly, William. *Political Theory and Modernity.* Oxford: Blackwell, 1988.
  "Nietzsche and the Nobility of Democracy." *International Studies in Philosophy* 32.3 (2000): 51–59.
Conway, Daniel W. *Nietzsche & the Political.* London: Routledge, 1997.
Daigle, Christine. "Nietzsche: Virtue Ethics . . . Virtue Politics?" *Journal of Nietzsche Studies* 32 (2006): 1–21.
Detwiler, Bruce. *Nietzsche and the Politics of Aristocratic Radicalism.* University of Chicago Press, 1990.
Drochon, Hugo. "Nietzsche and Politics." *Nietzsche-Studien* 39 (2010): 663–677.
  "The Time is Coming When We Will Relearn Politics." *Journal of Nietzsche Studies* 39 (2010): 66–85.
Hatab, Lawrence J. *A Nietzschean Defense of Democracy: An Experiment in Postmodern Politics.* Chicago: Open Court, 1995.
Hunt, Lester. "Politics and Anti-Politics: Nietzsche's View of the State." *History of Philosophy Quarterly* 2.2 (1985): 453–468.
Lukács, György. "Nietzsche as Founder of Irrationalism in the Imperialist Period," in *The Destruction of Reason*, trans. Peter Palmer. Atlantic Highlands, N.J.: Humanities Press, 1981.
McIntyre, Alex. *The Sovereignty of Joy: Nietzsche's Vision of Grand Politics.* University of Toronto Press, 1997.
Owen, David. *Nietzsche, Politics, and Modernity: A Critique of Liberal Reason.* London: Sage Publications, 1995.
Pippin, Robert B. "Deceit, Desire, and Democracy: Nietzsche on Modern Eros." *International Studies in Philosophy* 32.3 (2000): 63–70.
Schrift, Alan D. "Nietzsche for Democracy?" *Nietzsche-Studien* 29 (2000): 220–233.
Shaw, Tamsin. *Nietzsche's Political Skepticism.* Princeton University Press, 2007.
Siemens, Herman. "Agonal Communities of Taste: Law and Community in Nietzsche's Philosophy of Transvaluation." *Journal of Nietzsche Studies* 24 (2002): 83–112.

"Nietzsche's Critique of Democracy (1870–1886)." *Journal of Nietzsche Studies* 38 (2009): 20–37.

Siemens, Herman, and Vasti Roodt. *Nietzsche, Power and Politics: Rethinking Nietzsche's Legacy for Political Thought*. Berlin: Walter de Gruyter, 2008.

Siemens, Herman, and Gary Shapiro. "What does Nietzsche Mean for Contemporary Politics and Political Thought?" *Journal of Nietzsche Studies* 35 (2008): 3–8.

Strong, Tracy B. *Friedrich Nietzsche and the Politics of Transfiguration*. Berkeley: University of California Press, 1975.

"Tyranny, Tragedy, Cultural Revolution, and Democracy." *Journal of Nietzsche Studies* 35 (2008): 48–66.

Warren, Mark. "The Politics of Nietzsche's Philosophy of Power: Nihilism, Culture, Power." *Political Studies* 33:3 (1985): 418–438.

Nietzsche and Political Thought. Cambridge, Mass.: MIT Press, 1988.

PSYCHOLOGY AND PSYCHIATRY

Bornedal, Peter. "The Incredible Profundity of the Truly Superficial: Nietzsche's 'Master' and 'Slave' as Mental Configurations." *Nietzsche-Studien* 33 (2004): 129–155.

Chapman, A. H., and Miriam Chapman-Santana. "The Influence of Nietzsche on Freud's Ideas." *British Journal of Psychiatry* 166.2 (1995): 251–253.

Cowan, Michael. "Nietzsche and the Psychology of the Will." *Nietzsche-Studien* 34 (2005): 48–74.

Golomb, Jacob, Weaver Santaniello, and Ronald Lehrer. *Nietzsche and Depth Psychology*. Albany: State University of New York Press, 1999.

Lehrer, Ronald. *Nietzsche's Presence in Freud's Life and Thought: On the Origins of a Psychology of Dynamic Unconscious Mental Functioning*. Albany: State University of New York Press, 1995.

Parkes, Graham. *Composing the Soul: Reaches of Nietzsche's Psychology*. University of Chicago Press, 1994.

Pippin, Robert B. "Morality as Psychology, Psychology as Morality: Nietzsche, Eros, and Clumsy Lovers," in Richard Schacht, ed. *Nietzsche's Postmoralism*. Urbana-Champaign: University of Illinois Press, 2000, 79–99.

Nietzsche, Psychology, and First Philosophy. University of Chicago Press, 2010.

Schrift, Alan D. "Nietzsche's Psycho-Genealogy." *Journal of the British Society for Phenomenology* 14.3 (1983): 283–303.

Solomon, Robert C. *Living with Nietzsche: What the Great "Immoralist" has to Teach Us*. Oxford University Press, 2003.

Stambaugh, Joan. "Thoughts on Pity and Revenge." *Nietzsche-Studien* 1 (1972): 27–35.

Ure, Michael. "Stoic Comedians: Nietzsche and Freud on the Art of Arranging One's Humours." *Nietzsche-Studien* 34 (2005): 186–216.

Williams, Bernard. "Nietzsche's Minimalist Moral Psychology." *European Journal of Philosophy* 1 (1993): 4–14.

RELIGION

Aschheim, Steven E. "After the Death of God: Varieties of Nietzschean Religion." *Nietzsche-Studien* 17 (1988): 218–249.

Benson, Bruce Ellis. *Pious Nietzsche: Decadence and Dionysian Faith.* Bloomington: Indiana University Press, 2008.

Geffré, Claude, Jean Pierre Jossua, and Marcus Lefébure, eds. *Nietzsche and Christianity.* New York: Seabury Press, 1981.

Lippitt, John, and Jim Urpeth. *Nietzsche and the Divine.* Manchester: Clinamen Press, 2000.

McCullough, Lissa. "Nietzsche's Faith." *New Nietzsche Studies* 4.3/4 (2000): 55.

Roberts, Tyler T. *Contesting Spirit: Nietzsche, Affirmation, Religion.* Princeton University Press, 1998.

Santaniello, Weaver. *Nietzsche and the Gods.* Albany: State University of New York Press, 2001.

Stegmaier, Werner. "Nietzsche's Theology: Perspectives for God, Faith, and Justice." *New Nietzsche Studies* 4.3/4 (2000): 73.

Wienand, Isabelle. "God and Gold: On Nietzsche's Conception of God." *New Nietzsche Studies* 4.3/4 (2000): 91.

Young, Julian. *Nietzsche's Philosophy of Religion.* Cambridge University Press, 2006.

SCIENCE, NATURE, AND NATURALISM

Anderson, R. Lanier. "Nietzsche's Will to Power as a Doctrine of the Unity of Science." *Studies in the History and Philosophy of Science* 25.5 (1994): 729–750.

Babich, Babette E. *Nietzsche's Philosophy of Science: Reflecting Science on the Ground of Art and Life.* Albany: State University of New York Press, 1994.

Cox, Christoph. *Nietzsche: Naturalism and Interpretation.* Berkeley: University of California Press, 1999.

Del Caro, Adrian. *Grounding the Nietzsche Rhetoric of Earth.* Berlin: Walter de Gruyter, 2004.

Gallo, Beverly. "On the Question of Nietzsche's 'Scientism.'" *International Studies in Philosophy* 22.2 (1990): 111–119.

Moore, Gregory. *Nietzsche, Biology, and Metaphor.* Cambridge University Press, 2002.

"Nietzsche, Spencer, and the Ethics of Evolution." *Journal of Nietzsche Studies* 23 (2002): 1–20.

Moore, Gregory, and Thomas H. Brobjer. *Nietzsche and Science.* Aldershot: Ashgate, 2004.

Parkes, Graham. "Staying Loyal to the Earth: Nietzsche as Ecological Thinker," in John Lippit, ed. *Nietzsche's Futures.* New York: St. Martin's Press, 1999, 167–188.

Stack, George J. *Nietzsche's Anthropic Circle: Man, Science, and Myth.* University of Rochester Press, 2005.

Taffel, David. *Nietzsche Unbound: The Struggle for Spirit in the Age of Science.* St. Paul, Minn.: Paragon House, 2003.

STYLE AND INTERPRETATION

Babich, Babette E. "On Nietzsche's Concinnity: An Analysis of Style." *Nietzsche-Studien* 19 (1990): 59–80.
de Man, Paul. *Allegories of Reading: Figural Language in Rousseau, Nietzsche, Rilke, and Proust.* New Haven: Yale University Press, 1979.
Derrida, Jacques. *Spurs: Nietzsche's Styles,* trans. Stefano Agosti. University of Chicago Press, 1978.
Gilman, Sander L. *Nietzschean Parody: An Introduction to Reading Nietzsche.* Bonn: Bouvier Verlag H. Grundmann, 1976.
Higgins, Kathleen. "Nietzsche's View of Philosophical Style." *International Studies in Philosophy* 18 (1986): 67–81.
Howey, R. L. "Some Reflections on Irony in Nietzsche." *Nietzsche-Studien* 4 (1973): 36–51.
Kofman, Sarah. *Nietzsche and Metaphor,* trans. Duncan Large. London: Athlone Press, 1993.
Schrift, Alan D. *Nietzsche and the Question of Interpretation: Between Hermeneutics and Deconstruction.* New York: Routledge, 1990.
Shapiro, Gary. *Nietzschean Narratives.* Bloomington: Indiana University Press, 1989.

WOMEN AND FEMINISM

Burgard, Peter J. *Nietzsche and the Feminine.* Charlottesville: University Press of Virginia, 1994.
Diethe, Carol. *Nietzsche's Women: Beyond the Whip.* Berlin: Walter de Gruyter, 1996.
Helm, Barbara. "Combating Misogyny? Responses to Nietzsche by Turn-of-the-Century German Feminists." *Journal of Nietzsche Studies* 27 (2004): 64–84.
Irigaray, Luce. *Marine Lover of Friedrich Nietzsche.* New York: Columbia University Press, 1991.
Oliver, Kelly. "Woman as Truth in Nietzsche's Writing." *Social Theory and Practice* 10 (1984): 185–199.
  Womanizing Nietzsche: Philosophy's Relation to the "Feminine." New York: Routledge, 1995.
Oliver, Kelly, and Marilyn Pearsall. *Feminist Interpretations of Friedrich Nietzsche.* University Park: Pennsylvania State University Press, 1998.
Oppel, Frances Nesbitt. *Nietzsche on Gender: Beyond Man and Woman.* Charlottesville: University of Virginia Press, 2005.
Ostfeld, de Bendayan. *Ecce Mulier: Nietzsche and the Eternal Feminine: An Analytical Psychological Perspective.* Wilmette, Ill.: Chiron Publications, 2007.
Patton, Paul. *Nietzsche, Feminism, and Political Theory.* London: Routledge, 1993.

Platt, Michael. "Woman, Nietzsche, and Nature." *Maieutics* 2 (1981): 27–42.
Thomas, R. H. "Nietzsche, Women, and the Whip." *German Life and Letters* 34 (1980): 117–125.

WILL TO POWER AND THE *ÜBERMENSCH*

Ansell-Pearson, Keith. "Who is the *Übermensch*? Time, Truth, and Woman in Nietzsche." *Journal of the History of Ideas* 53:2 (1992): 309–331.
Clark, Maudemarie. "Nietzsche's Doctrine of the Will to Power." *International Studies in Philosophy* 32.3 (2000): 119–135.
Conway, Daniel W. "Overcoming the *Übermensch*: Nietzsche's Revaluation of Values." *Journal of the British Society for Phenomenology* 20.3 (1983): 211–224.
  "The Genius as Squanderer: Some Remarks on the *Übermensch* and Higher Humanity." *International Studies in Philosophy* 30 (1998): 81–95.
Crawford, Claudia. "Nietzsche's Overhuman: Creating on the Crest of the Time-point." *Journal of Nietzsche Studies* 30 (2005): 22–48.
Gillespie, Michael Allen. "'Slouching Toward Bethlehem to be Born': On the Nature and Meaning of Nietzsche's Superman." *Journal of Nietzsche Studies* 30 (2005): 49–69.
Magnus, Bernd. "Perfectibility and Attitude in Nietzsche's *Übermensch*." *Review of Metaphysics* 36 (1983): 633–660.
Mittelman, Willard. "The Relation between Nietzsche's Theory of the Will to Power and His Earlier Conception of Power." *Nietzsche-Studien* 9 (1980): 122–141.
Sedgwick, Peter R. "Nietzsche, Normativity, and Will to Power." *Nietzsche-Studien* 36 (2007): 214–242.
Stegmaier, Werner. "Nietzsche's Doctrines, Nietzsche's Signs." *Journal of Nietzsche Studies* 31 (2006): 20–41.
Williams, Linda L. *Nietzsche's Mirror: The World as Will to Power*. Lanham, Md.: Rowman & Littlefield Publishers, 2001.

Index

Index

decadent, Wagner as 238
Delian League 51
democracy 51–52
democratic enlightenment 6
democratic idiosyncrasy 205
denial of morality 131, 136
Derrida, Jacques 19
Descartes, René 13
Descent of Man 92
desirabilities 257–58
The Dialectic of Enlightenment 3–4
Dionysiac role in human life 66
The Dionysian Worldview 69
dithyramb, invention of 155
downfall 31
Duessen, Paul 77
the duty of truth 32
dynamic quanta 252

early notebooks 17–43
    1867–1872 26–29
    1872–1876 29–39
    1876–1879 39–43
Ecce Homo 7, 8, 9, 10, 13, 86, 88, 91, 94, 102,
    108, 116, 145, 153–54, 158, 163, 172, 182,
    215–39
English psychologists 149, 203–04
epistemology 30, 33, 35
essence of judgement 254
esteeming 160
Eternal Recurrence 141–43, 144–46
eternity 145
ethics 41
existence, as aesthetic phenomenon 27

Faber, Marion 99
faith, and intellectual conscience 218–19
false picture of agency 129–31
fatalism 11–12
Feuerbach, Ludwig 113–14, 116
Franco-Prussian War 92
The Free Spirit 83, 110
free spirit series 98, 105–06, 108–09
free spirited side of Nietzsche 109–11
free thinkers 202
freedom
    of the mind 256
    and tyranny of capricious laws 221
Freud, Sigmund 92, 130
*Friedrich Nietzsche and the Politics of
    Transformation* 4
Friedrich the Untimely One (inscription on
    photo) 89
Fritsch, E. W. 69
fundamental feelings 85

fundamental thought of work 172
future tasks/projects 87–88

Gast, Peter 138
The Gay Science/Joyous Science 1, 7, 8–9, 10, 13,
    98, 105–06, 108, 110, 137–51, 155, 162, 201,
    218, 220, 223, 224
genealogical analysis 89
genealogy and morality 201–06
Genealogy see On the Genealogy of Morals
German Materialism 113–17
Germany
    appeal to German youth 39
    cultural renewal 64
    Franco-Prussian War 35, 73
    National Socialism (Nazi Party) 2–3, 4, 17, 99
God, death of 91, 141–43, 146
good, bad and evil 206–07
Gospel of St John 20
great individuals 38
Greece
    archaic society 50–51
    dieties, and principles/forces 47–48
    philosophy 30
    poets 50–51
    tragedy in 47–48
The Greek State 52, 213
Greeks 9–10, 25–26, 150
Grillparzer, Franz 74, 75
growth in culture 200
guilt, moral concept of 207

Hartmann, Eduard von 74–75
healing instinct of life 211
Hegel, Georg Wilhelm Friedrich 4, 93, 113–14,
    144
Heidegger, Martin 4, 19
Helmholtz, Herman von 116
herd animal morality 202
higher humanity 93
historicism 75–76
history, approaches to 35–36
History of Materialism 116
history of morality 203
Hollingdale, R. J. 217–18
Homeric Question 213–14
Homer's Contest 213–14
Human, All Too Human (A Book for Free
    Spirits) 18, 26, 31, 39, 42, 77, 83, 88,
    91–111, 112, 123–29, 138, 147
    prefaces 103–04, 105, 109
human fate 55–56
human nobility 178
human possibility 79
human situation, as illusion 58–59

Printed in the United States
By Bookmasters